BENTHAM ON DEMOCRACY, COURTS, AND CODIFICATION

Drawing upon original manuscripts and *The Collected Works of Jeremy Bentham*, this collection represents the latest scholarship on Bentham's late and mature thought on constitutional law. The contributions cover a diverse range of major topics, from official aptitude or competency to the interests of women, and explore Bentham's writings on courts, codification, and cosmopolitanism. Together, its chapters challenge the received notion, based on early jurisprudential writings, that Bentham's constitutional thought is authoritarian and show that Bentham, as a constitutional theorist, offers a distinctive liberal perspective. Freeing Bentham's theories from their long sentences and unfamiliar terminology, these chapters make accessible Bentham's subtle and important ideas on liberal democracy. By shining a light on Bentham's mature thought, this collection offers a refreshingly comprehensive, detailed, and authentic account of Bentham's theory of democracy.

PHILIP SCHOFIELD is director of the Bentham Project, Faculty of Laws, University College London, and general editor of the new authoritative edition of *The Collected Works of Jeremy Bentham*. He is the author of *Utility and Democracy: The Political Thought of Jeremy Bentham* (2006) and *Bentham: A Guide for the Perplexed* (2009).

XIAOBO ZHAI is Associate Professor, Faculty of Law, University of Macau. He is the co-editor of *Bentham's Theory of Law and Public Opinion* (2014) and *Bentham Around the World* (2021). He also writes on legal philosophy, constitutional theory, and Chinese law.

BENTHAM ON DEMOCRACY, COURTS, AND CODIFICATION

Edited by

PHILIP SCHOFIELD

University College London

XIAOBO ZHAI

University of Macau

CAMBRIDGE
UNIVERSITY PRESS

CAMBRIDGE
UNIVERSITY PRESS

Shaftesbury Road, Cambridge CB2 8EA, United Kingdom

One Liberty Plaza, 20th Floor, New York, NY 10006, USA

477 Williamstown Road, Port Melbourne, VIC 3207, Australia

314–321, 3rd Floor, Plot 3, Splendor Forum, Jasola District Centre, New Delhi – 110025, India

103 Penang Road, #05–06/07, Visioncrest Commercial, Singapore 238467

Cambridge University Press is part of Cambridge University Press & Assessment, a department of the University of Cambridge.

We share the University's mission to contribute to society through the pursuit of education, learning and research at the highest international levels of excellence.

www.cambridge.org
Information on this title: www.cambridge.org/9781009013666

DOI: 10.1017/9781009031745

First published 2022
First paperback edition 2024

A catalogue record for this publication is available from the British Library

ISBN 978-1-316-51604-1 Hardback
ISBN 978-1-009-01366-6 Paperback

CONTENTS

CONTRIBUTORS

PHILIP SCHOFIELD is Professor of the History of Legal and Political Thought at University College London, Director of the Bentham Project, and General Editor of the *Collected Works of Jeremy Bentham.* He has edited or co-edited eleven volumes in the *Collected Works*, the most recent being *The Book of Fallacies* (2015) and *Preparatory Principles* (2016). His *Utility and Democracy: The Political Thought of Jeremy Bentham* (2006) won the prestigious WJM Mackenzie Prize. He is also the author of *Bentham: A Guide for the Perplexed* (2009).

XIAOBO ZHAI is Associate Professor at University of Macau. He has co-edited *Bentham's Theory of Law and Public Opinion* (with Michael Quinn, 2014) and *Bentham around the World* (with Simon Palmer, 2021). His books include *The People's Constitution* (2009) and *China's System of Constitutional Implementation* (2009).

MALIK BOZZO-REY is Research Professor at Lille Catholic University. His publications include the edited volumes *Bentham juriste: l'utilitarisme juridique en question* (with Guillaume Tusseau, 2011) and *Raisons politiques* (with Pierre-Yves Néron, 2014).

ANNE BRUNON-ERNST is Professor at Panthéon-Assas University and a member of the Centre Bentham. Her publications include *Utilitarian Biopolitics* (2012) and *Le Panoptique des pauvres* (2007) and edited volumes *Jeremy Bentham's Theory Today* (2011), *Beyond Foucault* (2012), *Concurrence des normativités* (2018), *Nudges et normativités* (2018), *Indirect Legislation: Bentham's Regulatory Revolution* (2017), and *Nudges: Better Choices?* (2016).

EMMANUELLE DE CHAMPS is Professor of British History and Civilization at CY Cergy Paris Université. Her publications include *Enlightenment and Utility: Bentham in France/Bentham in French*

(2015) and *La déontologie politique ou La pensée constitutionnelle de Jeremy Bentham (2008).* She co-edited, with Jean Pierre Cléro, *Bentham et la France: Fortune et Infortunes de l'utilitarisme (2009).*

BRIAN CHEN is Associate Professor at National Chengchi University. His publications include journal articles on Hume's and Bentham's moral, legal, and political theory.

STEPHEN ENGELMANN is Associate Professor of Political Science at the University of Illinois at Chicago. He is author of *Imagining Interest in Political Thought: Origins of Economic Rationality* (2003) and editor of *Selected Writings: Jeremy Bentham* (2011).

FRANCESCO FERRARO is Research Fellow at the University of Milan. His publications include *L'utilità dei diritti. Diritti morali e giuridici in una prospettiva ética utilitarista* (*The Utility of Rights: Moral and Legal Rights in a Utilitarian Perspective*) (2013) and *Il giudice utilitarista. Flessibilità e tutela delle aspettative nel pensiero giuridico di Jeremy Bentham* (*The Utilitarian Judge: Flexibility and Protection of Expectations in Jeremy Bentham's Legal Thought*) (2011).

MICHIHIRO KAINO is Professor of the History of Legal Thought at Doshisha University. He is the author of *Jeremy Bentham: Legislator of the World* (2007) and co-editor of *The Challenges of Jeremy Bentham* (2015).

TSIN YEN KOH is Assistant Professor of Political Science at Yale-NUS College. Her publications on Bentham have appeared in *History of Political Thought, Revue d'études benthamiennes,* and *History of European Ideas.*

DAVID LIEBERMAN is the James W. and Isabel Coffroth Professor of Jurisprudence at the University of California, Berkeley. He is the author of *The Province of Legislation Determined: Legal Theory in Eighteenth-Century Britain* (1989), and he edited Jean Louis De Lolme's *The Constitution of England; or, An Account of the English Government* (2007).

PETER NIESEN is Professor of Political Theory at the University of Hamburg. His publications include *Jeremy Bentham: Unsinn auf Stelzen. Schriften zur Französischen Revolution* (2013), *Immanuel Kant:*

Zum ewigen Frieden/Auszüge aus der Rechtslehre (2011) and *Kants Theorie der Redefreiheit* (2008).

MICHAEL QUINN is an Honorary Research Fellow at Philipps Universität Marburg (Fachbereiche Gesellschaftswissenschaften und Philosophie, Institut für Politikwissenschaft), and at Lille Catholic University. He was previously Senior Research Associate at the Bentham Project. He has edited four volumes in the *Collected Works* on poor relief (2001, 2010) and political economy (2016, 2019); co-edited a fifth on sexual morality (2014); while a sixth is awaiting submission to the press. Pre-publication versions of two further volumes on political economy have been freely available via UCL digital depository since 2019. He has published widely on many aspects of Bentham's thought, and his book on Bentham as a theorist of public policy (*Bentham*) appeared in 2021.

GUILLAUME TUSSEAU is Professor of Public Law at Sciences Po. His publications include *Contentieux constitutionnel comparé: une introduction critique au droit processuel constitutionnel* (2021), *Droit comparé et théorie générale du droit. Notes sur quelques allers-retours aporétiques* (2021), *Droit constitutionnel et institutions politiques* (2021), *Jeremy Bentham, La guerre des mots* (2011), *Jeremy Bentham et Le Droit Constitutionnel: Une approche de l'utilitarisme juridique* (2001), and edited volumes *Debating Legal Pluralism and Constitutionalism: New Trajectories for Legal Theory in the Global Age* (2020), *The Legal Philosophy and Influence of Jeremy Bentham: Essays on 'Of the Limits of the Penal Branch of Jurisprudence'* (2014), and *Bentham juriste: l'utilitarisme juridique en question* (with Malik Bozzo-Rey, 2011).

Introduction

PHILIP SCHOFIELD AND XIAOBO ZHAI

The present collection arises from a research project (MYRG2017-00140-FLL) funded by the University of Macau, where most of the papers were presented. It consists of fourteen chapters on related aspects of Bentham's constitutional theory written by scholars from eight countries. None of these chapters have been previously published.

The writings of Jeremy Bentham (1748–1832), philosopher and reformer, form a prominent landmark in the history of human thought. He made prodigious contributions to many fields, including language and logic, ethics, jurisprudence, codification, judicial procedure and evidence, punishment, education, provision for the poor, prison reform, colonialism, political economy, secularism, and sexual morality. Our focus is on his theory of constitutional law and democracy, with a particular emphasis on its relationship to his legal theory.

Philip Schofield explains that 'Bentham established the framework for his later writings on constitutional law in his work on jurisprudence in the 1770s and 1780s and 'had in fact developed important aspects of his constitutional theory in his early writings on jurisprudence'.[1] However, it is widely accepted that Bentham in the first half of his career paid little attention to constitutional theory as such. Following a long course of frustrating experiences in relation to his projects of legal reform and his attempt to build a panopticon prison, he came to realize in the 1810s that constitutional reform would have to precede legal reform.[2] His main focus thereafter was constitutional law. His late works on this subject, especially the three-volume *Constitutional Code*, represent one of the most ambitious and comprehensive contributions to constitutional theory. However, in contrast to his early writings on law, which have

[1] P. Schofield, *Utility and Democracy: The Political Thought of Jeremy Bentham* (Oxford: Oxford University Press, 2006), 221, 223.

[2] See ibid., 221–3.

been covered in a number of excellent studies,[3] Bentham's late writings on constitutional law have not received the attention they deserve and remain a rich mine for further discoveries. The chapters in this book embody the latest scholarship on this underexplored but important subject. They expand and deepen our understanding of Bentham's theory of constitutional law and democracy, on the one hand, and of major themes in constitutional theory in general, on the other hand.

The innovative aspects of this collection and hence its significance can be appreciated when situated against the current state of scholarship on Bentham's constitutional theory. The received and still prominent view sees Bentham as an authoritarian and sometimes as the forerunner of totalitarianism. This view originates in Elie Halévy's seminal *The Growth of Philosophic Radicalism* where he states, 'Bentham had never been a liberal . . . he merely passed from a monarchic authoritarianism to a democratic authoritarianism'[4] and has been extremely influential.[5] There has also been a tendency for scholars to focus on Bentham's writings from the 1770s and 1780s, when he was much more sympathetic to the British Constitution and generally did not worry too much about political reform, concentrating instead on legal reform. Bentham's friend and editor Étienne Dumont wrote in 1802: '[Bentham] does not give exclusive preference to any form of Government. He thinks that the best constitution for a people is the one to which it is accustomed . . . . He thinks that a people which has good laws can arrive at a high degree of happiness even without having any political power, and, on the contrary,

[3] For example, H. L. A. Hart, *Essays on Bentham: Studies in Jurisprudence and Political Theory* (Oxford: Clarendon Press, 1982); G. Postema, *Bentham and the Common Law Tradition* (Oxford: Clarendon Press, 1986; 2nd ed., 2019); D. Lieberman, *The Province of Legislation Determined: Legal Theory in Eighteenth-century Britain* (Cambridge: Cambridge University Press, 1989); M. Lobban, *The Common Law and English Jurisprudence 1760–1850* (Oxford: Oxford University Press, 1991).

[4] E. Halévy, *The Growth of Philosophic Radicalism* (corrected ed., London, 1952), 375–6. For a criticism of Halévy's interpretation, see F. Rosen, 'Elie Halévy and Bentham's Authoritarian Liberalism', in *Enlightenment and Dissent* 6 (1987), 59–76.

[5] See, for example, D. G. Long, *Bentham on Liberty: Jeremy Bentham's Idea of Liberty in Relation to His Utilitarianism* (Toronto: University of Toronto Press, 1977); C. F. Bahmueller, *The National Charity Company: Jeremy Bentham's Silent Revolution* (Berkeley; Los Angeles: University of California Press, 1981); G. Himmelfarb, 'The Haunted House of Jeremy Bentham', in *Victorian Minds: Essays on Nineteenth-Century Intellectuals* (New York: A. A. Knopf, 1968), 32–81; D. J. Manning, *The Mind of Jeremy Bentham* (New York: Barnes and Noble, 1968); C. Gere, *Pleasure and the Greater Good: From Panopticon to the Skinner Box and Beyond* (Chicago: University of Chicago Press, 2017).

that it may have the widest political powers and yet necessarily be unhappy, if it has bad laws.'[6]

The study of Bentham – his constitutional theory in particular – has been fundamentally transformed by the appearance of volumes in the new authoritative edition of *The Collected Works of Jeremy Bentham*, produced by the Bentham Project at University College London.[7] Ten volumes of the new edition are directly concerned with constitutional law or closely related to constitutional issues.[8] Thanks to the publication of these volumes, there is now a proper basis for better scholarship on Bentham's constitutional theory. Hence, the resources for the study of Bentham's constitutional theory are much broader and more 'authentic' than they were thirty years ago. First, we can now see that Bentham has a rich and comprehensive constitutional theory and, second, that his theory is open to a liberal interpretation, but that it is very different from the orthodox version of democratic liberalism.

Since the 1980s, Bentham has been increasingly recognized as a major constitutional theorist – a liberal constitutionalist of a very different kind – with considerable relevance for the twenty-first century. There has already been a considerable amount of revisionist scholarship,[9] but

[6] Translated from *Traités de Législation Civile et Pénale* (Paris, 1802), 'Discours Préliminaire', i. 16–17.

[7] For these volumes, see www.ucl.ac.uk/bentham-project/publications.

[8] *Constitutional Code: Vol. I* (1983); *First Principles Preparatory to Constitutional Code* (1989); *Securities against Misrule and Other Constitutional Writings for Tripoli and Greece* (1990); *Official Aptitude Maximized; Expense Minimized* (1993); *Colonies, Commerce, and Constitutional Law: Rid Yourselves of Ultramaria and Other Writings on Spain and Spanish America* (1995); *'Legislator of the World': Writings on Codification, Law, and Education* (1998); *Political Tactics* (1999); *Rights, Representation, and Reform: Nonsense Upon Stilts and Other Writings on the French Revolution* (2002); *On the Liberty of the Press, and Public Discussion and Other Legal and Political Writings for Spain and Portugal* (2012); *The Book of Fallacies* (2015).

[9] The most important works on Bentham's constitutional theory are P. Schofield, *Utility and Democracy*; and F. Rosen, *Jeremy Bentham and Representative Democracy: A Study of the Constitutional Code* (Oxford: Oxford University Press, 1983). Bentham's constitutional theory is summarized by P. Schofield, 'Jeremy Bentham', in *Constitutions and the Classics*, ed. D. J. Galligan (Oxford: Oxford University Press, 2014), 231–49. Other works include F. Rosen, *Bentham, Byron, and Greece: Constitutionalism, Nationalism, and Early Liberal Political Thought* (Oxford: Oxford University Press, 1992); O. Ben-Dor, *Constitutional Limits and the Public Sphere: A Critical Study of Bentham's Constitutionalism* (Oxford: Oxford University Press, 2000); P. J. Kelly, *Utilitarianism and Distributive Justice: Jeremy Bentham and the Civil Law* (Oxford: Oxford University Press, 1990); R. Harrison, *Bentham* (London: Routledge, 1983); Postema, *Bentham and the Common Law Tradition*, and *Utility, Publicity, and Law: Essays on Bentham's Moral*

there is now the opportunity to build on this revisionist scholarship and draw out its implications for Bentham's theory of democracy and constitutional law. This is what the present collection aims to achieve.

Bentham's constitutional theory can be distinguished into three complementary parts. First, an analytical part, which offers an original exposition of major notions of constitutional law, including the idea of constitutional law itself; the state or political society; law and sovereignty; the habit of obedience or disposition to obey; the distinction between legislative, executive, and judicial powers, and between constitutive and operative powers. Second, a sociological or descriptive part, which deals with the political reality that constitutional law addresses, including the origin of the state; the virtues and weaknesses of the people as political sovereign; political psychology or the psychology of officialdom; political corruption, misrule, and exploitation; the sinister interest of the ruling few; the differences between free and despotic government; and the juncture for resistance. Third, a normative part, which deals with constitutional design. Two major transitions in Bentham's normative constitutional theory can be identified: the first, from political conservatism, especially pronounced in the wake of the perceived threat to social order from the French Revolution, to political radicalism around 1804–1809; and the second, from 'democratic ascendancy' to uncompromising republicanism around 1818. Bentham's mature constitutional theory is a constitutional liberalism of a very different kind from the standard view. He criticized many ideas or principles accepted as orthodox in the liberal tradition, including the social contract, natural law and natural (human) rights, the entrenchment of fundamental constitutional rights, the mixed constitution, the balance of powers, the limited legislature, bicameralism, and judicial review. In place of these ideas or principles, Bentham developed the first utilitarian theory of democracy and proposed a comprehensive system of 'securities against misrule' to check the oppression of 'the subject many' by 'the ruling few'.

Bentham's constitutional design is based on three basic principles. The first is the principle of utility, which stipulates that the only right and proper end of government is the greatest happiness of the community; the second is the rulers' object-indicating principle, which states that all

and Legal Philosophy (Oxford: Oxford University Press, 2019); X. Zhai and M. Quinn, eds., *Bentham's Theory of Law and Public Opinion* (Cambridge: Cambridge University Press, 2014); J. E. Crimmins, *Utilitarian Philosophy and Politics: Bentham's Later Years* (London: Bloomsbury, 2011).

rulers will naturally pursue their own interest at whatever cost to the greatest happiness; and the third is the junction-of-interests prescribing principle, according to which the only way to ensure that the rulers pursue the greatest happiness is to make their own happiness depend upon the happiness of the governed. Bentham's constitutional design, therefore, consists of chains of subordination and superordination, which lead down from the democratic electorate and its organ the public opinion tribunal, through the legislature, to the executive, consisting of the administrative and judicial departments of government. Hence, at the foundation of Bentham's republican democratic theory lies popular sovereignty. He advocates virtual universal and equal suffrage (subject to a literacy test), equal electoral districts, annual elections, and the secret ballot, together with people's power to remove their deputies (his preferred term, rather than representatives or delegates) to the legislature and other high-ranking officials through petition and majority vote. Interestingly, Bentham aims to make the prime minister and other ministers more akin to civil servants than politicians. Hence, one of the central elements of his constitutional thought is captured in his aphorism 'official aptitude maximized, expense minimized', which he translates into a whole series of administrative provisions, such as public examination for offices, the economic auction, reward linked to attendance, and 'single-seated responsibility', as a means of ensuring democratic dependence and accountability.[10] As well as being recognized as the first theorist of bureaucracy,[11] Bentham is also recognized as a seminal thinker in the field of transparency.[12]

For Bentham, as important as, or perhaps more important than, the formal system of representative democracy is the public opinion tribunal,

[10] For a recent study drawing on Bentham's ideas in order to apply them to contemporary problems, see J. Elster, *Securities against Misrule: Juries, Assemblies, Elections* (Cambridge: Cambridge University Press, 2013).

[11] L. J. Hume, *Bentham and Bureaucracy* (Cambridge: Cambridge University Press, 1981).

[12] G. Bowrey and C. J. Smark, 'The Influence of Jeremy Bentham on Recent Public Sector Financial Reforms', *Journal of New Business Ideas and Trends*, viii (2010), 25–35; M. Bozzo-Rey, 'La transparence chez Jeremy Bentham: de l'invisibilité d'un concept à sa publicité', *The Tocqueville Review/La Revue Tocqueville*, xxxii (2011), 89–111; V. Rzepka, *Die Ordnung der Transparenz: Jeremy Bentham und die Genealogie einer demokratischen Norm* (Berlin: Lit, 2013); J. Domingo Sánchez Estop, 'Wikileaks: From Abbé Barruel to Jeremy Bentham and Beyond', *Cultural Studies↔Critical Methodologies*, xiv (2014), 40–9; S. Baume and Y. Papadopoulos, 'Transparency: From Bentham's Inventory of Virtuous Effects to Contemporary Evidence-Based Scepticism', *Critical Review of International Social and Political Philosophy*, xxi (2018), 169–92.

which is the source of the popular or moral sanction and gives ultimate binding force to constitutional law. For the public opinion tribunal to be effective, the freedom of political communication (including the freedom of the press and of association) must be secured. Throughout his writings, Bentham considered publicity to be the most effective guarantee for the subordination of the ruling few to the subject many. Inspired by the role of the public opinion tribunal in Bentham's system, scholars have recently argued that Bentham's theory of representative democracy has a strong deliberative tone, although it is not equivalent to participatory democracy.[13]

As noted above, compared with his early writings on law, Bentham's late writings and the many volumes of the *Collected Works* dealing with constitutional law, despite containing his 'fully developed or mature constitutional theory',[14] have not received the attention they deserve and there is much more that remains to be explored. Thanks to the appearance of *The Collected Works of Bentham*, scholars now have the opportunity to make new advances in understanding his constitutional theory. There are important topics that still need to be addressed and some existing interpretations that need to be enriched or revised. This is what our authors have begun to do in the present volume. Their chapters are thematically arranged under three headings: Democracy; Law and the Courts; and Codification. There follows a short description of the main themes of each of the chapters.

I.1 Democracy

In his chapter 'Intellectual Aptitude and the General Interest in Bentham's Democratic Thought' (Chapter 1), Philip Schofield presents a framework for understanding the significance of intellectual aptitude for Bentham's commitment to democracy. According to Schofield, Bentham's opposition to democracy in the wake of the French Revolution was the result of his concern that the people in general lacked the necessary intellectual aptitude to undertake the task of electing representatives and judging their policies. Between 1803 and 1809, Bentham realized that the imperfections in the law and the failure to

[13] Postema, *Utility, Publicity and Law*, chapter 13; J. Shafe, 'Challenges for a Revised View of Bentham on Public Reasoning', available at https://journals.openedition.org/etudes-benthamiennes/761#ftn21.

[14] Schofield, 'Jeremy Bentham', 235.

reform them were not because lawyers and politicians lacked intellectual aptitude but because they had a sinister interest in maintaining these imperfections. The emergence of the notion of sinister interest, Schofield points out, changed Bentham's previous assessment of the people's intellectual aptitude: he now believed that there was no other set of persons who possessed a greater degree of intellectual aptitude, combined with an equal degree of moral aptitude, as to possess an overall superiority in aptitude. If the people were ignorant and depraved, it was the result of the deliberate policy of rulers. In contrast to the people, the rulers had the least moral aptitude, while their sinister interest deprived them of any incentive to improve their intellectual aptitude. Besides, without appropriate moral aptitude, superiority in intellectual aptitude was detrimental to the aggregate of appropriate aptitude. With the discovery of the sinister interest of rulers, Bentham recognized that the promotion of the general interest of the community would only be implemented by a democratic government founded on chains of subordination together with the public opinion tribunal: only this form of democracy, the structure of which is outlined by Schofield, could bring about the identification of the rulers' particular interest with the community's general interest.

Michael Quinn's 'Bentham, Democracy, Free Government, and the Relationship between Rulers and Ruled' (Chapter 2) offers an account of Bentham's different and even conflicting attitudes towards democracy at various stages of his career. Bentham's early writings already contain the premises that form the basis for the utilitarian case for representative democracy. First, the purpose of government was the happiness of the community; second, the exercise of political power was a trust; third, self-interested motives were universally predominant over other motives; fourth, the conjunction of the interest and duty of those intended to obey a rule was the core task of the rule-maker. However, before the French Revolution, Bentham did not advocate representative democracy. When tailoring his argument for a French audience between 1788 and 1790, Bentham set out a utilitarian and egalitarian case for representative democracy in terms similar to those that he would employ again twenty years later. However, from the end of 1792, Bentham emphasized two dangers: first, that the concession of equality of right to representation would be superseded by the demand for equality of right to rule and then for equality of property and, second, that the poor majority were fit neither to govern nor to vote, owing to their ignorance. Bentham's anti-democratic reaction, Quinn points out, went beyond endorsement of limitations on liberty of association to advocate the surreptitious manipulation of public opinion. In 1817–18, Bentham advocated 'virtual universality' of male suffrage, and he offered three major responses to anti-democratic arguments that were effectively the same ones he himself had employed in 1799. First, he referred to American experience, where representative democracy had produced no anarchy. Second, he now believed that the poor had the equal right to representation but that demands for equalization of suffrage would not lead to demands for equalization of political power and demands for economic levelling or revolution. Third, the poor majority had sufficient knowledge of their own interests and of the fundamentals of political economy to qualify them to be voters, although not rulers. Bentham's expressions of fear about the ignorance of the poor disappeared around 1809, because, for Bentham, the dangers of democratic ignorance were a risk that had to be tolerated if progress against the sinister interest of the ruling few was to be achieved.

In *Constitutional Code*, Bentham proposes 'virtual universality' of suffrage which would include 'the whole body of the inhabitants … deduction made of certain classes'. One of the deducted classes is 'females'. An influential explanation for this is that the deduction is due to tactical reasons, namely, to compromise with the general and intense prejudice against women's suffrage, and to avoid the risk of derailing his project of universal male suffrage, but that as a matter of principle, Bentham's utilitarianism requires equal political rights for women. Emmanuelle de Champs agrees with this explanation. Building upon Bentham's non-gendered comments in *Constitutional Code*, his analysis of marriage, and his recently published writings on sexual morality, her chapter, 'The Interests of Women in Bentham's Late Constitutional Thought' (Chapter 3), discusses the utilitarian foundations of Bentham's anthropological theory of gender and women's interests as a whole and argues that his utilitarianism makes possible a unified approach to women as legal and political agents. De Champs presents Bentham's utilitarian justification of women's equal political rights, which has two steps. First, since women and men are equal in their sensibility to pain and pleasure and their desire and capacity for happiness, they therefore have equal right to happiness; second, 'each individual [including women] was the best judge of his [or her] best interests'. The exclusion of women from the constitutive authority cannot be justified by Bentham's principle of utility. As De Champs shows, in his writings dating from 1789, 1817–18, and the early 1820s, Bentham explicitly opposed contemporary arguments against women's suffrage, which, he argued, reflected male tyranny and was based upon dubious facts and prejudices. According to De Champs, Bentham throughout his writings does not essentialize gender difference. In his view, domestic powers are not natural but created by law; marriage and sexual relations ought to be based upon 'free and fairly obtained' consent and mutual interests, especially the interests of the 'weaker' and 'gentler' sex. The only limit on suffrage is the ability to form a rational judgement about one's interest, and women certainly have this ability. Due to tactical considerations, Bentham did not advocate women's suffrage, but as De Champs points out, he took care to establish some compensatory mechanisms to vindicate women's interests. One is the public opinion tribunal, which incudes women, and another is to introduce women into legal establishments, especially when disputes involving women are being dealt with.

In 'Religion and Judgment in Bentham's Political Thought' (Chapter 4), Tsin Yen Koh shows how Bentham's critique of the influence of religion is relevant to his championing of representative democracy as the only just form of government. Bentham believed that religion had the aim and effect of corrupting the judgement. The Church discouraged free criticism of its doctrines and practices and encouraged an uncritical reliance on its authority. Religion challenged the empirical basis of knowledge. Bentham pointed out that belief could be generated by the prospect of pleasure or pain, while the threat of eternal misery for disbelief could skew people's consideration of evidence. In both cases, Koh points out, the corruption of judgement had real effects on happiness in the present life. Bentham thought that the corruption of judgement was detrimental to representative democracy. Bentham distinguished between a 'self-formed' and a 'derivative' judgement and between the 'influence of will on will' and the 'influence of understanding on understanding'. He acknowledged that newly enfranchised voters might not be able to vote wisely on the basis of their 'self-formed' judgements but could do so on the basis of their 'derivative' judgements – most probably derived from public opinion. A secret ballot would eliminate the 'influence of will on will' and allow only the 'influence of understanding on understanding'. The functioning of representative democracy depended on the collective judgement of the voters, both individually and in the form of public opinion. The corruption of judgement, therefore, could harm representative democracy. Koh argues that Bentham thought of religion as a species of 'delusion', which was one of the 'instruments of misrule', and so contributed to the maintenance of oppressive political regimes.

Malik Bozzo-Rey's 'Organising the Utilitarian State: the Official Aptitude of Functionaries' (Chapter 5) is concerned with Bentham's theory of transparency and democracy, focusing on the management of functionaries or officials. A functionary must possess moral, intellectual, and active aptitude. To achieve this end, Bentham invented an institutional system for the management of functionaries. First, the procedure for the selection of functionaries needed to be transparent to the public, on the one hand, and to make the candidates' qualities transparent to the recruiters, on the other hand. Second, the power of a functionary and the money at his disposal should be minimized and his responsibility maximized: in this way, the candidate who lacked the necessary moral and intellectual aptitude would be discouraged from applying for the job. Third, there would be competitive examinations, ensuring that functionaries had the specific skills needed to perform particular functions. Fourth, to create a junction between the interest and duty of functionaries, the people should be given the power to dismiss and punish functionaries. Fifth, the public opinion tribunal, as a system of distrust, was necessary to align the interest of functionaries with that of the people. Bozzo-Rey then offers an account of the composition, force, and functions of the public opinion tribunal. Sixth, transparency – as a disciplinary technology – was also applied by Bentham to the spatial and temporal dimensions of the management of functionaries, so that their bodies were controlled with a view to promoting the greatest happiness. All these arrangements constituted a constitutional panopticon, with functionaries as its inmates and members of the public as its guardians. In this constitutional panopticon, functionaries were made transparent to the public: believing that they were being constantly watched by the public, they would internalize the principle of utility or the requirements of the greatest happiness.

Brian Chen's 'Bentham on the Corruption of Democracy' (Chapter 6) explores Bentham's views on the corruption of representative democracy. According to Chen, Bentham believes that representative democracy is exposed to the threat of two types of corruption. On the one hand, the executive department may endeavour to form a league of sinister interest with the legislature by bribing the latter. On the other hand, the subject many, like the ruling few, have their own particular interest, desiring not just security against depredation but also to engage in the depredation of all other men; they may gratify their desire of depredation by unjustly promoting their share in the universal interest and voting for candidates who will represent their particular interest. Besides, they may be bribed, manipulated, and deluded by the ruling few or be entirely occupied in promoting their private business. Chen points out that, in Bentham's writings, there are many ways in which both types of corruption are tackled. The process of socialization can help people realize that some of their particular interests are consistent with the universal interest and motivate them to cooperate with others. Elections can motivate both constituents and candidates to promote shared interests. The ideal legislator ought to tolerate and respect the plurality of citizens in their tastes and opinions. The ideal code, that is the Pannomion, can make justice accessible to all and perform the function of civic education. The principle of single-seatedness and a hierarchy of government organs can improve the accountability of rulers. Annual multi-candidate elections and the 'temporary non-relocability system' will make political life more competitive and participatory and meanwhile infuse fresh political knowledge and experience into the population, thereby improving the moral and intellectual character of the public mind. A system of official documentation, statistics and publication, and an 'all-comprehensive system of appropriate information-furnishing, from the Administrative authorities to the Legislature' will guarantee the publicity of government. All these arrangements will create and empower a robust public opinion tribunal that can enlighten the subject many, prevent them from being deluded, and even make them into good citizens. The public opinion tribunal may deviate from the principle of utility, but, as Chen suggests, Bentham is optimistic and confident that the deviations will become less and less.

The conventional view is that Bentham rejects the separation of powers and advocates instead the principle of the dependence of the governors on the governed and a supreme, omni-competent, and unicameral legislature. Xiaobo Zhai's contribution, 'The People's "Greatest Misfortune" and "All the Chance the People Have": Bentham on the Separation of Powers' (Chapter 7), revises this view and offers a more complete account of Bentham's thought on the separation of powers. According to Zhai, first, Bentham embraces the functional division of power and contributes to it by adding to the traditional tripartite division a new division between constitutive and operative powers. Second, for Bentham, the temporal fractionization of power is conceivable, and he adopts the simple fractionization of the supreme constitutive power and the legislative power. Third, Bentham's constitutional design takes the overall shape of the traditional tripartite division of power. This design, however, is based on the principle of popular sovereignty and subject to the scrutiny of a fourth power, namely, the public opinion tribunal. There is a relationship of dependence between the sharers of different and divided operative powers, which, instead of being co-ordinate, belong to different ranks, and among which the legislative branch is superior to the other branches and subject to no legal limitations, including those of entrenched basic rights. The administrative and judicial branches will normally operate autonomously, and the judicial branch can even exert some influence on the legislative; however, in extraordinary situations, the legislative branch can intervene and even take over the powers of the administrative and judicial branches. For Bentham, the tripartite distribution of power serves such values as the rule of law, efficiency, impartiality, and checking the abuse of power. Fourth, what Bentham really opposes are checks and balances. He denounces the idea as nonsense and argues that it leads to anarchy and the exploitation of the majority by the minority. When the polity is democratic, it will lead to complication, waste, and inefficiency. Bentham nevertheless argues that when the government is undemocratic and independent of the people, checks and balances may be all the chance that the people have to avoid oppression: it can weaken bad laws, contribute to public deliberation of laws, and force the power-holders to appeal to and thereby make them dependent upon the people. Zhai believes that a real political body is always a mixture of democracy and despotism, which seems to suggest that, in Bentham's eyes, there is a necessary role for the principle of checks and balances to play in our actual politics. Zhai concludes his chapter by suggesting that Bentham would agree that, before we enter the constitutional utopia of complete accountability, some kind of checks and balances is necessary and useful to the greatest happiness.

I.2 Law and the Courts

Bentham was perhaps the first author who thought that constitutional law was indeed law. Guillaume Tusseau's 'Between Constructivism and Immanentism: Bentham's Unsettled Conception of Constitutional Law' (Chapter 8) examines Bentham's pioneering notion of constitutional law and the tensions implicit in his position and shows how the perspectives of Paine and Burke can be productively combined in Bentham's theory. Tusseau points out that Bentham hesitated over two major issues regarding the nature of constitutional law. First, he was unsure whether constitutional law belonged to the civil or penal branch of law or formed an independent and third branch of law. Second, Bentham seems to have hesitated between modern constructivism and ancient immanentism. Modern constructivism is represented by Paine's notion of constitutional law, according to which the constitution is a document by which the people create, organize, and bind the government. As Tusseau suggests, Bentham's notion of constitutional law shares many key features with Paine's. On the other hand, Bentham's notion can be traced to the immanentist paradigm of constitutional thinking, famously articulated by Burke, who argues that constitutional law is a matter of national tradition and custom. For example, first, Bentham argues that the constitution is something already established and stable and not something to be made. Second, he thinks that the force of a constitution arises from the popular sanction imposed by the public opinion tribunal, which is based on a complex process of social interaction. Tusseau argues that, in terms of the nature of constitutional law, Bentham is paradoxically both modern and ancient. Tusseau does not think that Bentham's notion of constitutional law is inconsistent. His explanation is that, since the social interactions that serve as the basis of the popular sanction are not spontaneous but purposefully shaped, Bentham's Burkean immanentism turns out to be configured in a Paine-like constructivist way.

'Legisprudence' is the name given to the field of legal theory focusing on legislation, partly as a reaction to its traditional focus on the judicial dimensions of law. In Chapter 9, '"A Genius for Legislation": Bentham's "Art and Science" of Legislation, Legislative Justification, and Modern Legisprudence', Francesco Ferraro argues that Bentham is the father of modern legisprudence. One concern of modern legisprudence is to show that the study of legislation is a perfectly legitimate enterprise for legal theorists. After all, legal scholars do better to avoid meddling with substantive moral judgements and political debates, according to some prevailing views in legal theory. Generally speaking, studying the existing law seems very different from inquiring into the process of law-making and checking its conformity with substantive moral standards. Ferraro argues, however, that the exclusion of law-making from the field of legal theory would have made no sense to Bentham: not only did Bentham regard legislation as the most important of all intellectual enterprises, but he also considered it as central to jurisprudence. Ferraro suggests that Bentham's expository jurisprudence was instrumental to his 'art of legislation', which he regarded as a subdivision of normative ethics. Bentham addressed the need for justified law-making by proposing that each new law be accompanied by a rationale, which would serve as a guide (as well as a bridle) for judicial interpretation, besides displaying the usefulness of each law to the citizens. Bentham emphasized that the legislator was a potentially rational agent, whose rationality, however, was not to be taken for granted and was necessarily bounded by limitations of time and information. Legislative justification nowadays presents the legislator as engaged in a dialogue with the judicial power, especially with regard to judicial review. Bentham opposed judicial review. Nonetheless, Ferraro points out, in his late thought, Bentham in fact ascribed such 'judicial' control over legislation to the public opinion tribunal as the guardian of the constitution. Since the rationale of a law would always make reference to the greatest happiness principle, it would help shape public debate on legislation by reference to the language of utility, rather than that of fundamental rights.

Indirect legislation has recently become a significant area of interest in Bentham studies. Anne Brunon-Ernst's 'Indirect Legislation in Bentham's Constitutional Writings' (Chapter 10) is the first attempt to investigate indirect legislation in Bentham's constitutional writings. The phrase 'indirect legislation' emerges in Bentham's early writings on jurisprudence but rarely appears in his late constitutional writings. Nevertheless, Brunon-Ernst assumes that the mechanisms Bentham identified as indirect legislation are still at work there. She first presents an overview of the major points of Bentham's theory that are relevant to indirect legislation and then discusses the meaning of indirect legislation in Bentham's early writings. She goes on to describe the mechanisms akin to indirect legislation that are found in Bentham's late constitutional writings, including the public opinion tribunal, publication and registration schemes, and architectural arrangements. Three conclusions flow from Brunon-Ernst's discussion. The first is that a certain number of mechanisms, similar to early indirect policies, exemplify the shift in Bentham's theory from his early concern with defining law and sovereignty to his later normative political theory. The second is that the public opinion tribunal, which Bentham considered to be a system of law emanating from the body of the people, can be construed as indirect law. The third is that, in his late writings, Bentham does not need any longer to rely on indirect legislation because he has built a theory of law that embraces publicity. In short, Brunon-Ernst argues, the public opinion tribunal supersedes indirect legislation.

Bentham's three-volume *Constitutional Code* devotes nearly one-third of its space to judicial organization and procedure. David Lieberman discusses this striking but neglected feature of Bentham's constitutional design. Chapter 11 answers two questions: why the judicial establishment acquires such prominence in Bentham's reform program and how Bentham understood the democratic dimensions of his plan for the judiciary. Lieberman begins with an account of Bentham's lifelong preoccupation with courts and legal process, which received additional stimulus from the dynamics of judicial reform in the 1820s. In Bentham's view, the general goal of the judicial establishment was to secure justice for all members of a political community with the minimum of 'expense, vexation, and delay'. Lieberman then presents the basic principles and institutions of Bentham's blueprint for the judiciary. The key to the vices of the unreformed legal order, according to Bentham, was the practice of legal fee-taking, which cemented the common interests of Judge and Co., leading to a huge labyrinth of 'expense, vexation, and delay'. Lieberman points out that the evil especially condemned by Bentham was the fact that that law was turned into the weapon of the wealthy few to plunder the poor majority. Bentham's design aimed to offer justice to everyone. Lieberman sketches Bentham's measures for promoting equal justice. In this connection, he answers the question of how to understand the democratic dimensions of Bentham's design of the judiciary. Bentham's thought on the judiciary developed and matured well before he embraced representative democracy. Lieberman's view is that Bentham's endorsement of democracy did not lead to a revamping of his program of judicial reform, but it helped him to 'recognize and emphasize the democratic promise' that was already implicit in his program and to deepen his political analysis of it. Bentham's *Constitutional Code*, Lieberman says, 'supplied a democratic gloss on reforms that predated [his] embrace of political radicalism'. The old legal order was the tyranny of the minority. Judge and Co. was ideologically and institutionally a part of Britain's ruling elite. Bentham's judicial plan, Lieberman suggests, would align the interests of Judge and Co. with the interest of all the people and was an example of the logic of democracy applied to courts and judicial procedure.

I.3 Codification

'Pannomial Fragments', according to Richard Smith's editorial note in the third volume of Bowring's *Works of Jeremy Bentham*, is a collection of 'sketches' gathered from manuscript, some of it very late, that were intended for 'an Introduction to a Pannomion, or Complete Code of Laws'. Stephen Engelmann's contribution, 'Ending at the Beginning: Law and Political Theory in "Pannomial Fragments"' (Chapter 12), attempts to answer three questions. First, what are the main manuscript sources for this text? Second, given these sources and parallel materials from Bentham's final years, how well does the text serve as a statement of his intentions for an introduction to the pannomion? Third, given the inadequacy of 'Pannomial Fragments', what can we salvage from the text, that is, what is most useful in it for understanding Bentham's project as a whole as envisioned in his final years? Engelmann's answers to these questions drive three arguments. First, 'Pannomial Fragments' as a text testifies to the fundamental unreliability of the Bowring edition: its omissions and arrangement obscure Bentham's purposes and defy elementary standards of logic and coherence. Only the constitutional and the penal codes, without mention of the civil and the procedural, are introduced in chapter I, and the whole of 'Pannomial Fragments' gives little hint of the abiding concern of Bentham's final decade, namely, misrule. Second, Bentham's pannomion cannot finally be introduced because it cannot be completed as he came to envision it. In particular, his increasing preoccupations with 'nomography' – with reflections on the writing of the law, the method of adequate codification, and the reasons for that method – speak to the endlessness of his project. Third, the most useful material in 'Pannomial Fragments' appears in chapter IV on axioms of pathology, where they are related to the general happiness in its four subordinate ends of subsistence, abundance, security, and equality, thereby providing insight into both the special interdependence of art and science in Bentham's art-and-science of government, as well as how the four ends might successfully travel from their seemingly parochial origins in Bentham's political economy to shape the concerns of the pannomion as a whole. 'Pannomial Fragments' is deeply flawed, but, Engelmann concludes, it does contain concentrated nuggets of Bentham that belong at the heart of his late constitutional thought.

Bentham aspired to be 'legislator of the world'. His aim was to produce a Pannomion, which would include his Constitutional Code. In 'Bentham's Constitutional Code and His Pannomion' (Chapter 13), Michihiro Kaino considers two criticisms of Bentham's project of a pannomion. The first is that, in contrast to the common law, Bentham's pannomion would not keep up with social changes because of the limited role it gives to judges. The second is that his radical project of introducing his pannomion across the world was overly optimistic. Kaino defends Bentham against these criticisms. First, he argues that Bentham was fully aware that it was not possible to foresee every case that might arise and that his pannomion gave judges sufficient powers to enable them to update the legal system in response to social change. In his Constitutional Code, for example, Bentham proposed a 'contested-interpretation-reporting function', an 'eventually-emendative function', and a 'preinterpretative function', to empower judges to suggest amendments of the pannomion to the legislature. Kaino, moreover, points to Bentham's distinction between an individual offence and a species of offence. Bentham thought that, although not foreseeable individually, offences could be foreseen in species; adding a new species of offence to the pannomion would amount to legislation, but adding an individual offence to an existing species of offence could be left to judges. Second, Kaino argues that Bentham's late optimism regarding the pannomion can be reconciled with his early incrementalism, through his belief that utilitarian rationality would have a contagious influence if the freedom of the press and public discussion were established. In 1817 or 1818, Bentham realized that constitutional reform was a precondition for introducing his pannomion. Meanwhile, he began to advance the idea of the 'contagious influence of reason', namely, that if one government adopted his pannomion, it would soon be adopted by other governments. Bentham's strategy of legal transplantation in his early years was an incremental one. In 'Place and Time' written around 1780, Bentham discussed the problem of legal transplantation and emphasized the importance of the indirect means of freedom of the press and public discussion. Kaino suggests that Bentham then seems to have thought that, through freedom of the press and public discussion, people would come to know their true interests and would abandon laws that were at odds with his pannomion.

Peter Niesen's 'Bentham's Cosmopolitan Constitutionalism' (Chapter 14) lays out the cosmopolitan elements of Bentham's constitutional theory, by which Niesen means those elements that ascribe legal and political entitlements to all members of the human race. Regarding Bentham's thought on this subject, an undue focus, Niesen complains, has been placed on 'A Plan for an Universal and Perpetual Peace', which, Niesen suggests, propagates an international, not a cosmopolitan, order in that it relates states, not world citizens, to each other. Nevertheless, already in 'Plan', Bentham introduces the term 'citizen of the world', by which he refers to an impartial, nationally unattached optimal draughtsman of an international code. Niesen calls this feature Bentham's 'authorial cosmopolitanism', which is not his focus here, since it has been well-established in Bentham studies. For Niesen, it is in his constitutional writings that Bentham's most strikingly cosmopolitan elements are found, and which he terms 'cosmopolitanism within one country': its central feature is the organization of domestic constitutions and laws in an open, universalist, and omni-laterally accessible manner. According to Niesen, Bentham's 'cosmopolitanism within one country' has four features. First, the constitutional code should award mobility rights to both citizens and foreigners, and thereby make the political state 'an asylum to all, a prison to none'. Second, it should give passive suffrage to foreigners, secure cosmopolitan political participation, and allow foreigners to stand for and be appointed to administrative posts, parliamentary seats, and political offices. Third, it should allow political representation of foreigners, which would contribute to mutual understanding, mutual recognition, and peace, on the one hand, and improve domestic political expertise and deliberation, on the other hand. Fourth, it should grant all foreigners extensive rights to free border-crossing speech. Niesen notes that this feature, which opens up the public opinion tribunal to people of all nations, is the purest cosmopolitan entitlement in Bentham's democratic thought. Niesen concludes, first, that Bentham's greatest happiness principle should be seen to apply to all those 'encompassed' by a specific legal order, where some of those encompassed (foreigners) will not at the same time be 'subjected'; and second, that with states withdrawing from the global cosmopolitan institutional order, Bentham's 'cosmopolitanism within one country' forms an attractive alternative.

Focusing on Bentham's late writings on constitutional law, and building upon newly published volumes and unpublished manuscripts, our authors have broken new ground in Bentham studies, revised conventional readings, and offered more sophisticated and nuanced accounts of established themes. This volume will be a valuable addition to Bentham studies and hence to a wide variety of disciplines. At a time when traditional liberal values are facing many challenges, we have much to learn from Bentham's very different and unconventional theory of liberal democracy.

PART I

Democracy

1

Intellectual Aptitude and the General Interest in Bentham's Democratic Thought

PHILIP SCHOFIELD

1.1 Introduction

In my *Utility and Democracy*, I noted that an important difference between the pre-democratic and post-democratic Bentham consisted in his view of the relationship between property and the franchise. In the earlier phase of his career, he feared that the non-propertied, if given the vote, would in effect destroy civilized life by insisting on a redistribution of property, while in the latter phase he dismissed this threat as illusory and pointed to the United States of America as a functioning large-scale democracy where property was secure.[1] While there is no reason to question this account, there is arguably more to be said about how Bentham regarded the problem of bad government, or misrule, and the solution, in terms of the possession of intellectual aptitude – in other words, the possession of knowledge and judgement – one of the branches of appropriate aptitude. An individual possessed intellectual aptitude when he had the relevant knowledge and judgement to promote the general or universal interest, moral aptitude when he was motivated to do so, and active aptitude when he performed the relevant actions. As Bentham confessed, the branches of aptitude represented his interpretation of the attributes of wisdom, goodness, and power that William Blackstone had declared to be 'the requisites that ought to be found in

[1] See P. Schofield, *Utility and Democracy: The Political Thought of Jeremy Bentham* (Oxford: Oxford University Press, 2006), 88, 89, 107, 168–9. For Bentham's fears for the consequences of any attempt forcibly to redistribute property, see, for instance, J. Bentham, *Writings on the Poor Laws: Volume II*, ed. M. Quinn (Oxford: Clarendon Press, 2010 [*CW*]), 194–5. The non-existence of any threat to property from a universal franchise, or rather such a franchise subject to a literacy test, is the main theme of 'Radicalism not Dangerous' written in 1819–20. See J. Bentham, *The Works of Jeremy Bentham*, ed. J. Bowring, 11 vols. (Edinburgh: William Tait, 1843), iii. 599–622.

every well constituted frame of government'.[2] That the securing of intellectual aptitude was a prominent concern of Bentham can be seen in the various schemes he devised for securing information, the source of knowledge, for instance, in the political assembly envisaged in *Political Tactics*,[3] in the publication of accounts in the proposed panopticon prison,[4] in the reporting of crime in the proposed *Police Gazette* and *Calendar of Delinquency*,[5] and in the recording of official activity in the proposed *Constitutional Code*.[6] It is also worth noting that, in his proposals for political reform, Bentham insisted on the ability to read as a sine qua non for granting the vote. In this chapter, I attempt to present a framework for understanding the significance of intellectual aptitude – of knowledge and judgement – in Bentham's political thought and how it not only complemented but was a necessary adjunct to moral aptitude in securing good government. Since the key to securing good government was to bring about an identification of interests between rulers and subjects, I will explain Bentham's notion of interest and the main varieties of interest that feature in his political thought. I will then explain how Bentham hoped to bring about an identification of interests, before showing the place of intellectual aptitude in this process. First, however, I will show that Bentham's opposition to democracy in the period following the French Revolution was based on his concern that the people in general lacked the necessary intelligence to undertake the task of electing representatives and then outline the emergence of his commitment to a democratic form of government.

1.2 The People's Ignorance as a Bar to Democracy

Throughout his career, Bentham insisted that the general interest of the community – in other words, the greatest happiness of its members – was

[2] See Bentham Papers, British Library Additional MS 33,550, fo. 35 (25 October 1814), referring to W. Blackstone, *Commentaries on the Laws of England*, 4 vols. (Oxford: Clarendon Press, 1765–9 [*CW*]), i. 48.

[3] J. Bentham, *Political Tactics*, ed. M. James, C. Blamires, and C. Pease-Watkin (Oxford: Clarendon Press, 1999 [*CW*]), 33–4.

[4] Bentham, *Works*, iv. 29.

[5] S. Jacques and P. Schofield, eds., *Jeremy Bentham on Police: The Unknown Story and What It Means for Criminology* (London: UCL Press, 2021), 91–102. These proposals were an elaboration of a scheme that he had put forward in 'A View of the Hard-Labour Bill' in 1778. See Bentham, *Works*, iv. 48–9.

[6] J. Bentham, *Constitutional Code: Volume I*, ed. F. Rosen and J. H. Burns, (Oxford: Clarendon Press, 1983 [*CW*]), 218–67.

the only right and proper end of government.[7] He did, however, change his mind about which form of government would best achieve this end. Up to the time of the French Revolution, when he was mainly working on a complete penal code (the work published as *An Introduction to the Principles of Morals and Legislation* was written as the first part of the introduction to the penal code), he did not, as he himself confessed, overly concern himself with constitutional law.[8] He was indifferent as to the form of government, envisaging that once he had presented his penal code to an enlightened sovereign – whether that was the British Parliament or an absolute monarch such as Frederick the Great of Prussia or, more plausibly in his view, Catherine the Great of Russia – its merit would be recognized and it would be enacted accordingly. When the course of the French Revolution led him to consider political reform, except for one brief interlude, he opposed democracy, not because of any deficiency in the people's desire to promote the general interest – by definition there could not be, since the universal interest, as we will see in Section 1.4, was constituted by an aggregation of all the individual interests in a community – but because of a deficiency in intellectual aptitude. In 'Considérations sur la composition des États-Généraux', written in late 1788 or early 1789, for instance, Bentham argued in favour of political equality, on the grounds that each person's interest should be given equal consideration. He did, however, add the qualification that only those persons who were capable of correctly judging the nature of their interest should be enfranchised, and on this basis proceeded to exclude minors, the insane, females (though he pointed out that there was no valid reason for excluding them), non-proprietors, and non-readers. The problem in relation to non-proprietors was that they would demand a redistribution of property because they would only see the immediate advantage to themselves and not realize that the long-term consequences, by undermining security and hence the incentive to labour, would be disastrous for society as a whole. At the same time, Bentham rejected plural votes for those with large amounts of property. If the franchise were limited to those with the ability to make correct

[7] For two similar statements to this effect, written over half-a-century apart (1780 and 1823 respectively), see J. Bentham, *An Introduction to the Principles of Morals and Legislation*, ed. J. H. Burns and H. L. A. Hart (London: Athlone Press, 1970 [*CW*]), 13; and 'Constitutional Code: Matter Occasioned by Greece', in J. Bentham, *Securities against Misrule and Other Constitutional Writings for Tripoli and Greece*, ed. P. Schofield (Oxford: Clarendon Press, 1990 [*CW*]), 259.

[8] Bentham, *Introduction to the Principles of Morals and Legislation* (*CW*), 281.

judgements about their personal interest, then each such individual had neither more nor less than one personal interest, which should be given the same consideration as that of every other individual. Moreover, each person had only one understanding, and so each eligible person should have only one vote. This seems to have been his point when he asked whether a man had 'trois âmes pour sentir? deux, trois esprits pour juger?'[9]

When briefly flirting with political reform in the early period of the French Revolution, Bentham recommended a universal franchise (including females) for France and a universal male franchise for Britain but characteristically added the proviso that the vote should be limited to those with the ability to read.[10] Events in France in the autumn of 1792 thereupon led Bentham, like the vast majority of his countrymen, to adopt a much more politically conservative outlook.[11] He again opposed democracy on the grounds that the ignorance, or the lack of intelligence, of the people meant that they were incapable of conducting the affairs of government. Democracy obliterated the salutary distinction between legislators and members of the community generally: 'You employ one man to make laws for you as you employ another man to make shoes.' There were few even among the well-educated who were capable of governing well, and yet in a democracy everyone was required to take an interest in and understand public affairs. The intelligence needed to choose legislators, and hence to judge their policies, was beyond the capacity of the people, who were 'all *will* – they have no reason, no understanding'.[12] Moreover, the people, who had to labour for a living, lacked sufficient time to understand public affairs. A democratic government would require that each and every citizen employed themselves in the business of government: 'Either the major part of the whole labour of the state must be thus bestowed or those who take time to understand the business must be governed and outvoted by those who do

[9] J. Bentham, *Rights, Representation, and Reform: Nonsense upon Stilts and Other Writings on the French Revolution*, ed. P. Schofield, C. Pease-Watkin, and C. Blamires (Oxford: Clarendon Press, 2002 [*CW*]), 69–70, 83–5. As he later puts it in *Rationale of Judicial Evidence, specially applied to English practice*, ed. J. S. Mill, 5 vols. (London: Hunt and Clarke, 1827), iv. 475 (reprinted in Bentham, *Works*, vii. 334), 'every individual in the country tells for one; no individual for more than one'.

[10] Bentham, *Rights, Representation, and Reform* (*CW*), 248–9, 428–9.

[11] See I. R. Christie, *Stress and Stability in Late Eighteenth-Century Britain: Reflections on the British Avoidance of Revolution* (Oxford: Clarendon Press, 1984).

[12] Bentham Papers, University College London Library (hereafter UC), box xliv, fo. 2.

not and can not take time to understand it.'[13] Bentham praised the electoral system in Britain for placing government in the hands of the 'well-informed classes', thereby providing a security against anarchy and civil war[14] and criticized the 'system of the democrats' for subjugating 'the well-informed to the ill-informed *classes* of mankind'.[15] He made the same point when, in discussing pauper education in his writings on the poor laws in or around 1797, he argued that pauper children apprenticed to the proposed National Charity Company should be enjoined not only 'to be contented with their lot' but also 'to mind their own business', since the existing government was 'better than any other to the formation of which [the pauper child] can have any chance of contributing, were he even to . . . devote his whole time and attention to the accomplishment of the supposed improvement'. In order to establish a new form of government, the pauper child would need to possess as much knowledge about the law in all its branches – civil, penal, constitutional, financial, and ecclesiastical – and the administration of the armed forces, the government of colonies, and the conduct of foreign affairs, as did the Lord Chancellor and the judges, the bishops, the Lords of the Treasury, and all the rest of the government officials put together.[16]

1.3 The Emergence of Bentham's Commitment to Democracy

From the outbreak of the French Revolution until 1803, Bentham's life was dominated by the panopticon prison scheme and by other initiatives – such as his proposals relating to the poor laws, police, and finance – by which he aimed to help the British state through the various crises engendered by the French Revolutionary Wars. His bitterness at the rejection by ministers of the panopticon prison scheme, which, he claimed, amounted to the exercise of an unconstitutional dispensing power on the part of the executive,[17] and his development, in the context

13 UC xliv. 5.
14 UC xliv. 4.
15 UC xliv. 5.
16 Bentham, *Poor Laws: II* (*CW*), 193, 195–6.
17 Bentham gave a detailed account of his dealings with the administration in relation to panopticon between 1798 and 1802 in 'A Picture of the Treasury' (see UC boxes cxx and cxxi), which in turn gave rise to the three 'Letters to Pelham' and 'A Plea for the Constitution'. See J. Bentham, *Panopticon versus New South Wales and Other Writings on Australia*, ed. T. Causer and P. Schofield (London: UCL Press, 2022 [*CW*]), Editorial Introduction, pp. xvii–xviii.

of writings on judicial procedure and evidence between 1803 and 1809,[18] of the notion of 'sinister interest', eventually led to his 'transition' or 'conversion' to democracy.[19] The eighteenth-century Bentham thought that English law in general, and the law of evidence in particular, was so confused, complex, and chaotic because lawyers, trapped by habit and tradition, had been unable to see how to reform it. From 1803, he began to recognise that reform was not undertaken, not because lawyers lacked the requisite understanding but because they had a sinister interest in seeing it remain in its chaotic state. 'Judge & Co', as he disparagingly referred to the legal profession, made money from fees, and the more complex the legal procedure, the greater the number and value of the fees that they might harvest. This had the effect of denying justice to all but the richest part of the population. At first, Bentham believed that the lawyers had hoodwinked the politicians into thinking that legal reform was impossible; but by the summer of 1809, he had come to the conclusion that the politicians were in league with the lawyers.[20] The whole legal, political, and ecclesiastical establishment of the British state, in his view, shared a common sinister interest in oppressing the vast majority of the people. As he stated in the printed but unpublished 'Preface for the Second Edition' of *A Fragment on Government*, written in 1822, at the time of the work's first publication in 1776 he had regarded the 'imperfections' in the law as the result of nothing worse than 'inattention and prejudice', but 'the experience and observations of near fifty years' had revealed them to be 'the elaborately organized, and anxiously cherished and guarded products of sinister interest and artifice'.[21]

From 1809 until his death in 1832, Bentham's career was marked by political radicalism – at first advocating 'democratic ascendancy' within the British state and then from about 1818 advocating republicanism for each and every political community across the globe.[22] He now recognized that

18 The vast majority of the material for *Rationale of Judicial Evidence*, *Scotch Reform* (London: J. Ridgway, 1808 with a second edition in 1811) and *The Elements of the Art of Packing, as applied to Special Juries, particularly in cases of libel law* (London: Effingham Wilson, 1821), was written between 1803 and 1809.

19 A detailed account appears in Schofield, *Utility and Democracy*, 109–36.

20 See, for instance, J. Bentham, *Official Aptitude Maximized; Expense Minimized*, ed. P. Schofield (Oxford: Clarendon Press, 1993 [*CW*]), 376–7; and J. Bentham, *A Comment on the Commentaries and A Fragment on Government*, ed. J. H. Burns and H. L. A. Hart (London: Athlone Press, 1977 [*CW*]), 539–40.

21 Bentham, *Comment/Fragment* (*CW*), 508.

22 He addressed various publications to 'all nations professing liberal opinions', but his writings for Tripoli reveal his ambitions to have been universal.

utilitarian reform – the promotion of the general interest of the community – would only be implemented by a democratic government and even then only by a particular form of democratic government. Bentham rejected, for instance, a form of democracy based on the traditional doctrine of the separation of powers. To give the legislature, executive, and judiciary their own spheres of authority would tend to create interests that would run counter to the general interest.[23] In contrast, as we will see in Section 1.5, Bentham's scheme was founded on chains of subordination and superordination. The people would be sovereign. The legislature would be subordinate to the people in their role as electors or, in Bentham's terminology, as possessors of the supreme constitutive power. The administrative and judicial departments (together composing the executive power) would be subordinate to the legislature – the purpose of both administration and judiciary would be to put into effect the will of the legislature and that of the legislature to put into effect the will of the people.[24] The administrative department, headed by the prime minister and up to thirteen ministers, would constitute in effect a bureaucracy or civil service,[25] while judges would enforce the provisions of the enacted code and not, like English common law judges, make the law themselves, while claiming only to declare it.[26]

1.4 The Varieties of Interest

The promotion of the general or universal interest – in other words, the interest of the community – was, for Bentham, as we have seen above, the only right and proper end of government. What, then, did he mean by 'the general interest'? In *An Introduction to the Principles of Morals and Legislation*, having explained that by 'utility' he meant the tendency of

[23] Bentham, *Rights, Representation, and Reform* (*CW*), 405–18; J. Bentham, *First Principles Preparatory to Constitutional Code*, ed. P. Schofield (Oxford: Clarendon Press, 1989 [*CW*]), 101–12.

[24] Bentham, *Constitutional Code: I* (*CW*), 25–7.

[25] See L. J. Hume, *Bentham and Bureaucracy* (Cambridge: Cambridge University Press, 1981), 209–37.

[26] J. Bentham, *'Legislator of the World': Writings on Law, Codification, and Education*, ed. P. Schofield and J. Harris (Oxford: Clarendon Press, 1998 [*CW*]), 123–40. For a general account of Bentham's Constitutional Code, see F. Rosen, *Jeremy Bentham and Representative Democracy: A Study of the Constitutional Code* (Oxford: Clarendon Press, 1983); and for an assessment of the continuing relevance of Bentham's constitutional thought, see J. Elster, *Securities against Misrule: Juries, Assemblies, Elections* (Cambridge: Cambridge University Press, 2013).

any 'object' to 'produce benefit, advantage, pleasure, good, or happiness . . . or . . . to prevent the happening of mischief, pain, evil, or unhappiness to the party whose interest is considered', whether that of the community in general or that of a particular individual, Bentham continued:

> The interest of the community is one of the most general expressions that can occur in the phraseology of morals: no wonder that the meaning of it is often lost. When it has a meaning, it is this. The community is a fictitious *body*, composed of the individual persons who are considered as constituting as it were its *members*. The interest of the community then is, what? – the sum of the several members who compose it.
>
> It is in vain to talk of the interest of the community, without understanding what is the interest of the individual. A thing is said to promote the interest, or to be *for* the interest, of an individual, when it tends to add to the sum total of his pleasures: or, what comes to the same thing, to diminish the sum total of his pains.

In a note to the phrase 'interest of the individual' in the second of the quoted paragraphs, Bentham explained: 'Interest is one of those words, which not having any superior *genus*, cannot in the ordinary way be defined.'[27] He was alluding to his division of nouns substantive into the names of real and fictitious entities and to the Aristotelian method of definition *per genus et differentiam*, whereby, for instance, a human being was defined as an animal that possessed the quality of reason.[28] An entity was real insofar as it had physical existence, such as an animal, a chair, an apple, or a book, and as such was capable of being perceived through the senses. An entity was fictitious insofar as it did not have physical existence, and so was not perceptible, but yet it still made sense to speak of it – in short, the name of a fictitious entity was the name of an abstraction. Hence, an interest, like a right or a power or a duty, was not capable of being seen or touched, for instance, and neither could it be defined *per genus et differentiam* because it was not a sort of anything, as a human being was a sort of animal.

Hence, in order to give an 'exposition' (rather than 'definition') of the term 'interest', it was necessary to have recourse to the method of 'paraphrasis', which involved, as Bentham explained, not the translation of one word into another or other words, but rather the translation of one

[27] Bentham, *Introduction to the Principles of Morals and Legislation* (*CW*), 12 & n.

[28] See J. Bentham, *Preparatory Principles*, ed. D. G. Long and P. Schofield (Oxford: Clarendon Press, 2016 [*CW*]), 97–8, 157–8, 434–5.

whole sentence that contained the name or names of a fictitious entity or entities into another whole sentence in which the terms either represented real entities or were 'more immediately resolvable' into terms representing real entities. Propositions containing the names of fictitious entities only made sense if they could be translated into propositions containing 'terms calculated to raise *images* either of *substances* perceived, or of *emotions*; – sources, one or other of which every idea must be drawn from, to be a clear one'. Hence, if I have a duty to perform (or refrain from performing) some action, then another person has a right to make me perform (or refrain from performing) it, and if I do not perform it (or do perform it), I am liable to be punished, in other words, to suffer a pain administered in accordance with the expressed will of the legislator.[29] The notion of having a duty could only be understood by relating it to its 'real source' in physical reality,[30] which in this case consisted of certain persons, certain expressions of will on their part, certain pains and pleasures, and so forth. It should be noted that Bentham regarded the emotions of pain and pleasure as real entities, in that they had a physiological basis and were directly perceptible by the mind.

To understand what it meant to say that a person had an interest, it was necessary to translate a sentence in which the term 'interest' appeared into another sentence that contained only the names of real entities. To say that a person had an interest in some event or in some state of affairs was, therefore, to say that the person in question would receive some benefit from the event taking place or the state of affairs coming into existence, with the notion of benefit referring to the expectation that the person in question would experience a balance of pleasure over pain. To speak of 'the interest of the community' brought together the names of two fictitious entities – the term 'community' was just as much the name of a non-physical entity as the term 'interest'. A 'community', as a collective noun, only made sense when understood as the aggregate of the individuals who composed it. Hence, a political community consisted of the aggregate of the individuals who were subject to the same sovereign, and the interest of that community consisted in an aggregate of the pains and pleasures experienced or expected to be experienced by each of the individuals in that community. Given that the 'partisan' of the principle of utility approved of any action

29 Bentham, *Comment/Fragment* (*CW*), 494–5 n.
30 UC ci. 218 (23 August 1814), reproduced in Bentham, *Works*, viii. 246.

that augmented the happiness of the community and disapproved of any that tended to diminish it,[31] the notion of promoting the utility of the community, promoting the interest of the community, and promoting the general interest, amounted to the same thing, since these phrases only made sense when related to the promotion of pleasure and the diminution of pain. It should also be noted that the notion of interest was linked in Bentham's thought to that of motive. If one had an interest, for example, in the performance of a particular action, that was as much as to say that one had a motive to perform it. In *A Table of the Springs of Action* (1817), Bentham produced a list of pleasures and pains with their corresponding interests and motives: hence the pleasures and pains of curiosity were linked to the 'Interest of the Spying-Glass' and motives such as curiosity, inquisitiveness, and desire of information.[32]

Two pairs of contrasting interests were central to Bentham's democratic thought: the first, the general or universal interest as opposed to particular interests; and the second, a right and proper interest as opposed to a sinister interest. The general or universal interest, as we have seen, was equivalent to that of the community as a whole, while a particular interest was that of an individual or some group of persons less than the community as a whole. A right and proper interest consisted of an interest in performing an action or bringing about a state of affairs that increased the happiness of the community overall. A sinister interest consisted of an interest in performing an action or bringing about a state of affairs that, while it increased the happiness of the persons who possessed the sinister interest, decreased the happiness of the community overall. A sinister interest was a particular interest, though not every particular interest was a sinister interest. For example, it might be the particular interest of an individual to perform an action that gave that individual a degree of pleasure but that either affected no one else (it was a purely self-regarding action) or on balance benefited the other persons affected by it. In this case, the particular interest of the individual was a right and proper interest, since it led to an increase in the happiness of the community overall. A sinister interest was a particular interest that led to actions or states of affairs that diminished the general or universal interest. To act in such a way as to promote a sinister interest to the detriment of the general interest was to bring about 'the sinister sacrifice'

[31] Bentham, *Introduction to the Principles of Morals and Legislation* (*CW*), 13.

[32] J. Bentham, *Deontology together with A Table of the Springs of Action and Article on Utilitarianism*, ed. A. Goldworth (Oxford: Clarendon Press, 1983 [*CW*]), 82.

or, in other words, to act corruptly. Hence, in Bentham's view, it was in the sinister interest of lawyers to maintain the complexities and obscurities of the law because of the monetary gain it brought them, despite the greater harm it did in denying justice to the vast majority of the community. Similarly, it was in the sinister interest of rulers, or the ruling few, as we will see in Section 1.5, to oppress subjects, or the subject many, on account of the power, wealth, and reputation it brought them.[33]

1.5 The Identification of Interests

The problem that the utilitarian moralist had to address was how to ensure that rulers used their power to promote the general interest, rather than their own particular and sinister interest. As Bentham noted, 'Power in a certain quantity and in certain shapes is of the essence of the situation'. In the case of the power exercised by government, he explained that,

> power is the power of disposing of certain things and certain services of certain persons with a view to a certain end: under things, money being included: the object and problem is so to order matters that in each situation having power to make application of the things and human services in question to the benefit of the whole community or a certain portion of it according to the department to which the office of the functionary belongs, he should at the same time not have power to dispose of it to his own benefit exclusively or to the benefit of particular individuals connected with him by this or that special line of interest or sympathy.[34]

The solution lay in the identification of interests, whereby the actual end of government was brought into coincidence with the proper end. The whole point of constitutional law was to replace the natural opposition of interests that existed between rulers and subjects with an artificial identification of interests. Rulers were to be so placed that the only way in which they could promote their own particular interest was through the promotion of their share in the universal interest.[35]

In 'Identification of Interests' (1822), Bentham expounded the notion of the identification of interests as follows:

[33] Bentham, *First Principles* (*CW*), 17–20, 184–5, 192–3, 270.
[34] Ibid., 30.
[35] Ibid., 232–7.

> As between each individual and the whole community, identification of interests has place, in so far as when in consequence of any act on his part, or any other event or state of things, good in any shape happens to him, good in the same or any other shape happens to the whole community; or in so far as evil happens, evil: and in so far as in consequence of that same cause good happens to the community, good happens to him, or in as far as evil happens to the community, evil happens to him.
>
> As between individual and the community, identification of interests is constituted by communion in good, or by communion in evil, or by communion in both kinds.[36]

The opposite state of affairs, the opposition of interests between an official, or, in Bentham's terminology, a functionary, and the community, might arise either from the laws and institutions of the state themselves or from 'delinquency', that is, actions in contravention of laws and institutions. The first case was much the more serious, as it demonstrated that 'the root of the evil is in the form of government' and would not be remedied until 'the texture of the government' was changed. Yet the 'texture of the government' was itself dependent on the actions of those functionaries who supported it, whether they had created it or not, because it served their interests to do so. The result of this 'sacrifice of universal to particular and sinister interest' was that 'depredation and oppression are carried on with impunity' and on 'the very largest scale', that is, against all the members of the community, excepting only those to whom 'the self-constituted and self-licensed depredators and oppressors are please[d] to grant exemption'.[37] Where the evil-doing and delinquency lay with the people themselves or with lower-ranking functionaries, the problem lay in a lack of intellectual aptitude and the solution lay in the provision of information. Where it lay with 'the highest functionaries themselves', the problem lay in a lack of 'moral aptitude' and the only remedy was a change in the form of government. A change of the functionaries themselves was 'useless', since they would continue to be effectuated by the same sinister interests and would continue to pursue the same sinister course: 'The whole Official Establishment is in that case in the state of a ship infected with the plague.'[38]

According to Bentham, as noted above, the only form of government in which the identification of interests could be made effective was a

[36] Ibid., 125.
[37] Ibid., 126–7.
[38] Ibid., 127–8.

representative democracy, and even then, only a particular form of representative democracy. He outlined the principles on which his ideal republic would be based in 'Economy as applied to Office' (1822), where he combined an analysis of the various sorts of powers that might exist in a political state with his view concerning the best form that the distribution of those powers might take. He divided power in government into operative and constitutive power: the former performed the business of government, while the latter 'determined who the person or persons are by whom the operative power shall be exercised'. Taking the supreme power, as opposed to subordinate power, in a state, he divided supreme operative power into supreme legislative and supreme executive power. The former was the general power to impose upon 'persons of all classes, obligations of all sorts, for purposes of all sorts, and with reference to things of all sorts', without any other power in the state being capable of nullifying or altering the obligations in question. The purpose of the supreme executive power was to give 'execution and effect to the ordinances issued by the supreme legislative power', in other words, to apply the general ordinances of the supreme legislature to particular persons or particular classes of persons. The supreme executive power, though supreme with reference to all other persons, was subordinate to the legislature. The supreme executive power itself was divided into administrative and judicial power. Both powers, which were assigned to an administrative and judicial department respectively, as branches of executive power, were, therefore, concerned with applying the ordinances of the supreme legislative power, but in the latter case only where there was 'a contest between two or more parties in respect to the point of right', with the plaintiff complaining that, without the interposition of the judicial power, something that the defendant ought to do would not be done. The administrative power, however, could act on its own initiative, where authorized to do so by the legislative power, particularly in relation to the goods and services that had been 'rendered exigible for the use of the state'.[39]

The supreme constitutive power, argued Bentham, should be placed without any defalcation in 'the people at large', since it would thereby be placed in the hands of those persons whose interest constituted the universal interest. Each person, Bentham explained, was 'disposed . . . to take that course which in his judgment is most conducive to his own

[39] Ibid., 6–7.

individual interest' and hence would be 'disposed to take that course which is most conducive to the universal interest: for the universal interest is nothing else than the aggregate of all individual interests'. This was simple and straightforward, remarked Bentham, since the description of this group of persons would remain the same, even though the individuals themselves would change by birth and death and by immigration and emigration. In relation to the supreme constitutive power, therefore, each individual was left to pursue that course of action that in his view made 'the best provision possible for his own individual interest'. The position was far different in relation to the possessors of the supreme operative power, since they had to be prevented from pursuing their individual interests insofar as those interests were in conflict with the universal interest. The difficulty was to set 'the strictest limits' on such power, yet at the same time give it 'amplitude sufficient' for the promotion of the universal interest. This was achieved by not only giving the power of appointing the holders of supreme operative power to the people in their capacity of holders of supreme constitutive power but also the power of dismissing them. In general, while the rulers pursued the universal interest, the people would allow them to remain in office; if they failed to pursue the universal interest, the people would remove them.[40]

The mechanism envisaged by Bentham for such appointment and dismissal (or, in Bentham's terminology, location and dislocation) was through election to a representative legislative assembly, which would in turn, as we have seen, control the administrative and judicial departments of government. The elections to the legislature would be conducted annually by secret ballot, within roughly equal electoral districts. The right to vote would be subject to a literacy test and the electorate would consist of males over the age of twenty-one, until such time as the males themselves were enlightened enough to admit women to the suffrage.[41] Each constituent would choose that candidate who would sacrifice every one else's interest to his own, and in order to secure his vote, were he the only voter, the candidate would promise to do so. However, each individual constituent had some overlapping, but also some competing interests, and so, in order to be successful, the candidate had to appeal to as wide a range of those interests as possible. 'To recommend himself to all', noted Bentham, 'what is possible is – to promote the interest of each in those points in which it is not opposed by any other interests: this accordingly is

[40] Ibid., 132–4.

[41] Bentham, *Constitutional Code: I* (*CW*), 29–30; Bentham, *First Principles* (*CW*), 97–100.

what he does'. In the representative assembly, each member would vote in favour of the interest of the inhabitants of his district, whereupon 'arrangements which are favorable to the interests of the inhabitants of all the Districts, or at least to the majority of them' would 'be adopted and carried into effect'. To the extent that it depended upon government, the interest of each person insofar as it was not adverse to the happiness of any other person, would be secured, 'while all such portions of happiness as he could not be made to enjoy without depriving others of happiness to greater amount will not be given to him'. 'On this plan', Bentham noted, 'the identification of each man's individual interest with the several individual interests of all the other members of the community has place as far as the nature of man permitts'. With the supreme constitutive power in the hands of subjects (albeit acting as rulers when exercising the constitutive power itself), and the supreme operative power in the hands of persons chosen by them, the identification of interests between rulers and subjects would be as complete as possible.[42]

This structure represented the bare outline of the constitutional arrangements that Bentham thought necessary for the securing of good rule. Within this democratic structure, Bentham devised a whole series of 'securities against misrule', with a view to promoting the moral, intellectual, and active aptitude of government functionaries. The most important security against misrule was the maximizing of moral responsibility, in other words, exposing rulers to criticism through the medium of what Bentham termed the public opinion tribunal. Throughout his career, Bentham had recognized the importance of the capacity to criticize rulers as a vital security for good government.[43] In his later democratic writings, he recommended detailed provisions for the publication and dissemination of records detailing the actions of officials, from members of the legislature down to subordinate functionaries in the various ministries,[44] which would provide the basis for an informed and critical public opinion.[45]

42 *First Principles* (*CW*), 135–6.

43 See, for instance, Bentham, *Comment/Fragment* (*CW*), 485; and J. Bentham, *On the Liberty of the Press, and Public Discussion and Other Legal and Political Writings for Spain and Portugal*, ed. C. Pease-Watkin and P. Schofield (Oxford: Clarendon Press, 2012 [*CW*]), 1–52.

44 See Bentham, *Political Tactics* (*CW*), 29–44; Bentham, *First Principles* (*CW*), 292–8; and Bentham, *Constitutional Code: I* (*CW*), 162–8.

45 See G. J. Postema, 'The Soul of Justice: Bentham on Publicity, Law, and the Rule of Law', in X. Zhai and M. Quinn, eds., *Bentham's Theory of Law and Public Opinion* (Cambridge: Cambridge University Press, 2014), 40–62.

1.6 The People as the Possessors of Intellectual Aptitude

When Bentham turned to democracy, his assessment of the intelligence of the people was very different from that he had advanced in the 1790s. The change of mind is obvious enough, though the process that produced it requires further examination. Bentham himself, as we will see, pointed to the United States, as a large-scale functioning democracy where political debate thrived,[46] and to Ireland under the Volunteer Movement, as positive examples of popular participation in government. Be that as it may, in 'Identification of Interests', Bentham answered the objection – an objection that he had himself urged in the wake of the French Revolution – that the people neither did possess, nor could be made to possess, sufficient knowledge and judgement to qualify them to vote for members of the supreme legislative assembly. He responded that there was no other person or set of persons who possessed a greater degree of intellectual aptitude, combined with an equal degree of moral aptitude, or at least who were so far superior in the former, and so little inferior in the latter, as to possess an overall superiority in aptitude. Whether the supreme power was lodged in a single hand, in the hands of a few, or shared between the one and the few, or between 'a tricompound body, composed of the one, the few and the delegates of the people – or rather of a small portion of the people' (Bentham, of course, had the British form of government in mind), it was the interest of these rulers that all the 'external instruments, or say means, of felicity' – wealth, power, reputation, factitious dignity, vengeance, and ease[47] – be concentrated in their hands, whereas it was the interest of the greatest number that they be distributed 'in a manner as near to equality as is consistent with general subsistence, general abundance in the character of a security against accident, and general security in all its shapes'. In the case of the tri-compound system, 'the whole of the stock of knowledge, judgment, and active talent' would be used by rulers to augment their own share of the instruments of felicity, which was as much as to say to reduce that of the people in general. 'On the part of the people, appropriate aptitude in the shape of moral aptitude is at all times at a maximum: on the part of the one, at all times . . . at a minimum', while on the part of the people, intellectual aptitude was 'at all times naturally on the encrease', and, were

[46] See H. L. A. Hart, *Essays on Bentham: Studies in Jurisprudence and Political Theory* (Oxford: Clarendon Press, 1982), 53–78.

[47] Bentham, *First Principles* (*CW*), 152.

rulers actively to promote its development, was 'susceptible of great and continual encrease'. On the contrary, rulers had directed their efforts towards diminishing 'the stock of true, active knowledge: in the room of true conceptions to substitute false, fallacious and mischievous ones', especially the view that the maximum of moral aptitude was to be found in the ruling one and that it existed in 'the sub-ruling or jointly ruling few . . . in proportion to their respective altitudes in the conjoint scales of power, opulence and factitious dignity'.[48]

A point reiterated by Bentham was that, if the people were ignorant or incapable of perceiving their true interest (which, perhaps, in effect amounted to the same thing), it was a result of a deliberate policy on the part of the ruling classes not only in keeping them ignorant but in giving them false ideas – in other words, in deluding them. When, in the 'Postscript to the Second Edition' of *A Fragment on Government*, he reflected on the significance of the work in terms of its offering, when it appeared in 1776, the first critique of English law, he noted that one of the strategies used by lawyers was to argue that legal fictions – in short, lies – were necessary to the provision of justice. Outside the law, falsehood was 'painted in its proper colours' as a vice, but in lawyers it was regarded as a virtue, with a view to showing that rulers possessed 'the power of making *wrong* and *right* change natures, and determining what shall be *morality* as well as what shall be *law*', and to determine what should be truth. 'To produce ductility', Bentham stated, 'produce debility . . . . But for this [debility in the people], how could judges have been suffered to make law, or priests gospel, as they have been and still are?'[49] In *The Book of Fallacies*, Bentham pointed out that the lawyers tried to ensure that the law could not be known by those whose fate was determined by it, while the clergy obstructed the means of teaching the art of reading by their opposition to the Lancasterian schools.[50] It was a prominent theme of *Church-of-Englandism and its Catechism Examined* that the point of forcing children to recite the catechism in the Church's own National Society schools was to produce moral and intellectual depravity. The poor children whose parents would not send them to a Church-of-England school would be abandoned to 'ignorance, vice, and wretchedness', while those who were sent would come under the

48 Ibid., 142–4.

49 Bentham, *Comment/Fragment* (*CW*), 511.

50 J. Bentham, *The Book of Fallacies*, ed. P. Schofield (Oxford: Clarendon Press, 2015 [*CW*]), 132.

dominion of the Church, with the catechism employed for corrupting both the intellectual and the moral part of their minds:

> the *intellectual* … that by weakness they might be rendered *unable*, because by terror they had been rendered *unwilling*, to discern the mischievousness of the dominion exercised at their expense: the *moral* part, that by their being themselves habituated to the practice of mendacity and insincerity in their own sphere, the spectacle of those vices, when practised at their expense in higher spheres, might in their eyes be rendered an object of indifference.[51]

In 'Constitutional Code Rationale', Bentham emphasized the importance of delusion, that is, the engendering of 'erroneous conception or opinion', to misrule. The purpose of delusion was to engender the opinion that those who held the highest offices in government were possessed of appropriate aptitude for exercising the powers of government and that the higher the office, the greater the aptitude. In truth, remarked Bentham, the opposite was usually the case.[52]

In 'Identification of Interests', Bentham went on to deal with a second objection to the involvement of the people in the political process – again one that he had himself advanced in the 1790s – namely, that the people, given that most of their 'disposable waking time' was 'unavoidably preoccupied by labour for subsistence, and a small quantity for recreation', did not have enough time to form a correct judgement concerning the aptitude of candidates for election, especially in light of the fact that the business of legislation might comprise 'little less than the whole field of thought and action'. Bentham gave the same answer as he had to the first objection, namely, that any such deficiency in intellectual aptitude was no objection unless it could shown that some other persons had greater intellectual aptitude, together with an equal degree of moral aptitude, 'without which superiority in intellectual aptitude is detrimental, and not contributory, to superiority in the aggregate of appropriate aptitude'. Bentham distinguished between self-seated and derivative or borrowed aptitude, that is, between one's own knowledge and that which the 'least instructed' person could obtain from the person 'of whom general estimation points out as the best qualified for giving such advice of all who are within his reach'. He suggested that 'an all-comprehensive and rationalized Code', of the sort

[51] J. Bentham, *Church-of Englandism and its Catechism Examined*, ed. J. E. Crimmins and C. Fuller (Oxford: Clarendon Press, 2011 [*CW*]), 67–8, 88.

[52] Bentham, *First Principles* (*CW*), 261–3.

that he himself was producing, would give 'all possessors of the art of reading' a greater stock of intellectual aptitude than had hitherto existed in 'the best instructed minds'. The code would form 'the standing table' of the people's knowledge, with daily transactions reported in the newspapers furnishing their 'daily bread'.[53]

In *The Book of Fallacies*, he discussed the question of authority, and in particular whose authority might be most reliable, that is, whose authority might possess the greatest 'legitimately persuasive force'. He pointed out that sinister interest affected not only the declaration of an opinion, in that it provided a motive for insincerity, but affected the opinion itself, by keeping 'the relevant means and materials of information ... out of the mind', or, if this did not prove possible, not giving them the weight they deserved. He noted that the correctness and completeness of the information possessed by a man depended on the means he enjoyed for collecting it and the motives he possessed for making use of those means and coming to an accurate opinion based upon them. On these grounds, the most trustworthy opinion was that 'constituted by what may be termed *scientific* or professional *opinion*', since the professional would be likely, for instance, to profit financially if his opinion were seen to be correct and suffer financially if it were seen to be erroneous. In descending order beneath professional authority, Bentham listed authority derived from power, from opulence, and from reputation. A powerful man had greater facility in terms of 'obtaining the means conducive to rectitude of decisions' than the man of opulence, and the man of opulence than the man of reputation. However, none of these classes had 'any motive sufficient to the production of that desire and that energy by which alone he can be, to an adequate degree, put in possession of the means'. In fact, the more power that a man possessed, and the more his desires were thus satiated, the less incentive he had to exert himself. An oriental despot, for instance, had more of the means of information at his command than any other individual, but having no motives to make use of those means, 'the general result is a state next to infantine imbecillity and ignorance'. 'In England', noted Bentham, 'the King – the Peer – the opulent Borough-holding or County-holding Country Gentleman – would ... present an instance of the sort of double scale in question, in which, while means decrease, motives rise'. All this was on the supposition of an absence of sinister interest. Where

53 Ibid., 144–5.

a man's understanding was 'under the dominion of sinister interest', then the more complete the information at his disposal, the less the confidence that should be placed on his expressed opinion, whether pretended or real. Hence, in the case of an opinion expressed by a minister of state, 'the probative weight of the authority' was 'so far from being greater than that in the case of an average man' but rather 'so much below' to the extent that there was reason for supposing that the opposite opinion was 'the right and true one'.[54]

In 'Identification of Interests', Bentham again noted that the acquisition of intellectual aptitude depended on mental labour, while 'the quantity of labour is proportioned to the force of inducement'. The class of monarchs was the class of persons with the least inducement to mental labour, since there was no need for it: the whole time of a monarch was 'spent in the enjoyment of the pleasures of power, none in acquiring aptitude for the exercise of it'. Monarchs were a thousand times more likely than all other classes taken together to suffer from 'mental incapacity', and yet, until his condition rendered it necessary to confine or to banish him, he 'remains in the eyes of all his subjects the same perfect and inimitable seat and model of appropriate moral, intellectual and active, and, in full, all-exalting aptitude'.[55] In practical terms, in the United States, the supreme operative power had been in the hands of the delegates of the people for over forty years, and no where had appropriate aptitude ever approached so nearly to perfection, and no where had the people ever enjoyed such felicity or had there existed on their part 'so great a measure of good morals'. He continued:

> In all places at all times, not in the inverse but in the direct ratio of the quantity of power left in the hands of the many has been the aggregate of appropriate official aptitude, the moderateness of official expence, the stock of actual felicity and intelligible virtues.

Bentham also pointed to the state of Ireland under the Volunteer Movement between 1778 and 1783 and more particularly to the National Convention that met at Dublin in November 1783, where representatives, albeit 'self-appointed', came in from 'all classes promiscuously' but 'all of them actuated by . . . the universal interest', when the result was not a 'scene of universal disorder and universal mischief' but one of 'universal innocence, universal tranquillity, universal felicity and

[54] Bentham, *Book of Fallacies* (*CW*), 124–9.
[55] Bentham, *First Principles* (*CW*), 145.

universal moral virtue'.[56] Bentham turned the view he had expressed in the 1790s on its head. The problem of a lack of intelligence now lay not with the subject classes but with the ruling classes.

1.7 The People's Enemy and the People's Friend

On 6 February 1831, Bentham drafted a letter under the title of 'The People's Enemy Unmasked' intended for anonymous publication in the *Examiner* newspaper. The people's enemy, he noted, claimed that only the owners of substantial property should be represented in Parliament. What this claim amounted to, explained Bentham, was that the '*relatively opulent*, relation had to the rest of the people ... the *relatively unopulent*', were 'the only persons to whose welfare any regard ought to be paid: the only persons whose happiness ought to be the end in view: aimed at as such by the legislative authority in the exercise of its functions'. In other words, both in the form of government and in the exercise of its powers, the greatest happiness of the whole community ought to be sacrificed to that of the smaller number.[57] The people's enemy, continued Bentham, would deny that he aimed to promote the greatest happiness of the smaller number, but rather claim that he aimed to promote the greatest happiness of the greater number, on the grounds that 'appropriate intellectual aptitude' was necessary in order to do so, that the opulent were the class who possessed intellectual aptitude in 'the largest proportion', and that the government should, therefore, be placed in their hands.

In Bentham's imaginary debate, the people's friend responded by pointing out that intellectual aptitude was merely one of the three branches of appropriate aptitude relevant to the situations of legislator and elector, the others being moral and active aptitude. The possession of relative opulence might be taken as 'presumptive evidence' of intellectual aptitude, but it was 'very far from being conclusive' evidence. Moreover, it was only when intellectual and active aptitude were combined with moral aptitude that they were 'contributive to the maximization of all-comprehensive appropriate aptitude'. If the aim of the legislator or the elector was the greatest happiness, not of the subject many but of the ruling few, then the greater his knowledge and the more profound his judgement, 'the greater will be the contribution made by him to the

[56] Ibid., 145–6.
[57] UC cxlix. 278 (6 February 1831).

encrease of the happiness of the ruling few, at the expence of . . . that of the subject many; and thereby of the whole number taken together'.[58]

In order to maximize the happiness of the whole community, the people's friend argued that it was necessary to maximize intellectual aptitude on the part not merely of the greater number but of the whole number of the members of the community, while at the same time not reducing moral aptitude. The possession of riches in itself did not secure intellectual and active aptitude, but what did give likely evidence of it was the possession of 'the art of *reading*'. Hence, it was not property but the capacity to read that should form the basis of representation. The capacity to read was 'moreover conducive to the possession of moral aptitude', since it exposed the reader to 'such discourse' that showed the 'inducements' encouraging him to pursue 'a course of good moral conduct'. The only qualification for the franchise that the people's friend would require 'on the part of an individual of a competent age' would be the ability to read. This was what Jeremy Bentham (as the letter was intended to be anonymous, Bentham referred to himself in the third person) had recommended in his Parliamentary Reform Bill.[59] The people's friend urged that the legislature make provision for teaching the art of reading (whether to the whole population or just to males is not made explicit), and, presumably to illustrate the feasibility of the proposal, pointed to Bavaria and Denmark as countries in which everyone was able to read and write. Having admonished the admirers of the British Constitution for straining 'every nerve to keep your fellow men of this Your Country in the state and condition of beasts of the field', the people's friend concluded:

> In the possession of every man an equal share in the means of having his welfare attended to – this is one good thing; in the hand of every man a key to useful knowledge in every shape – this is another good thing: and of these two good things, on the plan of Mr Bentham, the one is effected by the instrumentality of the other: thus are two birds killed (as the phrase is) with one stone.[60]

This short letter presents a summary of Bentham's case for democracy, and it puts intellectual aptitude at the centre of it.

[58] UC cxlix. 279 (6 February 1831).

[59] UC cxlix. 280 (6 February 1831). For Bentham's recommendation, see 'Radical Reform Bill, with Extracts from the Reasons', in Bentham, *Works*, viii. 558–97 at 560, 565.

[60] UC cxlix. 281 (6 February 1831).

1.8 Conclusion

In this chapter, I have attempted to present a framework for understanding the place of knowledge and judgement, or intellectual aptitude, within Bentham's political thought and in particular its importance in terms of Bentham's commitment to democracy. In the earlier part of his career, while acknowledging that government should be conducted in the interest of the whole community, he did not think that it could be entrusted to the people because of their lack of intelligence and the means to acquire it. In the later part of his career, he thought that it was the rich and powerful who lacked any incentive to undertake the necessary labour to acquire knowledge and to exercise judgement, or if they did so, that it would be directed towards their own sinister ends. They did, however, have every incentive to maintain the people in ignorance. The sinister interest of rulers would be overcome by the identification of interests, made possible by the introduction of a democratic form of government, where the diffusion of the art of reading would promote the intellectual aptitude of the people. While the identification of interests between rulers and subjects was made possible by a democratic structure, it did not necessarily achieve it without further securities against misrule. One of the most important securities was that provided by the people in their role as members of the public opinion tribunal, which required them to be informed – with newspapers playing a critical role – to debate, to express their views, and then to give effect to their views. Bentham always supported the promotion of the general interest, but it was only when he reconciled himself to the fact that the people themselves best understood their own interest that he was able, consistently and coherently, to advocate democracy.

2

Bentham, Democracy, Free Government, and the Relationship between Rulers and Ruled

MICHAEL QUINN

> The Sedition Act may be regarded as a second *Magna Charta*, preserving against attacks still more destructive that security which the first had formed . . .. The Sedition Act has silenced the mob of inflammatory tongues: but howsoever necessary, and . . .exempt from real danger, it can not be denied to have been a measure of the strongest . . . kind.[1]

> For the destruction of everything by which the constitution of this country has ever been distinguished to its advantage, no additional measures need be employed: let but the principles already avowed continue to be avowed – let but the course of action . . . be persevered in – the consummation is effected.
>
> Gagging Bills – suspension of the Habeas Corpus Act – interdiction of all communication between man and man for any such purpose as that of complaint or remedy – all these have already become precedent.[2]

Jeremy Bentham wrote both these passages, although eighteen years separated them. The first, praising the Seditious Meetings Act of 1795, which banned large political meetings unless licensed by a magistrate, appears in Bentham's little-known writings of 1798–9 on preventive police.[3] The second, in critique of both the Seditious Meetings Act of 1817, which repeated the provisions of the Act of 1795 and added new penalties, and the suspension of *habeas corpus*, appears in the work by publication of which, eight years after initial drafting, Bentham declared

[1] 'Notes to the Police Bill', 1799, University College collection of Bentham manuscripts (henceforth UC), cl. 585–6.

[2] 'Plan of Parliamentary Reform: with an introduction, showing the necessity of radical, and the inadequacy of moderate, reform' (first published 1817), in *The Works of Jeremy Bentham, edited under the supervision of his executor, John Bowring*, 11 vols. (Edinburgh, 1843) (henceforth Bowring), iii. 433–552, at 435.

[3] See *Writings on Political Economy, Volume III: Preventive Police*, pre-publication version (Bentham 2018) at http://discovery.ucl.ac.uk/10055084/.

himself a proponent of radical parliamentary reform. How is the contradiction to be explained, or how did the Bentham of 1799 come to view draconian restraints on liberty of association as a guarantor of security, when at all other times he viewed that liberty as a crucial characteristic of free governments? An examination of Bentham's attitude to democracy sheds light upon this question and on ambiguities and developments in Bentham's thinking about the exercise of political power and the appropriate means for its control.

In Section 2.1, the distinction between democracy understood (as it traditionally had been) as 'rule by the many' and the kind of representative democracy that Bentham explicitly, though briefly, espoused in the early stages of the French Revolution, and consistently in print from 1817, is introduced. This distinction informs everything that follows, since Bentham always regarded the former as characterized by a high risk of conflict and political violence and as incompatible with the existence of political society in any but small agrarian communities. During his period of anti-democratic reaction in the 1790s, he insisted that democracy in the second sense would be quickly corrupted into democracy in the first sense, and it was as a bulwark against the dangers of democracy in that sense that he eulogized the Sedition Act. Section 2.2 argues that three premises that form the basis of the utilitarian case for representative democracy, advanced by Bentham in 1788–9 and consistently from 1817, are all present in his early writings. Despite this, before 1789, Bentham developed no argument for extending the very limited franchise in Great Britain and thus apparently failed to draw plausible inferences from his own premises.[4] Section 2.3 addresses Bentham's democratic interlude of 1788–90, during which, albeit in tailoring his argument for a French audience to whom only something akin to universal suffrage would appeal, he set out a utilitarian case for

[4] The literature has been centrally concerned with whether Bentham's alleged conversion to democracy in 1788–9 was either substantive or enduring, and if not, what other factors led to his later espousal of wholesale electoral reform. See M. Mack, *Jeremy Bentham: An Odyssey of Ideas, 1748–1792* (London: Heinemann, 1962), 407–43; J. H. Burns, 'Bentham and the French Revolution', *Transactions of the Royal Historical Society*, 16 (1966), 95–114; J. R. Dinwiddy, 'Bentham's Transition to Political Radicalism, 1809–10', *Journal of the History of Ideas*, 36 (1975), 683–700; M. James, 'Bentham's Democratic Theory at the time of the French Revolution', *Bentham Newsletter*, 10 (1986), 5–16; J. E. Crimmins, 'Bentham's Political Radicalism Reexamined', *Journal of the History of Ideas*, 55 (1994), 259–81; P. Schofield, *Utility and Democracy: The Political Thought of Jeremy Bentham* (Oxford: Oxford University Press, 2006), 78–108.

representative democracy in terms strikingly similar to those he would employ twenty years later. Section 2.4 provides new evidence of the strength of Bentham's anti-democratic reaction, which went beyond endorsement of limitations on liberty of association to advocate the manipulation of public opinion. Section 2.5 focuses on Bentham's advocacy of 'virtual universality' of male suffrage in 1817 and examines his responses to the self-same anti-democratic arguments earlier employed by him. Section 2.6 connects Bentham's developing understanding of the necessary conditions for rendering rulers dependent on the ruled with his own priorities as a reformer of law and with his ongoing efforts to turn his theoretical insights into recommendations for practice.

2.1 Democracy What?

Rosen emphasizes that the later democratic Bentham never advocated 'rule by the people', in the sense that the people as a body would function as law-makers or active wielders of political power, but rather advocated popular control of the exercise of public power and of the elite who would inevitably exercise it.[5] Bentham drew a central distinction between governors (those exercising political power), on the one hand, and subjects (those not exercising political power), on the other:

> The power of making laws, of carrying on the business of government, and the power of determining who shall make them, who shall carry it on, are powers perfectly distinct in themselves, and which ... should be kept so in practice. In the former it is not possible that each man should have a share, in the latter it is not only possible but easy and expedient.[6]

Following a classification of constitutions according to the number and proportion of the population empowered to make laws, which was employed by Blackstone and dates back to Aristotle,[7] the early

[5] See F. Rosen, *Jeremy Bentham and Representative Democracy: A Study of the Constitutional Code* (Oxford: Clarendon Press, 1983), 12: 'A major thesis underlying his argument is that all rulers, however they are chosen, form a class apart by virtue of their wealth and political power and are potentially at odds with the people whose happiness they are supposed to secure.'

[6] UC cxxvii. 2 (1790[?]).

[7] Aristotle recognized multiple varieties of democratic constitution, according to the proportion of the population permitted to participate in the deliberative or judicial functions of the state and eligible to hold the highest magistracies. See *Politics*, 1289a, 1297b–1298a, 1316b. He further distinguished between democracy and oligarchy in terms of wealth rather than number: in democracies, the poor held sway (see ibid., 1279–80, 1290).

Bentham understood democracy as equalization of political power, that is, equality in the making of laws.[8] Bentham ridiculed Blackstone's discussion, noting that where all rule the division into rulers and subjects on which the defining characteristic of political society depends (namely, the existence of a settled habit of obedience on the part of subjects to the mandates of the sovereign),[9] has disappeared. Either there is nobody left over whom 'all' might rule, or the power of ruling has been annihilated by division into infinitesimal shares. The project of 'rule by the people' was close to incoherent, entailing the abolition of political power, since such power, like all power of command, depended for its existence on a relation of inequality.[10]

In the 1780s, Bentham discussed what he termed constitutional liberty, which, properly understood, meant 'the absence of danger to individuals from abuses of power on the part of persons exercising the powers of government'.[11] He rejected the 'party sense' of the idea, which asserted that such liberty existed 'in exact proportion to the share which the whole body of the people possess in the exercise of the powers of government' and entailed 'a chance of power: the power of coercing other individuals' (UC c. 154).[12] This understanding invited only a violent struggle for control of the coercive apparatus, undermining all expectations and producing chaos. The knowledge required to make good laws and the knowledge required to be a good subject were different. Bentham advanced an argument as old as Plato that government, especially law-making, is a specialist activity requiring skills not possessed by everyone: for the people to insist on governing would be as sensible as insisting that everyone make their own shoes.[13] Empowering the people to legislate was practically a guarantee of bad law-making, while the constitutional endorsement of equality in the political sphere invited demands to extend the principle to the economic, with dire consequences.

[8] See 'A Fragment on Government' (henceforth *Fragment*), in *A Comment on the Commentaries and a Fragment on Government*, ed. J. H. Burns and H. L. A. Hart (London: Athlone, 1977 [*CW*]), 391–551, at 455.

[9] See ibid., 428–9.

[10] Ibid., 459.

[11] UC c. 153 (no date).

[12] UC c. 154 (no date).

[13] See UC cxxvii. 2 (1782[?]); clxx. 175 (March 1793); Bowring, iv. 52. For Plato's argument see *The Republic*, 331d–336b.

2.2 The Premises of the Utilitarian Case for Representative Democracy in the Early Bentham

Three premises present in Bentham's early writings constitute the core of the case for representative democracy which he later made assiduously. The first was the proposition that the purpose of government was to deliver happiness to the community. The point of government action, as of all action, was happiness. As Bentham put it in 1782, 'The end of government, wherever it is what it ought to be, is to provide for the happiness of the governed.'[14] The second was the proposition that the exercise of political power was a trust, and the holders of such power were trustees for the welfare of the ruled.[15] Governments that pursued other ends than general happiness were guilty of 'misrule', abuse of public trust, which included both conscious perversion of the end and unconscious selection of mischievous means.[16] Bentham distinguished between deliberate and accidental confusion of ends according to whether the problem was one of probity or wisdom, that is, whether it lay in the will or the understanding, in failure of what he later called moral aptitude or failure of intellectual aptitude. The third premise is the proposition that, empirically speaking, self-interested motives were universally operative and usually predominated over all others: every individual was liable to prefer his particular interest to the general interest and to be willing to sacrifice the latter to the former.[17]

[14] 'Indirect Legislation', UC lxxxvii. 2.

[15] See *An Introduction to the Principles of Morals and Legislation* (henceforth *IPML*), ed. J. H. Burns and H. L. A. Hart (Oxford: Clarendon Press, 1996 [*CW*]), 263n; and see *Preparatory Principles*, ed. D. G. Long and P. Schofield (Oxford: Oxford University Press, 2016), 185. For discussion, see J. H. Burns, 'Bentham on Sovereignty', *Northern Ireland Political Quarterly*, 24 (1973), 133–51.

[16] See UC xcix. 133 (1782[?]), a brouillon for 'Indirect Legislation'.

[17] If this were not the case, Bentham's project for modifying behaviour through rewards and punishments would collapse. See his discussions of the necessary conditions for voluntary human actions in, for instance, *IPML* (*CW*), 244; 'Indirect Legislation', UC lxxxvii. 4, 7–8, 13; *Rights, Representation and Reform, Nonsense upon Stilts and Other Writings on the French Revolution*, ed. P. Schofield, C. Pease-Watkin, and C. Blamires (Oxford: Clarendon Press, 2002 [*CW*]), 415–6; *Writings on Political Economy*: I, ed. M. Quinn (Oxford: Oxford University Press, 2016), 176–8; 'Method of an Institute of Political Economy', UC xvii. 208, 244 (*Jeremy Bentham's Economic Writings*, ed. W. Stark, 3 vols. [London: Allen & Unwin, 1952–4], iii. 334–5). For the prevalence of pecuniary interest, see, for instance, *IPML*, 174; *Writings on the Poor Laws*: II, ed. M. Quinn (Oxford: Oxford University Press, 2010), 371–3.

In designing constitutions, the crucial question concerned the necessary and sufficient conditions for uniting the interests of rulers with their duty. Put the three premises together and a case for representative democracy emerges. Self-interested governors possessed the power and the motivation to abuse their trust and subvert the proper end of government, and only the institutionalized operation of the moral sanction of public opinion might ensure that fear of punishment by electoral defeat or removal prevented such abuse. From the first, Bentham recognized that public power-holders were a potential source of evil to their subjects.[18] Indeed, the conjunction of the interest and duty of those intended to comply with a rule was the core task of the rule-maker in all fields, from drafting of penal laws, through design of institutions, to design of constitutions: 'To have compleated the junction between interest and duty in every line of human conduct would be neither more nor less than to have brought the science and art of government to perfection.'[19]

The early Bentham did not advocate representative democracy, which may not be surprising in a writer who hoped to influence the existing holders of political power. He did, however, discuss sovereignty and therein the foundation of governmental authority. He came close to viewing the existence of a functioning government as evidence of popular endorsement, since sovereignty, and the very existence of political society, was constituted solely by the habit of obedience. 'The only thing that gives the sovereign body the power it possesses is the habit of submission. The only thing that can limit the same power is the same habit of submission.'[20] If the people ceased to obey the sovereign, that sovereign ceased to be sovereign, in that their writ no longer ran. The passages in *Fragment* that discussed the habit of obedience appear in Bentham's critique of the fiction of the original contract as the foundation of government. Crediting Hume with opening his eyes, Bentham noted that on reading this part of Hume's *Treatise of Human Nature* he 'learnt to call the cause of the people the cause of Virtue'.[21] To modern ears, the cause of the people has a democratic ring, but Bentham did not elaborate

[18] Bentham recognized in 1776 that governments might oppose the happiness of the people: see *Fragment* (*CW*), 443. See also 'Indirect Legislation' (1782), UC lxxxvii. 2; and, for detailed analysis of expedients for the prevention of misrule, lxxvii. 102–3, 122, 104–6, 123–6, 107–21.

[19] *Writings on the Poor Laws*: II, 353.

[20] *Preparatory Principles*, 180.

[21] *Fragment* (*CW*), 439–40n.

his statement, which may simply indicate endorsement of popular feeling over philosophical abstractions.[22] Hume had argued that no one believed in a duty to obey government founded on a promise, because there was a simpler explanation: men obeyed because they recognized the benefits of the stability consequent on general obedience. Bentham might have summarized his own argument by quoting Hume: 'all men … are sensible, that they owe obedience to government merely on account of the public interest'.[23] And further,

> This interest I find to consist in the security and protection, which we enjoy in political society …. As interest, therefore, is the immediate sanction of government, the one can have no longer being than the other; and whenever the civil magistrate carries his oppression so far as to render his authority perfectly intolerable, we are no longer bound to submit to it.[24]

Bentham added only a new name for the point where political authority becomes intolerable, namely, the juncture of resistance. Until that juncture was reached, the good citizen should 'obey punctually' but 'censure freely'.[25]

For the early Bentham, there was no necessary connection between achieving the end of government, the people's happiness, and the form of government or the constitution, a name for 'the System or Distribution of Public Powers in a State'.[26] A good constitution delivered the subordinate ends of the civil law, and security in particular,[27] by making the operations of the law and its agents public and thus predictable, and limited,

[22] See D. Hume, *A Treatise of Human Nature: being an attempt to introduce the experimental method of reasoning into moral subjects,* 3 vols. (London, 1739–40), (Bk. III, Pt. II, § VIII) iii. 153–4, where no mention is made of either the people or their cause. Hume does argue that although wishing to avoid appeals to authority, in this case he would 'appeal to popular authority, and oppose the sentiments of the rabble to any philosophical reasoning. For … the opinions of men, in this case, carry with them a peculiar authority, and are, in great measure, infallible. The distinction of moral good and evil is founded on the pleasure or pain, which results from the view of any sentiment, or character; and as that pleasure or pain cannot be unknown to the person who feels it, it follows, that there is just so much vice or virtue in any character, as every one places in it'.

[23] Ibid., 164 (Bk. III, Pt. II, § IX).

[24] Ibid., 160.

[25] *Fragment* (*CW*), 399.

[26] *Preparatory Principles*, 107.

[27] See UC clxx. 173 (1793), where Bentham listed desirable two desirable properties in a constitution: 'I. Subserviency to Subsistence, Abundance, Security and Equality. II. Stability.'

or at least non-arbitrary: 'A Government may be said to be more or less free, as more or less care is taken in it of the security of the people.'[28] A government that observed legal process and refrained from arbitrary interference in the non-coercive interactions of its subjects was a free government, irrespective of its electorate or formal rules for appointing political and legal officials.

In *Fragment*, Bentham asserted that distinguishing free from despotic states depended on:

> the *manner* in which that whole mass of power, which, taken together, is supreme, is ... *distributed* among the several ranks of persons that are sharers in it: – on the *source* from whence their titles to it are successively derived: – on the frequent and easy *changes* of condition between govern*ors* and govern*ed*; whereby the interests of the one class are more or less indistinguishably blended with those of the other: – on the *responsibility* of the governors; or the right which a subject has of having the reasons publicly assigned ... of every act of power that is exerted over him: – on the *liberty of the press*; or the security with which every man ... may make known his complaints ... to the whole community: – on the *liberty of public association*; or the security with which malecontents may communicate their sentiments, ... and practise every mode of opposition short of actual revolt, before the executive power can be legally justified in disturbing them.[29]

Although mention of the source from which titles to power derived might involve questions of popular election of law-makers, Bentham pursued neither this question nor the related ease and frequency of gaining and losing positions of power, that is, changes of condition between governors and governed.

In *Preparatory Principles*, written at around the same time, Bentham made a connection between popular government and free government,[30] before turning to the conjunction of rulers' interests with their duty as the condition of good government and again suggesting that an easy transition from the status of 'ruler' to that of 'ruled' and back again would effect that conjunction: 'It is the interest of persons in Government to consult the interest of the subjects, when the same persons are alternately Governors and subjects.' It is difficult to avoid the conclusion that Bentham is advancing the sort of alternation between government and opposition that characterized the British House of Commons as among

[28] *Preparatory Principles*, 199.
[29] *Fragment* (*CW*), 485.
[30] *Preparatory Principles*, 214.

the guarantors of non-despotic government and as serving to blend indistinguishably the interests of rulers and ruled. He was at this time prepared to assert that the British constitution 'is found by experience to . . . be more highly conducive to the happiness of those who live under it than any other yet exemplified'.[31] In effect, the assertion is that the septennial opportunity for a tiny fraction of the people to exercise their will in appointment of one of two legislative houses was sufficient to insure them all against oppression, at least while press freedom and liberty of association prevailed.

Elsewhere in *Fragment*, Bentham hinted at sympathy for extension of the franchise[32] but declined to offer any prescription for reform, thinking it 'not worth the giving'.[33] One reason it was not worth giving was simply that he viewed radical parliamentary reform as neither necessary nor sufficient for good government. More important were the remaining characteristics of free government: responsibility of the governors, liberty of the press, and liberty of association. The first, responsibility, the right to demand public justification of every exercise of public power, served to protect the subject against arbitrary treatment. The second, liberty of the press, facilitated both public knowledge of evasions of responsibility and communication concerning the possible approach of the juncture of resistance. The third, liberty of association, performed a similar role, protecting all opposition short of 'actual revolt'. By comparison, rendering rulers electorally responsible to the body of the people seemed immaterial.[34]

Any government that delivered the ends of the civil law was a good one: 'if one supposed that the purposes of private [i.e., civil] law were accomplished, it would scarcely matter what was done with constitutional law, or even that there was such a thing as constitutional law'.[35] This is Bentham at his most Humean, and the conservatism of his approach rests on its strikingly binary nature: stability versus chaos. For the early Bentham, 'under the worst government . . . everyone enjoys protection for their properties; and it is only here and there that some exceptions are seen . . .. But the civil war once started, there is no longer

[31] 'A Comment on the Commentaries', in *A Comment on the Commentaries and a Fragment on Government* (*CW*), 1–273, at 56.

[32] *Fragment* (*CW*), 488.

[33] Ibid., 472–3.

[34] A further reason was that existing institutions, however, seemingly irrational in form, possessed utility simply by virtue of their existence and the people's experience of it.

[35] UC clxx. 199 (1785[?]).

security for anyone'. In the 1780s, Bentham effectively asserted that the juncture of resistance could never arrive: no government was 'so bad that a friend of humanity would be justified in advising a revolt to substitute any another form whatsoever in its place'.[36]

In 1782, Bentham devoted a long chapter in 'Indirect Legislation' to the prevention of misrule, in which it is noteworthy that popular election hardly features and no sympathy for extension of the franchise is expressed.[37] By contrast, liberty of the press and of association do feature. In regard to the former, Bentham noted that it had developed in Britain in consequence of governmental inattention and had no firm basis in law. He recommended heeding the 'common sense' advice to 'hear what any body has to say: you may be the better, and you can not be the worse'.[38] Like a sovereign refusing to receive petitions, governments that sought to limit public discussion denied themselves access to alternative opinions. Again, reporting of legal cases and government accounts facilitated informed discussion. Bentham coupled liberty of association with the right to possess weapons, describing the dual entitlement as the most important right, 'which should be reserved at the institution of a government ... as being the basis of the rest'.[39] He rejected the charge that armed associations would lead to political instability, responding that 'this is an argument not against the expediency of establishing the right ... but against the impropriety of suffering a people to remain in ignorance'.[40]

In short, the early Bentham recognized the dangers of abuse of power by self-interested rulers but viewed other means than frequent risk of rejection by a wide electorate as the best means of aligning their interest with their duty.

2.3 The Penny Drops (or Not)

In 1788, bankruptcy of the French state led to the summoning of the Estates General for the first time since 1614. Bentham seized the opportunity to advise on reform in France and addressed the question of

[36] UC clxx. 200; 199.

[37] Lack of space prevents a detailed analysis of the subject, but for oblique references, see 'Indirect Legislation', UC lxxxvii. 103, 114–6 (1782[?]).

[38] Ibid., UC lxxxvii. 107.

[39] Ibid., UC lxxxvii. 119. For a similar sentiment, see *Preparatory Principles*, 180.

[40] 'Indirect Legislation', UC lxxxvii. 120.

representation directly. While again declaring the British constitution perfect, he considered in the abstract the claims of the people to appoint law-makers. He asserted both an equal desire and equal capacity for happiness, the latter on the basis that the assertion was less false than any other.[41] From egalitarian premises he drew the egalitarian inference: 'Hence, in the choice of representatives or proxies in the business of making laws, every person not naturally disqualified ought to have a right of suffrage. And every such person ought to have an equal right: since no reason can be given why one person should have a greater influence ... than another.'[42] Justifiable exclusions from the franchise fell into two categories, the first being cognitive incapacity. Those clearly lacking capacity, children and the insane, should be excluded, as should those unable to read, who were thereby unable to access the resources necessary to rational judgement concerning the merits of candidates.[43] The second exclusion concerned the class of 'non-proprietors', on the basis that they were likely to conclude, quite erroneously, that coercive equalization of property would benefit them:

> By non-proprietors must be understood to this effect not those who have absolutely nothing ... but those to whom it must appear that, if they could succeed in making a redistribution of the total mass of property among everyone, they would find themselves better-off.
>
> However, unfortunately the majority of the human race must be always and everywhere in the position in question: at least no-one will deny that it is so at present (and this will suffice) in France.[44]

Schofield notes that on Bentham's estimate his scheme would exclude nine-tenths of the population from the franchise.[45] The ground for the

[41] 'Considérations d'un Anglois sur la composition des États-Généraux', in *Rights Representation and Reform* (*CW*), 63–146, at 68.

[42] UC clxx. 50 (1788[?]). Bentham made exactly the same argument in 1817. See 'Plan of Parliamentary Reform', Bowring, iii. 452.

[43] In 1788, Bentham made a third major exclusion from the franchise, namely, women, despite failing to endorse any of its alleged justifications. See 'Considérations d'un Anglois', 70. In 1789, he rejected those justifications and reversed the exclusion ('Project of a Constitutional Code for France', in *Rights, Representation and Reform* (*CW*), 227–61, at 231, 246–8). After committing himself to radical reform, Bentham continued to dismiss the arguments for the exclusion of women but, in the interests of maximizing the chances of success, again refrained from proposing their inclusion ('Plan of Parliamentary Reform', Bowing, iii. 463).

[44] 'Considérations d'un Anglois', 73 (my translation).

[45] See Schofield, *Utility and Democracy*, 88.

exclusion of the propertyless was the threat to security of property (and thereby to abundance and subsistence).

Within a year of presenting an argument that began with egalitarian premises but concluded by excluding the vast majority of the population, Bentham wrote a new work for France proposing annual elections and universal adult suffrage, subject only to a literacy qualification.[46] Of concerns over possible expropriations by the ill-informed dispossessed, there is no sign, quite probably, as Schofield argues, because Bentham hoped that his proposals might be adopted, and universal suffrage was now an established fact that had to be accommodated.[47] At around the same time, in discussion of the ostensibly unconnected subject of the division of power, and its failure as a security against misrule, and almost certainly with such a suffrage in mind, Bentham explicitly linked constitutional liberty with the 'originative power' of the people: 'Constitutional liberty depends upon and is proportioned to the dependence of the possessors of efficient public power upon the will of the body of the people, in virtue of the originative power they possess.'[48] In other words, security against misrule could not be left to the salutary restraining influence of freedom of the press and of association but varied directly with the degree to which the rulers were subject to appointment by the body of the people. In the same work, he combined the three premises that formed the core of his mature case for representative democracy:

> Government is good in proportion to the measure of happiness of which it is productive on the part of the body of the people subject to it.
>
> The accomplishment of good government . . . depends upon the concurrence of the three requisites of intelligence, power and inclination. Government will be good in proportion as those who stand invested with the power possess inclination to render it so, and in addition the measure of intelligence necessary to that purpose.
>
> The degree of inclination will be in exact proportion to the dependence of the governors on the governed: to the dependence of the persons intrusted with the power, on the persons by whose obedience the power is constituted: to the dependence . . . of those who exercise power on those on whom it is exercised. In as far as a man who has power is independent, his inclination will be [to] make use of it for his own benefit: in as far as he is dependent upon any one, he will find himself obliged to employ it for

[46] See 'Project of a Constitutional Code for France', in *Rights, Representation and Reform* (*CW*), 230–1.

[47] See P. Schofield, *Utility and Democracy*, 88.

[48] 'Division of Power', in *Rights, Representation and Reform* (*CW*), 405–18, at 408.

> the benefit of him on whom he depends. In this there is no . . . obscurity. It is founded on the universal, necessary, undisputed . . . property in human nature—the predominance of the self-regarding affections over the social.[49]

In 1790, Bentham began planning a work advocating parliamentary reform in Britain, including annual Parliaments, equal electoral districts, and universal male suffrage, but quickly abandoned it.[50] By the end of 1792, escalating violence and property confiscations in France had terminated Bentham's enthusiasm for electoral reform on either side of the Channel. In March 1793, he sketched plans for defending the existing electoral system. He conceded that 'a priori, nothing would have been rational or just but equal representation'[51] but cautioned that concession of the principle would invite 'the mischiefs of popular government' and lead inevitably to the disorders seen in France: 'I look upon excess as essential to the form of government in a nation so full of manufacturers and other day labourers as Britain.'[52] Equal rights to representation would generate demands for equal access to political power, because demands for reform 'could not stop at any of the changes as yet proposed, since the principle would go on requiring further changes with accumulated force'.[53] The only logical stopping point for political reform was a pure republic in which his own distinction between rulers and ruled would disappear and the concession of equality of right to representation would be trumped by the demands for equality of right to rule on one hand, and equality of property on the other. Violence, disorder, and chaos would ensue, and security, subsistence, and abundance would be forfeited.

By 1794, Bentham was noting: 'The people are all *will* – they have no reason, no understanding . . .. A proposition must be extremely simple or their minds can not take hold of it – and when they do, it can only be

49 Ibid., 415.

50 See 'Parliamentary Reform', in *Rights, Representation, and Reform* (*CW*), 428–34. Schofield (*Utility and Demcoracy*, 239) notes correctly that Bentham viewed his proposals of 1789 as taking place within the context of a constitutional monarchy, but that is hardly conclusive: the French constitution of 1789 was adopted in the context of constitutional monarchism, while republican constitutional forms are only the defining feature of democracy if democracy itself is properly understood solely in the sense of rule by many or by all.

51 UC clxx. 175 (1793).

52 UC clxx. 176.

53 UC clxx. 173.

through the medium of their affections.'[54] His confidence in the educative potential of association, so evident in 1782, had evaporated: 'for the ignorance inseparable to popular government there is no cure: for instruction, by the slowness of its operation, may to this purpose be reckoned as nothing'.[55] In 1795, he argued: 'The system of the democrats is absurd and dangerous: for it subjugates the well-informed to the ill-informed classes of mankind.'[56]

Bentham had always fretted over the limited intellectual capacities of the poor, always attributing it to lack of education and of time.[57] In early 1793, in a rasping critique of stamp-duties on legal instruments for putting legal redress beyond their reach, he asserted: 'The poor, on account of the ignorance and intellectual incapacity inseparably attached to poverty, are debarred generally, as perhaps it is necessary, were it only for their own sake, they should be universally, from the sweets of political power.'[58] In one sense, this is simply a reprise of his distinction between rulers and ruled, between the knowledge necessary to proper utilization of the tools of power and knowledge of one's own interests. In 1794, he noted that 'scarce any political power can, consistently with their own good, be trusted'[59] even to members of Friendly Societies, the wisest of

[54] UC xliv. 2 (1794), brouillon for a projected work 'Reform no Improvement'.

[55] UC clxx. 175.

[56] UC xliv. 5 (8 July 1795).

[57] Even in 1776 there is evidence of Bentham's concern about the ignorance of the poor: 'In the members of a Democracy in particular, there is likely to be a want of wisdom – Why? The greater part being poor, are when they begin to take upon them the management of affairs, uneducated: being uneducated, they are illiterate: being illiterate, they are ignorant. Ignorant, therefore, and *unwise*, if that be what is meant by ignorant, they *begin*. Depending for their daily bread on the profits of some petty traffic, or the labour of some manual occupation, they are nailed to the work-board, or the counter' (*Fragment* [*CW*], 466). It is true that the comment is made in a parody of Blackstone's argument, but it would be an error simply to disregard it as offering no clue to Bentham's attitude. Of course Bentham is parodying Blackstone, but the consistent structure of that parody throughout his commentary is, first, to complain that Blackstone's expression is too oblique to be comprehensible; second, to reconstruct that argument in comprehensible form; and third, to parody the specific elements which he finds absurd. The quotation comes from the second phase, while it is noteworthy that Bentham neither dissents from it nor subjects it to parody. What he does parody is the next step in Blackstone's reconstructed argument, namely, the assertion that the ignorance of the democratic branch (House of Commons) is compensated for by the wisdom of the aristocratic branch (House of Lords).

[58] 'A Protest against law taxes', in *Writings on Political Economy*: I, 276.

[59] See 'Proposals Relative to Divers Modes of Supply', in *Writings on Political Economy*: II, ed. M. Quinn (Oxford: Oxford University Press, 2019), 151–262, at 200n.

the poor, who had demonstrated 'the sacrifice of the present to the future', the 'great desideratum in morality'.[60] Again, this is no new departure: the direct exercise of political power required knowledge the poor lacked. What Bentham did not now consider, however, was whether they might be trusted with control over the holders of political power. The point is that in reversing his position Bentham set aside his combination of premises from 1789 and reverted to discussion of democracy as government by all, or the literal equalization of political power.

In his poor law writings, Bentham tendentiously equated demands for extension of the franchise with demands for equality of right to govern and a claim to universal competence in all branches of legislation.[61] On the arguments he had advanced in 1788–9, concerning not the right to rule but to elect rulers, the critique had no apparent purchase. In 1787, Bentham had compared the capacity of the indigent man in cases 'untinctured with simplicity' to that of other men: 'He knows what is his interest as well as they do, and is as . . . able to pursue it as they are.'[62] His case for representative democracy relied on a similar assertion, united with the insistence that such knowledge was sufficient for representative democracy to perform its primary function in preventing misrule.

2.4 Dissemination of Facts, Manipulation of Opinion: The Police Gazette of 1799

In 1798–9, Bentham drafted a Bill for his friend the magistrate Patrick Colquhoun, proposing the establishment of a Board of Police in London to administer a licensing system for dealers in second-hand goods, to serve as indirect legislation against a range of offences.[63] The Board would publish weekly a *Police Gazette* containing reports of offences, appeals for information, and descriptions of suspects. The *Gazette* would be sold cheaply and supplied free to all licensees under the new system,

[60] See 'Defence of Lotteries as they might be ordered, with a plan for ordering them', in ibid., 263–8, at 267.

[61] *Writings on the Poor Laws*: II, 193.

[62] 'Defence of Usury; Shewing the Impolicy of the present legal restraints on the terms of pecuniary bargains', in *Writings on Political Economy*: I, 43–121, at 58.

[63] For a fuller discussion, see M. Quinn, 'Bentham on Preventive Police: The *Calendar of Delinquency* in evaluation of policy, and the *Police Gazette* in manipulation of opinion', *International Criminal Justice Review* 31 (2021), 229–56 https://journals.sagepub.com/doi/10.1177/1057567719827343.

all public houses, and local civil and religious officials. The central function of the *Gazette* was to provide information, to disseminate knowledge of criminality by communication of facts from understanding to understanding. However, it had a further function, 'as an instrument for the propagation and maintenance of social dispositions and affections, and for the preservation of tranquillity, harmony, and loyalty among the great body of the people'. This purpose 'though but collateral, and *not proper to be mentioned in the Bill*' was '*still more important, perhaps, than even the direct one*'.[64]

Bentham noted that since newsworthy events happen at irregular intervals, newspapers suffer from quiet days, but all had expedients for filling space on such days to produce a paper of standard size. In the *Gazette*, 'this collateral part would, therefore, pass not as a novelty, nor as directed to any special end, but as coming in as a matter of course, in conformity to the custom of the trade'. Government should exploit this space to speak not merely to people's understanding but to their will:

> The occasional superstructure, the *didactic* part, will have at any rate the circumstance of contiguity, to cement the idea of it in the mind with the idea of the other part, and thus obtain for it a portion of the same favour: and by grafting it upon the other, as the moral is upon the fable, the sermon upon the text … the association will be rendered still more intimate and indissoluble.[65]

Bentham thus advised government to add moral to fable, sermon to text, conscious direction of moral and political preferences to provision of factual information. In other words, the communication of will to will is facilitated both by familiarity with the *Gazette* and by its popular identification as *purely* a channel of communication between understanding and understanding. To its ostensible role as conduit of information is added an esoteric role as shaper of opinions, and it is general acceptance of its fulfilment of the first that creates the opportunity to exploit its potential for the second. In a cancelled passage, this dissembling was explicit:

[64] 'Notes on the Police Bill', UC cl. 576 (Bentham [2018], 323), emphasis added. The intended audience for Bentham's arguments consisted of government ministers, while one reason for omitting this use from the Bill is that announcing it would make successfully manipulating people's affections more difficult.

[65] Ibid., UC cl. 579 (Bentham [2018], 324–5).

> But the sort of Sermon which might be practiced ... without ceasing in the *Police Gazette*, this *unannounced and unsuspected Sermon, cautiously, sparingly, and in a manner imperceptibly, though at the same time unremittingly, insinuated* into a publication composed principally, and *to appearance exclusively*, of that sort of matter which ... can never lose ... its hold upon the affections ... of those *otherwise untutored minds, for whose direction it is more especially designed* – there would be neither end nor limit to its influence.[66]

Bentham estimated that 500,000 readers would receive this sermon and argued that no paper declaring its political allegiance could aspire to such influence: 'Hanging out such a sign, it presupposes on the part of its customers the presence of those very dispositions the absence of which is the cause that produces the demand for it ... [and] gives warning to those ... who are neutral or indifferent, to put themselves upon their guard against its influence.'[67] The Sedition Act had failed to regulate the written word, but the *Gazette* presented a gentle alternative to licensing the press directly.

The contrast between the Bentham of 1799 and Bentham the apostle of conjunction of rule with rationale, of exposure of exercises of public power to public scrutiny, could not be clearer. This was the Bentham who had argued consistently that liberty of the press and of association, and the public judgement of public power they facilitated, were defining characteristics of a free state. In 1782 he noted:

> There are but two plans of dealing with the people that bear any tolerable colour of propriety: perfect mystery or perfect unreserve. To exclude the people perfectly and absolutely from the knowledge of their affairs, or to give them as perfect a state of them as possible: ... to keep them from forming any judgment at all, or to enable them to form a right one: in a word, to deal with them like beasts, or to deal with them like men.[68]

66 UC cl. 279^{v}, drafted for 'Notes to the Police Bill' (emphasis added).

67 'Notes to the Police Bill', UC cl. 587 (Bentham [2018], 329). In November 1776, during the American War of Independence, when public opinion was divided over the war, and Bentham keen to advertise his credentials as an advisor to legislators, he drafted a proposal for a newspaper, ostensibly independent but in fact 'conducted under the eye of the Minister' and serving as the mouthpiece of government, under the name of '*The Candid Chronicle or Impartial Post*'. See UC cxlix. 1–9. To maintain a reputation for impartiality, the paper would publish articles from moderate opposition politicians and criticize government occasionally (if only by complaining that it had not already introduced measures which it actually planned to introduce soon). Among the paper's functions would be publishing 'observations of a general aspect, and thrown in apparently without design, and tending to sooth the temper of the people' (UC cxlix. 3).

68 'Indirect Legislation', UC lxxxvii. 110; see also *Fragment* (*CW*), 441.

Yet in 1799 he was recommending a thoroughgoing dissembling as a necessary bulwark to political stability, though in the event neither Board of Police nor Bentham's *Police Gazette* were adopted, so this resource for surreptitious guidance of the multitude remained unexploited.

2.5 Bentham versus Bentham

It is worth discussing the anti-democratic arguments advanced by defenders of the existing system in 1817 and Bentham's responses to them. Bentham summarized one objection that captured his own attitude of 1799: 'Objection: – Universal suffrage, universal hostility and anarchy.'[69] After pointing out the non-violent means advocated by leaders of the reform movement, Bentham imagined such evidence being rejected by anti-democrats in terms that echo his own fears of 1799: 'But what you perhaps don't see, and we do see is – the mob which is still behind them.'[70] The resonances multiply when the words of the opponents to reform are examined:

> The destructive objects which the leading members of these societies have in view are demonstrated by their publications ... all equally *calculated to inflame the minds ... of the poorer classes of the community.* At the ordinary meetings of these societies ... their time is principally employed in listening to speeches *tending to the destruction of social order, recommending a general equalization of property, and at the same time endeavouring to corrupt the morals of the hearers*, and to destroy all reverence for religion.[71]

Except only concern over reverence for religion, and these words might have been written by Bentham himself twenty years earlier.

In response, Bentham first referred to the experience of the United States, where representative democracy had produced not anarchy but 'the best government that is or ever has been'.[72] What was the secret of America's success? In 1795, in the midst of his anti-democratic reaction, Bentham answered this question thus, 'American Republic, why so quiet? – Because there are no very large towns. No towns affording mobs

69 'Plan of Parliamentary Reform', Bowring, iii. 465.

70 Ibid., 471.

71 'Report of the Secret Committee of the House of Lords respecting certain Dangerous Meetings and Combinations', in *Parliamentary Debates* (1817) xxxv. 417 (emphasis added).

72 'Plan of Parliamentary Reform', Bowring, iii. 472; see also 'Radicalism not dangerous', Bowring, iii. 599–622, at 612.

large enough to influence the whole country . . .. Being chiefly husbandmen, their business keeps them separate and quiet. No swarms of professional men out of practice'.[73] The recipe for a flourishing representative democracy then, involved the combination of a largely agrarian society and the absence of cities. American democracy worked because the poor were too isolated and too busy securing subsistence to worry about politics but would, Bentham had argued, 'be ruinous in a nation so full of manufacturers and other day labourers as Britain'. In 1817, Bentham did not address this difference in circumstances,[74] pointing out instead that two more decades of experience had failed to produce anarchy in America. However, if his argument had had any merit in 1795, the contrast on which it depended had only become stronger in the interim.

Bentham's second response also engaged with his own past fears. Redeploying his distinction between rulers and ruled, he pointed out that the reformers' demand was not for an equal share in law-making but merely an equal share in appointing the law-makers, that is, in 'the unimperative faculty of deputation . . . a power which, if such it must be called, is but the fraction of a fraction'.[75] The anti-democratic Bentham had insisted that once the egalitarian genie was out of the bottle there could be no controlling it: equalization of suffrage would give way to demands for equalization of political power in its coercive sense and to demands for economic levelling. The democrat Bentham insisted on the justice and utility of the first demand and divorced it from the second. Only thus could he argue that the mass of people possessed the necessary knowledge of their own interests to qualify them for admission to the suffrage. The knowledge necessary for representative democracy to perform its prophylactic task of preventing misrule was not that of how to legislate to maximize happiness. No more knowledge was required on the part of individual voters than knowledge of their own interests. Assuming each to vote in pursuit of their own interest rather than in pursuit of their understanding of the universal interest, competing interests tended to cancel each other out, so that the victorious candidate

[73] UC xliv. 2 (1794).

[74] In 1801, in arguing that the Americans would have been better advised to remain British colonists, Bentham had painted a less flattering picture of America as an 'unvaried scene of sordid selfishness, of political altercation, of discomfort, of ignorance, of drunkenness': see 'Method of an Institute of Political Economy', UC xvii. 205 (*Jeremy Bentham's Economic Writings*, iii. 356–7).

[75] 'Plan of Parliamentary Reform', Bowring, iii. 465.

would be he who appealed most successfully to common interests.[76] Where interests were not reflected in votes, the interests of those excluded could not motivate legislators, since they were not accountable to them, were unremovable by them, and could safely ignore them. The making of good legislative decisions depended upon correct calculation of the pleasures and pains liable to ensue therefrom. Given the predominance of self-interested motives, the limitation of the franchise implied the exclusion of some interests from the calculation. The knowledge necessary to governing the people did not have, but, since they made no demand to govern, this deficit was no disqualification.

For the later Bentham, representative democracy was no guarantor of achieving maximum happiness but a machine for preventing the systematic oppression of a majority by a minority. It is in this sense that 'among the peculiar excellencies' of representative democracy was that 'to good government in this form nothing of *virtue*, in so far as *self-denial* is an ingredient in virtue, is necessary'.[77] By now, Bentham was prepared to state explicitly that, 'The actual end of government is in every political community the greatest happiness of those . . . by whom the powers of government are exercised.'[78]

Bentham's final response to the charge that democratic reform would lead to property expropriations and violent disorder rehearsed an argument he had developed in the 1780s in comparing the happiness available to men outside political society with that available to the poor in 'civilized' societies. Both depended on labour for subsistence, and if the labour of the latter was more uniform,

[76] See *First Principles Preparatory to Constitutional Code*, ed. P. Schofield (Oxford: Clarendon Press, 1989 [*CW*]), 135–6. In 1789, Bentham had argued explicitly that 'it is impossible the majority of the grown persons in a nation can have each of them an interest distinct from that of the whole': see *Rights, Representation and Reform* (*CW*), 69, 430. It is entirely arguable that Bentham's identification between the interest of the majority and that of the whole leaves open the possibility that the interests of minorities could be disregarded, as later argued by J. S. Mill. Bentham finessed this possibility in his later writings, perhaps because his identification bestowed on the democratic cause the role of champion of the universal interest and perhaps because his overriding priority was to overthrow the systematic oppression of the majority by a minority under the unreformed system.

[77] See Rosen, *Jeremy Bentham and Representative Democracy*, 54: 'Popular sovereignty by no means ensures that the society will be well governed, but Bentham argues that without popular sovereignty it will never achieve this goal.'

[78] *First Principles Preparatory to Constitutional Code* (*CW*), 232. A similar conclusion had been implicit in 1789. See *Rights, Representation and Reform* (*CW*), 415.

> the reward is more certain; the lot of the woman is more gentle, infancy and old age have more resources; the species multiplies in a proportion a thousand times greater, and this alone would suffice to show on which side is the superiority of happiness. Hence the laws, in creating property, have been benefactors to those who remain in their original poverty. They participate more or less in the pleasures, advantages, and resources of civilized society: . . . they enjoy the pleasures of acquisition: hope mingles with their labours.[79]

In 1817, Bentham argued that that the poor in Britain were too sensible of the benefits of 'civilized society' to risk not only the loss of their existing property but potential starvation by joining violent convulsions of the social order.[80] He asserted that they were now better informed of the consequences of equalization of property than they had been in 1799 but offered no further details of the reasons for his change of mind.

2.6 Theory and Practice

Bentham always sought to use his intellect to make a difference, to improve the lives of human beings. Since law in its most extensive sense was the mechanism that delivered the benefits of social life, his focus settled on thoroughgoing reform of law. As Lieberman and Schofield emphasize, Bentham was prepared to countenance any political system that would grant him a hearing, in the belief (or hope) that those in power must surely perceive the merit in his plans.[81] Schofield argues that it was above all the perfidy of government in relation to the panopticon that convinced Bentham of the systematic nature of sinister interest, first in relation to the legal establishment and only several years later in relation to the political establishment. Having realized that the necessary condition for radical legal reform was radical reform of the political system, Bentham became an adherent of representative democracy.[82] There is much to be said for this position, although given that the rejection of panopticon was a *political* and not a *legal* decision, Bentham would seem to have assembled the elements of his conspiracy of corruption in a somewhat perverse order.[83] Further, while the earliest

[79] 'Principles of the Civil Code', Bowring, i. 309.
[80] 'Plan of Parliamentary Reform', Bowring, iii. 475.
[81] See Schofield, *Utility and Democracy*, 83, 139–40; D. Lieberman, 'Jeremy Bentham: Biography and Intellectual Biography', *History of Political Thought*, 20 (1999), 187–204.
[82] See Schofield, *Utility and Democracy*, 109–36.
[83] See ibid., 120–1.

appearance of sinister interest in Bentham yet uncovered dates from 1794, the assertion of the ubiquity of private (hence potentially sinister) interest had appeared in his earliest writings.[84] Finally, while his recognition of the conspiracy of sinister interest goes a long way towards explaining Bentham's 'conversion' to democratic radicalism, the thesis remains incomplete, in that it does not explain the apparent disappearance of his anxiety over the ignorance of the poor.

Crimmins astutely connects Bentham's changes of position on democracy with his earlier investigation of the necessary conditions for transplanting laws.[85] There Bentham contrasted abstract utility – which considered the pains and pleasures liable to be experienced by human agents as such, and was calculated using empirical generalizations about human psychology – with final or concrete utility – which took account of the influence on pleasures and pains of prevailing customs, beliefs and attitudes.[86] In terms of abstract utility, the case for representative democracy was obvious, as Bentham admitted even as he rejected it in 1793: 'a priori, nothing could be more reasonable'. However, abstract utility was not the utility that counted, which was rather the final utility of any proposed reform in a given context. In the context of Britain in the 1770s and 1780s, Bentham, on his own premises, might have endorsed representative democracy, or at least significant political reform in that direction, but through a combination of seeing no urgency in the need, a concentration on legal reform, and finally a recognition that such endorsement would not enhance his chances of influencing governments, he did not, instead echoing eulogies of the perfection of the constitution. Between 1788 and 1790, he did endorse such a programme, initially for France, where a democratic franchise was contextually inevitable, but then, albeit very briefly, for Britain too. The violent disorder of the revolution in France transformed the context and postponed any such endorsement on his part. His bitter experience at the hands of government over the panopticon certainly contributed to that endorsement, as did his development of the notion of sinister interest as the shared motive of the overlapping political, legal, and religious elites who oppressed the

84 See Crimmins, 'Bentham's Political Radicalism Reexamined', 277.

85 See ibid., 270.

86 For fuller discussion, see M. Quinn, 'Popular Prejudices, Real Pains: What Is the Legislator to Do When the People Err in Assigning Mischief?', in X. Zhai and M. Quinn, eds, *Bentham's Theory of Law and Public Opinion* (Cambridge: Cambridge University Press, 2014), 63–89.

subject many. Yet the notion that rulers (like everybody else) possessed motives to sacrifice the interest of the public to their own could hardly have come as a shock.

As Bentham noted in 1793, reform was only justifiable if its capacity for curing grievances outweighed 'the danger of its introducing greater mischiefs in the attempt'.[87] The anti-democrat Bentham argued that, given the susceptibility of the poor to simplistic arguments, the proposed democratic cure was worse than existing constitutional imperfections. He had argued since the 1780s that the poor *ought to be* convinced that their interest lay in maintaining existing property titles, but in the 1790s became alarmed that their conviction might be easily overturned. In that popular ignorance obstructed a potential democratic solution to the mischief of misrule, a critical analysis of Bentham's change of mind on the level of threat posed by the uninformed poor remains necessary. Democracy (at least in representative form) was, on Bentham's premises, a corrective to misrule by the elite, but democracy, because of the enfranchisement of ignorance, itself presented a threat to social order. The test of any theory was its application to practice; the test of abstract utility was final utility. The anti-democrat Bentham was convinced that the ignorance of an enfranchised poor would pose a clear and present danger to political stability and was therefore driven to argue that representative democracy would inevitably degenerate into anarchy. By 1817, he was confidently asserting that this danger had abated.

There is some evidence that Bentham's anxieties over popular ignorance persisted, but since the edifice of privilege was rotten to the core, that ignorance was a risk that had to be accepted and mitigated if progress was to be achieved. In 1819, in an unsent letter to the press, he was candid about elements in the reform movement that anticipated with glee the economic upheavals consequent on a systematic failure of credit and indicated that he too would welcome that failure if he thought it would accelerate the achievement of democratic ascendancy:

> Of those who think with me . . . on the subject of Parliamentary Reform there are many, I believe, who look to the destruction of the Bank paper money and the extinction of the . . . property in government annuities with . . . anxious desire, regarding the two connected events as . . . certainly productive of Parliamentary Reform in a radical shape. For my part, though with a tolerably distinct view . . . of the extempore calamity which would be produced . . . by that double Catastrophe, yet having a not less

[87] See UC clxx. 173.

> distinct view of the all-pervading ... mischiefs produced by the absence of that exclusively effective remedy, *I should regard the purchase as an extremely cheap one if, at the price of the ... that double Catastrophe, the Establishment of Parliamentary Reform in its radical shape ... were to be accomplished.*[88]

When set alongside Bentham's usually unfaltering commitment to the benefits of stability, this prioritization of political over economic consequences in the utilitarian calculus is startling. He did not, however, endorse provoking economic crisis to produce political change and, in a contemporary pamphlet unpublished until after his death, conceded that although the cancellation of government debt formed no part of *his* plan, it had been mentioned in enthusiastic terms in reform meetings. As 'a known radicalist', Bentham cautioned his more extreme fellows that the consequences would be ruinous, especially for those dependent on sale of their labour. If the dangers of democratic demagoguery had not gone away, Bentham might at least seek to mitigate them from inside the radical tent.[89]

In 1809, the newly democrat Bentham reflected on how the excesses of the French Revolution had paralyzed rational reform in Britain: 'Scared out of our wits by distant anarchy, we have been drawn into the ever open arms of domestic despotism.'[90] By then, he was arguing in private that those excesses offered a salutary lighthouse to guard reformers from the rocks of social strife, rather than an insuperable objection to political reform. Later, in his blueprint for a democratic state, he embedded a series of measures to ensure that all public officials possessed the knowledge and judgement requisite for the exercise of public power, including systematic efforts to put such power beyond the reach of the poor, ignorant or otherwise.

88 'Paper and Gold', UC iii. 511 (May 1819), emphasis added.
89 'Radicalism not dangerous', Bowring, iii. 609.
90 UC cxxvii. 47 (18 August 1809).

3

The Interests of Women in Bentham's Late Constitutional Thought

EMMANUELLE DE CHAMPS*

In *Constitutional Code, Volume 1*, Bentham proposed 'virtual universality' of suffrage, giving the right to vote to 'the whole body of the inhabitants, who, on the several days respectively appointed for the several Elections . . . are resident on the territory of the state, deduction made of certain classes'. Among the 'classes thus deducted', alongside minors and non-readers, stood '[F]emales'.[1] Women were thus excluded from the 'constitutive authority', the founding authority in the State. Unlike other provisions of the code deemed to require explanation, this 'enactive' law was not justified by any corresponding 'ratiocinative' text. This cursory exclusion would have passed unnoticed in the context of nineteenth-century dismissals of women's political rights, had it not contradicted other statements in which Bentham openly justified female suffrage. For instance, as late as 1822, at the time he was working on *Constitutional Code*, he lamented in manuscripts that 'the gentler half of the species stand as yet excluded [from the suffrage] by tyranny and prejudice'.[2]

As Bentham scholars have noted, the position expressed in his manuscripts is consistent with the universalist principles on which utilitarianism rests. Since sensitivity to pleasure and pain were universal, Bentham argued that each individual was the best judge of his – and her – interests. Moreover, Bentham's early case for democracy was built precisely on this anthropological foundation: equal political rights were justified by the fact that 'everyone has an equality of right to happiness, an equality of

* Emmanuelle de Champs thanks Monica Biberson for translating part of this text.

[1] J. Bentham, *Constitutional Code: Vol. I*, ed. F. Rosen and J. H. Burns (Oxford: Clarendon Press, 1983 [*CW*]), 29.

[2] 'Securities against Misrule', in J. Bentham, *Securities against Misrule and Other Constitutional Writings for Tripoli and Greece*, ed. P. Schofield (Oxford: Clarendon Press, 1990 [*CW*]), 58.

capacity for happiness, and equality of desire for happiness', in Philip Schofield's words.[3] This commitment to making interests the foundation for suffrage is the linchpin of his later theory of political representation. In *Securities against Misrule* he repeated it and made its implications for the political status of women clear:

> As to persons of the female sex, if the only proper mode of receiving the declaration of a person's will, namely that of *secret suffrage openly delivered*, be employed, no reason consistent with the principle of general utility as above can be assigned why they or any of them, being of relatively mature age, should stand [excluded].[4]

The link between interests and political rights were thus a defining feature of Bentham's ideas concerning women. In his 1824 article 'On Government' for the *Supplement to Encyclopedia Britannica*, James Mill, on the other hand, argued against including female voters in the electorate on the grounds that their interests were to be thought of as included within men's, a position strongly opposed by Anna Wheeler and William Thompson and later by John Stuart Mill. In his *Autobiography*, John Stuart Mill noted that 'it is pleasant to be able to say that Mr. Bentham, on this important point, was wholly on our side'.[5]

The extract from *Securities against Misrule* quoted above, however, ends with the following caveat: 'But no prepossession, however adverse to the principle of general utility, can on the sudden be eradicated: and it would be idle to propose to all that to which acceptance it is certain would not be given by any one.'[6] With this statement, Bentham provisionally closed the debate: though female suffrage was in the greatest interest of the greatest number, advocating it would ultimately be self-defeating. Similar statements can be found in Bentham's writings from the time he made his commitment to radical reform public in 1817. The cursory exclusion of women from the electorate in *Constitutional Code*, written from 1822 and published in 1830, therefore followed naturally.

[3] P. Schofield, *Utility and Democracy: The Political Thought of Jeremy Bentham* (Oxford: Oxford University Press, 2006), 149–50.

[4] 'Constitutional Code, matter occasioned by Greece', in Bentham, *Securities against Misrule* (*CW*), 260 For similar arguments, see Bowring, IX, 108.

[5] J. S. Mill, *Autobiography and Literary Essays* (Toronto: University of Toronto Press, 1981), 107.

[6] 'Constitutional Code, matter occasioned by Greece', in Bentham, *Securities against Misrule* (*CW*), 260.

Bentham's retreat has played a part in scholarly assessments of his feminism. In 1975, Miriam Williford explained that he was in favour of 'an almost total emancipation' of women.[7] Drawing on published texts and manuscripts, she stressed the innovative nature of his ideas on gender equality in three areas where the issue of equality was at stake: politics (the right to vote), legal rights (equality in civil and penal law), and sexuality (marriage and procreation). She also highlighted the pages in which Bentham attacked the preconceptions of his time and denounced the clichés about women's supposed psychological and intellectual inferiority. These analyses were taken further by Lea Campos Boralevi who mined manuscript sources and convincingly showed that Bentham's stance on women's emancipation was consistent with his utilitarianism and culturally ahead of their time.[8] This view was shared by Annie Cot for whom Bentham's writings 'demonstrate[d] that, aside from some physical differences, the situation of inferiority of women is socially constructed and determined' and the situation should be remedied.[9] More recently, in 1994, Nicola Lacey called Bentham a 'proto-feminist'; like Annie Cot, she was careful about attributing a 'feminist' label that appears largely anachronistic but insisted on the way in which Bentham's utilitarian arguments could help structure a critical reflection on women's rights.[10] Conversely, in a series of articles published in the 1980s written in order to defend James Mill's position, Terence Ball argued that Bentham 'almost certainly was not a feminist'.[11] According to him, Bentham's ultimate exclusion of women from the suffrage had its root not only in tactical choices but in assumption of what he considered to be women's inferiority.[12]

All scholars involved in this debate, however, agree that there is a close connection between the anthropological foundations of utilitarianism and the treatment of women's rights. In order to understand

[7] M. Williford, 'Bentham on the Rights of Women', *Journal of the History of Ideas*, 36 (1975), 167.

[8] L. Campos Boralevi, 'In Defense of a Myth', *Bentham Newsletter*, 4 (1980), 33–44; L. Campos Boralevi, *Bentham and the Oppressed* (Berlin: W. de Gruyter, 1984).

[9] A. Cot, '"Let there be no distinction between the sexes": Jeremy Bentham on the Status of Women', in R. W. Dimand and C. Nyland, eds., *The Status of Women in Classical Economic Thought* (Cheltenham: Edward Elgar, 2003), 165–89, at 165.

[10] N. Lacey, 'Bentham as Proto-feminist? Or an Ahistorical Fantasy on "Anarchical Fallacies"', *Current Legal Problems* 51 (1998), 441–66.

[11] T. Ball, 'Was Bentham a Feminist?', *The Bentham Newsletter* 4 (1980), 25–31.

[12] T. Ball, 'Utilitarianism, Feminism and the Franchise: James Mill and His Critics', *History of Political Thought* 1 (1980), 91–115.

how women's interests were taken into account in Bentham's later constitutional thought – a period starting with his radical writings of the late 1810s – this chapter takes a longer view and examines the foundations on which his anthropological view of gender rests. Indeed, as far as the status of women and of their rights is concerned, Bentham's position remained remarkably consistent throughout his career. Another thread is provided by his interest in the ways the law frames sexual relations between men and women, especially through the institution of marriage. Bentham's utilitarianism made possible a unified approach to women as legal and political subjects and agents. If their exclusion from the suffrage can indeed be ascribed to precautionary reasons in the polemical context of British radicalism, Bentham took care to establish other mechanisms to vindicate women's interests as individuals in the political community.

3.1 Gender, Interests, and Utility

Bentham opened *An Introduction to the Principles of Morals and Legislation* with the statement that 'nature has placed mankind under the governance of two sovereign masters, pain and pleasure'. The equal ability of individuals to feel pleasure and pain meant that legislators had to pay equal attention to all of them as sentient beings: '*each person*', he wrote in French in 1789, 'has an equal right to all the happiness one's nature is capable of'.[13] Thus, the starting point of Bentham's philosophy of interest was the individual as a sentient being apt to experience pleasure and pain. To what extent was this individual gendered? This question has been posed by the feminist critique of the political philosophy of the Enlightenment in general. Indeed, the phrase 'false universal' has been used to denounce the use of the generic masculine that prohibits conceiving female specificity and obliterates it from political discourses. As Joan Wallach Scott has pointed out, in classical political thought

[13] 'Composition des États-Généraux', in J. Bentham, *Rights, Representation, and Reform: Nonsense upon Stilts and Other Writings on the French Revolution*, ed. P. Schofield, C. Pease-Watkin, and C. Blamires (Oxford: Clarendon Press, 2002 [CW]), 68. On this subject, see also M. E. L. Guidi, '"Everybody to count for one, nobody for more than one". The Principle of Equal Consideration of Interests from Bentham to Pigou', *Revue d'études benthamiennes* 4 (2008), doi.org/10.4000/etudes-benthamiennes.182.

> the political individual ... was taken to be both universal and male; the female was not an individual, both because she was nonidentical with the human prototype and because she was the other who confirmed the (male's) individual individuality.[14]

It is true that Bentham frequently uses the masculine to refer to both men and women, especially as subjects of penal and civil law. In 'A View of the Hard Labour Bill', printed in 1778, he takes care to make it clear:

> In regard to *sex*, I make, in general, no separate mention of the *female*; that being understood (unless where the contrary is specified) to be included under the expression used to denote the *male*.[15]

It can, however, be argued that Bentham did not consider this an obvious move and took care to consider gender differences. Throughout *An Introduction to the Principles of Morals and Legislation*, he used the neutral terms 'mankind', 'individual', 'person', or 'human creature' much more readily than the generic 'man'. The biological distinction between the sexes came up in the sixth chapter of *Introduction* under the title of 'circumstances influencing sensibility'. It ranked twenty-fifth after other characteristics such as '1. Health. 2. Strength. 3. Hardiness. 4. Bodily imperfection. 5. Quantity and quality of knowledge. 6. Strength of intellectual powers ... 10. Moral sensibility ... 12. Religious sensibility ... 19. Habitual occupations. 20. Pecuniary circumstances ....'[16] Whilst it was not one of the first determinants of sensibility, the gender criterion was nevertheless far from ineffective:

> Among such of the primitive modifications of the corporeal frame as may appear to influence the quantum and bias of sensibility, the most obvious and conspicuous are those which constitute the *sex*. In point of quantity, the sensibility of the female sex appears in general to be greater than that of the male. The health of the female is more delicate than that of the male: in point of strength and hardiness of body, in point of quantity and quality of knowledge, in point of strength of intellectual

[14] J. W. Scott, *Only Paradoxes to Offer* (Cambridge, MA: Harvard University Press, 1997) 8; H. L. Smith, *All Men and Both Sexes: Gender, Politics, and the False Universal in England, 1640–1832* (University Park: Penn State University Press, 2002).

[15] 'Advertisement', in J. Bentham, *View of the Hard-Labour Bill; being an abstract of a pamphlet intituled 'Draught of a bill, to punish by imprisonment and hard labour, certain offenders; and to establish proper places for their reception'. Interspersed with observations relative to the subject of the above draught in particular, and to jurisprudence in general* (London: T. Payne, 1778).

[16] J. Bentham, *An Introduction to the Principles of Morals and Legislation*, ed. J. H. Burns and H. L. A. Hart (Oxford: Clarendon Press, 1996 [*CW*]), 52.

> powers, and firmness of mind, she is commonly inferior: moral, religious, sympathetic, and antipathetic sensibility are commonly stronger in her than in the male.[17]

Bentham's approach indeed gave centre ground to physical, intellectual, and moral characteristics without ever making gender the sole criterion.

However, the move from physical to moral characteristics had significant consequences: 'the female is rather more inclined than the male to superstition', Bentham wrote, and 'her sympathetic biases are in many respects different' since 'her affections are apt to be less enlarged seldom expanding themselves so much as to take in the welfare of her country in general ... unless it be in virtue of her sympathy for some particular individuals that belong to it'.[18] The different imprint of sympathy in women – which is important because it conditions the hypotheses they made to calculate maximum utility – was not due to any structural biological difference, nor to the experience of motherhood; Bentham discarded these arguments and indicated that the disparities were due to 'some deficiency in point of knowledge, discernment, and comprehension'.[19] It was the result, he explained, of the political, social, and moral situation to which women were confined in a world ruled by men and for men's interests: 'legislators seem all to have been of the male sex, down to the days of Catherine [of Russia]'.[20]

> In certain nations, women, whether married or not, have been placed in a state of perpetual wardship: this has been evidently founded on the notion of a decided inferiority in point of intellects on the part of the female sex, analogous to that which is the result of infancy or insanity on the part of the male. This is not the only instance in which tyranny has taken advantage of its own wrong, alleging as a reason for the domination it exercises, an imbecility, which, as far as it has been real, has been produced by the abuse of that very power which it is brought to justify.[21]

These ideas are not in themselves utilitarian, nor were they specific to Bentham. A strand of the Enlightenment saw women's moral deficiencies as the product of their education, socialization, and laws made by men. Helvétius, for instance, pointed out that 'it is unreasonable to reproach women for insincerity, when decency and laws combine to force them to

[17] Bentham, *IPML* (*CW*), 64.
[18] Ibid., 65.
[19] Ibid.
[20] Ibid., 238n.
[21] Ibid., 245n.

embrace it; and that effects cannot change as long as the causes subsist', while Voltaire cursorily pointed out that 'none other than men have made the laws'.[22]

Specific to Bentham's utilitarianism, however, is the intellectual and legal approach to groups and categories, which helps us understand why he did not essentialize gender characteristics, or at least no more than any other characteristic. According to a distinction made in his earliest writings, the power of legislators was twofold: they commanded and named the individuals to whom their laws applied. Naming and specifying individuals endowed those individuals with rights and duties.[23] Whilst some categories may coincide with observable characteristics ('women', or 'men aged over 21', for example), most of them were artificial, created by legislators for their own ends and subject to change depending on their objectives. This focus on the power of naming structured Bentham's legal thinking. By treating gender alongside other types of categories, many of them socially, legally, and politically constructed, Bentham paved the way for de-essentializing gender. Thus, among the circumstances that affect sensibility, gender could be taken into account but alongside other specifications, such as 'the primary circumstances of bodily imperfection,[24] and insanity . . . the secondary circumstance of sex; perhaps . . . that of age; at any rate . . . those of rank, of climate, of lineage, and of religious profession'.[25] This refusal to essentialize natural characteristics is consistent with Bentham's deconstruction project: the principle of utility served as a tool for questioning existing categories, particularly where morality was concerned.

Defined early on in Bentham's writings, this approach to individuals and categories remained operative in his late constitutional thought,

[22] 'Je dis seulement qu'on ne peut raisonnablement reprocher aux femmes une fausseté dont la décence et les lois leur font, pour ainsi dire, une nécessité; et qu'enfin l'on ne change point les effets, en laissant subsister les causes.' C.-A. Helvétius, *De l'esprit* (Paris: Fayard, 1988), 149; 'Ce sont les hommes qui ont fait les lois'; Voltaire, *Prix de la justice et de l'humanité* (Oxford: Voltaire Foundation, 2008), 148.

[23] H. L. A. Hart, *Essays on Bentham: Studies in Jurisprudence and Political Theory* (Oxford: Clarendon Press, 1982), 200–6; G. Tusseau, 'Jeremy Bentham on Power-Conferring Laws', *Revue d'études benthamiennes* 3 (2007), doi.org/10.4000/etudes-benthamiennes .160; E. de Champs, *'La déontologie politique' ou La pensée constitutionnelle de Jeremy Bentham* (Geneva: Droz, 2008), 150–55.

[24] E. de Champs, 'Propriété et statut personnel chez Jeremy Bentham', in B. Bachofen, ed., *Le libéralisme au miroir du droit. L'Etat, la personne et la propriété*, (Paris: ENS éditions, 2008), 117–43.

[25] Bentham, *IPML* (*CW*), 69.

which relied on a complex system through which individuals were invested with powers depending on their legal status or situation. In *Constitutional Code*, Bentham paid close attention to the way in which categories of the population are made assignable or, to put it another way, defined as legal subjects.[26] He often made a deliberate effort to take an inclusive view of political communities, mentioning, for instance, that 'every person, elector, inhabitant, or foreigner . . . every individual of the human species' was a member of the Public Opinion Tribunal.[27] This was not general, of course, and he continued to use 'man' to mean 'persons of both sexes' in many articles of the *Code*.[28]

3.2 Family, Marriage, and the Civil Law

The artificiality of the categories constructed by the legislator concerned the private sphere ruled by civil law. In a collection of texts from the 1770s in preparation for a project for a utilitarian code, Bentham insisted on the fact that, like all other legal powers, domestic powers were all created by legislators and could not be considered natural:

> Relations stiled Natural are also constituted by the Powers called Civil. For they are constituted by Powers given by the State.
>
> A Man and Woman copulate: in this the State, indeed, has no part: but this does not render them Husband and Wife. It does not give to either any of those powers which alone make the relation an object of notice.[29]

The statuses of husband and wife, of child and ward, did not pre-exist the law. In this, as the editors of *Preparatory Principles* noted, Bentham broke with Blackstone and the natural law tradition which deemed these statuses to have been initially natural and only subsequently sanctioned by legislators. For Bentham, domestic powers were above all artificial and had to be defined on the basis of utility. In this regard, he took a particular interest in the situation of women within the family (mainly

[26] 'First Lines of a Proposed Code of Law', in J. Bentham, *Legislator of the World: Writings on Codification, Law, and Education*, ed. P. Schofield and J. Harris (Oxford: Clarendon Press, 1998 [*CW*]), 191–2.

[27] Bentham, *Constitutional Code* (*CW*), 39.

[28] Unlike Blackstone, who made a point to state 'Under the word homo also, though a name common to both sexes, the female is however excluded, propter defectum sexus.' S. W. Blackstone, *Commentaries on the Laws of England* (Chicago: University of Chicago Press, 1975), IV, 362, n. 66.

[29] J. Bentham, *Preparatory Principles*, ed. D. G. Long and P. Schofield (Oxford: Oxford University Press, 2016), 67.

in their role as wives rather than householders). Marriage was the point where the state created the status of each spouse within marriage and defined their respective powers:

> What makes the Man and Woman Husband and Wife is *powers* given by Law, in consequence of the contract of their Marriage. Powers given to the Wife over the possessions of the Husband. Powers given to the Husband over the possessions and person of the Wife. 'Tis punishment creates those powers.[30]

Bentham's insistence on the contractual character of marriage has been studied by Mary Sokol.[31] This idea was familiar to Enlightenment readers: Pufendorf had insisted on it, followed by Montesquieu and Voltaire. In 1791, the French Revolution recognized marriage as a civil contract, which was confirmed by Napoleon's Civil Code a decade later. In his later constitutional writings, Bentham insisted on the purely civil nature of this contract and sought to exclude the undue meddling of religion. He provided the bureaucratic structure that allowed the conformity of this contract to utilitarian ideals under the administrative authority of the 'Local Registrar' who was placed in charge of the 'recordation … as they occur, of all marriages celebrated within his territory'. In this section of *Constitutional Code* published only after his death by John Bowring, Bentham seized on the opportunity to quip at the undue influence of the Church and at its monopoly on marriage, christenings, and burials.[32]

A few years later, in his examination of James Humphreys's proposal for a new property code, Bentham examined the marriage contract with a clear focus on the bride's interests: intelligibility, especially that of the economic implications of the marriage settlement, was key to her expressing informed consent:

> Miss Campbell [the fictitious bride in Humphreys's draught of a marriage contract] is the chief object of my care. And why? Even because – whatsoever is either not understood or misunderstood, is in proportion mischievous; mischievous, in the joint proportion of the importance of the matter, and the number of persons interested, from whose minds the true import is in either way excluded. For, from nonunderstoodness or

30 Ibid., 67.

31 M. Sokol, *Bentham, Law and Marriage: A Utilitarian Code of Law in Historical Contexts* (London: Continuum, 2011).

32 'Constitutional Code', Bowring, IX, 629. Bowring considered that Bentham had inspired the Registration system which came in force in England in 1841, see 625n.

> misunderstoodness comes oppositeness to expectation; from oppositeness to expectation, disappointment; from disappointment, suffering, in proportion to the importance of the consequences.[33]

Consent, therefore, appears as a key theme in Bentham's writings on marriage – in his early as well as in his later texts. Beyond the marriage contract, consent was also the main term around which sexual relations hinged. This notion is central in understanding Bentham's writings on sexual relations that occupied the second half of the 1810s. Indeed, within his utilitarian system, he attributed an intrinsic value to sexual pleasure, with significant consequences for morals as well as for legislation. The goal of utilitarian legislators was to maximize pleasure, whatever its source:

> The pleasure that comes from the union of the sexes is a form of pleasure; leaving aside the evils, if any, that may result from the same source, that is [enough?] for a legislator to do whatever is in his power to ensure that there is the greatest possible quantity of it in society.[34]

In order to assess whether or not an act created pleasure, legislators in effect had to examine the sum total of the pleasure produced. If one's pleasure was obtained at the expense of another's pain, then the sum total of pleasure was zero or less. More broadly, from a civil and criminal point of view, Bentham made consent the criterion for the legality of any act that had an impact on another. In *An Introduction to the Principles of Morals and Legislation*, it was the first criterion for determining whether or not an act should be punished. Or rather, punishment was unfounded when the act was consensual:

> this consent, provided it be free, and fairly obtained, is the best proof that can be produced, that, to the person who gives it, no mischief, at least no immediate mischief, upon the whole, is done. For no man can be so good a judge as the man himself, what it is gives him pleasure or displeasure.[35]

If the principles were laid out early on in Bentham's career, their implications in the field of sexual morality were only fully worked out in the

[33] 'Commentary on Humphreys's Real Property Code', Bowring, V, 405. In his later works, Bentham had more consideration for married women's property than in his early manuscripts, in which he did not frontally oppose Blackstone's statement that the husband was the only legal owner of property in a married couple (see *Preparatory Principles* [CW]), 68.

[34] UC 32, f. 103.

[35] Bentham, *IPML* (*CW*), 159.

1810s, with his attack on the domination of ascetic principles in morals and legislation, especially in the third, unpublished volume of *Not Paul, but Jesus*.[36] Consent and pleasure were intrinsically linked. The importance given to consent guided all of Bentham's proposals in sexual matters, particularly the decriminalization of homosexuality and adultery 'on one side or other'[37].

In these later writings, though his main object was to lift the moral stigma and legal penalties attached to male homosexual acts, Bentham showed explicit awareness of the issues associated with consent on the part of women. He reflected on the conditions in which it could be considered to have been given (excluding inebriation, force, insanity, or age) and provided a long list of 'evils to the female' attached to sexual gratification that took both physical and verbal harm into account, as well as injuries to reputation.[38] Though Bentham noted that all these evils could also be imposed on men, women were specifically considered in this respect. Rape, tellingly, was described as 'the sort of war thus waged against one half of the species'.[39] Conversely, consent could lead individuals to enter into sexual relations outside marriage, or in open marriages, or in temporary marriages.[40]

It must be said that Bentham's later constitutional writings did not go so far as to provide the legal framework that would have made such sexual freedom possible, except perhaps for the casual remark that it was also the function of the Local Registrar to record divorces.[41] Making divorce an everyday administrative matter was consistent with his calls for the simplification of divorce proceedings. Bentham's position on divorce was recurringly framed in the 1810s and 1820s in terms of interests, as when he discussed Jesus's prohibition of the repudiation of his wife by her husband:

[36] J. Bentham, *Not Paul, but Jesus. Vol. III. Doctrine*, ed. P. Schofield, M. Quinn, and C. Pease-Watkin (London: University College London, 2013).

[37] 'Of Sexual Irregularities', in J. Bentham, *Of Sexual Irregularities, and Other Writings on Sexual Morality*, ed. P. Schofield, C. Pease-Watkin, and M. Quinn (Oxford: Oxford University Press, 2014 [*CW*]), 3.

[38] 'General Idea of … Not Paul, but Jesus', in Bentham, *Of Sexual Irregularities* (*CW*), 138–9.

[39] 'Sextus', in Bentham, *Of Sexual Irregularities* (*CW*), 67.

[40] Or, to take up Bentham's words, 'sexual intercourse without cohabitation'; 'cohabitation without marriage'; 'marriage polygamous on both sides', Bentham, *Not Paul, but Jesus (CW)*, 57.

[41] Bowring, IX, 629.

> The will of the male alone would have in this case for its source the interest of the male alone: the interest of the strongest, to which the interest of the weakest of the parties would thus be sacrificed: thus saith the law of utility: thus saith the law of Jesus.[42]

Bentham's utilitarian logic, guided by the notions of interest and consent, was innovative insofar as he rigorously examined the interests of women in the civil relations that united them to men. The current provisions of English law and Christian morality were repeatedly indicted as 'tyranny': tyranny on the part of the legislator for the criminalization of sexual acts considered harmless or pleasurable by the persons involved[43] but also tyranny on the part of the male sex upon the female, as in the extracts quoted above.

3.3 Interests and Citizenship in the Code

The aim of Bentham's constitutional architecture is to check the operation of sinister interests, an objective that is often equated with a fight against 'tyranny', a theme common to radical writing of the early nineteenth century.[44] In Bentham's political vocabulary, only the proper recognition of the interests of the greatest number can act as a check against the tyranny of the few. The centrality of interests to politics is stated in Bentham's early writings, for instance, in *An Introduction to the Principles of Morals and Legislation*, where he explained the conditions under which one might logically move from individual to group interests:

> The interest of the community is one of the most general expressions that can occur in the phraseology of morals... When it has a meaning, it is this. The community is a fictitious *body*, composed of the individual persons who are considered as constituting as it were its *members*. The interest of the community then is, what? – the sum of the interests of the several members who compose it.[45]

However, it was only after 1789 and in view of the events unfolding in France, that the democratic conclusions of such a definition of the political community were worked out. As with civil matters, he made consent the mark of the public expression of a political interest. Thus:

[42] Bentham, *Not Paul, but Jesus* (*CW*), 67.

[43] 'Sextus', in Bentham, *Of Sexual Irregularities* (*CW*), 53, 56, 64, 68, 75.

[44] This theme has recently received attention in T. Y. Koh, 'Bentham on Asceticism and Tyranny', *History of European Ideas* 45 (2019), 1–14.

[45] Bentham, *IPML* (*CW*), 12.

> The purpose of the constitutional branch of law, as of all other branches, must be general utility, that is, the greatest possible happiness for the members of the community in question. The surest sign, the most evident proof of general utility is general consent.[46]

In 1789, Bentham developed a theory of democracy based on the representation of interests.[47] The role of the ballot in declaring interests was but one of the mechanisms that he put forward: in his constitutional plans, voting was done by secret ballot, the electoral mandate was short (one year). A system for publishing the Assembly's debates allowed for democratic control and petitions gave voters the opportunity to remove their representatives before the end of their annual term.[48] Interests, consent, and representation were therefore inseparable.

Bentham's reflections on women's political participation were directly stimulated by revolutionary debates. In Projet of a Constitutional Code written for France, very likely after having read Condorcet's plea for the admission of women to full voting citizenship, Bentham wrote: 'The Right of election shall be in every French citizen, male or female, being of full age, of sound mind, and able to read.'[49] Not only could women vote, they could also be elected: 'from the capacity of being elected no human creature whatsoever can be excluded'.[50] In these manuscripts, Bentham did not dispense with justifications for supporting women's vote. The universalist argument was repeated: 'there is no a priori reason which justifies the fact that [the right to vote] should be denied to some or others': the only ones who could be legitimately excluded were those who were unable to use it 'for their own benefit or that of others', that is, those who were not sound of mind or were too young. The illiterate were the final category to be excluded, as they were deemed unable to 'form a

[46] UC 176, f. 3. See also de Champs, *'La déontologie politique' ou La pensée constitutionnelle de Jeremy Bentham*, 183–91.

[47] Schofield, *Utility and Democracy*, 98–9; E. de Champs, *Enlightenment and Utility. Bentham in France/Bentham in French* (Cambridge: Cambridge University Press, 2015), 115–9.

[48] 'Considérations d'un Anglois' and 'Projet of a Constitutional Code for France', in Bentham, *Rights, Representation and Reform* (*CW*), 142–5, 248.

[49] 'The Right of election shall be in every French citizen, male or female, being of full age, of sound mind, and able to read.' Ibid., 231. Compare with Condorcet, 'On the Admission of Women to the Rights of Citizenship', 3 July 1790, in *The French Revolution and Human Rights: A Brief Documentary History*, translated, edited, and with an introduction by Lynn Hunt (Boston; New York: Bedford; St. Martin's, 1996), 119–21.

[50] Ibid.

rational judgement' by accessing printed information independently.[51] Did any of these criteria justify the exclusion of women from the suffrage, Bentham asked, reversing the burden of proof? His conclusion was unambiguous:

> As to the usage which has prevailed so generally to the disadvantage of the softer sex, it has tyranny for its efficient cause and prejudice for its sole justification.[52]

In a short passage he rebutted common arguments: the supposed inferiority of women's intellectual faculties ('the fact is dubious'); they should not be taken away from their domestic tasks ('the men have their domestic duties as well as the women'); and, finally, that the idea itself of giving women the vote was intrinsically ridiculous ('not so truly as that of excluding them from it').[53] Though they were deeply consistent with Bentham's system and with the utilitarian rationale for democracy, these plans remained unpublished.

In 1817, when Bentham publicly came out in support of radical reform and published *Plan of Parliamentary Reform*, he again grounded the right to vote on the equality of sensibility to pain and pleasure, from which equality of interests derives.[54] Thus, the greatest happiness of the greatest number required universal suffrage and exceptions needed to be justified. Here, he proposed the exclusion of minors, criminals, and idiots on the same ground as in his earlier writings for France.[55] In discussing the place of women in the body of electors, he noted the difficulty there was in grounding their exclusion on any utilitarian reasoning:

> The great leading considerations above brought to view – viz. the universal-interest-comprehension principle, the quality of appropriate probity and appropriate intellectual aptitude – these guides to decision, if they apply not with propriety to both sexes, it seems not easy to say with what propriety they can be applicable to either.[56]

His manuscripts were even more explicit: the principle of utility made it impossible to justify the exclusion of women from the suffrage.[57] Only

[51] Ibid., 246–9.
[52] Ibid., 247.
[53] Ibid., 247–8.
[54] 'Plan of Parliamentary Reform', Bowring, III, 439.
[55] Ibid., 450.
[56] Ibid., 463.
[57] UC 127, f. 261.

by presuming or assuming that women's interests were comprised in those of men might such a move be justified, which Bentham rejected.

> Upon experience and examination, should it ever be established that an adequately strong connection of interests has not place, and that for want of it, more evil is produced by injury done by the exclusion to the interests of the female sex than is atoned for by the exclusion of the mass of Election evil abovementioned, the propriety of abolishing this exclusion, and accordingly giving admission to the votes of females will have been established.[58]

In *Plan of Parliamentary Reform*, including women in the electorate was, however, characterized as 'premature' and as something that would cast 'scorn' upon the entire reform proposal.[59] Six years later, Bentham still believed this to be the case. In a manuscript dated 16 March 1823, he justified his choice:

> Why exclude the whole female sex from all participation in the constitutive power?
>
> – Because the prepossession against their admission is at present too general, and too intense, to afford any chance in favour of a proposal for their admission.[60]

Putting forward such a measure would be bound to fail and risked derailing the demand for the considerable extension of the suffrage to 'virtually universal' suffrage. Interestingly, Bentham himself provided evidence of such disparaging comments by quoting Charles Fox in a footnote to *Plan of Parliamentary Reform*.[61]

However, the idea of female suffrage was being aired in radical circles at the time, especially after 1815.[62] In 1820 the trial of Queen Caroline provided a platform for radical female societies, which opposed George IV in his behaviour both as a husband and a ruler – this occasioned a conservative backlash against the involvement of women in politics.[63] Bentham's reluctance to bring up the topic might have been part of his

[58] UC 127, f. 277, dated 25 November 1818.

[59] 'Plan of Parliamentary Reform', Bowring, III, 463.

[60] UC 37, f. 120 dated 16 March 1823; and 'Supreme Operative', Bowring, IX, 108.

[61] 'Plan of Parliamentary Reform', Bowring, III, 463n.

[62] A. Chernock, 'Extending the "Right of Election": Men's Arguments for Women's Political Representation in Late Enlightenment Britain', in S. Knott, B. Taylor, eds., *Women, Gender and Enlightenment* (Basingstoke: Palgrave Macmillan, 2005), 587–609.

[63] L. Davidoff and C. Hall, *Family Fortunes: Men and Women of the English Middle-Class, 1780–1850* (London: Routledge, 1987), 149–55; A. Clark, *Scandal: The Sexual Politics of the British Constitution* (Princeton: Princeton University Press, 2003), 177–207.

campaign to make 'radicalism not dangerous', which involved rejecting accusations that radical reform would subvert private property and, more generally, the avoidance of association with the revolutionary branch of the reform movement.[64]

Accordingly, Bentham's Election Code, as published in *Radical Reform Bill* in 1819 did not contain any provision for women's vote (though it continued to justify it on principle in a footnote). It explicitly rejected, however, the possibility for women to be elected, on the grounds of 'the absurdity of the mixture betwixt sex and sex',[65] which sounded unlike the tone employed in the manuscripts. The Election Code provides a link between Bentham's radical reform projects and the Constitutional Code: in 1830, when he had *Constitutional Code: Vol. 1* printed, he omitted the sections on eligibility and the organization of elections, referring readers to *Bentham's Radical Reform Bill* published in 1819 for the details of each article.[66] Women were neither electors nor eligible for election in *Constitutional Code*, where their exclusion was not justified.

Nevertheless, in *Constitutional Code*, Bentham provided compensatory mechanisms in order to accommodate women's interests. Indeed, it rested on a double democratic mechanism for representing interests, of which suffrage was but one part. Bentham stressed that control of political activity was a major counterweight for preventing the abuse of power and guiding votes. Thus, even though women were excluded from the category of voters, they were involved in the Public Opinion Tribunal to which Bentham ascribed a major constitutional role in controlling and directing political action.[67] The Public Opinion Tribunal was made up of 'all individuals, of whom the Constitutive body of this state is composed', and, he continued, of 'all those classes, which under §1, article 3 stand excluded from all participation in such supreme power'. The Tribunal played a key part in this constitutional mechanism: 'To the pernicious

64 'Radical Reform Bill', Bowring, III, 559–622.

65 Ibid., 567n.

66 Bentham, *Constitutional Code* (*CW*), 48n.

67 Recent studies of Bentham's late constitutional theory focus on the role given to public opinion. See G. J. Postema, 'The Soul of Justice: Bentham on Publicity, Law and the Rule of Law', in X. Zhai and M. Quinn, eds., *Bentham's Theory of Law and Public Opinion* (Cambridge: Cambridge University Press, 2014), 40–62; D. Lieberman, 'Declaring Rights: Bentham and the Rights of Man', in I. Hunter and R. Whatmore, eds., *Philosophy, Rights and Natural Law. Essays in Honour of Knud Haakonssen* (Edinburgh: Edinburgh University Press, 2019), 306–37.

exercise of the power of government it is the only check; to the beneficial, an indispensable supplement.'[68]

Whilst one might fear that the Public Opinion Tribunal would structurally attach less importance to what women rather than men had to say (an objection Bentham did not address), concrete suggestions were made for the inclusion of women in legal institutions, particularly when their interests as women were concerned. The 'quasi-jury', a key element in Bentham's reform of the judiciary, was such an institution. Contrary to the traditional English jury, the quasi-jury was not responsible for giving a verdict: instead, acting as observers in court, the members of the quasi-jury assessed the conduct of the judge and reported on it. It therefore played a central role in the shaping of public opinion and increased the power of publicity over legal decisions. This institution, Bentham suggested, would include women when 'those cases in which the interests of the two sexes antagonize' were at stake. This measure was expressly presented as an opportunity for women to make their own interests heard:

> On this occasion, it would be among the objects of consideration for the legislature, whether anything, and what, can be done for the alleviation of the tyranny hitherto, in a greater or less degree, so universally exercised over the weaker by the stronger sex. Suppose for this purpose, amongst other things, a modification of the Quasi-Jury. The number of the males (the total number being minimized as it has been) would scarcely, it would be thought, admit of retrenchment. If so, the next least number affording a certainty of a majority is five. Reserving in every case the predominance to the stronger sex, here then would be the foreman as before, a male erudite, ordinaries two males: of the female sex, erudite one, ordinary the other.[69]

Bentham can be criticized for keeping men in the majority, allowing for three jurors as opposed to, at most, two female jurors – this however appears strikingly innovative, as women were not allowe– to serve on juries in England until 1931. Such a proposal expanded significantly on an existing English institution, that of the 'Jury of Matrons', more precisely a group of women who were called upon by the judge in situations where a woman's pregnancy needed to be asserted or disproved, either in the case of a woman sentenced to the death penalty or

[68] Bentham, *Constitutional Code* (*CW*), 36.
[69] 'Constitutional Code', Bowring, IX, 566–7.

in cases relative to inheritance.[70] Bentham's proposal to reserve specific places for women on juries was also interesting because it supposed some community of interests between women – something that was not necessarily implied by his writings on women in other contexts (see above).

Similarly, the 'Local Headman', whose role was to prevent a case from going to trial through the use of mediation, was encouraged to enlist the services of a female assistant.

> *Instructional.* Art. 5. In the case of husband and wife, and in other cases, where the parties are of different sexes, he will do well to call in, as his assistant, a person of the female sex, wife or widow, and past the age of child-bearing.
>
> *Instructional.* Art. 6. Where both, or all parties are of the female sex, at the desire of any one, he may do well to call in, or refer them from himself to some person of the female sex, circumstanced as per Art. 5.[71]

The officers in charge of carrying out judicial measures also had to be female when the accused were women.[72] As before, Bentham did not immediately question the conditions of male dominance since judges were still men and women only their assistants; however, in the early-nineteenth-century political and legal context, the visibility he intended to give women in these albeit secondary judicial roles was significant – as was its connection to public morality.

In *Constitutional Code*, Bentham displayed both pragmatism and consistency: accepting that including women as voters would damage his reform strategy, he put forward mechanisms that allowed their sensibility and interests to be taken into account and debated in the Public Opinion Tribunal. He thereby established mechanisms, which,

70 For a presentation of Jury of Matrons in the eighteenth century, see J. M. Cornett, 'Hoodwink'd by Custom: The Exclusion of Women from Juries in Eighteenth-Century English Law and Literature', *William and Mary Journal of Race, Gender and Social Justice* 4 (1997), 2–89.

71 'Constitutional Code', Bowring, IX, 620.

72 See 'Constitutional Code', Bowring, IX, 639: 'Where the proposed Prehendee is of the female sex, the Judge will, if he thinks fit, make appointment of a person of that same sex, to act as attendant on the person of the proposed Prehendee, whether she be a foreigner or a native: this, for the purpose of minimizing the annoyance to which a person of the female sex may unavoidably be subjected, by being in the mode in question placed under the power of a person of the male sex: of which annoyance the intensity will naturally be in proportion to the degree of affluence to which she has been habituated.'

whilst they did not make up for women's exclusion from the franchise, testified at least to the constant attention that their interests deserved.

3.4 Conclusion

Taken as a whole, Bentham's writings provided a sustained and rigorous case for women's political and legal rights, be it in private or in political matters. Starting from the equal consideration of interests and making consent an explicit sign of this interest, he exposed the inconsistency of contemporary laws regarding sexuality and marriage. As far as political rights were concerned, his vindication of women's participation in politics through the vote was strikingly modern. Indeed, utility provided a unifying principle that operated in the private and in the public spheres and acted as a genuine alternative to right-based theories of gender equality, which often found it difficult to reconcile women's biological inferiority in the family with claims to equal political rights. Bentham saw women's political rights as making up for the domination from which they still suffered in the private sphere:

> Again, in domestic concerns, males derive greater power from physical force: here, then, is a means of injury: for security against it, if in respect of political power, there be a difference, it should rather be in their favour than in the favour of males.[73]

Whilst it would be anachronistic to see Bentham as a 'feminist' in any of the senses this word has had since the twentieth century, it seems important to acknowledge the fact that he systematically explored ways in which hedonistic individualism provided a foundation for the inclusion of women's interests in the decisions of the legislator. Moreover, he tried to put forward a consistent analysis of the various statuses of women, who he always defined as rational individuals able to act in keeping with their interests and worthy of the legislators' protection, without this protection being based on an essentialization of gender traits. The notion of consent was at the heart of his argument and sets the main methodological limit to Bentham's 'feminism' since the social and political conditions in which consent was expressed were not subject to a specific analysis in the case of women – even though Bentham noted

[73] Ibid., 108.

the domination they suffered and put forward, in a work like *The Book of Fallacies*, a critical theory of power in discursive contexts.[74]

Utilitarian arguments in favour of equal political rights for women were carried forward by the next generation, that of Anna Wheeler, William Thompson, and John Stuart Mill. But before that time, Bentham's deference to public opinion on the issue of women's suffrage probably contributed to delay the placing of the issue on the political agenda in Britain.

[74] J. Bentham, *The Book of Fallacies*, ed. P. Schofield (Oxford: Clarendon Press, 2015 [*CW*]).

4

Religion and Judgement in Bentham's Political Thought

TSIN YEN KOH

4.1 Introduction

One of the charges Bentham made against the Church of England was that it aimed at, and achieved to some degree, the 'prostration of understanding and will'. The phrase was taken from a visitation sermon by Bishop Howley, in which he warned against the dangers of Unitarianism as a shelter for 'infidelity'. Fortunately, in Howley's view, the appeal was as yet confined to men of limited education who had not spent much thought on religion, or who, 'loving rather to question than to learn, [had] approached the oracles of divine truth without that humble docility, that prostration of the understanding and will, which [were] indispensable to proficiency in Christian instruction'.[1] Bentham took the phrase to represent the Church's desiderata in its followers more generally. 'Prostration of understanding and will', he declared, was 'in one word *slavery*', and a more absolute slavery than that to be found in Barbary or the West Indies. The only reason he could think of for the establishment of a system of slavery was the exercise of a corresponding tyranny over the people enslaved.[2] Despotism and slavery were but two sides of the same coin: 'He who as towards one man acts the part of a despot, is but the more fitted for acting towards another man that of a slave. So many men as there are, one above another, standing in these relations to one another, so many links are there in the chain of slavery.'[3] The prostration of understanding and will was, then, a two-part act: the prostration of will was sufficient to form links in the chain of despotism

[1] W. Howley, *A Charge Delivered to the Clergy of the Diocese of London* (London: T. Bensley, 1814), 16.

[2] J. Bentham, *Church-of-Englandism and Its Catechism Examined*, ed. James E. Crimmins and Catherine Fuller (Oxford: Oxford University Press, 2011), 47, 258.

[3] Bentham, *Church-of-Englandism*, 419.

and slavery, but the prostration of understanding was necessary to make the chain perpetual.

Contemporary reviews of *Church-of-Englandism* fell along predictable lines: the *Examiner*, which was generally supportive of Bentham, praised it for striking 'a great number of irresistible blows' at the 'roots of bigotry and worldliness'; the *British Critic* and the *Quarterly Review*, which were not, attributed its composition to insanity and malevolence respectively.[4] This last review ended with the complaint that the 'worst part' of the book was not the 'deep-seated malignity' it displayed towards the Church and its officers but the 'indecent levity' with which it treated sacred subjects. The reviewer concluded with a recommendation to the author to consider 'whether the decline of life [could not] be better spent than in captiously cavilling at the doctrines of religion, and in profane ridicule of its most holy rites?'[5]

In this chapter, following the *Examiner* and departing from the *Quarterly Review*, I propose to take Bentham's charge seriously. I argue that Bentham thought that religion, referring to the Church of England in particular and Christianity in general, had a corruptive effect on the faculty of judgement. More specifically, the Church discouraged free criticism of its doctrines and practices and encouraged an uncritical reliance on its authority. On this view, *Church-of-Englandism* can be read not so much as a defence of the right of private judgement (which is not the topic of this chapter) but a critique of the Church's claim to intellectual authority. A second way in which religion could corrupt judgement, even without the benefit of an established church, was by challenging the empirical basis of knowledge. The main text used here is *Analysis of the Influence of Natural Religion* (*AINR*).[6] Bentham argued

[4] 'Shocking and Pernicious Absurdities of Bigotry', *Examiner* 559 (13 September 1818), 578–9; 'Art V. Church-of-Englandism, and Its Catechism Examined', *British Critic* 10 (November 1818), 519–28; 'Art VIII. Church-of-Englandism and Its Catechism Examined', *Quarterly Review* 21, no. 41 (1 January 1819), 167–77. The *Examiner* also published a laudatory review of *Mother Church Relieved by Bleeding* (London: R. Carlile, 1823), which comprised an extract from *Church-of-Englandism* recapitulating the vices of the established church: 'never was there a more striking *exposé* of a mass of corruption' ('Church Establishment', *Examiner* 894 [20 March 1825], 177).

[5] 'Church-of-Englandism', *Quarterly Review*, 177. Bentham called the journal 'Saint Quarterly Review' in his book (*Church-of-Englandism*, 386).

[6] P. Beauchamp [George Grote], *Analysis of the Influence of Natural Religion* (London: R. Carlile, 1822). *AINR* was composed by George Grote from Bentham's manuscript material on natural religion and the utility of religion. Catherine Fuller, after an examination of the *AINR* and Bentham's manuscripts, concluded that 'a fair summation of

that while belief could not be compelled, it could be influenced, and, in particular, it could be influenced by the prospect of pleasure or pain. The promise of eternal happiness in return for belief in the deity, and the threat of eternal misery for disbelief, could skew one's consideration of the evidence and encourage believers to pay selective attention to evidence (if evidence it was) that supported their preferred conclusion. In both cases, the corruption of judgement had real and deleterious effects on happiness and misery in this present life.

The corruption of judgement also had a detrimental effect on the effectiveness of representative democracy in bringing about the 'greatest happiness of the greatest number'.[7] We might turn here to two useful distinctions Bentham made with respect to judgement, both from *Plan of Parliamentary Reform*.[8] The first distinction is between a 'self-formed' and a 'derivative' judgement. In the *Plan*, as part of his argument for universal (manhood) suffrage, Bentham acknowledged the potential objection that newly enfranchised voters might not know enough about the business of government to vote wisely in an election. That is, their 'self-formed' judgement might be inadequate for the task. The solution, however, was to depend on their 'derivative' judgements – derived, for example, from public opinion. After all, many people relied on 'derivative' opinions for many important decisions in private life, such as those to do with medicine, law, or religion; it should not be a stretch for them to do so when voting as well.[9] The second distinction is between 'the

Grote's work as a whole is that it echoes Bentham's text and summaries, but it is rewritten to accommodate Grote's own thoughts, and in his own style' (C. Fuller, 'Bentham, Mill, Grote, and *An Analysis of the Influence of Natural Religion on the Temporal Happiness of Mankind*', *Journal of Bentham Studies*, 10 [2008], 10). See also J. E. Crimmins, *Secular Utilitarianism: Social Science and the Critique of Religion in the Thought of Jeremy Bentham* (Oxford: Clarendon Press, 1990), 208–10; and P. Schofield, 'Political and Religious Radicalism in the Thought of Jeremy Bentham', *History of Political Thought*, 20, no. 2 (1999), 276, on the composition of the *AINR* and its fidelity to Bentham's views. For a survey of the manuscript material, see Catherine Fuller, '*Utility of Religion a Subject Yet Little Examined*: A Survey of Bentham's Writings on the Utility of Religion', *Revue d'études benthamiennes* 6 (2010), 1–16. It seems reasonable to treat the *AINR* as reflective of Bentham's thought generally, especially where it is consistent with his other writings.

7 The phrase is found in a number of Bentham's works, such as J. Bentham, *A Comment on the Commentaries and a Fragment on Government*, ed. J. H. Burns and H. L. A. Hart (London: The Athlone Press, 1977), 393. See J. H. Burns, 'Happiness and Utility: Jeremy Bentham's Equation', *Utilitas* 17, no. 1 (2005), 46–61, on the history and interpretation of the phrase.

8 J. Bentham, *Plan of Parliamentary Reform* (London: R. Hunter, 1817).

9 Ibid., xlv.

influence of will on will' and 'the influence of understanding . . . on understanding'.[10] As part of his argument for a secret ballot in the *Plan*, Bentham noted that a vote should ideally be a free expression of the voter's will – that is, of 'his *self-formed* will . . . [which is] the product of his own *judgment*, *self-formed* or *derivative* as the case may be' – and not, for example, an expression of the will of the person who had bought or otherwise directed his vote.[11] The secrecy of the ballot would protect the freedom of the ballot, by eliminating the 'influence of will on will' in elections – as manifested, for example, through bribery or intimidation – and leaving only the influence of understanding on understanding.[12] Representative democracy depended on the collective judgement of the voters, both individually and in the form of public opinion (public judgement, as it were). The corruption of judgement by religion, therefore, could have detrimental effects on the effectiveness of representative democracy in furthering public happiness.

More generally, I argue that Bentham treated religion as a species of delusion, where delusion was one of the 'instruments of misrule'.[13] As such, delusion worked to weaken the moral and intellectual faculties of those who propagated or accepted the delusion and so justified the prevailing power asymmetry between the governors and the governed. The 'prostration of understanding', in other words, led to the 'prostration of will'. In this reading, I follow recent (and less recent) scholarship in reading Bentham's writings on religion as part of his political thought.[14] The focus on this chapter, however, is not on the Church as an example of the influence of will on will – in the sinister influence of the episcopacy over the wills of their followers, for example, or in the opposition between the interest of churchmen as a class and the

10 Ibid., xlviii.

11 Ibid., lx.

12 Ibid., lxi–lxv.

13 J. Bentham, 'Supreme Operative' and 'Constitutional Code Rationale', in *First Principles Preparatory to Constitutional Code*, ed. Philip Schofield (Oxford: Clarendon Press, 1989 [*CW*]), 184, 261.

14 The scholarship in question includes James Steintrager, 'Morality and Belief: the Origin and Purpose of Bentham's Writings on Religion', *Mill Newsletter* 6, no. 2 (1971), 3–15; J. Steintrager, 'Language and Politics: Bentham on Religion', *Bentham Newsletter* 4 (1980), 4–20; Crimmins, *Secular Utilitarianism*; Schofield, 'Political and Religious Radicalism'; J. E. Crimmins, 'Bentham's Religious Radicalism Revisited: A Response to Philip Schofield', *History of Political Thought* 22, no. 3 (2001), 494–500; and P. Schofield, *Utility and Democracy: The Political Thought of Jeremy Bentham* (Oxford: Oxford University Press, 2006), ch. 7.

universal interest – but on the influence of understanding on understanding. The writings on religion draw our attention to the ways in which judgement could be systematically distorted and manipulated in support of an oppressive political regime.

Sections 4.2 and 4.3 discuss the corruption of 'derivative' and 'self-formed' judgement, in the context of the Church and natural religion respectively. Section 4.4 concludes with implications for Bentham's theory of representative democracy.

4.2 Authority and the Church

There seemed, Bentham observed in the *Book of Fallacies*, to be a 'universal propensity' among human beings to take not only facts, but also opinions, on trust.[15] In morality and politics, for example, 'ninety-nine out of one hundred [people] have an adoptive judgment'.[16] This was not a denunciation of 'derivative' judgement, exactly; as Bentham implied in the *Plan*, there was a place for 'derivative' judgement on issues on which the person was not competent to form, or confident of forming, her own opinions. The more important question was, from what source of authority was the adoptive judgement derived? How should one distinguish between 'legitimate' and 'illegitimate', or more trustworthy and less trustworthy, sources of authority?[17]

Bentham proposed a scale of authoritative trustworthiness in the *Book of Fallacies*. The trustworthiness, or 'legitimately persuasive force', of the authority depended on several factors, including the intelligence and probity of the authority figure, her access to information, and her interest in collecting and evaluating evidence. At the top of the scale was intellectual, professional, or scientific authority: the professional or scientist, assuming she had 'relative and adequate' intelligence and probity, was likely to have the means to gather information and a professional interest in forming a well-reasoned judgement based on this information.[18] Bentham put himself forward as an example of an intellectual authority in the legal sphere: in an open letter to American citizens, offering to

[15] J. Bentham, *The Book of Fallacies*, ed. Philip Schofield (Oxford: Oxford University Press, 2015), 51.

[16] J. Bentham, 'A Table of the Springs of Action', in Bentham, *Deontology together with A Table of the Springs of Action and The Article on Utilitarianism*, ed. Amnon Goldworth (Oxford: Clarendon Press, 1983 [*CW*]), 58.

[17] *Book of Fallacies*, 121.

[18] Ibid., 124–7.

draw up legal codes for several American states, he noted that 'intellectual authority', the 'source of the influence of understanding on understanding', was 'the sole and indispensable foundation for a *derivative* judgment'. To aid the judgement of his audience on this occasion, he set out his principles and proposals in the letter and provided testimonials on his codification credentials from James Madison, John Quincy Adams, and other American dignitaries.[19] Next in the scale after intellectual (or professional or scientific) authority, in descending order of trustworthiness, came authority from power, authority from opulence, and authority from general reputation.[20]

In this section, I propose to read *Church-of-Englandism* as a challenge to the authority of the Church. On this reading, the Church professed, and was commonly thought, to have intellectual authority – on the basis of which, for example, Howley recommended the 'prostration of the understanding' before the 'oracles of divine truth'. However, Bentham challenged the intellectual authority of the Church in two ways: by exposing the moral and intellectual contradictions of the Church of England Catechism, which was used to teach both reading and religion to young children, and by arguing that the Church had substituted its own religion, 'Church-of-Englandism', for the genuine 'religion of Jesus', just as it had substituted its Catechism for the Bible as a teaching text. One advantage of this reading is that it gives Bentham's examination of the Catechism, which is ostensibly the main text of the book even though it comprises about 10 per cent of it, a central role in the book (the rest of the book consists of two Prefaces, a Plan, a long Introduction, and several Appendices, including one that runs for over a hundred pages).

The first challenge to the Church was based on a line-by-line critique of the Catechism.[21] The Catechism was used to teach children to read and write in schools established by the National Society for the Education of the Poor in the Principles of the National Church, which was itself set

[19] J. Bentham, 'Papers Relative to Codification and Public Instruction' in Bentham, *'Legislator of the World': Writings on Codification, Law, and Education*, ed. Philip Schofield and Jonathan Harris (Oxford: Clarendon Press, 1998 [*CW*]), 114–7.

[20] *Book of Fallacies*, 127–8.

[21] Bentham used much the same method for other works. See, for example, his criticism of Blackstone's *Commentaries* in *Fragment on Government* and (the longer, unfinished) *A Comment on the Commentaries*, as well as his criticism of the Declaration of Rights in 'Nonsense upon Stilts', in Bentham, *Rights, Representation, and Reform: Nonsense upon Stilts and Other Writings on the French Revolution*, ed. P. Schofield, C. Pease-Watkin, and C. Blamires (Oxford: Clarendon Press, 2002 [*CW*]), 317–402.

up under the auspices of the Church of England. This was in contrast to the Bible, which was used for the same purposes in schools established earlier by Joseph Lancaster, the Quaker educationist.[22] The problem with the Catechism as a teaching text, on Bentham's account, was that it taught children things that were useless in practical life, unintelligible to young minds, inconsistent with clerical practice, or simply mendacious. This was not (or not merely) captious cavilling at doctrines of religion, as the *Quarterly Review* put it, but a demonstration of the unfitness of the Catechism as a source of intellectual authority.

For example, the Catechism taught children that their godparents had committed them to renouncing, among other things, 'the devil and all his works', as well as 'the pomps and vanity of this wicked world'. But it did not go on to explain what the devil or his works were, or what renunciation required. The 'pomps and vanity' of the world might require no explanation, perhaps, but the injunction to renounce them was inconsistent with experience, if not downright hypocritical: the monarch, aristocrats, and bishops – these 'sitting and walking pageants' with sceptre and crown, mitre and robe – had demonstrably failed to renounce ostentatious displays of power and wealth in this world.[23] For another example, the Catechism also taught children to rehearse the articles of their belief, including the crucifixion and resurrection of Jesus Christ, and to declare that they had learned, from this recitation, to believe in God the Father, who had created the world; God the Son, who had redeemed mankind; and God the Holy Ghost, who had sanctified his elect people.[24] This, however, in Bentham's view, was not a useful thing for children to know: learning about the crucifixion and resurrection, for example, would not help them contend with the death of persons who were only human.[25] Nor was it clear what it meant to believe in God as father, son, and spirit. The ideas of creation and redemption were, perhaps, comprehensible, but the idea of sanctification was not intelligible without further explanation. It was as if, Bentham remarked, the authors of the Catechism felt that they had to assign unique roles to each member of the Trinity, and, after assigning the 'less plainly incomprehensible functions of *creation* and *redemption*', could only come up with 'sanctification' for the Holy Ghost – a

22 *Church-of-Englandism*, xi–xii.
23 Ibid., 204, 207–10.
24 Ibid., 212, 222.
25 Ibid., 215.

remark that illustrates Bentham's scepticism towards the Catechism and Christian doctrine in general.[26]

More generally, the Catechism sought to teach children to believe in things they could not yet understand, because their 'faculty of reason' was not sufficiently developed. Belief required the ability to consider the opinions put before the mind, and come to a judgement on them.[27] At this point in their lives, however, the children were 'completely incompetent to the forming of any *judgment* or so much as a *conception*' on these matters and so were not truly able to believe in the articles of the Catechism.[28] What the Catechism could and did teach them to do was to profess belief in its articles. In other words, as Bentham put it, the 'duty and practice of *lying* formed part of every Church of England child's first lesson.'[29] On this view, the Catechism was not an effective instrument of education, but it was an effective 'instrument of corruption', for 'corrupting altogether the intellectual part, and to a great extent the moral part, of the minds thus impregnated'. It did so by habituating the young minds to the 'practice of mendacity and insincerity' and in that way weakening their ability and willingness to recognize and protest against abuses of power.[30] The 'prostration of the understanding' thus led to the 'prostration of the will' to the authority of the Church.

This brings us to the second way by which Bentham sought to undermine the intellectual authority of the Church. He argued that the Catechism lacked intellectual authority because it was a 'substitute' for the Bible, not only as a teaching text in schools but also as the foundational text of a religion. The Catechism was a poor substitute for the Bible as an 'exposition' of it: it did not, for example, provide any biblical quotations or references to demonstrate the fidelity of its exposition and more generally did not give a 'true picture' of the 'religion of Jesus'.[31] It was, in fact, so poor a substitute for the Bible that Bentham concluded that the religion taught by the Catechism was not the 'religion of Jesus'. The Catechism was not effective at conveying the content or the spirit of the Bible to children, but it was effective as the foundational text

[26] Ibid., 224, 222–5.
[27] Bentham's conception of belief is discussed in Section 4.3.
[28] *Church-of-Englandism*, 203 (original emphasis).
[29] Ibid., 211 (original emphasis).
[30] Ibid., 67–8.
[31] Ibid., 67–9.

of an alternative religion, 'Church-of-Englandism': it propounded the doctrines of the Church to children and prepared them to submit uncritically to the authority of the Church.[32]

On this view, the 'prostration of the understanding' that Howley called for was not to God, before whom prostration was rightly due, but to man.[33] The 'oracles of divine truth' the bishop referred to were not the literal word of God, nor even of scripture, but, in his words, doctrines 'deducible by the established laws of interpretation from Scripture' – established, that is, by Church officers.[34] It was not clear, however, what these laws might be, unless they were nothing more than the artistry of the interpreter.[35] Bentham was willing to concede that the formularies of the Church, including the Catechism, might have been useful at an earlier stage in human development but to continue to use them in a more enlightened time was to perpetuate error – to encourage believers to prostrate their understandings and wills before the 'blindly assumed infallibility of a comparatively unenlightened age' and to commit to keeping themselves 'debarred from the free exercise of their judgments' in these matters.[36] But if the authority of the Church was not based on intellectual expertise, what was it based on? Towards the end of his sermon, Howley urged clergymen to pay close attention to the National Schools.

> In proportion to the success of your attention to this important point, the course of your ministry will become smooth and easy. Your parishioners, from their infancy initiated in the principles, and inured to the practice, of pure Christianity, will crowd with pious affection to the altars of their Mother Church; and will learn to regard the pretences and artifices of corrupt or illiterate instructors with indifference or disdain. Your instructions and exhortations received with humble docility, as the oracles of God, by congregations who revere in your persons the dispensers of divine truth, will no longer be wasted on a barren soil.[37]

From the passage above, it appears that Bentham and Howley were in agreement on the effects of the Catechism in indoctrinating young minds

32 Ibid., 82–3.

33 Ibid., 258–9.

34 Howley, *Charge*, 15; *Church-of-Englandism*, 260.

35 *Church-of-Englandism*, 264–71.

36 Ibid., 471–2. See M. Schwartzberg, 'Jeremy Bentham on Fallbility and Infallibility', *Journal of the History of Ideas* 68, no. 4 (October 2007), 563–85, on Bentham's arguments against infallibility.

37 Howley, *Charge*, 22–3; partially quoted in *Church-of-Englandism*, 259.

and cultivating in them a reverence for the Church and its officers. From Bentham's perspective, however, these were not beneficial effects. The Catechism did not only fail to teach children anything of practical use but actively contributed to their moral and intellectual depravation: by detaching the profession of belief from the formation of judgement, it taught children to lie and so weakened their ability to detect or defend themselves against mendacity. It prepared them, in other words, for the submission of their judgement, and so of their will, to the authority of the Church. On this account, the authority of the Church was not based on intellectual expertise but on power. The desired outcome of the bishop, and of the Church more generally, was 'the establishment of a state of things, which, when described in plain English, is neither more nor less (for, what else is it?) than a system of slavery; – of intellectual, and thence, as a necessary consequence, of moral and corporeal slavery', in which the officers of the Church were the tyrants, the lay members the subjects and all other people 'enemies'.[38] The Catechism, as an instrument for the corruption of judgement, was thereby an instrument of tyranny.

4.3 Belief and Natural Religion

This section considers the corruptive influence of Christian doctrine on 'self-formed' judgements. Bentham had a judicial conception of judgement: a person should ideally only form an opinion or judgement on an issue after a careful consideration of the facts and of different arguments, much as a judicial tribunal should only pronounce on a matter after a careful consideration of the evidence and arguments presented to it. As Bentham put it in *AINR*, 'in the natural state of things, a man assents to that which he thinks is the best evidence – dissents from what appears to be refuted by the best evidence. Under such circumstances, there is nothing to guide his choice except the evidence'.[39] We might also use the 'Public Opinion Tribunal' as an illustration of this conception of judgement. Bentham suggested that public opinion could be represented as an informal tribunal, headed by someone who could inform and direct public opinion, such as a newspaper editor. Much like a judge on an actual tribunal, a newspaper editor should form an opinion on a matter after receiving

[38] *Church-of-Englandism*, 260.
[39] *AINR*, 110.

different claims, collecting evidence, and reading or hearing arguments from the various parties involved.[40] Religion could corrupt this process of judgement-formation in two ways: by providing incentives for specific beliefs, and so skewing the process of collecting and considering evidence and arguments, and more generally by challenging the empirical basis of knowledge.

In *AINR*, Bentham considered the utility of natural religion – characterized by belief in the existence of a deity, in the agency of the deity in this world, and in a system of eternal rewards and punishments in the afterlife – and concluded that it was harmful both to individual believers and to society at large. (These are arguably also the foundational beliefs of revealed religion.)[41] One of the mischiefs of natural religion was that it disqualified the understanding 'for purposes useful in this life', by promising eternal happiness as a reward for belief in the deity (and associated beliefs) and threatening eternal misery as a punishment for disbelief.[42] Bentham reasoned that the point of offering reward or punishment for specific beliefs was to influence judgement; if men and women would naturally have adopted the beliefs in question, there would then be no need to offer incentives of any kind.[43]

[40] J. Bentham, 'Securities against Misrule', in *Securities against Misrule and Other Constitutional Writings for Tripoli and Greece*, ed. P. Schofield (Oxford: Clarendon Press, 1990 [*CW*]), 45, 60–61. See also the functions of an official judicatory at 54–5; and the functions of the Public Opinion Tribunal in J. Bentham, *Constitutional Code, Vol. 1*, ed. F. Rosen and J. H. Burns (Oxford: Clarendon Press, 1983 [*CW*]), 36.

[41] Blackstone, for example, listed some of these beliefs in his explanation of the importance of revealed religion to civil society: 'The belief of a future state of rewards and punishments, the entertaining just ideas of the moral attributes of the supreme being, and a firm persuasion that he superintends and will finally compensate every action in human life (all which are clearly revealed in the doctrines, and forcibly inculcated by the precepts, of our saviour Christ) these are the grand foundation of all judicial oaths ... all moral evidence therefore, all confidence in human veracity, must be weakened by irreligion, and overthrown by infidelity.' (W. Blackstone, *Commentaries on the Laws of England* [Oxford: Clarendon Press, 1769], Vol. 4, 43–4.) It is not surprising that *AINR*, despite its title, should encompass a critique of revealed religion as well. George Grote followed Bentham's instruction to focus on natural religion in editing the *AINR*, but also drew from Bentham's manuscript material on revealed religion. There was, in any case, a tradition of criticizing revealed religion under cover of natural religion (Fuller, 'Utility of Religion', 9, 11).

[42] *AINR*, 92–109.

[43] Ibid., 110. Bentham employed the same reasoning in *Constitutional Code Rationale* to justify the absence of an established religion in his proposed constitutional code. See 'Constitutional Code Rationale' in *First Principles* (*CW*), 325–31.

It was not the case that reward or punishment could directly influence belief; the will could not act quite so directly on the understanding.[44] One could not, for example, make a man believe that he was *not* sitting in a chair when he was doing so, or not holding a book in his hand when he was doing so.[45] However, not all judgments were as obvious or immediate as these. While it was not possible, on Bentham's account, to make a person 'really and immediately' believe in the truth of a thing he knew to be false, it *was* possible to make him do any or all of the following: 1. to refrain from declaring his disbelief of it: 2. to make him declare his belief in it: 3. to make him turn instantly aside from all considerations tending to confirm him in his disbelief of it: 4. to look out for, and fix his *attention* on, all considerations tending to induce him to believe in it: especially authority, an instrument by which, in so many instances, men have contrived to force themselves into the belief of [... ?] facts in repugnancy [to] the concomitant evidence of their own senses.[46] A key term in the passage above is 'attention'. In Bentham's view, the faculty of judgement was a faculty of the understanding, whereas the faculty of attention was a faculty of the will; to pay attention to something was to 'fasten' one's mind, as it were, by an act of the will, to the thing in question.[47] Even if there were universal agreement that judgements should be based on evidence, it was not always clear what counted as evidence in the particular case or how much weight should be accorded to contradictory evidence or contrary arguments. In such cases, paying selective attention to different evidence or arguments could lead to different judgements on the matter.[48]

What one paid attention to, however, often depended not on one's understanding but on one's motives, that is, on prospects of pleasure or pain.[49] In the case of religious doctrine, the relevant motives were hope

[44] The following account was influenced by the discussion of the influence of interest on belief (or of the will on the understanding) in R. Harrison, *Bentham* (London: Routledge, 1983), 144–6.

[45] *Book of Fallacies*, 160; *AINR*, 111.

[46] *Book of Fallacies*, 160 (my emphasis).

[47] 'This operation [of the faculty of attention] ... has place in so far as by an act, by a more or less continued exertion of the *will*, and the psychological active faculty its servant, the mind is as it were fastened upon the object or subject from which a perception or conception is derived to it.' (J. Bentham, 'Essay on Logic', in *The Works of Jeremy Bentham*, Vol. 8, ed. John Bowring [Edinburgh: William Tait, 1843], 224; see also 281.)

[48] *AINR*, 111.

[49] On motives, see J. Bentham, *An Introduction to the Principles of Morals and Legislation*, ed. J. H. Burns and H. L. A. Hart (Oxford: Clarendon Press, 1996 [*CW*]), 96, 100.

and fear: hope of eternal happiness and fear of eternal misery.[50] In *Church-of-Englandism*, for example, Bentham accused the Church of depraving the minds of children through the introduction of 'groundless and useless terrors' in the Catechism.[51] Children, as mentioned above, were made cognizant of the devil and all his works. Stories and pictures of the devil might not be frightening to adults but were surely terrifying to children. 'How many', he demanded, 'to whom this [the devil's] ideal presence is sufficient to render *solitude*, at least when coupled with *darkness*, a situation of never-ceasing torment?'[52] (Bentham knew whereof he spoke; he had been afraid of ghosts since childhood.)[53]

The situation was no better in natural religion. Bentham argued in *AINR* that, in the absence of revelation, all we could conceive of the supreme deity was that it was omnipotent, invisible, essentially unknowable, and had agency in this world; we could not tell if this agency was benevolent or malevolent. That is, all we could conceive of the supreme deity was as a 'capricious tyrant', modelled on our conception of capricious human tyrants but with unlimited power at its disposal.[54] In such a scenario, our imaginations would naturally tend towards scenes of terror and suffering – fear being, as Bentham suggested, the 'never-failing companion and offspring of ignorance'.[55] We might try to placate the supernatural tyrant, as we would a human tyrant, by offering to it our privations and sufferings or, better yet, the privations and sufferings of other people.[56] At any rate, the terrors conjured up by religion might

[50] *AINR*, 111.

[51] *Church-of-Englandism*, 254.

[52] Ibid., 208–9.

[53] *The Works of Jeremy Bentham*, Vol. 10, ed. J. Bowring (New York: Russell & Russell, 1962 [1843]), 18–20, 39, 64. Bentham told Bowring he had cured himself of his fear by reasoning that if ghosts appeared to him wearing clothes (as ghosts did), then there had to be ghosts of clothes as well as of people, which was a stretch too far for belief. *Works*, Vol. 10, 587.

[54] *AINR*, 20, 25.

[55] Ibid., 5.

[56] Ibid., 33, 54–7. On divine despotism, see also Fuller, 'Utility of Religion', 3. On human despotism, see also Bentham's discussion of the principle of sympathy and antipathy in *IPML*: he argued that the 'various systems that have been formed concerning the standard of right and wrong [including moral sense, common sense, the law of nature, right reason, the doctrine of election, and others], may all be reduced to the principle of sympathy and antipathy'. The principle of sympathy and antipathy could more accurately be called the 'principle of caprice', because it did not rely on an external standard of right and wrong, but only on the author's own sentiment or opinion. Caprice was a defining characteristic of despotism; the upshot of the different systems of sympathy and

push us into forming opinions (such as the opinion that a supreme deity existed) that we might not, with a clearer mind, have formed.

More generally, Bentham argued that people paid attention to things that tended to be pleasurable and avoided thinking about things that tended to be painful. A system of reward for belief and punishment for disbelief would therefore tend to skew judgement towards belief, by skewing one's consideration of the evidence. We might draw an example from the discussion of witchcraft in Blackstone's *Commentaries*. Blackstone appears to have been divided in his opinion: on the one hand, he felt that the empirical evidence for witchcraft was sketchy at best and that 'the ridiculous stories that are generally told, and the many impostures and delusions that have been discovered in all ages, are enough to demolish all faith in such a dubious crime'. On the other hand, he acknowledged that the 'contrary evidence', especially from the Bible, was 'extremely strong' and that the legal prohibition of witchcraft in many countries implied at least 'the possibility of a commerce with evil spirits'.[57] Bentham, on the contrary, judging from his sardonic remarks comparing Blackstone's discussion to his own grandmother's belief in witches, did not appear to think that biblical references to witches were good evidence for their existence, or any evidence at all.[58] With respect to Bentham's theory of selective attention motivating belief, we could say that religious belief skewed judgement in this area, by encouraging a person to pay selective attention to evidence, such as biblical references to witches, which supported their preferred conclusion.

We might draw a second example of this theory in action from Blackstone's *Commentaries*, this time from his discussion of sodomy. Should the destruction of Sodom and Gomorrah in the Bible be considered as evidence for the harmfulness of sodomy? Blackstone answered

antipathy, the 'mischief common to all these ways of thinking and arguing ... is their serving as a cloak, and pretence, and aliment, to despotism: if not a despotism in practice, a despotism however in disposition: which is but too apt, when pretence and power offer, to show itself in practice'. (*IPML*, 21n, 25, 25–8nn).

57 Blackstone, *Commentaries*, Vol. 4, 60.

58 The comments in question are in J. Bentham, *White Bull*, Vol. 1 (London: J. Bew, 1774), lxix; and *Works*, Vol. 10, 18. See also Bentham's manuscript musings on the evidence (or lack thereof) for the truth of Christianity in Fuller, 'Utility of Religion', 6–7. The *White Bull* is testimony to Bentham's lack of faith in this respect. Bentham's view of the evidential basis of biblical events is neatly encapsulated in Cardinal Newman's remark that 'Mr. Bentham made a treatise on Judicial Proofs a covert attack on the miracles of Revelation' (J. H. Newman, *The Idea of a University Defined and Illustrated* [London: Longmans, Green and Co, 1893], 96).

in the affirmative: he pointed out that sodomy was a capital offence, according to 'the voice of nature and of reason, and the express law of God', as evidenced by the destruction of Sodom and Gomorrah by 'fire from heaven'.[59] Bentham addressed this point in his arguments against the punishment of sodomy and other non-conformist sexual practices. In the third *Not Paul, But Jesus* volume, for example, he argued that the sin of the cities was not sodomy but violent rape and the violation of the rules of hospitality.[60] Perhaps, if one took seriously the threat of the devil and all his works, and of the prospect of eternal misery, one would put more weight than Bentham did on the burning of the cities as evidence of the sinfulness of sodomy. Or perhaps, a non-believer, free from the inducements of religion, would not consider the biblical event to be evidence at all, much less evidence in favour of the punishment of an otherwise harmless sexual act (if between consenting adults). The non-believer might even conclude, with Bentham, that 'the religious premium offered for faith tends . . . to corrupt the judgment of an individual.'[61]

The second way in which religion could corrupt judgement was by challenging the empirical basis of knowledge. In *AINR*, Bentham defined knowledge, at least in the sense of 'useful' knowledge of pleasure and pain in this world, as consisting in 'believing facts conformable to experience'.[62] Religion, however, demanded belief in things for which there was no empirical evidence and could not be empirical evidence. In the Catechism, for example, children were asked to believe in things for which there was neither evidence nor explanation. In natural religion, people were similarly asked to believe in a deity who, by definition, could not be seen or heard or even truly comprehended by human minds. The 'very basis' of natural religion could only be said to be 'an article of *extra-experimental belief*, or belief altogether unconformable to experience'.[63] (The same might be said of revealed religion.)

59 Blackstone, *Commentaries*, Vol. 4, 216.

60 J. Bentham, *Not Paul, But Jesus, Vol. 3: Doctrine* (London: Bentham Project, UCL, 2013), 134–8, 147–8. See also Bentham's discussion of the destruction of the two cities in his notes to the essay on paederasty, published in 'Jeremy Bentham's Essay on "Paederasty"', ed. L. Crompton, *Journal of Homosexuality* 4, no. 1 (1978), 104–6.

61 *AINR*, 111.

62 Ibid., 93.

63 Ibid., 97–9, 95. The term 'extra-experimental belief' is from Grote, not from Bentham (Fuller, 'Bentham, Mill, Grote', 9). However, I think Bentham would have agreed with the idea that religious belief was not derived from experience and could not be substantiated by empirical evidence.

But if experience were not the basis of knowledge, then past experience would not be a good predictor of future events. There would be no way, for example, to refute falsehoods based on their inconsistency with past events or to establish means of reliably producing pleasure and avoiding pain. There would be no way, in other words, to acquire 'useful' knowledge of pleasure and pain in this world.[64] The influence of religion on judgement had therefore 'the most destructive consequences' in this present life:

> It discredits and renders inadmissible the lessons of experience: It vitiates irrecoverably the processes both of proof and refutation, thereby making truth incapable of being established, and falsehood incapable of being detected: It withdraws us from the power of distinguishing the true methods, of procuring enjoyment or avoiding pain, from the false ones; and plunges us into the naked, inexperienced and helpless condition of a new-born child – thereby qualifying us indeed for the kingdom of heaven, but leaving us wholly defenceless against the wants and sufferings of earth.[65]

One could object to the generalizations: even if we accepted that there was a disjunct between belief and experience with regard to religious belief, it was confined to the sphere of religion and would therefore have limited effect on the ordinary course of human life. However, Bentham argued that mistakes tended to follow one another; a person who had a 'mind so constituted' as to believe in the account of Lilliput, for example, was likely to believe in the account of Brobdignag as well.[66] The disconnect between belief and experience in the sphere of religion was likely to spill over to other spheres of life. 'Extra-experimental' beliefs could produce, and had produced, harmful effects in the world. The belief in witches, for example, despite being unsupported by empirical evidence, had led to the persecution and condemnation of many innocent women – women who had been 'sacrifice[d]' to extra-experimental belief, and to the 'thorough depravation of the intellect, and erasure of the distinction between truth and falsehood' that it brought about.[67]

Another example offered by Bentham was trial by ordeal. On his account, trial by ordeal was invented when men were 'unable to discover satisfactory criteria of guilt and innocence, by a just comparison of

[64] *AINR*, 99–101.
[65] Ibid., 106.
[66] Ibid., 94–5.
[67] Ibid., 101–2.

conflicting testimony' and so turned instead to a 'blind reliance on *extra-experimental* belief'. The effect was to protect the guilty from appropriate punishment and maximize the suffering of the innocent.[68] Trial by ordeal is the exact opposite of the process of judgement-formation discussed at the beginning of this section and as such offers a good illustration of the ways by which religion corrupts judgement: instead of carefully considering evidence and arguments, the judges in a trial by ordeal *surrender* judgement entirely and leave it in the hands of an invisible, incomprehensible, and unaccountable being – which is to say, they leave it without judgement and without justice.

4.4 Judgement and Representative Democracy

In *Book of Fallacies*, Bentham observed that the distinction between a 'self-formed' and a 'derivative' judgement was critical to representative democracy. As he put it, 'upon [this distinction] depends not only the pre-eminence of democratic above every other form of government, but, upon a scale of any considerable extent, especially if for any considerable length of time, the possibility of its existence'.[69] I take this to mean that the benefits of representative democracy as a form of government, and indeed its existence itself, depended on the collective judgement of the electorate. In this section, I consider the ways in which the corruption of judgement compromised the effectiveness of representative democracy in furthering public happiness. To the extent that religion contributed to the corruption of judgement, it should be thought of as a species of delusion, and thereby one of the 'instruments of misrule'.

One major benefit of representative democracy over other forms of government was that it was more likely to result in the alignment of interests between the governors and the governed. In his essay on the 'Identification of Interests', Bentham stipulated that the greatest happiness of the greatest number required, to the greatest extent possible, the identification of interests between 'each individual and the whole community' and especially between public officials and the community at large.[70] In his view, however, this situation had failed to obtain in

[68] Ibid., 104–5.

[69] *Book of Fallacies*, 121.

[70] J. Bentham, 'Identification of Interests', in *First Principles* (*CW*), 125–6. Bentham argued that the greatest happiness of the greatest number required the identification of interests between parliamentary representatives and government officials, on the one hand

England, at least at the time of his writing. Bentham argued in *Plan of Parliamentary Reform* that the two 'domineering interests' in England, the monarchical and the aristocratic interests, were at odds with the universal or 'democratical' interest. The ruling classes worked together to further their partial and sinister interests to the detriment of the universal interest, through such expensive projects as the pursuit of foreign wars and the maintenance of overseas colonies.[71] It was, perhaps, not unexpected that the ruling classes should govern in their own interests. But where their interests diverged from the universal interest, the result was not the greatest happiness of the greatest number but, conversely, 'the greatest happiness of the ruling few, at the expense of the subject many'.[72] What was needed, therefore, was a system of government in which the interest of the ruling few was aligned with that of the subject many.

Accordingly, in *Plan of Parliamentary Reform*, Bentham called for a number of measures aimed at the establishment of 'democratic ascendancy' in England, one of which was the introduction of 'virtual universality of suffrage'. One advantage of (virtually) universal suffrage was that it could serve as a 'security' for misrule, as the universal interest was more likely to be accurately represented by a wider suffrage.[73] The realization of the benefits of (virtually) universal suffrage, however, depended on the collective judgement of the voters, in knowing their interest and in choosing candidates who would work to promote their interest. The corruption of judgement could therefore have a detrimental effect on the effectiveness of representative democracy in advancing the universal interest.

As mentioned earlier, Bentham reassured his readers that voters who were ignorant of the business of government might still be trusted to vote wisely on the basis of their 'derivative' judgement. The wisdom of derivative judgement depended on the source of authority from which it was derived. As discussed in the Section 4.2, Bentham identified intellectual, scientific, or professional authority – that is, authority from the understanding alone – as the most trustworthy source of authority,

('possessors of the Supreme Constitutive power'), and the whole community, on the other (125–7). See also Schofield, *Utility and Democracy*, for a discussion of the role of sinister interest in Bentham's political thought.

71 *Plan of Parliamentary Reform*, xi–xv, xviii–xx.

72 J. Bentham, 'Economy as Applied to Office', in *First Principles* (*CW*), 61.

73 *Plan* of *Parliamentary Reform*, lxxx–ci, and especially xc–xcvii for acceptable 'defalcations' from the 'universal-interest-comprehension principle'.

followed in descending order by authority from power, from wealth, and from general reputation. On this view, religion was not a trustworthy source of authority. This was in part because the interest of churchmen as a class was opposed to the universal interest: churchmen, no less than members of the monarchical and aristocratic factions, were interested in power, money, and factitious dignity, 'the good things of this wicked world', and sought to obtain them at the expense of their followers.[74] And it was in part because the religious premium for faith corrupted the collection and consideration of evidence in the process of coming to a 'self-formed' judgement and so brought judgement into contempt altogether.

In the case of voting, voters were likely to derive their opinions from public opinion.[75] Public opinion was in general a trustworthy source of authority, at least where the universal interest was concerned, and in addition acted as a security against misrule, by holding public officials to account.[76] There were, however, a few notable exceptions to the rule: cases in which public opinion had turned against innocuous acts. Examples of such cases included public antipathy to religious dissent, to divorce by mutual consent (especially if initiated by the wife), and to sexual non-conformity.[77] Religion could have a corruptive effect on public judgement, as on private judgement, in two ways: by encouraging public sympathy for acts that did not actually increase the greatest happiness of the greatest number (such as the persecution of so-called witches) and by encouraging public antipathy for acts that were not actually harmful (such as sodomy and other unconventional sexual practices).[78] Take sodomy, for example: Bentham argued in *Sextus*, an unfinished essay on sexual non-conformity, that 'spurious' moral demands, such as those generated by the unwarranted antipathy towards sodomy, often crowded out 'genuine' moral demands, such as those generated by the principle of utility – a 'genuine' morality being one that aimed at the *increase* of public happiness, rather than its decrease. He argued that the decriminalization of sodomy, and the

[74] *Plan of Parliamentary Reform*, xvii–xx; *Book of Fallacies*, 146; *Church-of-Englandism*, *passim*, but see especially Appendix 4.

[75] *Plan of Parliamentary Reform*, xliv.

[76] 'Constitutional Code Rationale', 283, 286–92; 'Securities against Misrule', 25–9. See also M. Quinn, 'Popular Prejudices, Real Pains: What Is the Legislator to Do When the People Err in Assigning Mischief?', in X. Zhai and M. Quinn, eds., *Bentham's Theory of Law and Public Opinion* (Cambridge: Cambridge University Press, 2014), 63–89.

[77] 'Constitutional Code Rationale', 290.

[78] *AINR*, 84–92.

institution of sexual liberty more generally, would lead to the exclusion of a 'false and spurious morality' and thereby to a boost for 'genuine morality'.[79]

The effect of religion on judgement mirrored the effect of delusion on judgement, in giving credence to fictions and otherwise untenable propositions and so encouraging belief in spurious moral and political principles. Religion, then, to the extent that it corrupted judgement, could be understood as a species of delusion, where delusion was one of the instruments of misrule. In his essays on the *Supreme Operative* and *Constitutional Code Rationale*, Bentham catalogued two kinds of instruments of misrule: 'corporeal' instruments, such as the soldier, the lawyer, and the priest, and 'incorporeal' instruments, such as force, intimidation, corruption, and delusion.[80] Delusion was the instrument both of the lawyer and the priest and was used by them for the same purposes – to promote their particular interests, as well as the interest of the monarch – but in different ways. The terrors invented by the lawyer, for example, were limited to the present life, whereas the terrors invented by the priest knew no such bounds.[81]

One example of delusion in action was in the use of legal fictions. This had the effect of 'demoralizing' the moral faculties of the people who used them, by establishing an alternative moral principle: that the approbation or disapprobation of acts did not depend on the greatest happiness of the greatest number but on the 'practice, consequently on the will, and thence on the interest, real or supposed' of the class of lawyers.[82] The purpose, and ultimate effect, of the principle of demoralization was to inure people to 'the perpetration of injustice, and in a word political evil in all its shapes' and also to the use of 'mendacity' in perpetrating this injustice.[83]

Another example of delusion was that generated by 'factitious honour'. In *Plan of Parliamentary Reform*, after reassuring readers that voters could vote wisely on the basis of their derivative judgements, Bentham offered additional reassurance by observing that the same men who

[79] J. Bentham, 'Sextus', in *Of Sexual Irregularities, and Other Writings on Sexual Morality*, ed. P. Schofield, C. Pease-Watkin, and M. Quinn (Oxford: Clarendon Press, 2014 [*CW*]), 114–5. On antipathy and sexual non-conformity, see T. Y. Koh, 'Bentham and the Pleasures of Cruelty', *History of Political Thought* 40, no. 4 (2019): 699–716.

[80] 'Supreme Operative', 183–5, 'Constitutional Code Rationale', 252.

[81] 'Supreme Operative', 185.

[82] 'Constitutional Code Rationale', 268.

[83] Ibid., 268.

presently determined the course of elections 'by the influence of *will* on *will*' would, for the most part, continue to exercise the same power 'by the influence of *understanding*, real or imputed, on *understanding*'.[84] This was explained by the common, if mistaken, tendency to equate high social position with aptitude for high political office and generally to place an outsized and unjustifiable importance on birth and wealth as indicators of appropriate aptitude for political office.[85] (Whereas the fact of the matter was that birth, wealth, and social connections were not only irrelevant qualifications for office, but were likely to be found in inverse proportion to any actual aptitude.)[86] Bentham pointed out that election results confirmed the ubiquity of this tendency: even in boroughs where the radical candidate won the election, the successful candidates were still men of birth or wealth, such as Sir Francis Burdett and Lord Cochrane in Westminster, Sir Samuel Romilly in Bristol, and Lord Brougham in Liverpool.[87]

Bentham adopted a less sanguine tone when discussing the effects of this tendency in 'Constitutional Code Rationale', where he argued that one effect of factitious honour was to generate the delusion that men in positions of power deserved their positions, because they possessed the appropriate aptitude for such positions, and because they had more social affection and benevolence than the people they governed.[88] The convention not to speak ill of the dead was one instance of this delusion, as was the convention to represent 'the powerless, the unopulent, the undignified' as 'less benevolent, less knowing, less judicious, less able' than they were and, conversely, to represent men of power, wealth, or dignity as more benevolent and more able than they were.[89] The result of this delusion was to make people 'dupes' and so make them 'slaves' – to discourage people from questioning the qualifications of the men in power and so reconcile them to their subordinate status. The purpose and effect of factitious power was therefore to delude people: 'Deluded? and to what further end? only that by means of the delusion they may with the less discontent submitt to be plundered and oppressed.'[90]

84 *Plan of Parliamentary Reform*, xlviii.
85 Ibid., xlviii, cxv.
86 'Constitutional Code Rationale', 261–3.
87 *Plan of Parliamentary Reform*, cxv.
88 'Constitutional Code Rationale', 261–3, 65.
89 Ibid., 265–7.
90 Ibid., 266.

More generally, the use of delusion was to justify the current political system and to confirm the relative positions of the governors and the people they governed. The effect of delusion – whether in the form of religious or legal fictions, or of unjustifiable beliefs (the empty intellectual authority of the Church, the false equivalence between social position and political office) – was to discourage people from questioning the grounds of power, and so reconcile them to their subordinate status, while bolstering the claims of the ruling classes to power (as well as to wealth and honours). That is to say, in the somewhat hyperbolic language of *Church-of-Englandism*, the effect of delusion was to produce the prostration of understanding and will and so forge links in the chain of despotism and slavery. On this reading, Bentham's writings on religion illustrate one more way in which power could be used and abused and specifically in which judgement could be corrupted and manipulated to further the partial and sinister interests of the ruling classes, at the expense of the universal interest.

5

Organizing the Utilitarian State

The Official Aptitude of Functionaries

MALIK BOZZO-REY*

5.1 Introduction

This chapter examines the way in which, in his constitutional writings, Jeremy Bentham argues for democracy as the best form of government, while also analyzing his ability to envision the organization and structure of the state. In specific terms, a central theme of Bentham's thinking is the management of functionaries. What is their role and to what end should they be managed? Functionaries are an integral part of the utilitarian state, which, as such, must maximize its efficiency and minimize its expenditure while also ensuring the greatest happiness for the greatest number. Therefore, one can speak of the state's primary end, which is set by the principle of utility and concerns society as a whole, and of a secondary end, still set by this same principle but that has to do with a particular group of individuals: functionaries. Consequently, the latter are actors among others in the social theatre Bentham attempts to construct.

In order to fully understand the mechanics at work in this evolving space, this chapter will first identify precisely what Bentham means by a functionary, from its characteristics to its role. This will then provide an understanding of how the functionary fits into the general economy of Bentham's thought, in particular through the connection between the theory of motivation, the maximization of aptitudes, and the minimization of expense. The issue of aptitudes is deeply tied to which interests functionaries must pursue. Failing to strive for the maximization of the community's interest would call into question the very nature of functionaries and undermine the functioning of democracy. This perspective brings to light the dynamic of control that governs, at least in part, the managerial

* I would like to thank Katya Long, PhD for translating this chapter into English.

techniques advocated by Bentham. Their sole purpose is to guarantee the transparency of the state apparatus and of its mechanisms as the only means of defending the interests of all citizens. The underlying question of this chapter concerns the normative dimension that should be given to this requirement of transparency. Indeed, one can observe that it applies not only to all the elements of what could be called Bentham's management of functionaries but also that it operates differently when it is addressed to individuals, to a class, or to an organization. Section 5.5 will offer a re-reading of Bentham's panopticon. Indeed, the norm internalization that is the purpose of his conception of the management of functionaries draws the outline of a Constitutional Panopticon.

5.2 Being a Functionary: Between Utility and Sacrifice?

5.2.1 What Is a Functionary?

The very word 'functionary' conforms to the imperatives of Bentham's dichotomous method of classification. It must therefore be understood as belonging to the pair functionary/non-functionary. This distinction overlaps with those of rulers/subjects, the ruling few/the subject many[1] or governors/governed. The opposition between functionaries and non-functionaries is thus associated with various divisions elaborated by Bentham to classify and categorize reality and divide society into classes. His understanding of society, and especially of political society, is always based on a division into two groups with opposing interests and assumes that each class, like individuals, pursues its own interest.[2] The meaning of the term 'functionary' is extremely broad in Bentham's writings: he understands it to mean any person who holds official responsibilities or a duty connected with an official office, regardless of their position in the hierarchy. They belong to the 'Official Establishment' – 'the vast fictitious receptacle which includes all functionaries' in Bentham's own words.[3] The people, who are then considered as the 'constitutive power', create the class of functionaries through the two powers conferred upon them: the power to 'locate' or 'dislocate' functionaries. As an individual

[1] On the articulation of different classes, see E. de Champs, 'Les fonctionnaires dans le Code Constitutionnel', *Revue d'études benthamiennes* 1 (2006), doi.org/10.4000/etudes-benthamiennes.

[2] This point will be developed in a later part of this chapter.

[3] J. Bentham, *Constitutional Code: Volume I*, ed. F. Rosen and J. H. Burns (Oxford: Clarendon Press, 1983 [*CW*]), 195.

belonging to a specific and defined class, a functionary must, according to Bentham, possess 'official aptitude', which covers three categories: moral, intellectual, and active.[4]

Moral aptitude represents the capacity to act in conformity to the principle of utility; intellectual aptitude involves knowledge and appropriate judgement, that is, the ability to master specific skills; and finally, active aptitude entails dedication and assiduity at work.[5] For Bentham, every functionary must possess and develop these three branches of aptitude.[6] They must therefore ideally follow and apply the tenets of the principle of utility, possess the skills and knowledge necessary for the tasks assigned to them, and be present at their place of work. In other words, Bentham's functionary is a technician, an expert who seeks only the interest of the greatest number. Thus, Bentham constructs the ideal functionary and the question is then the extent to which this optimum can be realized – how to find or train such people and ensure that the quality of their work will endure.

5.2.2 Functionaries' Selection Procedure

The state faces – like any manager who handles recruitment – a problem of asymmetric information. Indeed, knowing beforehand whether a person is truly competent is impossible. Their value will only be revealed after the fact, once their skills have been tested, which may then lead the manager to review their judgement and reverse their initial decision. This means managing an uncertainty which is an integral part of the recruitment process and which does not, and should not, intrinsically preclude the decision to hire. In the case of functionaries, things are slightly different. Indeed, there can be no room for error when hiring a judge, a customs officer or a Minister of Finance, since consequences for society as a whole may be disastrous. Reducing - or even eliminating - the possibility of error and managing uncertainty are therefore the objectives that Bentham set himself. His aim was to resolve the issue of asymmetric information regarding the moral, intellectual, and active aptitude of candidates for office. This endeavour results in a requirement for transparency: to reveal what might be hidden by an individual during

[4] Bentham, *Constitutional Code* (*CW*), 21.

[5] J. Bentham, *First Principles Preparatory to Constitutional Code*, ed. P. Schofield (Oxford: Clarendon Press, 1989 [*CW*]), 4 and 51.

[6] Bentham, *Constitutional Code* (*CW*), 19.

the recruitment process. It aims to reduce uncertainty and to make available all the information necessary to decision-making. However, Bentham knows perfectly well that such a requirement cannot be based on a choice made by the individual in question; it will therefore be a matter of making the individual himself transparent. This explains why the individual is reduced to the three dimensions identified by the aptitude described by Bentham.

There is a second set of problems inherent to the recruitment of functionaries and directly related to the following statement: "The greatest happiness for the greatest number requires that no functionary be located by chance: much less by birth: in no case otherwise than by nomination or election."[7] Is it then possible to ensure that no mistakes are made in the recruitment of functionaries? How can a system of mechanisms and procedures be created that will focus on identifying the appropriate aptitude in applicants and not on legitimizing class candidates?[8] Bentham goes even further: how is it possible to ensure that only the right candidates wish to become functionaries? These questions need to be answered before, during, and after recruitment.

5.2.3 *Dissuasion and Self-Selection*

The first step is to discourage applicants who lack the necessary moral and intellectual aptitude. For Bentham, this is possible by making public service less attractive. He identifies two ways of doing this: one direct, the other indirect.[9] The direct method is to minimize the advantages of each position. Indirectly, it is about maximizing the moral and legal responsibility of each functionary. It is therefore necessary to minimize the power in the hands of each one of them – what Bentham terms 'minimisation of power'[10] – and limit the sums of money at their disposal[11] because these are the two main reasons for maladministration. The direct consequences are the 'principle of minimising trust' and the 'principle of maximising control',[12] that is, the actions of individuals are necessarily known and

[7] Bentham, *First Principles* (*CW*), 117.

[8] Bentham's desire for reform can be seen clearly here, as aristocrats must be excluded from state office.

[9] 'The first points to be ascertained are: [1.] the duties attached to the Office: 2. The emolument and benefit in all shapes attached to it.' Bentham, *First Principles* (*CW*), 92.

[10] Bentham, *First Principles Preparatory* (*CW*), 30.

[11] Bentham, *First Principles* (*CW*), 40.

[12] Bentham, *Constitutional Code* (*CW*), 118.

identified as such. Bentham believes indeed that only those who apply for positions in public service will be capable of combining their interests with those of the majority. Nevertheless, it is necessary to discourage unsuitable applicants for public employment, which is tantamount to ensuring the moral aptitude of functionaries.

5.2.4 *Education and Public Examinations*

The second step involves intellectual aptitude. It is based on two mechanisms: education and competitive examinations. They both obey the same principle: a strict and precise evaluation of the candidates' knowledge based on the skills – or talents, in Bentham's words – required for each position.[13] The various applicants are therefore clearly compartmentalized and individualized: the objective is to identify the skills needed to perform a specific function and not to rely on the general competencies and versatility of individuals. Every test, interview, or examination is designed to eliminate any external element that could disrupt the recruitment process with the aim of creating a procedure for finding the ideal functionaries: in other words, a kind of pure and perfect process that is not subject to the vagaries of circumstances and context. Individuals are thus judged solely on their intellectual ability, with no consideration of social level or class. Bentham describes the examiners, the organization of the examination, and ranking in great detail. He also suggests that the entire procedure should be made public: the recruitment of functionaries must be absolutely transparent. Perfect procedures and absolute transparency are the two elements that should ensure only competent individuals are recruited; they are also supposed to guarantee their future efficiency. We can see here that Bentham is again trying to minimize the uncertainty of the recruitment process. But the effectiveness of the hiring leads him to seek guarantees that too much unchecked power is not placed in the hands of functionaries.

5.2.5 *Functionaries and Power*

The people have real power over the constitution of the functionary class. This is Bentham's theory of power-conferring.[14] Functionaries have two

[13] Ibid., 314–5.

[14] For a pointed analysis, see G. Tusseau, 'Jeremy Bentham on Power-Conferring Laws', *Revue d'études benthamiennes* 3 (2007), doi.org/10.4000/etudes-benthamiennes.

types of obligations: the first is a moral obligation to strictly follow the principle of utility, while the second, which is both a moral and political one, requires them to respect the wishes that may be expressed by the people. These obligations are inherent to their functions.

However, this understanding of the delegation of power implied by Bentham's conception of functionaries is not without its difficulties. Indeed, Bentham considers that whatever the circumstances, individuals pursue their own interests, rather than those of others or of the majority. There is therefore a latent conflict between various interests within society. However, considering a group of individuals as a whole raises the issue of the transformation of individual interests by virtue of their aggregation. Bentham considers that a new interest emerges: that of the class constituted by those individuals. It is the sum of the individual interests that compose it and is different from those of the greatest number. The conflict between individual interests and class interests is then revealed and is one of the great problems facing utilitarianism. Already identified within the framework of utilitarian ethics, it takes on another dimension when it becomes a social and political problem. This is particularly true in this case when it is applied to functionaries and their duties. Functionaries constitute, as such, a class that pursues its own interest and can therefore come into conflict with the interest of the people. In other words, functionaries are constantly tempted to sacrifice the interest of the people they are supposed to serve to satisfy their own. Bentham speaks here of 'sinister interests' – which conflict with the interest of the many – which leads to the sinister sacrifice.[15] The power to dismiss and sanction functionaries naturally belongs to the people, to the greatest number – at least according to Bentham's logic – insofar as the aim is to maximize this interest: collective utility rather than the individual interests of a few. Every functionary is therefore constantly subject to the confidence of the greatest number, and their position depends on the choice made by the people.

5.2.6 *Issues Related to the Actions of Functionaries*

There are two aspects to the management of functionaries: first, how to ensure that they will act in all cases and at all times in the interest of the people and not pursue their own personal interests. Second, how the

[15] Bentham, *First Principles* (*CW*), 151 and 276.

interests of functionaries and those of the greatest number can be made to coincide in a certain and genuine manner so as to avoid the sacrifice of the former for the latter? Bentham provides only one possible answer to these two challenges and that is to structure and organize the state apparatus in such a way that it is in the interest of the functionary to increase the happiness of the greatest number of people. The individual or class interest is then in harmony with the public interest. Bentham's theory of motivation should be interpreted precisely in such a context: it is the foundation of the legislator's main task, which is to create an artificial harmony of interests within society in order to increase the total sum of pleasure.

5.3 The Theory of Motivation or How to Use Punishment and Reward

5.3.1 Pleasure and Pain: The Two Sources of Motivation

Bentham argues that a single principle accounts for motivation: people seek pleasure and avoid pain.

> Nature has placed mankind under the governance of two sovereign masters, *pain* and *pleasure*. It is for them alone to point out what we ought to do, as well as to determine what we shall do. On the one hand the standard of right and wrong, on the other the chain of causes and effects, are fastened to their throne. They govern us in all we do, in all we say, in all we think: every effort we can make to throw off our subjection, will serve but to demonstrate and confirm it. In words a man may pretend to abjure their empire: but in reality he will remain subject to it all the while. The principle of utility recognizes this subjection, and assumes it for the foundation of that system, the object of which is to rear the fabric of felicity by the hands of reason and of law. Systems which attempt to question it, deal in sounds instead of sense, in caprice instead of reason, in darkness instead of light.[16]

Bentham's theory of motivation is based on the descriptive axioms of mental pathology and the normative principle of utility, the former reflecting the drivers of human action and the latter dictating the proper end of actions.[17] The only possible way to influence people's behaviour is

[16] J. Bentham, *An Introduction to the Principles of Morals and Legislation*, ed. J. H. Burns and H. L. A. Hart (Oxford: Clarendon Press, 1996 [*CW*]), 1.

[17] For a detailed analysis, see R. Harrison, *Bentham*, (London: Routledge, 2008) and especially 106–34 and 167–94.

by acting on pleasures and pains, whether they be real or imagined.[18] Bentham's conception of human action is based on the individual's transparency, not to himself but to others; in this case, the others being the legislator. In other words, if the latter wishes to influence the behaviour of its subjects, it must necessarily distribute pleasures and pains, attribute rewards, or inflict punishment. And it is through these that the potentially conflicting interests of the different classes that make up society can be brought into line. As far as functionaries are concerned, this means associating pleasure with the satisfaction that comes from interest in the position at hand as well as its specific activities and duties. If the state wishes to work towards maximizing the greatest happiness of the greatest number, it will need to attain two objectives that cannot be dealt with separately: maximizing the aptitudes of functionaries and minimizing expenditure.

5.3.2 Limiting Public Expenditure

State organization is based on satisfying the interests of functionaries[19] as a means of maximizing their efficiency. This management principle goes hand in hand with its counterpart: a decrease in public spending that contributes to increasing the happiness of the greatest number. Indeed, a careful and disciplined stewardship of the public budget results in lower taxes that lead to a higher standard of living and therefore greater happiness for taxpayers. According to Bentham – and his theory of motivation – there is no need to offer high salaries for bureaucratic positions to attract the best people because their prestige is more important than the proposed salary. However, Bentham is very clear on one point: it is both necessary and important to take an interest in the happiness of functionaries. Considering soldiers as an example: they are psychologically prepared to face the greatest dangers and they expect wages and periods of rest in return. This expectation must be met because of the following maxim: the better their expectations are met, the better the soldiers will do their duty. Dissatisfaction and

[18] This addition is quite important, particularly in the framework of Bentham's theory of punishments. 'It is the real punishment which produces all the evil: it is the apparent punishment which produces all the good. It is proper to diminish the first, and to augment the second, as much as possible. Humanity consists in the appearance of cruelty.' J. Bentham, Principles of Penal Law. In J. Bowring, ed., *Works of Jeremy Bentham* (Edinburgh: William Tait, 1843), 549.

[19] Insofar as those interests coincide with the general interest.

disappointment are avoided, working conditions are improved, and there is no longer a need to increase their salaries in order to ensure their effectiveness.[20] Even if public offices are attractive, Bentham is nevertheless well aware that the pleasure of being a functionary may not be enough when confronted with a number of temptations, resulting in corruption. A balance, perhaps a precarious one, must therefore be struck between the salary that must be high enough to avoid corruption, while still being reasonable enough so as not to be too great an expense. This balance is necessary to ensure the proper functioning of the state.

The salary of civil servants must therefore be set in such a way as to ensure as perfect a match as possible between their duties and their interests.[21] In other words, the pairing of duty and interest is made possible through wages by creating 'such a species of interest [which] can be formed as shall combine the *force* which is peculiar to punishment with the *certainty* which is peculiar to reward'.[22] The salary is thought of as a reward granted to functionaries for fulfilling their duty, that is, maximizing the general interest. The balance between wages and government spending is part of an attempt to find a more general equilibrium and resulted in a comprehensive book: *Official Aptitude Maximized, Expense Minimized.*[23]

5.3.3 *Maximizing Aptitudes*

Bentham's view on the management of aptitude within the civil service is threefold: one must first ensure that the candidates applying for a position possess these three branches of aptitude; then that they are selected on that basis; and finally, once in their position, he seeks to guarantee the maximization of aptitude. It is important to understand that the use and effectiveness of a branch of aptitude does not depend solely on natural and individual ability. In fact, it only acquires a tangible and useful meaning through the relationship between individual aptitude and the general institutional structure. For example, the moral aptitude of a functionary is only effective when their particular interest is identified with that of the majority through the use of punishment and a certain amount of

[20] Bentham, *Constitutional Code* (*CW*), 244 and 356.

[21] J. Bentham, *Rationale of Reward*, ed. R. Smith (London: John and H. L. Hunt, 1825), 150–5.

[22] Ibid., 24–5.

[23] J. Bentham, *Official Aptitude Maximized, Expense Minimized*, ed. P. Schofield (Oxford: Clarendon Press, 1993 [*CW*]).

control. Bentham, however, seeks to maximize aptitude through reward, if such and such an action is effectively carried out, implying that failure to do so or carrying out some other action would result in a sanction. In other words, he believes that the strict application of what is advocated by the principle of utility, that is, acting on pleasures and pains, will make it possible to positively influence and maximize moral aptitude. The state becomes an ethical space ruled by the principle of utility, where the individual interests of functionaries, especially if considered as a class, are made to coincide with the greatest happiness of the greatest number.

Active aptitude is directly tied to the motivation inherent in the position and its place in the general organization of the state: experience and the motivation to perform certain tasks make it increasingly rewarding. Intellectual aptitude, on the other hand, depends to a certain extent on natural talents but is developed through the education system and an interest in public affairs.

It is well understood that the architecture of constitutional law has a dual relationship with the official aptitude of functionaries: it must promote them while simultaneously being their *raison d'être*. Neither can be considered without the other. What is to be administered, and the way in which it is administered, both depend on the aptitude of the functionary in charge.[24] It is, therefore, quite fitting that Bentham focuses on the aptitude of individuals who are potential or actual functionaries and that he makes explicit the extent to which the principle of utility should guide their actions; this provides an insight into the significance of his motivational theory in the organization of the state. However, the existence of 'sinister interests' means that Bentham must focus on creating safeguards against abuses of power. This is the level at which one can grasp the normative importance of transparency, both at the structural and the individual level. It will also be the means of putting the people back at the heart of the process of locating and dislocating functionaries, thus strengthening the coherence of Bentham's theory of democracy.

5.4 The Dynamics of Interests as a Justification for Democracy

5.4.1 The Interest of Functionaries

While the issue of interests is central to understanding Bentham's position on aptitude, it is equally crucial to grasping their place in his

[24] Bentham, *First Principles* (*CW*), 4.

justification of the democratic system. The challenge lies in understanding how all the interests at work within a political society and the universal interest will be articulated.[25]

If the interests of functionaries and those of the community as a whole are not matched or not identical,[26] Bentham speaks of a 'sinister sacrifice':

> In so far as, in the instance of the functionary in question, this identification fails to have place, the consequence is – on his part, in so far as depends on his endeavours, the sacrifice of the universal interest to his personal or other particular interest: say, for shortness, *the sinister sacrifice.*[27]

The establishment and functioning of a good government depend upon two different groups of interests being aligned with the universal interest: the interest of those who possess the 'constitutive authority' and that of those who have the 'operative power'.[28] In other words, the interests of the people and of the functionaries or the rulers themselves must be aligned. The constitutive authority is the electoral body of the people that has the power to 'locate' (appoint) and 'dislocate' (dismiss) functionaries, whereas the operative authority is formed by the whole of the functionaries and officials and is divided into the legislative and the executive branches.[29] This division is far from trivial. Indeed, the people who hold the constitutive power – the people – are also those whose interests make up the universal interest. The operative power is subordinate to the constitutive power, which implies that the interests of functionaries and rulers are subordinate to those of the constitutive power. Or more precisely, the interests of the former may be made to align with the universal interest through or via the interest of the people. The universal interest is defined by the aggregate of the interests of the people. Consequently, the legislature can only be thought of as a true representation of the people. An electoral system based on universal suffrage is therefore necessary. Bentham thus constructs an argument in which the

[25] This issue is discussed in a contrasting way in P. Schofield, 'Bentham on the Identification of Interests', *Utilitas* 8 (1996), 223–34; and G. J. Postema, *Bentham and the Common Law Tradition* (Oxford: Clarendon Press, 1989), 361–2 and 389–90. See Bentham, *First Principles* (*CW*), 125.

[26] To use a terminology similar to Bentham's.

[27] Bentham, *First Principles* (*CW*), 17.

[28] Ibid., 6 and 239.

[29] The executive branch is itself divided into two departments: the judiciary and the administration. For a more detailed analysis, see de Champs, 'Les fonctionnaires'.

dynamic of interests serves as a justification for representative democracy. He reverses the power relationship between the rulers and the ruled: the rulers become the subjects of the people because it is the interests of the latter that make up the universal interest.[30] For Bentham, this universal interest can be thwarted by another type of interest: sinister interest,[31] which it thus becomes vital to guard against.

5.4.2 *'Sinister Interests'*

So, what is the nature of this sinister interest that may potentially undermine Bentham's architecture? This notion is one that Bentham explores starting in his 1803 writings on judicial procedure and evidence. One can identify the emergence[32] of a theoretical focus on the term in his 1807 work *Scotch Reform.*[33] Although he first used it to support his critique of English law, it became strategic in demonstrating that representative democracy allowed for the establishment of good government. Bentham realizes that sinister self-interest is at work in both the legal and political establishments.[34] As already mentioned, he stresses the importance of fighting it in order to ensure the proper functioning of government and presents democracy as the most effective way of rendering the rulers dependent on the ruled.

[30] J. Bentham, *First Principles* (*CW*), 135–7.

[31] Here is Bentham's explanation of his use of the word 'sinister' (quoted by P. Schofield in *Utility and Democracy: The Political Thought of Jeremy Bentham: The Political Thought of Jeremy Bentham* [Oxford: Oxford University Press, 2009], 109): 'Like bad, sinister is here employed for the expression of disapprobation. When motive is the name of the subject or the object marked for reprobation, bad is the adjunct most commonly, though *sinister* also is sometimes employed for that purpose: when interest is the name given to the subject or object, sinister is the only one of two names that is given to the adjunct. Of sinister motives we hear sometimes: of bad interests never.' UC civ. 346 (29 May 1811). This numbering system refers to the Bentham Papers at University College London Library. The first digit refers to the number of the box in which the manuscripts are located and the second to the number of the manuscript itself.

[32] For a thorough historical analysis, see Schofield, *Utility and Democracy*, 109–36.

[33] J. Bentham, *Scotch Reform; considered, with reference to the Plan, proposed in the Late Parliament, for the regulation of the Courts, and the Administration of Justice, in Scotland: with Illustrations from English Non-reform: in the course of which divers imperfections, abuses, and corruptions, in the Administration of Justice, with their causes, are now, for the first time, brought to light. In a series of Letters, addressed to the Right Hon. Lord Grenville,* (London: Richard Taylor and Co., 1808).

[34] This connection is clear in J. Bentham, *The Elements of the Art of Packing: As Applied to Special Juries, Particularly in Cases of Libel Law* (London: Effingham Wilson, 1821). In the rest of this chapter, I will refer to the version available in J. Bentham, *Works of Jeremy Bentham*, ed. John Bowring, 11 vols. (Edinburg: William Tait, 1843), vol. 5, 61–186.

But what exactly does Bentham mean by sinister interest?

> In every line of legislation, the true, the proper end – the only true, the only proper *end* – will at this time of day be generally – not to say universally – acknowledged to be the happiness – the well-being – the welfare – the prosperity – the interest – all these words mean the same thing, of the community: of the aggregate body of human beings under consideration.
>
> In every line of legislation, the interest and so forth of any minor assemblage of individuals forming part of that aggregate will, if put in opposition to the general interest, be in alike manner recognized as being a false – an improper – a *sinister* end. The pursuit of the sinister end will, in so far as the result is considered as sure to be or likely to be the loss of a greater quantity of happiness of the *whole* body taken together than is gained to the *part*, will accordingly be recognized as being an improper, a sinister pursuit: and the accomplishment of such sinister end, an undesirable result: undesirable to wit to any person, who, considering himself on the occasion and for the purpose, as the representative, or guardian, or agent, or advocate of the whole community considers for that same purpose and on that same occasion its interests as coinciding with his own.[35]

This sinister interest, which is contrary to the universal interest and often the prerogative of a minority class seeking to perpetuate its power or privileges without regard for the greatest number, is all the more dangerous when it is not limited to a particular individual, since a class will pursue it with all the more force and determination. In this context, the 'apt' functionary is seen as contributing to the safeguard that a democratic state can offer against the confiscation of power by an elite and the pursuit of sinister self-interest by the government. However, and in line with his conception of the interests at work within a political society, Bentham also believes that the publicity of the actions of officials and rulers will be a structuring element in the fight against sinister interest.[36]

The Public Opinion Tribunal also aims to play this role with its moral sanction.[37] Ensuring that the actions of those who govern are made

[35] UC lxix. 162–74 (13 August 1804). Quoted by Schofield in *Utility and Democracy*, 125.

[36] In the rest of this chapter, I will refer to the version available in Bentham, *Works*. J. Bentham, 'Scotch reform', in *Works of Jeremy Bentham*, ed. J. Bowring (Edinburg: William Tait, 1843), 91.

[37] In his early writings, Bentham identifies three types of sanctions: political, moral, and religious, see J. Bentham, *A Comment on the Commentaries and a Fragment on Government*, ed. J. H. Burns and H. L. A. Hart (Oxford: Oxford University Press, 2008 [*CW*]), 42 and 82. He later will identify four by adding a physical sanction, see

public forces them to be accountable for them, to be responsible to the people. This publicity is a fundamental element of the proper functioning of society and the alignment of interests within it by guaranteeing the moral aptitude of functionaries.[38]

> Is it objected against the regime of publicity, that it is a system of distrust? This is true; and every good political institution is founded upon this base. Whom ought we to distrust, if not those to whom is committed great authority, with great temptations to abuse it? Consider the objects of their duties: they are not their own affairs, but the affairs of others, comparatively indifferent to them, very difficult, very complicated, – which indolence alone would lead them to neglect, and which require the most laborious application. Consider their personal interests: you will often find them in opposition to the interests confided to them. They also possess all the means of serving themselves at the expense of the public, without the possibility of being convicted of it. What remains, then, to overcome all these dangerous motives? what has created an interest of superior force? and what can this interest be, if it be not respect for public opinion – dread of its judgments – desire of glory? – in one word, everything which results from publicity?
>
> The efficacy of this great instrument extends to everything – legislation, administration, judicature. Without publicity, no good is permanent: under the auspices of publicity, no evil can continue.[39]

Without necessarily carrying out a complete analysis of the Public Opinion Tribunal,[40] it is worth identifying its modalities and functions for the purposes of this chapter. All subjects can potentially be members of this Tribunal. It is important to emphasize that while Bentham

J. Bentham, *Introduction* (*CW*), 34–7; J. Bentham, *Traités de législation civile et pénale*, ed. E. Dumont, pref. M. Bozzo-Rey, A. Brunon-Ernst, E. de Champs (Paris: Dalloz, 2010), 28–30. He will finally add, at the end of his life the sympathetic sanction that he mentions in his correspondence: J. Bentham, *Correspondence, Volume 11: January 1822 to June 1824*, ed. C. Fuller (Oxford: Clarendon Press, 2000 [*CW*]), 86.

[38] F. Rosen, *Bentham, Byron, and Greece: Constitutionalism, Nationalism, and Early Liberal Political Thought* (Oxford: Clarendon Press, 1992), 69.

[39] J. Bentham, *Political Tactics*, ed. M. James, C. Blamires, and C. P. Watkin (Oxford: Clarendon Press, 1999 [*CW*]), 37.

[40] For a more detailed account, see, among others, M. Bozzo-Rey, 'La transparence chez Jeremy Bentham: de l'invisibilité d'un concept à sa publicité', *The Tocqueville Review/La revue Tocqueville* 32 (2011), 89–111; M. Bozzo-Rey, 'Bentham et le management des fonctionnaires: utilité, transparence et management de soi', *www.raison-publique.fr*', Oren Ben-Dor, *Constitutional Limits and the Public Sphere: A Critical Study of Bentham's Contitutionalism* (Oxford: Hart, 2000), 191–233; F. Rosen, *Jeremy Bentham and Representative Democracy, a Study of the Constitutional Code* (Oxford: Clarendon Press, 1983), 19–40.

acknowledges the fictitious nature of this court, he nonetheless insists on the reality of its power.

> When announced it will be apt to present itself as nothing more than the offspring of imagination and language: – a purely fictitious and verbal entity. The cause and reason of this is – that on no occasion are the several members of it sitting all together in their official and judicial capacity, or so much as capable of sitting and taking part in the business at the same time and in the same edifice or enclosure, or when at a distance maintaining anything like a regular course of correspondence.
>
> It wears therefore the colour of fictitiousness. But it possesses the substance of reality.[41]

This tribunal thus possesses quasi-judicial powers[42] and is precisely the means by which the constitutive authority can exercise its power to locate and dislocate officials. Bentham elaborates on this comparison since he considers that the moral sanction that may be issued by the Public Opinion Tribunal is similar to the legal sanction and may have the same degree of influence on the will of functionaries.[43] More specifically, he identifies nine commonalities in the way they operate, even though the manner of their application may differ:

> 1. Receiving claims and accusations. 2. Receiving oppositions and defences. 3. Receiving, compelling, collecting and storing evidence. 4. Receiving and hearing or reading arguments of parties litigant or advocates. 5. Forming opinions or judgments on ditto: with correspondent *will*. 6. Giving expression to such judgments and will. 7. Giving impression to such expression. 8. Giving diffusion to such impression. 9. Giving execution and effect to such judgment[s] and will.[44]

The Public Opinion Tribunal is a separate body that is meant to include 'all those classes which . . . stand excluded from all participation in such supreme power';[45] it is made up of 'all individuals of whom the Constitutive body of this state is composed'.[46] 'All other political communities, all such members, to whom it happens to take cognizance of

[41] J. Bentham, *Securities against Misrule and Other Constitutional Writings for Tripoli and Greece*, ed. P. Schofield (Oxford: Clarendon Press, 1990 [CW]), 54.
[42] J. Bentham, *Constitutional Code* (*CW*), 35.
[43] Bentham, *First Principles* (*CW*), 301–3 and 306–9. For a general comparison of the effects of their decisions, see also Bentham, *Securities* (*CW*), 54–73.
[44] Bentham, *Securities* (*CW*), 60.
[45] Bentham, *Constitutional Code* (*CW*), 35.
[46] Ibid.

the question, whatever it may be'[47] may take part, which potentially gives it an extremely broad constitution.

Bentham points to three functions of the tribunal: any person should be allowed to seek information and evidence on a particular public issue; the tribunal makes judgements, it punishes and rewards those involved in political actions by building – or destroying – their reputations; and it formulates propositions on public issues. Thus, one cannot summarize its role as merely monitoring those in power. Underestimating its role in shaping government policy would be a mistake. Information is both 'in' and 'out': it must enter the tribunal's process, but this also produces information without which legislators cannot make choices that are in the best interests of the greatest number.[48] The preferred medium used by the Public Opinion Tribunal is, of course, the press.[49]

With the Public Opinion Tribunal, Bentham reaches the ultimate conclusion of his initial defence of publicity,[50] since one of the main reasons in favour of publicity consists in presenting it as a guarantee for the governed that the members of political assemblies would perform their duty well. Applied to all functionaries, this defence takes shape in the Public Opinion Tribunal, the purpose of which is to ensure that, by maximizing moral aptitude, the alignment of interests is effective and that sinister interest does not guide the decisions of government officials. In so doing, he confirms the reversal of the relationship between those who govern and those who are governed and provides an additional tool to ensure the proper functioning of government and, ultimately, of democracy. Bentham thereby extends his thinking on the safeguards to be provided for utilitarian democracy to function properly and for the uncertainty of human behaviour, and of functionaries in particular, to be minimized. Such a purpose can be interpreted as a dynamic between externality and internalization: the externality of tools and procedures and the internalization of utilitarian moral standards through a specific architectural technology.

5.5 The Constitutional Panopticon: Transparency as a Disciplinary Technology or the Internalization of Moral Norms

Bentham regards the various tools and procedures discussed above as insufficient because their externality cannot guarantee their

47 Ibid..
48 Ibid., 36–7.
49 Ibid., 86–7 and 427.
50 Bentham, *Tactics* (*CW*), 29–44.

internalization. For example, if carrying out an action is the result of a utilitarian calculation that compares and measures pleasures and pains, an individual may still miscalculate, misjudge, or simply be wrong. There is no room for such uncertainty at any level in Bentham's system, as evidenced by the attention paid to the entire process of functionary recruitment. Hence, Bentham's managerial model can also be considered as a system of uncertainty management or, more precisely, as an attempt to eradicate all uncertainty. He seeks to impose a constraint that is not only external but also internal: he wants functionaries to integrate, to internalize moral norms so that they act in a specific way, perform certain precise actions in specific circumstances, and implement the principle of utility.

The normativity inherent in Bentham's system can, therefore, be understood as a normalization of behaviour: constraints are an integral part of the behaviour of functionaries. To achieve his ends, Bentham relies on the 'disciplinary technologies' described by Michel Foucault in *Discipline and Punish* and that can be identified in the Panopticon writings. The specific variation of these technologies that is of interest here can be called the Constitutional Panopticon.[51] Foucault's 'eye of power' is no longer unique but multiple: there is not one guardian of the constitutional panopticon, but many guardians. Every citizen, through the Public Opinion Tribunal, becomes a potential guardian; the eyes of the people guard this panopticon. The different disciplinary mechanisms at work will now be identified in order to determine their impact on behaviour through the internationalization of norms.

Discipline is an art. It consists in controlling the distribution of bodies in space, it is based on a precise chronology of acts, and it seeks to increase both collective utility and individual docility through the articulation of bodies in a specific arrangement.

5.5.1 *The Spatialization of Bodies*

The first characteristic of disciplinary technology is its ability to order bodies in space. A closed space is necessary in most cases as it allows the concentration of heterogeneous forces. The technology will then seek to maximize their utility, all the more so as the closure of the space in which the bodies move allows for a more effective surveillance of them.

[51] A. Brunon-Ernst, 'Les métamorphoses panoptiques: de Foucault à Bentham', *Cahiers critiques de philosophie* 4 (2007), 61–72.

A confined space has a double advantage: each individual is placed in the most useful position and is separated *a priori* from anything that could potentially constitute a group with strengths and dynamics of its own and thus liable to produce social values and collective standards.

Controlling the organization of space has a single purpose, namely, to control all the relationships that may take place within it. In this respect, the architectural organization of ministers' offices is a particularly telling example. The offices form a crescent, allowing the Prime Minister to potentially see all of his staff. The architecture and spatial organization of the different offices and floors where functionaries work is extremely precise: division into offices and corridors with single or double entrances, door mechanisms assigned to specific functions, and porters responsible for monitoring comings and goings. This has no other purpose than to ensure that individuals are in the right place to carry out the task assigned to them or to pass on the appropriate information.[52] The space created and arranged in this way offers a tangle of places allowing the precise localization of each individual. The control over bodies is not merely a matter of individual control of actions but also provides for the constant surveillance of a political institution that brings into play a dialectic between the one and the many, the individual and the community. This kind of control is only possible because each individual is identified and identifiable with open offices – which today would be called open-space – that ensure maximum visibility.[53] The space in which functionaries move is strictly defined, delimited, and drawn. It deconstructs and reconstructs the bodies[54] by prescribing which acts must be carried out with a programmatic aim.

5.5.2 *A Programmatic Chronology*

Time management is a second and equally important characteristic. Disciplinary institutions are like network nodes: times, like spaces, are constantly intertwined. To control time is to impose a rhythm that people must follow. Every moment must be useful and used. In *Discipline and Punish*, Foucault explains very clearly that time optimization is imposed by an external source that will divide and organize it. But he also insists on the fact that discipline will seize on the inner time that

[52] Bentham, *Constitutional Code* (*CW*), 285.
[53] Ibid., 442.
[54] M. Foucault, *Surveiller et punir – Naissance de la prison* (Paris: Gallimard, 1975), 162.

each individual sets for himself, that is, the time necessary to accomplish such or such an action, such or such a movement. This is how disciplinary power seeks to permeate the individual temporality of bodies: the external evaluation of the movements that must be carried out in succession is internalized by the subjects, and the pace imposed for such and such an action must become the spontaneous, somewhat natural rhythm that each body adopts as it carries out and repeats this same act. One temporal order is thus replaced by another, and this substitution is all the more effective as it is internalized.

The challenge also lies in the ability to extract as many available moments as possible from a given time[55] in order to control the sequences of actions carried out by bodies over a certain period while disciplinarily managing the pace of these actions. Decomposing, segmenting, individualizing time and space amounts to recomposing 'an overall movement and a joint progression that is neither carried out by a genuine whole nor experienced in a true collective'.[56] The buildings' organization should be understood in exactly the same way. They are designed to optimize the transmission of information, that is, to remove any delay: Bentham's ideal is one of immediacy. Efficiency means eliminating any time gaps, in other words, it is the constant search for instantaneity.[57]

After being spatially distributed, subjected to a specific pace through the internal time and duration imposed by an external measurement, the bodies must be brought together as rationally as possible in order to constitute a group, a class that is more powerful and efficient than the sum of its individuals. It is thereby necessary to 'build a machine'. Each individual becomes an individual with its own time and these multiple 'body-times'[58] must be integrated into this corporeal and disciplinary machine. The aim is to maximize the utility of these groups while minimizing their political strength. Applied to the state, this means that the control of functionaries involves maximizing their efficiency while minimizing their role, their political power, which equates to strengthening the political power of the people. A transparent architectural structure allows the activities of functionaries to be controlled: the

[55] Foucault, *Surveiller et punir*, 180.
[56] S. Legrand, *Les normes chez Foucault* (Paris: Presses Universitaires de France, 2007), 54.
[57] Bentham, *Constitutional Code* (*CW*), 440.
[58] This translates the concept of 'corps-durée' as developed by Stéphane Legrand.

state machine must be controlled or, more specifically, its productive force and efficiency must be made visible in order to be controlled.

5.5.3 Discipline as Training

The primary function of the disciplinary power is to train.[59] It is based on three elements: hierarchical surveillance, normalizing judgement, and examination. Hierarchical surveillance transforms architecture into a tool of power over individuals through total and constant visibility. Indeed, every individual is subjected to power because of their visibility, but this visibility is only possible through the exercise of power. Hierarchical surveillance articulates acts of looking and states of visibility. Everyone watches everyone else while also feeling constantly watched by others, thereby eliminating the need for any obligation to watch: the spatial interlocking of hierarchical surveillance results in self-surveillance and the group being under control and docile.[60]

However, establishing a constant state of surveillance is not enough; it is also essential to identify what is to be monitored. In this case, one might think that others are the object of this surveillance, but this is not the case: in fact, it is about monitoring whether people's actions are in line with what the power requires them to do, in other words, whether they are in conformity with the norm. Any inadequacy must be punishable, leading to the emergence of a punitive mechanism[61] that results in 'making the slightest departures from correct behaviour subject to punishment, and of giving a punitive function to the apparently indifferent elements of the disciplinary apparatus'.[62] This implies that any individual action is susceptible of being visible. Offences are now seen as failures to conform to the norm set as a model, and the purpose of punishment is to correct, to rectify: behaviour must be made to conform to this standard. The purpose of punishment in a disciplinary system is therefore to correct; 'in short, it *normalizes*'.[63] This is why Bentham insists on functionaries being present at their posts: their circumvention of the normative requirement of transparency, that is, their possible invisibility within the state system, must necessarily result in punishment.

[59] Foucault, *Surveiller et punir*, 200.
[60] Ibid., 201–8.
[61] Ibid., 210.
[62] Ibid.
[63] Ibid., 215.

Examination allows for a combination of hierarchical surveillance and normalizing punishment. It is defined by Foucault as 'a normalizing gaze, a surveillance that makes it possible to qualify, to classify and to punish'.[64] Stéphane Legrand's formulation is particularly accurate when he states that 'it is the scheme that links the verification of aptitudes and the sanctioning of subjects'.[65] Foucault reverses the general economy of power relations with this analysis of examination. The one who holds power is no longer the one who must be visible: it is the subjects of this power who must be seen, observed, constantly monitored thanks to a 'mechanism of objectification'. Individuals are now part of a documentary field, a network of writings, which records all their actions in a potentially infinite set of documents that classify and compare them in order to create disciplinary codes. These will formalize knowledge about individuals by accumulating information. Such a mass of data is consistent with Bentham's project of minimizing information asymmetry. Indeed, the transparency demanded by this type of operation is a political norm that not only underpins Bentham's theory of democracy but also ensures its proper functioning. The 'visible everything' is matched by a 'known everything'; the management of functionaries is not so much governed by an optimization of efficiency as by one of epistemological transparency. The shrinking of the invisible and the unknown is in fact an almost desperate attempt to make the non-visible invisible – to eradicate the unknown.

With hierarchical surveillance, 'every gaze is an element of power at work': the subjects' visibility ensures the power's control over their actions and behaviour. The space is now organized around an 'interlocking hierarchical surveillance' that generates a systematic and internalized self-surveillance of the group. In this case, the group covers two realities: functionaries and functionaries plus non-functionaries. The surveillance and visibility network created in this way can operate autonomously: 'Discipline makes possible a relational power that sustains itself through its own mechanisms.'[66] This is precisely the logic behind the organization of offices in public buildings: they are spaces whose interlocking is made possible by information transmission tubes that allow for hierarchical surveillance.[67] The constitutional panopticon

64 Ibid., 217.
65 Legrand, *Les normes chez Foucault*, 63.
66 Foucault, *Surveiller et punir*, 208.
67 Bentham, *Constitutional Code* (*CW*), 443–50.

dictates specific actions and behaviours to functionaries while penetrating each subject. Internalization produces a particular mode of behaviour. The management of functionaries – the maximization of their efficiency – is based on the management of the self, that is, on the normalizing power of disciplinary technologies. The requirement of transparency integrates this system in two ways: it makes the organization of the state transparent to the people and it obliges functionaries to be transparent to all those with whom they are likely to have a hierarchical or power relationship.

5.5.4 *The Control of Information*

For Bentham, the management of functionaries is an important field of interest since their behaviour can affect their efficiency and lead to additional costs. In this case, the individual interest would override the general interest and its pursuit would be the guiding principle for action. Since every individual, and moreover every functionary, as a rational agent, will seek to maximize pleasure and minimize pain, one can assume – from a basic utilitarian perspective – that they will try to find ways to increase their power, influence, and earnings while minimizing their efforts. As a result, they will use all the information at their disposal to create the illusion that their every action is in line with the utility principle and that they are seeking to maximize the general interest. This is typically the sort of situation that occurs in the case of asymmetric information between the functionary and the person controlling their work. There is a very strong link in Bentham's writings between transparency and information. Indeed, transparency is the key to resolving an asymmetry of information. Hence, controlling functionaries necessarily requires that the latter lose any monopoly they may have on information. Their activities and work must be made completely transparent in order to remove the possibility of concealing their true nature. If Foucault's analysis has shown that the relationship between the organization of individual and collective bodies, spaces, and times should work towards making actions visible, and one should add made visible to the public, then the issue of information asymmetry between functionaries and the public, the citizens, can be resolved. However, two points should be added in this regard: first, functionaries should wear clothes that allow anyone to identify them as such; second, there should be better communication with citizens, especially regarding the rules of public institutions. Secrecy must be completely abolished,[68] everything must be transparent because those who are most affected by the work of functionaries are the people.[69] Transparency is an integral part of Bentham's theory of democracy and a managerial norm that ensures the smooth functioning of such a regime.

5.6 Conclusion

Bentham's management of functionaries can only be understood if it is placed in the more general framework of utilitarianism, and more specifically in the ethical, political, but also legal fields, which all seek to influence individual behaviour. It is clear that the principle of utility plays an important role in this dynamic, particularly in laying the foundations of a theory of motivation that identifies pleasure and pain as the sole driving forces behind actions. Influencing behaviour is then simply a matter of acting on pleasure and pain, that is, of distributing rewards and inflicting punishments. This is indeed one way of managing functionaries and Bentham does not fail to emphasize both the importance of wages as a reward and the superior influence of rewards compared to punishments.[70] And yet, Bentham's approach can also be described as a search for ways in which the state, on the one hand, and society, on the other, can ensure that functionaries behave in a way that is consistent with the principle of utility. However, the implementation of the panoptic mechanism used in prisons and analyzed by Michel Foucault suggests a new approach to the management of functionaries. Disciplinary power penetrates people's bodies, and it is the internalization of disciplinary processes that changes behaviour. In this way, normativity becomes a procedure for normalizing behaviour. The ethical norms defined by the principle of utility are thus internalized, force is no longer necessary to constrain action, and no one needs to manage functionaries as they are now able to self-manage. The aim is to develop ways of normalizing the behaviour of functionaries that will lead them to adopt a specific form of behaviour in accordance with the ethical prescriptions of the utilitarian theory. However, such a normalization of

[68] Except in very specific cases, which are not at issue here. Bentham, *Constitutional Code* (*CW*), 440–8.

[69] Bentham, *Tactics* (*CW*), 52; Bentham, *Constitutional Code* (*CW*), 539.

[70] Although he does agree that the systematic use of rewards can lead to corruption, which he has consistently fought against.

behaviour can only be effective if the organizational or management techniques that Foucault described as disciplinary technologies are applied to the state apparatus. The management of functionaries, as described and recommended in Bentham's writings, is a means or an attempt to normalize the conduct of a specific and determined group of individuals through the internalization of ethical norms prescribed by the principle of utility. The bureaucratic space then becomes an ethical space of self-management,[71] made both possible and effective through constant monitoring as well as the intrinsic and necessary transparency of individuals and organizational arrangements. But this raises a further question: to whom should they be transparent? With regard to the organization, it has been said often enough that it is the eyes of the people, constituted as a Public Opinion Tribunal, that monitor the activity of functionaries with a view to realizing the principle of utility and continuously improving the effectiveness of democracy. As far as individuals are concerned, there are two aspects. First, as the focus is on particular individuals, namely, functionaries, and it has been made clear that transparency is required in the selection of candidates for civil service, in their recruitment, and in their activities. Second, Bentham initially assumes that individuals as such are intrinsically and necessarily transparent: there can be no hidden motives for action or even invisible actions. Anything that is hidden is concealed from knowledge and increases uncertainty, which increases concern and decreases happiness within society.[72] The transparency of individuals fuels the legislator's knowledge, a knowledge without which he cannot bring about the artificial harmony of interests within society. Therefore, the combined promotion of official aptitude, procedures for the recruitment of functionaries, the Public Opinion Tribunal, and the Constitutional Panopticon guarantee the proper functioning of the utilitarian and democratic state envisioned by Bentham.

[71] This concept is particularly analyzed in the following book: E. Pezet, *Management et conduite de soi. Enquête sur les ascèses de la performance* (Paris: Vuibert, 2007).
[72] See, on this point, Bentham, *Traités*, 258–71.

6

Bentham on the Corruption of Democracy

BRIAN CHIEN-KANG CHEN

> As is the blood of man to the tiger who has once tasted of it, so are the sweets of office to the functionary who has once tasted of them. Seldom by any thing but hopelessness of re-enjoyment will the appetite be extinguished.[1]

6.1 Constitution and the Dynamic Processes of Politics

The purpose of this chapter is to explore Bentham's observation of the tendency of representative democracy towards corruption. In his constitutional theory, Bentham's chief concern is to prevent corruption, and he consistently maintains that the antidote for that political evil is representative democracy. However, Bentham indicates that representative democracy is not immune from corruption, and I suggest that this insight is derived from his observation of the dynamic processes of politics. For that reason, Bentham's constitutional theory can be interpreted as an analysis of political processes and an offering of normative guidance on them and their development as influenced by the political psychology of members of political society.

In the framework that Bentham adopts for analyzing political phenomena such as corruption, he divides political society into two major groups of agents: the ruling few, who are endowed with political power and political resources, and the subject many, the vast mass of the people who remain vulnerable to oppression and depredation at the hands of the rulers. In turn, this framework helps Bentham to reveal the central tension between the rulers and the people, namely, that the ruling few, driven by selfishness and contempt for the subject many, will forever endeavour to maximize their particular interests at the expense of the interests of the subject many. Bentham describes that situation as the 'sinister sacrifice', which, wherever it prevails, indicates the corruption of

[1] J. Bentham, *Constitutional Code: Volume I*, ed. F. Rosen and J. H. Burns (Oxford: Clarendon Press, 1983, [*CW*]), 78.

political society. To prevent such a state, Bentham proposes the normative practice of the identification of interests, such that 'on every occasion if in consequence of the man's conduct, whatsoever good befalls the whole community, good, in the same proportion, befalls him: as also whatsoever evil befalls the whole community, in the same proportion befalls him'.[2]

The identification of interests involves intricate social interactions, for the interests of various members of political society are not only diverse but usually in conflict. First, according to Bentham, the interests of the ruling few naturally oppose the interests of the subject many. Second, the interests of aristocrats do not naturally align with the interests of the monarch, because they compete for political resources with the monarch, including money, power, and factitious dignity.[3] Third, even among the subject many, every individual has their particular interests that others do not share. Bentham provides his solution to these problems in his constitutional theory.

Following a careful investigation of the strengths and weaknesses of various polities, Bentham endorses the superiority of representative democracy, whose pivotal strength is a structure of power distribution that facilitates the identification of interests. According to Bentham, in a representative democracy, political power is composed of constitutive power and operative power; whereas operative power is ascribed to the functionaries, constitutive power is located in the electorate. Although legislation and policymaking are mostly achieved by exercising operative power, members of society with constitutive power determine who will exercise that operative power.[4] In this way, Bentham seeks ways to limit the authority of a government and subordinate it to the power of the people.

Subordinating operative power to those with constitutive power can prevent the sinister sacrifice. For example, in Bentham's *Constitutional Code*, electors are empowered to locate and dislocate members of the legislature and to dislocate the chiefs of the judiciary and administrative departments.[5] However, to maintain their superiority of power and

[2] J. Bentham, *First Principles preparatory to Constitutional Code*, ed. P. Schofield (Oxford: Clarendon Press, 1989, [*CW*]), 125.

[3] *First Principles* (*CW*), 190–1.

[4] Ibid., 6.

[5] *Constitutional Code: I (CW)*, 30–2. In Bentham's constitutional theory, the judicial and administrative departments both exercise executive power, which along with legislative power compose the operative power. See *First Principles* (*CW*), 6–7.

position, the executive department may endeavour to form a league of sinister interests with the legislature. For its main task, the league would seek to consolidate the functionaries' arbitrary power over society, thereby allowing the legislature and executive department to continue benefiting from the depredation and oppression of the subject many. In that 'game of corruption',[6] Bentham theorizes, the executive department is the corrupter, given the wealth of offices, honours, and money under its command. Meanwhile, the legislature is the corruptee: the body tempted by the executive department's political resources and willing to serve that department in exchange for them. Bentham remarks: 'In no form of government, to this bad purpose any more than to any good one, can profit in any shape be conveyed for a continuance into individual hands otherwise than through the intervention of a Supreme Executive, doing or professing to do the will of the Supreme Legislative.'[7]

The supreme executive – in Bentham's terminology, the 'corrupter general'[8] – is embodied not only in the monarch of a monarchy but also in the president of a representative democracy. In that light, Bentham maintains that representative democracy, albeit in ways somewhat unlike monarchy and aristocracy, is nevertheless exposed to the threat of corruption. In a democratic society, the corrupter general, along with bribing and manipulating the legislature, will not hesitate to subvert social morality by undermining the collective mind of the people. At first glance, that tendency may seem to enlarge the league of sinister interests, the consequence of which would be to compound the interests of the ruling few with the interests of the subject many. However, such a conclusion would misunderstand Bentham's analysis of political evil. The corrupter general's intention is to weaken constitutive power and, by means of delusion, turn its constituents into the willing victims of sinister sacrifice. By extension, 'on the will and agency of these same constituents will, in a greater or less degree, depend the composition of the body of these representatives and to this, as to other purposes, the conduct of the several members'.[9] In other words, because deluded people are not capable of electing virtuous representatives, the subject many need to be employed as instruments in a corrupted democracy. In that role, the masses contribute the 'chief matter' of corruption – above all, power and

[6] *First Principles* (*CW*), 24.
[7] Ibid., 23–4.
[8] Ibid., 24.
[9] Ibid., 24.

money – to the corrupter general, who distributes those resources among the representatives.[10] As people continue to elect immoral representatives who cooperate with the corrupter general, the security of the subject many continues to be sacrificed, and the greatest happiness of the greatest number never becomes the concern of the government. Worse still, blinded by prejudice and false expectation, the people remain unaware of their critical situation.[11] And so 'it is that exposure to corruption is of the very essence of the representative system. It is of the very essence of a Representative Democracy'.[12] Bentham goes on: 'To found, to establish, any such mixt Monarchy is therefore to establish Corruption – to establish it, and even by law: to establish any such Representative Democracy is to establish Corruption, to establish it even by law: in this respect, between a Representative Democracy and a mixt Monarchy with a Representative body in it there is no difference.'[13]

For Bentham, the merit of representative democracy is not that it is incorruptible but that it institutionalizes arrangements capable of preventing the tendency towards corruption. For example, democratic arrangements instil moral aptitude into functionaries as well as secure the publicity of governmental affairs, both of which can afford security to the people against corrupt governments. A mixed monarchy, by contrast, is not equipped with such arrangements. Thus, the corruption of democracy can be prevented and its pernicious effects neutralized by political arrangements, whereas the corruption of monarchy usually ends in the extreme: either the monarch becomes an absolute monarch or the government is abolished by the people infuriated by its corruption.[14]

6.2 The Identification of Interests and Social Convention

For Bentham, the prevention of corruption does not end with the establishment of a democratic regime. Instead, the rulers in a democracy,

[10] Ibid., 19–20, 24.

[11] As Bentham states in *Constitutional Code*: 'Here, as elsewhere, let it never be out of mind—it is not so much by the actual receipt of these objects of desire that the corruptedness is produced, as by the eventual expectation of them: for, by the receipt in one instance, it is not produced any otherwise than in so far as receipt is necessary to engender and keep alive expectation in other instances.' See *Constitutional Code: I* (*CW*), 77.

[12] *First Principles* (*CW*), 25–6.

[13] Ibid., 26.

[14] Ibid.

like monarchs and aristocrats, have strong motives to corrupt political society. Bentham observes that:

> No man ought to be presumed actually guilty to the purpose of judicial punishment: every man ought to be presumed disposed to be guilty and endeavouring to be guilty to the purpose of legislative enactment: every man, and most of all he who, having it most in his power to be guilty, and most assured of being guilty with impunity, has the strongest propensity to be guilty, and at the same time is most vehement in his assurance that in his breast no such propensity has place.[15]

Bentham's analysis of political evil is insightful because it incorporates the dynamic processes of politics. He is fully aware that corruption is always possible, and the significance of a democratic constitution, as he depicts it in *Constitutional Code*, is not merely to restrict the evil intention of politicians but also to instruct the people to remain cautious about the threat of corruption.[16]

The dynamic nature of Bentham's constitutional theory is also reflected in his view that the identification of interests is a multilevel practice. The tendency of democracy towards corruption means that establishing a democratic constitution does not guarantee that the identification of interests will be achieved. On the contrary, the significance of having a democratic constitution, according to Bentham, is that it structures the government and distributes political power in a way that makes it possible to prevent political evil. Of course, the recognition of political evil is a pillar of classical liberalism and a tradition that Bentham inherits from John Locke, insofar as they both regard political evil as inherent in politics and locate its remedy in the empowerment of civil society.[17] For Locke, a society is empowered when its members are aware of their mission of self-preservation; of their right to enjoy property; of their duties derived from their familial, social, and political relations; and of their right to elect representatives and, if necessary, to resist tyranny.[18] For Bentham, by comparison, the empowerment of civil society is accomplished first by the identification of interests among the possessors

[15] Ibid., 15.

[16] For more on the tendency of democracy towards corruption, see F. Rosen, *Jeremy Bentham and Representative Democracy: A Study of the Constitutional Code* (Oxford: Clarendon Press, 1983), ch. 2.

[17] For an elaboration on that theme, see F. Rosen, *Classical Utilitarianism from Hume to Mill* (London: Routledge, 2003), 19–20, 54, 239–40, 254–5.

[18] J. Locke, 'Second Treatise of Government', in *Two Treatises of Government*, ed. P. Laslett (Cambridge University Press, 1988), 267–428.

of constitutive power and second by the identification of interests between those with constitutive power and those with operative power. Only when those elements are in place can constitutive power be an effective counterforce to operative power.

It is worth noting that, for Bentham, the practice of the identification of interests occurs at two levels, if not more: 'The course most conducive to this identification of interests on the occasion of the establishment of the supreme constitutive power is one thing: the course most conducive to this same end on the occasion of the establishment of the supreme operative power is another thing.'[19] In Bentham's view, the interests of those with the supreme constitutive power should be made identical to the universal interest, and the intervention of law is not necessary to force those with constitutive power to pursue the general interest. In that case, the aggregate of their individual interests is the universal interest. Thus, Bentham contends, 'the constitutive power therefore can not be placed in any other set of individuals so aptly as in that set of individuals of the aggregate of whose several individual interests the universal interest is constituted'.[20] However, the interests of the possessors of operative power – that is, the interests of the ruling few – are not identical to the universal interest but in conflict with it. Bentham states:

> For the accomplishment of the universal end in the case of the possessors of the supreme constitutive power, the provision made can not be well-adapted otherwise than in so far as facility is left or given to each individual to make what in his eyes is the best provision possible for his own individual interest: in the case of the possessors of the supreme operative power, unless in so far as the utmost difficulty is opposed to his endeavours to make what in his eyes is the best provision possible for his own individual interest, to the detriment of the interest of the other individuals of that same community, that is to say in so far as mutual incompatibility and competition have place, making provision for his own interests to the detriment of theirs.[21]

The difference between the possessors of constitutive power and the possessors of operative power lies not in their human nature but in their situations. On the topic of human nature, Bentham argues that every human has two kinds of desires: the desire for security against depredation and oppression and the desire to exercise, for their personal

[19] *First Principles* (*CW*), 132.
[20] Ibid., 133.
[21] Ibid., 133–4.

interest, 'depredation and oppression to an indeterminate amount at the expence of all other men without distinction, and in particular at the expence of his fellow-citizens'.[22] He indicates that both of those desires – the desire for security and the desire for depredation – are inherent in human nature. However, the advantage of the possessors of operative power is that they simultaneously possess instruments to gratify their sinister desire. Thus equipped, they recognize that, with incorporeal and corporeal instruments at their disposal, they can bribe the representatives and corrupt the public. In this way, those who hold executive power form a league of sinister interests with the representatives that not only legislates to secure their sinister interests but also subverts public morality. In turn, the subject many will cast their votes for candidates who promise to gratify their desire of depredation:

> If it were possible, each constituent would cause to be chosen such a Candidate as would sacrifice the interests of all the constituents to his: each Candidate, his own personal interests and connections out of the question, rather than not succeed, [would] engage himself to that same constituent to make that same sinister sacrifice, and, rather than not have his vote and interest in the next Election, perform that engagement.[23]

As a consequence, civil society becomes composed of individuals who seek to gratify their desire of depredation and support candidates who are most likely to represent their sinister interests. Such a society is too weak to resist the arbitrary power of the ruling few, however, and constitutive power becomes enslaved by operative power. In that way, the rulers have their desires for both security and depredation gratified, whereas the people's desire for depredation is gratified at the expense of their security.

Similar to functionaries, the possessors of constitutive power seek to gratify their desires for security and depredation; however, they cannot secure cooperation to gratify their sinister desires for two reasons. First, because every individual's particular interest is at odds with that of every other, it is difficult for any individual to muster support from others who have contrasting interests. Second, unlike the possessors of operative power, the possessors of constitutive power lack instruments to bribe or intimidate and thus do not anticipate gratifying their sinister desires by restructuring their relations with others – that is, by converting competitors into allies, similar to the way in which the executive power

22 Ibid., 214.
23 Ibid., 135.

leagues with the legislature. Due to those limitations, the possessors of constitutive power redirect their efforts towards promoting their share in the universal interest, for in this respect 'each man finds all others in general disposed to become co-operators and supporters'.[24] As Bentham explains:

> What follows is – that having no expectation of promoting by his vote that particular and sinister interest which either is peculiar to himself, or can not be shared in with him but by a comparative few, he restricts his endeavours to the employing of it in giving support to his share in the universal interest: to that interest which finds in every other voter an interest by which he is urged to contribute his endeavours towards the accomplishment of that same all-comprehensive and universally beneficial end: he gives his vote to that Candidate whom by all means taken together he expects to find willing and able to contribute in a greater degree than any other to the accomplishment of it.[25]

Accordingly, the universal interest is not only the aggregate of electors' interests but also the interest collectively shared by electors, which can be identified through the dynamic processes of politics and social interactions.

From that dynamic, at least three features of Bentham's constitutional theory can be derived. First, the difference between the ruling few and the subject many is not that the former are naturally evil and the latter naturally naïve. After all, the rulers and the people both have the propensity to seek the sinister sacrifice. Instead, the difference is that the rulers are endowed with the political power and instruments needed to pursue and realize the sinister sacrifice, whereas the people are not. On that account, Bentham demonstrates that tension and conflicts of interest forever exist between the rulers and the people as well as among the people as a whole. Moreover, the conflict between the rulers and the people is not necessarily more intensive than the conflict among the people, because, as mentioned, the rulers have corporeal and incorporeal instruments at their disposal to delude the people and prevent the people from opposing the rulers' pursuit of their sinister interest. That strategy of the rulers is an expedient one, not because they are prepared to share the sinister interest with the people but because it will destroy the

[24] Ibid., 213. However, Michael James argues that those limitations would be conquered by a sinister coalition of group interests; see M. James, 'Public Interest and Majority Rule in Bentham's Democratic Theory', *Political Theory* 9 (1981), 49–64.

[25] *First Principles* (*CW*), 214.

people's mutual trust and undermine social unity. For the rulers, it also reduces the threat of social criticism against their sinister sacrifice and reverses the ideal structure of the distribution of power by subordinating constitutive power to the possessors of operative power: 'To this purpose it will be their [i.e., the rulers'] constant aim to preserve and increase abuses by which this, their sinister interest, is promoted, [and] to prevent every improvement by which it may be thwarted – thence to give currency to whatsoever notions tend to reconcile men to this sacrifice, or to prevent their seeing it.'[26]

In discussing the means to accomplish good government, Bentham underscores the need for those governing to be inclined to make the government good. However, because the affection of self-regard is the strongest affection, as Bentham supposes, in his conception of human nature, such an inclination will likely not grow spontaneously in the functionaries. Therefore, constitutional law should be so arranged as to render the rulers dependent on the people: 'In as far as a man who has power is independent, his inclination will be [to] make use of it for his own benefit: in as far as he is dependent upon any one, he will find himself obliged to employ it for the benefit of him on whom he depends.'[27]

Second, seeking the 'convergent interests'[28] of members of society involves a long, iterative process of social interaction. After all, an individual cannot identify which part of his interest aligns with the interests of others and which part is in opposition, without first learning from social experience. That dynamic suggests that the progress of social life is the accumulation of social experience from which individuals can learn to identify the general interest of the society. In that process of socialization, as individuals learn to differentiate their particular interest from the interest that they share with others, they also learn that, in some circumstances, certain individuals are indeed willing to lend them support, whereas in others such support is not available. In time, the universal interest of the society becomes explicit to its members, as do the particular interests of individuals. In Bentham's account of the identification of

[26] J. Bentham, 'A Table of the Springs of Action', in *Deontology together with a Table of the Springs of Action and the Article on Utilitarianism*, ed. A. Goldworth (Oxford: Clarendon Press, 1983 [*CW*]), 5–115, at 65.

[27] J. Bentham, 'Appendix A: Division of Power', in *Rights, Representation, and Reform: Nonsense upon Stilts and Other Writings on the French Revolution*, ed. P. Schofield, C. P. Watkin, and C. Blamires (Oxford: Clarendon Press, 2002 [*CW*]), 405–18, at 415.

[28] That concept is used by Postema. See G. J. Postema, *Utility, Publicity, and Law: Essays on Bentham's Moral and Legal Philosophy* (Oxford University Press, 2019), ch. 6.

interests, he seems to place individuals in a situation akin to the prisoner's dilemma: either they choose to cooperate with others in securing their common interest or they choose to strive for their particular interest and ultimately suffer from the resistance of others. In that situation, the choice of cooperating with others seems to be the rational one. In a society, once that consensus is formed, individuals learn not only to cooperate with each other in securing their common interest but also to respect each other's personal security and property. Beyond that, they learn to defend each other when facing common threats, whether from burglars or foreign enemies. We might call that consensus and the social practices derived from it a social convention.[29]

Third, such a convention enables the identification of people's interests upon the establishment of the supreme constitutive power. As mentioned, the course most conducive to one's personal interest is to cooperate with others for the sake of security. Even though that option is rational, individuals are liable to occasionally make irrational decisions. Put differently, although pursuing the universal interest is the most beneficial pursuit for all and, as such, for each individual, sinister interest may be so alluring that some individuals are willing to sacrifice the universal interest in exchange for it. In that case, if enough members of society cannot resist the allure of sinister interest, then a social convention will likely not arise, and if it does nonetheless, it will be ineffective due to its frequent violation. Accordingly, to preserve the general interest, a social convention should thus be preserved, an undertaking that may be achieved by distinguishing those individuals who are 'better disposed' to cooperate from those who are vulnerable to the temptation of the sinister interest. Nevertheless, Bentham rejects making that distinction and instead argues:

> So far then as regards the supreme constitutive power, that which the legislator has to do is – not the taking men by selection and rendering the aggregate of their individual interests in a state of identification with relation to the universal interest, but the taking at once that class of individuals the aggregate of whose interests constitutes the universal interest – the taking those individuals belonging to this all-comprehensive groupe, and lodging the power in their hands.[30]

[29] For an elaboration on the significant role of convention in Bentham's thought, see G. J. Postema, *Bentham and the Common Law Tradition*, 2nd ed, (Oxford University Press, 2019), ch. 5.

[30] *First Principles* (*CW*), 133.

This argument suggests that the practice of the identification of interests with relation to constitutive power occurs and is maintained spontaneously among citizens. Therefore, the legislature's intervention is unnecessary.

What the legislature should do, however, is distribute political power to the general members of society and allow them to identify society's best interests. Furthermore, Bentham's argument suggests that the process of social interaction sufficiently motivates people not only to establish a convention but also abide by it. Even though some members of society, tempted by their sinister interest, may occasionally take advantage of others' contributions to social security, they would be exceptions to the rule and, as such, not undermine the social convention.[31]

However, the course most conducive to the identification of interests on the occasion of the establishment of operative power differs from a social convention starkly. Bentham states:

> But in contact with the sharers in the supreme Operative power to place a functionary with money and money's worth at his disposal, that is to say placing within reach of the Legislative functionary good gifts at the disposal of the Chief Executive functionary, is to plant in the Constitution the seeds of corruptive influence: which influence, unless the most anxious precautions be taken, will sooner or later, as surely as flesh made putrid by summer heat, prevail and render the Chief Executive functionary, be he who he may, and the majority of the possessors of the supreme Operative power, accomplices with one another in the betraying of their trust.[32]

Bentham's observation demonstrates that, with political power and resources at hand, the ruling few in democracy are liable to bring their sinister design into effect. An effective way to prevent that outcome is to empower civil society with a constitutional code that allows the subject many to be the 'limitative power' of operative power.[33] In that light,

[31] Whereas Harrison suggests that Bentham avoids dealing with the problem of free riders, Bentham also seems to solve the problem by convention as described here. See R. Harrison, *Bentham* (London: Routledge and Kegan Paul, 1983), 235. For recent discussions on whether Bentham favours the natural or artificial identification of interests, see P. Schofield, 'Bentham on the Identification of Interests', *Utilitas* 8 (1996), 223–34; and F. Ferraro, 'Moral Aptitude and the Moral Sanction in Bentham's Institutional Architecture: Is There Any Room for Non-egoistic Motivation?', *Philosophy and Public Issues–Filosofia E Questioni Pubbliche* 1 (2011), 11–9.

[32] *First Principles* (*CW*), 42.

[33] Ibid., 134.

Bentham's *Constitutional Code* can be seen as a means of empowering the public by means of both a democratic system and publicity.[34] For that reason, albeit aware of democracy's tendency towards corruption, Bentham considers representative democracy as the antidote to corruption. Thus, in reference to Bentham's account of corruption, Philip Schofield has argued that, 'though a representative democracy, like a mixed monarchy, contained a representative body which was equally liable to corruption, in this case by the president, the difference was that in the representative democracy effective securities against corruption were capable of being instituted'.[35]

For Bentham, democracy is a polity capable of defending itself from the threat of corruption as long as utilitarian guidance is secured for it. A good example is Bentham's *Constitutional Code*, in which corruption is prevented by the constitutional arrangements developed on the core values of Bentham's utilitarian political theory such as publicity, accountability, and political empowerment. The league of sinister interests is always ready to corrupt political society, and the intention of the ruling few to delude the subject many and conceal corruptive transactions from the oversight of the possessors of constitutive power never ceases. It is also undeniable that, under the influence of delusion and the temptation of sinister interest, some individuals will become corrupt and abandon security for an illusory interest. However, the norms embedded in social convention and the political arrangements offered by Bentham's *Constitutional Code* are meant to maximize official aptitude and minimize official power and expense. Those arrangements, as well as public space for open, free discussion, and critical judgement provided by, for example, Bentham's notion of the Public Opinion Tribunal, can help to maintain the dynamic equilibrium between constitutive power and operative power. The former has to be empowered, while the latter has to be confined 'within the limits corresponding to the universal end'.[36] Otherwise, the identification of interests will be overturned, such that sinister interests prevail and the people's security is undermined.

[34] Therefore, it is misleading to argue that Bentham neglects the people's power and the critical character of publicity in his constitutional theory; see S. Splichal, 'Bentham, Kant, and the Right to Communicate', *Critical Review* 15 (2003), 285–305, at 292.

[35] P. Schofield, *Utility and Democracy: The Political Thought of Jeremy Bentham* (Oxford University Press, 2006), 291.

[36] *First Principles* (*CW*), 134.

6.3 Constitutional Arrangements and the Prevention of Corruption

Understanding how Bentham deploys constitutional arrangements to prevent political corruption requires reviewing his *Constitutional Code*, a work that captures his mature thought on the subject. In Chapter VII of *Constitutional Code*, Bentham provides an inaugural declaration for elected legislators. Although the possessors of operative power, legislators stand for the people's interest and are expected to speak for the public as their agents in the government. As candidates for office, they are also pivotal to the process of the identification of interests, because to earn people's votes, each needs to persuade their respective electors that they will defend the shared interests of the constituency. Bentham posits that the electoral system also motivates electors as well as candidates to both identify their mutual interest in security and abandon the pursuit of sinister sacrifice, for electors prefer part of their interests to be represented instead of none. Meanwhile, candidates will have no means to win the majority of votes other than by promoting the shared interests of the majority of electors. As a result, the legislature, with each deputy representing the interests of his constituency by means of voting, discussion, and other political arrangements, produces the convergent interests of the country. Thus, Bentham writes:

> In this way, in the instance of each individual such part of the whole mass of his happiness as is not adverse to the happiness of any other individual will be, in so far as depends on the agency of the government, secured to him: the correspondent part of his interest will be provided for: the correspondent part of his desires, of his wishes, will receive its gratification: while all such portions of happiness as he could not be made to enjoy without depriving others of happiness to greater amount will not be given to him.[37]

Bentham goes on to praise representative democracy as 'the perfection of government', for therein 'the identification of interests of rulers taken in the aggregate with that of subjects taken in the aggregate is as compleat as possible'.[38] His argument that 'all rulers should be subjects'[39] thus corresponds with the interpretation developed here, namely, that the possessors of operative power should be subordinate to the possessors of constitutive power by means of constitutional arrangements.

[37] Ibid., 135–6.
[38] Ibid., 136.
[39] Ibid.

In Bentham's constitutional theory, because 'the Supreme Legislature is omnicompetent',[40] if legislators lack appropriate aptitude, then the general interest suffers. In the 'Legislator's Inaugural Declaration', Bentham describes his ideal legislator, who should, for example, appreciate the plurality of fellow citizens in all of their tastes and opinions. That characterization suggests that Bentham's model representative is self-restrained and open-minded and, as such, will not consider his own taste and opinion as the sole standard of legislation: 'By no such means will I ever seek to constitute my opinion the standard of other men's opinions, my taste the standard of other men's tastes.'[41] The ideal legislator is also mindful to prevent the law from being a 'dead letter' or 'cruel snare'.[42] To achieve these ends, the law needs to be kept in a form 'as clear, correct, complete, concise, and compact as possible', one that is open to the inquiry of citizens and forms teaching materials at schools.[43] To promote that undertaking, Bentham's purposes are twofold: to eliminate the public's suspicion of the law by elevating the law's publicity and to enlighten the public by means of legal education.[44]

Not only should the text of the law be explicit and instructive, but justice should also be done equally to all. For the public, because judicial functionaries are the only means through which they can seek redress and security, Bentham's ideal legislator abstains from imposing taxes on judicial services, lest security and redress be denied to members of society who cannot afford judicial services and justice be sold to the rich for the depredation and oppression of the poor. When the public appeals to the law in order to seek security and redress, they abide by the social conventions of the political community in question and, in turn, the principle of utility. Supposing that their interests will not be protected due to the prohibitive taxation, members of the public become cynical about the efficacy of law and consider gratifying their sinister desire at the expense of the universal interest. Such tendencies not only bring about the corruption of democracy but also impair social stability. Thus, Bentham observes that not making justice accessible to all is 'to sell to the rich the means of irresistible and unpunishable aggression, – to deny to

[40] *Constitutional Code: I* (*CW*), 41.
[41] Ibid., 140.
[42] Ibid.
[43] Ibid., 141.
[44] Ibid.

the poor the possibility of self-defence, – to establish oppression, to join in depredation, and to produce by law the evils of anarchy'.[45]

Along with the legislator's public spirit as demonstrated in the inaugural declaration, other political arrangements that preclude the corruption of democracy appear in Bentham's *Constitutional Code*. A good example is Bentham's design of the electoral system. Deploying aptitude as a standard for evaluating the quality of functionaries, Bentham proposes that the longer the term of service, the higher the probability of corruption and moral inaptitude; therefore, the term of service in the legislature should be one year. However, he also realizes that such brief service will not sufficiently prevent corruption. For instance, in its annual election, as the Common Council of the City of London barely enhanced the competition for its posts, the result was 'imbecility, corruption – inaptitude in a word in every shape'.[46] That example suggests that enhancing competition is an effective way to prevent corruption but that enhancing competition means increasing the number of candidates for the offices available. For that reason, Bentham proposes that, after serving for one year, a legislator should be barred from participating in an election until the number of experienced candidates for deputies is increased by two- or threefold.[47] The 'temporary non-relocability system' reveals Bentham's concern for preventing the corruption of representative democracy through moral inaptitude. However, the moral inaptitude of representative democracy originates from the league of sinister interests formed by the executive power as 'Arch-corruptors' and the relocated deputies and leading electors as corruptees. Bentham comments that: 'without non-relocability – and *that* for a term sufficient to present to the Electors two sets at least of competitors, the number of whom, when added together, shall be little or nothing less than the double of that of the situations to be filled, – any supposed opening, for improvement or correction of abuse, will be but illusory'.[48]

At the same time, though limiting the terms of legislators to one year in order to minimize the risk of corruption, Bentham has no intention of downplaying the role of experience in politics. Aware that the newly elected deputies will need time to develop their legislative skills and may potentially abandon good measures, he proposes a 'Continuation

[45] Ibid.
[46] Ibid., 74.
[47] Ibid., 72.
[48] Ibid.

Committee' to compensate for the lack of experience in the legislature. Under the direction of the legislature, the Continuation Committee is composed of seven to twenty-one members elected by legislators before the expiration of their term. Although the members, thus elected not by the public but by the deputies, lack the right to vote, they may exercise the right of speech and make motions, which are indispensable to their chief function: offering counsel based on experience. In that way, the Committee is designed to prevent the delay of policies and the abolition of good measures. Bentham's plan of having the Committee's members determined not by the public but the deputies, who are familiar with the process of legislation and apt to know who is most qualified to exercise 'influence of understanding on understanding' in supporting new deputies,[49] reveals his respect for knowledge and experience in legislation.

To further address Bentham's concern for preventing corruption, the 'temporary non-relocability system' also affords the benefit of empowering society by broadening the paths for citizens to participate in elections and acquire political knowledge. In Bentham's words,

> Another reason that pleads in favour of non-reeligibility is the advantage that will accrue to the aggregate of the public mind by the perpetual infusion made of a fresh stock of political knowledge and experience into the aggregate mass of the population .. . . The advantage which the bulk of the population may be expected to reap in the article of moral character and conduct from such diffusion of political knowledge and the habit of attention to political subjects is neither less important nor less manifest than in the article of intellectual vigour.[50]

It is conceivable that the temporary non-relocability system will weaken the influence of politicians by restricting them from re-entering elections for a certain number of years. Moreover, along with the diffusion of political knowledge and experience among social members, more of the opinions and interests of civil society are infused into the process of legislation and into law themselves. This democratization of the political system will encourage more citizens to compete for the posts and cultivate their active aptitude. In this way, Bentham's temporary non-relocability system not only prevents corruption but also stimulates citizens to participate in politics. As a case in point, if electors ever have to choose between a candidate who has served in the legislature and a

[49] Ibid., 71.

[50] *First Principles* (*CW*), 140–1.

candidate who has not, then they will have to consider the conduct of the candidates in determining which one has the aptitude to appropriately represent the constituency's convergent interests. This process will not only regulate the candidates, supposing that they plan to compete for the posts again, but also stimulate the electors and the public to pay close attention to politics. More broadly, it preserves the security of the public by preventing corruption and by expanding political knowledge and the public spirit of civil society. As Gerald Postema has summarized, 'Bentham sought not merely to make governmental actions of all kinds transparent, but also to encourage, enable, educate, and empower the Public Opinion Tribunal's oversight of governmental actions.'[51]

In Bentham's design, the temporary non-relocability system also applies to the election of the prime minister, elected by the legislature for a four-year term and not again eligible for election until the number of competing candidates multiplies by two or three.[52] In electing the prime minister, legislators vote twice: once in secret and once in public. When the results are declared, if the majority has favoured a different candidate in each poll, then the person who secured the majority of votes in the public poll becomes the prime minister. In proposing the system, Bentham acknowledges the respective strengths and weaknesses of the two modes of voting. The strength of voting in secret, on the one hand, is that legislators are free from the influence and pressure of their colleagues and the candidates. What it cannot guarantee, however, is that legislators will not sell their votes for candidates who will pursue their particular interests. On the other hand, although open voting exposes legislators to the pressure of candidates and colleagues alike, it also allows the superintendence of the Public Opinion Tribunal over the process to secure the general interest. As experience accumulates, Bentham believes that the legislature and the public will be able to decide which mode of voting most benefits the general interest.[53]

Another indication of Bentham's concern for the corruption of democracy is his proposed arrangement of official documents. In *Constitutional Code*, significant space is devoted to discussing the importance of developing a system of official documentation and a system for managing public property. To Bentham, all of these arrangements – for instance, the registration system and the statistic function – are indispensable to

[51] Postema, *Utility, Publicity and Law*, 272.
[52] *Constitutional Code: I (CW)*, 156.
[53] Ibid., 158–9.

democracy as well as have political implications. For one, they keep the records of all governmental operations faithfully and are open to the inquiry of the public and the legislature, which expands the publicity of the government and subordinates the administrative department to the superintendence of the legislature. For another, to foretell the future, in Bentham's view, one needs to examine the past. By analogy, to avoid making similar mistakes in governance, the ministers need to study the historical records of the government: 'the more clear, correct, and complete, the information possessed by them, under the several appropriate heads, the greater the probability of their preventing the like losses in the future'.[54] Thus, from Bentham's perspective, publicity is the soul of justice,[55] and when the government is more open to the inquiry and criticism of the people, the more unlikely it is to hide sinister sacrifice from the Public Opinion Tribunal. In short, maximizing publicity maximizes the appropriate aptitude of functionaries and thus the prevention of corruption and the preservation of people's security. As David Lieberman has remarked: 'What made codification, for Bentham, such a powerful tool for the advancement of public happiness was not simply the substantive rules that comprised the content of the law. Of equal importance was the code's distinctive function and strengths as an instrument of communication and publicity.'[56]

Bentham also recommends that ministers keep 'loss books' to keep track of the losses of various public properties in administrative proceedings, whether lost by accident, want of adequate attention, embezzlement, theft, or other cause.[57] Although acknowledging that the causes and authors of losses may be difficult to ascertain, the records of the losses can offer sufficient evidence to 'produce and warrant *censure*, or at least *tutelary suspicion*, at the hands of the *Public Opinion Tribunal*' of the suspected authors, even if insufficient for legally convicting them.[58] In that way, to prevent the corruption of democracy, Bentham relies on both the legal and the moral sanction, and when the lack of evidence renders the legal sanction ineffective, the moral sanction can serve to criticize officials who deviate from the principle of utility. The moral

[54] Ibid., 219.

[55] Postema, *Utility, Publicity and Law*, ch. 12.

[56] D. Lieberman, 'Bentham's Jurisprudence and Democratic Theory: An Alternative to Hart's Approach', in *Bentham's Theory of Law and Public Opinion*, ed. X. Zhai and M. Quinn(Cambridge University Press, 2014), 119–42, at 138.

[57] *Constitutional Code: I* (*CW*), 224–5.

[58] Ibid., 225.

sanction stems from the conventions underlying civil society that shape people's idea of justice, such that functionaries suspected of violating that idea fall into disrepute even if they can evade legal punishment.

Aside from the Public Opinion Tribunal, Bentham promotes a system of accountability within the structure of the government. Arguing that functionaries should be held accountable to their superordinates and to the public and that every office should thus be single-seated, Bentham proposes an arrangement capable of preventing functionaries from shifting their responsibilities. In this context, he recognizes that the need for accountability justifies hierarchy and admits that 'correspondent and concomitant to subordinateness is *accountableness*', which 'supposes correspondent *powers* or *rights* on the part of the *superordinate*'.[59] Even so, Bentham is also aware that the division of grades or degrees in the administrative department will inevitably generate 'complication, delay, vexation, and expense', all of which, he argues, strongly favour corruption. Therefore, he indicates that 'unless for special and preponderant need, – between the grade occupied by the functionary by whom the course of operation is carried on, and the Minister of the Subdepartment, establish no intermediate grade'.[60] An example of that prescription is the legislation minister, whose subordinates will include only writing clerks and his deputy. By contrast, the sub-departments with the most complex hierarchies are those of the military. Even though Bentham does not deny the need of subordination in the military, he refers to the relative simplicity of subordination-grades in American military as an example, in order to criticize that how the redundancy of grades in the British military creates unnecessary costs. In that way, Bentham seeks to strike a balance between the accountability of the government and the prevention of corruption. Because the division of grades is necessary in some sub-departments, one means to reduce government expenditure is to lower the pay of superordinates, for whom power, Bentham argues, will incentivise them to labour, whereas subordinates, without any power, labour only for money. Thus, the emoluments of writing clerks should exceed those of their superordinates.[61]

To establish the accountability of the government, it is equally important to ensure transparency in the circulation of official information.

[59] Ibid., 206–7.
[60] Ibid., 214.
[61] Ibid., 207, 214.

As Lieberman puts it, 'publicity and transparency became the steady drum-beat of government routines'.[62] Whereas the registration system is useful in forming a database of official information, the publication system facilitates the circulation of information between different departments and sub-departments.[63] Meanwhile, the 'officially informative function' is meant to supplement the gap in the system of communication, such that information not registered or circulated in time can be requested by legislators or other functionaries in the administrative department.[64] The democratic implication of the officially informative system is that it prevents the administrative department from evading the superintendence of the legislature. As Bentham observes, 'in English practice, no such all-comprehensive or generally-comprehensive system of appropriate information-furnishing, from the Administrative authorities to the Legislature, has place'.[65] In the English government, the result was that the party in office, in order to avoid the legislature's censure, often refused to supply the information requested.[66] For a solution, Bentham proposes that the officially informative function will overcome information asymmetry between the legislature and the administrative department. In this way, the officially informative function enhances the accountability of the administrative department to the legislature and curbs corruption.

6.4 The Public Opinion Tribunal and Political Empowerment

For Bentham, delusion should be excluded not only from the legislature by means of its officially informative function but also from the minds of the people. As discussed above, in the process of corrupting democracy, the corrupter general and the representatives will endeavour to distort social morality and undermine people's understanding by delusion, which is the most efficient way of maintaining the structure of political corruption – that is, the preponderance of the possessors of operative power over the possessors of constitutive power. Bentham writes: 'Delusion, by means of false lights, – and the encouragement given for

62 Lieberman, 'Bentham's Jurisprudence and Democratic Theory', 140.

63 *Constitutional Code: I (CW)*, 162–8.

64 Ibid., 285. Cf. L. J. Hume, *Bentham and Bureaucracy* (Cambridge University Press, 1981), 235.

65 Ibid., 288.

66 Ibid., 288–9.

the reception of them by the application of the matter of reward in the character of matter of corruption, – are the principal means employed for preventing the *subject many* from endeavouring to substitute a form of Government favourable, to one, hostile, to their interests.'[67] To eliminate the influence of these 'false lights' is to enlighten and empower the people and, in turn, safeguard the subject many from the deception of the ruling few and motivate them to criticise the sinister sacrifice. While convergent interests are to be pursued, the sinister sacrifice is to be prevented by the pressure of public opinion imposed upon government officials. This dynamic shows that Bentham's constitutional theory requires, on the one hand, the political structure of representative democracy and, on the other, an instructional system for the people. Whereas the former is meant to create arrangements to exclude unapt individuals from holding office, the latter is meant to cultivate good citizens by means of arrangements aimed at equipping them with political experience and political knowledge. For example, in Bentham's discussion of the 'publication system', he indicates that it has two dimensions. The internal dimension is for circulating information within the government, whereas the external one is for conveying information to persons without any official relationship with the specific department or office. In that light, external publicity benefits 'mankind at the time in question and all succeeding ones'.[68] This dynamic demonstrates the instructional function of Bentham's *Constitutional Code*: to nourish people with political experience and political knowledge is to strengthen the Public Opinion Tribunal's capacity to judge public affairs according to the principle of utility and to prevent it from being deluded by the ruling few.

The dynamic processes implied by Bentham's constitutional theory feature the Public Opinion Tribunal, because the tension between the ruling few and the subject many continues to influence the judgement of the Public Opinion Tribunal. In describing the Public Opinion Tribunal, he writes, 'to the pernicious exercise of the power of government it is the only check' and that 'able rulers lead it; prudent rulers lead or follow it; foolish rulers disregard it',[69] to which may be added 'pernicious rulers manipulate it'. Although Bentham does not articulate it, he demonstrates that the Public Opinion Tribunal's purpose of checking political evil emerges from its increasingly coming into coincidence with the principle of utility:

[67] Ibid., 362.
[68] Ibid., 166.
[69] Ibid., 36.

> Even at the present stage in the career of civilization, its dictates coincide, on most points, with those of the *greatest happiness principle*; on some, however, it still deviates from them: but, as its deviations have all along been less and less numerous, and less wide, sooner or later they will cease to be discernible; aberration will vanish, coincidence will be complete.[70]

Parallel with Bentham's view on representative democracy, the Public Opinion Tribunal is not incorruptible. The reason that Bentham defends both of them is that, compared with other polities, representative democracy and the Public Opinion Tribunal converge on the principle of utility 'in so far as the conception entertained by the several Members in relation to their respective interests is correct'.[71] That implies that both representative democracy and the Public Opinion Tribunal should, and have great potential to, fulfil the greatest happiness of the greatest number, even if it requires an intricate process of social interaction and political empowerment.[72] In that process, because the threat of corruption is not precluded, representative democracy and the Public Opinion Tribunal need to be empowered to resist delusion and the temptation of sinister interest. For that reason, Bentham recommends a legal status for the Public Opinion Tribunal, even though its function is to dispense the moral sanction: 'Public Opinion may be considered as a system of law, emanating from the body of the people.'[73] For Bentham, the strength of the Public Opinion Tribunal, unlike the legal sanction, lies in that it 'neither is, nor ought to be, nor can be, fettered, by those formalities [i.e., the legal formalities of trials]'.[74]

However, the Public Opinion Tribunal is not without its challenges, and Bentham's analytical framework for examining corruption illuminates the dynamics of the Public Opinion Tribunal when conceived as being composed of two sections: the Democratical and the Aristocratical.[75] At root, the interests of the two sections are opposed. Whereas members of the Aristocratical Section want to maximize the depredation and oppression of the subject many, members of the Democratical Section desire their minimization. In short, the former

[70] Ibid.

[71] *First Principles* (*CW*), 68.

[72] For a psychological account of empowerment, see L. Cattaneo and A. Chapman, 'The Process of Empowerment: A Model for Use in Research and Practice', *American Psychologist* 65 (2010), 646–59.

[73] *Constitutional Code: I* (*CW*), 36.

[74] Ibid., 36, 134n.

[75] *First Principles* (*CW*), 68.

desires the 'right of doing wrong',[76] whereas the latter desires justice. Bentham acknowledges that their opposition of interests is due to their different situations. One is more exposed to the temptation of sinister interest, whereas the other is not; one has instruments to conduct the sinister sacrifice that the other lacks. As a consequence, in terms of moral aptitude, the Democratical Section is superior, although Bentham also recognizes that the Aristocratical Section is superior in intellectual aptitude: 'The judgment of the Democratical Section has many errors in it: it has some that are common to it and the Aristocratical Section: it has some which are peculiar to itself. But in proportion as it becomes more and more mature, it becomes more and more conformable to the universal interest.'[77] For that reason, Bentham argues that, in forming juries, a single member of the Aristocratical Section, as opposed to two members of the Democratical Section, is sufficient to fulfilling the function of improving the intellectual aptitude of the Democratical Section. In the development of democracy, the deficient intellectual aptitude of the Democratical Section will be improved gradually, at which time the demand for aristocratic assistance will decrease.

In short, Bentham's constitutional theory is concerned with securing a political structure for democracy to grow and mature. It takes experience for people to form and remain faithful to convergent interests; it takes knowledge and judgement for them to eliminate prejudice and delusion; it takes public spirit for them to communicate political information and pay attention to public affairs; and it takes time, effort, and precautions for people to acquire those properties and for democracy to mature. In that light, Bentham's aim is to secure a utilitarian foundation for democracy, while it is the people's choice whether or not to adopt it.

[76] Ibid., 74.
[77] Ibid., 76.

7

The People's 'Greatest Misfortune' and 'All the Chance the People Have'

Bentham on the Separation of Powers

XIAOBO ZHAI*

7.1 Introduction

A bill of rights and the separation of powers have widely been accepted as two basic safeguards of constitutional liberty.[1] Bentham, however, denounces both notions as nonsense. His criticism of the discourse of entrenched and inalienable rights is well-known and has been fully discussed.[2] In contrast, his discussion of the principle of the separation of powers has not been as fully treated as it deserves. The conventional view is that Bentham in his constitutional design rejects the separation of powers and advocates instead the principle of the dependence of the governors on the governed and a supreme, omni-competent, and unicameral legislature.[3] However, this view of Bentham's position is imprecise and incomplete for at least two reasons. First, the phrase

* Many thanks to Philip Schofield for his comments and suggestions on an early version of this chapter.

[1] J. Rawls, *A Theory of Justice* (Cambridge, MA: Harvard University Press, 1999), 197, 201.

[2] P. Schofield, 'A Defence of Jeremy Bentham's Critique of Natural Rights', in *Bentham's Theory of Law and Public Opinion*, ed. X. Zhai and M. Quinn (Cambridge: Cambridge University Press, 2014), 208–30; 'Jeremy Bentham's "Nonsense upon Stilts"', *Utilitas* 15 (2003), 1–26; G. Postema, *Utility, Publicity, and Law: Essays on Bentham's Moral and Legal Philosophy* (Oxford: Oxford University Press, 2019), 221–46; H. A. Bedau, '"Anarchical Fallacies": Bentham's Attack on Human Rights', *Human Rights Quarterly* 22 (2000), 261–79; H. L. A. Hart, *Essays on Bentham* (Oxford: Oxford University Press, 1982), 79–104; W. L. Twining, 'The Contemporary Significance of Bentham's Anarchical Fallacies', *Archiv fur Rechts-und Sozialphilosophie* 61 (1975), 325–56.

[3] E. Halevy, *The Growth of Philosophic Radicalism*, trans. M. Morris (London: Faber & Faber, 1934), 403–12; M. J. C. Vile, *Constitutionalism and the Separation of Powers* (Indianapolis: Liberty Fund, 1998), 123–4; F. Rosen, *Bentham, Byron, and Greece: Constitutionalism, Nationalism, and Early Liberal Political Thought* (Oxford: Oxford University Press, 1992), 41–58, 80–4; P. Schofield, *Utility and Democracy: The Political Thought of Jeremy Bentham* (Oxford: Oxford University Press, 2006), 94, 232–40.

'the separation of powers' was ambiguous. Bentham accepts the separation of powers in some forms and rejects it in others. Second, Bentham's rejection of the separation of powers in certain forms is conditional, not outright: he admits that it might be useful and necessary in real politics.[4]

This chapter aims to provide a more precise, complete, and thereby more faithful account of Bentham's thought on the separation of powers. Before I proceed with this account, some terminological clarification is necessary.

First, the notion of the separation of powers has been historically associated with that of the mixed or balanced government, which says that power should be shared among different classes. The mixed or balanced government has to be predicated upon, or operate through, some version of the separation of powers, namely, the separation between different government organs, because different classes have to be represented by different institutions, whether the Monarch, the House of Lords, and the House of Commons, on the one hand, or the executive, the judicial, and the legislative, on the other hand. Bentham says that 'the phrase – balance of power, supposes division of power, and expresses a modification of it'.[5] However, these two notions are logically distinct.[6] Bentham has criticized the view that the British Constitution is matchless because it is mixed or balanced.[7] My concern in this chapter is not his thought on mixed government per se: otherwise, this chapter would be a discussion of his theory of monarchy, aristocracy, and democracy. My focus is the separation of powers as a principle of constitutional organization, even though it is not free from class bias.

[4] Halevy (*Philosophic Radicalism*, 413), Vile (*The Separation of Powers*, 125–6), and Schofield (*Utility and Democracy*, 236, 280) are aware that there is a place in Bentham's constitutional design for the division of power in some form, but they only mention this point in passing.

[5] J. Bentham, *Constitutional Code: Book I*, in *The Works of Jeremy Bentham*, ed. J Bowring, 11 vols. (Edinburgh: William Tait, 1843) ix, 1–145, at 123. This text is one of the major sources for my discussion in this chapter. It was edited by Richard Doane, who says: 'The MSS. of this part of the work were very voluminous, having been written at various times between the years 1818 and 1830 . . .. The plan adopted in arranging and classifying them in the present order, was, – to incorporate into one chapter all that related to the same subject-matter.'

[6] Vile, *The Separation of Powers*, 37.

[7] J. Bentham, *A Comment on the Commentaries and A Fragment on Government*, ed. J. H. Burns and H. L. A. Hart (London: Athlone Press, 1977 [*CW*]), 461–73; J. Bentham, *First Principles Preparatory to Constitutional Code*, ed. P. Schofield (Oxford: Clarendon Press, 1989 [*CW*]), 206–10; also Schofield, *Utility and Democracy*, 238.

Second, Bentham's use of terms regarding the separation of powers is unfortunately very loose. His preferred term is 'the division of power', which he uses interchangeably with 'the separation of powers'.[8] He also uses 'the division of power' in a specific sense, denoting two ways of power distribution: '1st. by dividing it into three different branches, and giving each body a different branch; or [2nd.] by keeping it in one mass, and requiring the concurrence of each of the three bodies in every instance of its exercise.'[9] Schofield calls the first 'the separation of powers' and the second 'the balance of powers'.[10] By 'the balance of powers', Bentham means sometimes the balanced government as a class theory of powers[11] and sometimes 'checks and balances' as a constitutional theory of the organization of powers.[12]

In this chapter, I will not strictly follow Bentham's terminology. The phrase 'the separation of powers' in common use carries various significations, including but not exhausted by Bentham's 'division', 'separation', and 'balance' of powers. There are six versions of separation of powers discussed in Bentham's writings. Section 7.2 presents Bentham's theory of the functional separation of power, according to which political power can be distinguished into four basic functions, that is, legislative, judicial, administrative, and constitutive; in contrast to the constitutive function, the former three are operative functions. Section 7.3 shows why Bentham rejects a strict separation of powers. Section 7.4 discusses Bentham's notions of temporary and simple fractionization, and explains why he welcomes simple fractionization of the supreme constitutive power and the legislative power, but opposes simple fractionization of the executive power. Section 7.5 offers an account of the separation of powers that Bentham embraces in his constitutional design, which can be characterized as a division of labour based on popular sovereignty together with legislative supremacy. Section 7.6 is a reconstruction of Bentham's theory

[8] For example, Bentham composed in 1789 a fragment with the marginal heading of 'Division of Power', criticizing the French's separation of powers. When ridiculing 'the separation of powers' in art. 16 of the French Declaration of Rights in his famous 'Nonsense upon Stilts' written in 1795, Bentham used the words 'divide' to refer to 'separation'. See J. Bentham, *Rights, Representation, and Reform: Nonsense upon Stilts and other Writings on the French Revolution*, ed. P. Schofield, C. Pease-Watkin, and C. Blamires (Oxford: Clarendon Press, 2002 [*CW*]), lxv, xlvi, 373, 405–18. See also Bentham, *Constitutional Code*, ix. 123.

[9] Bentham, *Rights, Representation, and Reform* (*CW*), 410.

[10] Schofield, *Utility and Democracy*, 232, 235.

[11] Bentham, *Comment/Fragment* (*CW*), 461–73; *First Principles* (*CW*), 206–10.

[12] Bentham, *The Book of Fallacies*, in Bowring, ii. 445–7.

of checks and balances, in which I explain why Bentham says that checks and balances is the people's 'greatest misfortune', on the one hand, and 'all the chance the people have', on the other hand.

7.2 Functional Separation

One of the meanings of the separation of powers is that political power can be and should be distinguished into three main functions, performed in successive phases of governance, that is, legislation, administration, and adjudication, even if all of them are united in one body, and that each of these functions has its own distinctive character or standards of excellence. Power here is treated as a fictitious entity, contrasted to the real entities that possess power, that is, power-holders.[13] I will call this idea 'functional separation'. Only when functional separation is adopted can the exercise of power be articulated and ordered, and the rule of law is made possible; otherwise, the exercise of power would simply be impromptu coercion motivated by caprice.[14]

Bentham clearly thinks that functional separation is possible and desirable. When political power is not so divided, he says, it is autocratic, because the business of government will be carried on 'solely by particular commands', and the exercise of power will be without rule or law.[15] This is illustrated by the lawlessness in many Mahometan countries and in absolute governments.[16] When the power is exercised by rule, it has to be divided into legislative and executive:[17] they are clearly distinguishable from each other and 'in practice do often require to be distinguished'.[18] However, the terms are 'vague and obscure':[19] 'To describe accurately the limits between the legislative and executive powers', Bentham says, 'is a task the most novel and the most arduous', the accomplishment of which

[13] Bentham, *Comment/Fragment* (*CW*), 476.

[14] See J. Waldron, *Political Political Theory* (Cambridge, MA: Harvard University Press, 2016), 62–70.

[15] J. Bentham, *An Introduction to the Principles of Morals and Legislation* (*IPML*), ed. J. H. Burns and H. L. A. Hart (London: The Athlone Press, 1970 [*CW*]) 263; J. Bentham, *Preparatory Principles*, ed. D. G. Long and P. Schofield (Oxford: Oxford University Press, 2016), 108, 216.

[16] J. Bentham, *The Limits of the Penal Branch of Jurisprudence*, ed. P. Schofield (Oxford: Clarendon Press, 2010 [*CW*]), 162. Bentham, *Preparatory Principles*, 107, 109, 216.

[17] Bentham, *IPML* (*CW*), 263–4n. Also Bentham, *Rights, Representation, and Reform* (*CW*), 407.

[18] Bentham, *Preparatory Principles*, 109.

[19] Bentham, 'General View of a Complete Code of Laws', in Bowring, iii. 198.

is 'a great thing'.[20] In his view, the former has for its object classes of actions, things, and persons, and it is the power of imposing permanent 'obligations of all sorts upon persons in sorts for actions in sorts', whereas the latter has for its object 'individual actions'.[21] The legislative power 'as such of itself reaches no man .... It can only direct, and point out, sorts of persons as objects for punishment. It cannot punish any person'.[22] Executive power, by appointing individuals, fills up the sorts or classes marked out by legislative power. The difference here concerns the nature of power as a fictitious entity, not the person or body exercising power. A single person or body may exercise both powers, but they are still different powers.[23]

Executive power gives execution and effect to legislative ordinances.[24] Bentham considers judicial power to be a branch of executive power,[25] which is characterized by two features. First, a judicial authority can only issue a command on the ground of an act already done contrary to some pre-existing law, whether real or fictitious. Second, judicial execution or application of law takes place 'in the case of a contest between two or more parties in respect to the point of right' and at the request of some party. A judicial order can be general, and the duration of it indefinite.[26]

The other branch of executive power is the administrative.[27] Bentham sometimes uses 'executive' and 'administrative' interchangeably. In *Projet of a Constitutional Code* of 1789, he hesitated as to whether judicial power can be called executive,[28] pointing out that legislative and judicial power admit of 'the most simple and precise' description, while executive power can be defined as 'whatever branch of power is not included under one of the two other great divisions'.[29] The executive here is in fact the administrative. Administrative power is the power of applying law to

[20] Bentham, *Preparatory Principles*, 207. For a brief discussion of this subject, see P. Schofield, 'Jeremy Bentham', in *Constitutions and the Classics*, ed. D. J. Galligan (Oxford: Oxford University Press, 2014), 246.

[21] Bentham, *Preparatory Principles*, 103, 208, 259; also Bentham, *First Principles* (*CW*), 6; *Limits* (*CW*), 5; 'General View of a Complete Code of Laws', 198–9.

[22] Bentham, *Preparatory Principles*, 206.

[23] Ibid., 295; 103; also 205–6.

[24] Bentham, *First Principles* (*CW*), 6.

[25] Bentham, *Preparatory Principles*, 104, 207.

[26] Ibid., 63, 65, 179, 219; *Limits* (*CW*), 27; *First Principles* (*CW*), 7; 'General View of a Complete Code of Laws', 198–9.

[27] Bentham, *First Principles* (*CW*), 6.

[28] Bentham, *Rights, Representation, and Reform* (*CW*), 253, 405.

[29] Ibid., 253. See also Schofield, *Utility and Democracy*, 232.

dispose of things and personal services for the service of the state.[30] A measure of administration is temporary and undurable.[31]

Blackstone identifies the supreme legislative power with the sovereign power.[32] Bentham disagrees and points out that executive power, by its nature, is not necessarily subordinate to legislative power: 'It is as easy to form an idea of a Power Legislative, and a Power merely Executive exerting a supremacy over that, as what we are most accustomed to see actually exemplified, a Power Executive acting under the direction of a Legislature.' Bentham here has introduced a further bifurcation of executive power: the former type of executive power, that is, 'a power *merely* executive', or a power of 'issuing commands concerning individual actions *only*' (emphasis mine), can be called 'pure executive power', whereas the latter can be called 'applied executive power', which is the power to apply general legislative provisions to particular objects, and is thereby subordinate. A pure Executive power can be the Supreme power in the State, as a Legislative power can. A typical example of 'pure executive power' is the autocratic executive power, which, as discussed above, is exercised without rule. However, 'a Legislative [power] can never be the lowest in a chain of Public Powers. It must always have an Executive to carry . . . it's general commands into effect'.[33]

Bentham no doubt thinks that the three functions – even if they are possessed by one person or body – should be divided and exercised methodically. A functional division, in Bentham's view, can prevent partiality both in legislation and in its execution.[34] Self-binding laws are possible only when a functional division obtains. Bentham detests common law and denounces it as dog-law. The reason is that under common law, the functions of law-making and adjudicating are not separated. People, under common law, are not guided by pre-existing laws and are punished, without warning, after having done what judges dislike. They are treated like dogs: 'when your dog does anything you want to break him of, you wait till he does it, and then beat him for it'.[35] This is

[30] Bentham, *First Principles* (*CW*), 6.
[31] Bentham, *Limits* (*CW*), 26.
[32] W. Blackstone, *Commentaries on the Laws of England* (Oxford: Clarendon Press, 1765), 49.
[33] Bentham, *Preparatory Principles*, 107–9, also 210.
[34] Ibid., 296.
[35] Bentham, 'Truth versus Ashhurst', in Bowring, v. 235.

perhaps what Montesquieu means by 'arbitrary power'.[36] In a word, Bentham believes that a functional separation of power is necessary to the ideal of the rule of law. Otherwise, people will be ruled autocratically.

Apart from the above tripartite functional division of power, Bentham introduces the distinction between operative and constitutive power: comprising the legislative, administrative, and judicial powers, the former is the power 'in the exercise of which the business [is] done', including the power to issue directions to subjects, to punish and reward them, whereas the latter is the power to locate and dislocate, 'by the exercise of which it is determined who the person or persons are by whom the operative power shall be exercised': it does not '[take] direct and particular cognizance of that which requires to be done'.[37] This bifurcation of power later became one of the conceptual foundations of Bentham's constitutional design.

7.3 Strict Separation

Bentham embraces a functional separation of power. However, he rejects the strict organizational division of power, which means that functionally separate powers are lodged in hands 'totally separate and distinct'[38] and 'perfectly independent'.[39] M. J. C Vile has offered the following description of a strict separation of powers:

> the government [is] divided into three branches or departments, the legislature, the executive, and the judiciary. To each of these three branches there is a corresponding identifiable function of government, legislative, executive, or judicial. Each branch of the government must be confined to the exercise of its own function and not allowed to encroach upon the functions of the other branches. Furthermore, the persons who compose these three agencies of government must be kept separate and distinct, no individual being allowed to be at the same time a member of more than one branch.[40]

36 Montesquieu, *The Spirit of the Laws*, ed. A. M. Cohler, B. C. Miller, and H. S. Stone (Cambridge: Cambridge University Press, 1989), 157.

37 Bentham, *First Principles* (*CW*), 6; See also Bentham, *Constitutional Code* (*CW*), vol. I, ed. F. Rosen and J. H. Burns (Oxford: Oxford University Press, 1983), 26; Bentham, *Securities against Misrule and Other Constitutional Writings for Tripoli and Greece*, ed. P Schofield (Oxford: Clarendon Press, 1990 [*CW*]), 226.

38 Madison's phrase, see A. Hamilton, J. Jay, and J. Madison, *The Federalist*, ed. G. W. Carey and J. McClellan (Indianapolis: Liberty Fund, 2001), 250.

39 Bentham, *Rights, Representation, and Reform* (*CW*), 373, also 406, 410–1. Schofield, *Utility and Democracy*, 235.

40 Vile, *The Separation of Powers*, 14.

Bentham clearly rejects these notions. He does not accept that 'division of power is the only safeguard of constitutional liberty, the only efficient cause of good government . . .. The more the power is divided . . . the more the liberty'. On the contrary, he says that strict separation of powers is 'nonsense' and 'no more at variance with reason than it is with practice and with itself'. He condemns it as a 'thick confusion and gross error in theory', the consequence of which will be 'frequent and pernicious errors in practice'.[41]

First, Bentham argues that the purpose of the executive and the judicial powers is to give execution and effect to legislative ordinances. Strict separation will make this entirely impossible.[42]

Second, some union of any two powers is necessary to the normal operation of government and does not lead to despotism or the arbitrary exercise of power, as mistakenly claimed by supporters of strict separation.[43] Bentham even suggests that lodging in the same hand different branches of power will not by itself result in despotism or the arbitrary exercise of power.[44]

Third, the principle of strict separation of powers had been 'repeatedly violated in practice. It would have been rather extraordinary if they had not: for without violating them no government can be carried on'.[45] 'It is certain', he notes again, 'that each of these three bodies has exercised and does exercise, and that without dispute, those which are commonly spoken of as being the peculiar functions of the other two'.[46]

7.4 Fractionization

In Bentham's view, the possible modes of power-holding are either integral or fractional: 'integral where the power is all in *one hand*; fractional where in divers, not acting but in conjunction'.[47] Fractionization of power concerns the allocation of different functions or branches of power to different persons or bodies. Bentham disapproves of the integral mode of power-holding and dismisses it as

[41] Bentham, *Rights, Representation, and Reform* (*CW*), 406–7.
[42] Bentham, *Constitutional Code*, in Bowring, ix. 123–4.
[43] See Rosen, *Bentham, Byron, and Greece*, 53.
[44] Bentham, *Rights, Representation, and Reform* (*CW*), 405–6.
[45] Ibid., 406.
[46] Bentham, *Preparatory Principles*, 207, and also 103; Bentham, *Comment/Fragment* (*CW*), 464.
[47] Bentham, *First Principles* (*CW*), 7–8.

'primitive'.[48] To effect the identity of interests between rulers and subjects, and to remove obstacles to the greatest happiness of the greatest number, the possessors of the supreme operative power must be rendered punishable for any abuse of power, which in Bentham's view requires fractionizing the power, that is, breaking it into fractions and lodging them in 'more hands than one'.[49]

Bentham explicitly discusses two types of fractionization: simple and complex. However, there is in his writings a third type of fractionization, which can be called temporal fractionization. It refers to the arrangement by means of which the supreme operative power – which by nature cannot be punished by any power simultaneously existing with it – is made punishable by the succeeding supreme operative power.[50] This type of punibility, Bentham suggests, guarantees that the holders of the previous supreme operative power are subordinate to 'the functionaries sharing in the supreme constitutive power'.[51]

The fractional mode of power-holding that Bentham explicitly discusses is either simple or complex. It is simple 'where it is only among one set of functionaries acting together in a body that the power is divided: so that to give validity to an act of [the power] . . . nothing more is required than the concurrence of a majority of that same body'.[52] Examples of simple fractionization of power include popular elections and unicameral legislatures.[53]

Bentham argues that, first, the supreme constitutive power should be fractionized in the simple mode, so that the power be given to those whose interest it is that happiness be maximized: this arrangement is intended to enhance the appropriate moral aptitude of the supreme constitutive functionaries.[54]

Second, the legislative power should be fractionized in the simple mode. Bentham thinks that if the whole of the operative power were lodged in the hands of a single individual, that individual would possess 'absolute power'. The counterforce provided by the people's constitutive power 'would be plainly insufficient', because this power is normally dormant,

[48] J. Bentham, *Theory of Legislation*, trans. from the French of Etienne Dumont by R. Hildreth (London: Kegan Paul, Trench, Trubner & Co., 1896), 449.

[49] Bentham, *First Principles* (*CW*), 238.

[50] Ibid.

[51] Ibid., 31.

[52] Ibid., 7–8.

[53] Ibid., 8; *Constitutional Code* (*CW*), 25.

[54] Bentham, *Constitutional Code* (*CW*), 21; *Theory of Legislation*, 450.

and the people are clumsy when they occasionally exercise this power: absolute power thereby tends to and may easily persist forever. As a remedy against this type of absolutism, Bentham suggests that the supreme legislative power be 'shared among a multitude of individuals', that is, be simply fractionized: each member of the legislative assembly being elected by a single constituent district.[55] Moreover, the simple fractionization of the legislative power will help to ensure that its exercise is all-comprehensive and continuous, deliberative and rational, benefiting from debate, supported with reasons and checked by the public, and thereby democratic – that is, representative of the population as a whole.[56]

The executive power, including the judicial, however, must be located in a single hand, in order to secure responsibility, maximize the appropriate moral aptitude of the power-holders, and minimize complication and expence.[57] Bentham calls this the principle of single-seatedness. In contrast, the simple fractionization of power produces many-seatedness.[58] Bentham points out that the greater the number of judges that adjudicate a case, the more likely they will deviate from the law: 'the probability of good judicature is everywhere not directly, but inversely, as the number of the judges. Few moral rules have ever received so full a proof from experience'.[59]

Single-seatedness promotes responsibility, whereas many-seatedness leads to blame-shifting: everybody's business is nobody's business. This logic applies equally to Bentham's legislative assembly: as Madison contends, 'being at once exempt from the restraint of an individual responsibility for the acts of the body . . . unauthorized measures would of course be more freely hazarded, than where the executive department is administered by a single hand, or by a few hands'.[60] It is perplexing that Bentham does not address this problem of responsibility regarding his many-seated supreme legislature. Perhaps he thinks that the subordination of the legislature to the people (including annual elections), the publicity of its proceedings, debates and voting, and the public opinion tribunal, will help to reduce the irresponsibility of the many-seated legislature.[61]

55 Bentham, *First Principles* (*CW*), 36–7.
56 Ibid., 120, 238; *Constitutional Code* (*CW*), 28
57 Bentham, *First Principles* (*CW*), 40, 118; *Securities against Misrule* (*CW*), 242, 245.
58 Bentham, *Constitutional Code* (*CW*), 28; see Schofield, *Utility and Democracy*, 296.
59 *Securities against Misrule* (*CW*), 245.
60 *The Federalist*, 260.
61 For Bentham on public voting, see *Political Tactics* (*CW*), 147; see also A. Vermeule, 'Open-Secret Voting', in *Secrecy and Publicity in Votes and Debates*, ed. J. Elster (Cambridge: Cambridge University Press, 2015), 217–8.

7.5 Separation of Powers as Division of Labour

Bentham rejects strict separation, but he does not oppose dividing power into different branches and allocating them to different bodies: 'division ought not to result in *separate* and *independent* powers; for that would bring on a state of anarchy'.[62] 'Not separate' means that a partial mixture or a blending of agency between them is necessary; and 'not independent' means that checks between them are necessary, which presupposes some degree of agency sharing.

Bentham occasionally says that all power in one individual will not lead to despotism or tyranny if that individual is entirely dependent upon the people.[63] However, this kind of comment serves mainly for polemical purposes, rather than to express Bentham's considered position. As mentioned above, he claims that to place all power in one hand is a 'primitive' arrangement. In his constitutional design, Bentham does not concentrate different powers in one hand or one body. He believes that the division and dispersal of power into different bodies and the minimization of power are precautions against the abuses of authority[64] – that the difference between free and despotic government turns on the manner in which the supreme power is *distributed* among the several ranks of sharers in it.[65]

Powers that are divided but not separate or independent can be connected through either a chain of dependence or co-ordinate checks and balances: the latter Bentham terms complex fractionization. Bentham on the whole prefers the former and rejects the latter. This section discusses the form of the separation of powers that Bentham embraces, which flows from his philosophy of constitutional design.

7.5.1 *Bentham's Philosophy of Constitutional Design*

The major propositions of Bentham's philosophy of constitutional design are as follows:

(1) The principle of utility is the standard of the rightness and wrongness of every action, including the making of a constitution.

[62] Bentham, *Theory of Legislation* (*CW*), 450. Emphasis is mine.
[63] Bentham, *Rights, Representation, and Reform* (*CW*), 410.
[64] Bentham, *Theory of Legislation* (*CW*), 449–50.
[65] Bentham, *Comment/Fragment* (*CW*), 485.

(2) According to the principle of utility, the legitimate end of a constitution is the greatest happiness of the greatest number.[66]

(3) In order to achieve this end, the constitution should maximize the appropriate aptitude of rulers.[67] Aptitude is divided into three branches – moral, intellectual, and active – among which moral aptitude, that is, 'the disposition to contribute, on all occasions and in all ways, to the greatest happiness of the greatest number', is foundational:[68] if deficient, 'the more able the functionary, the more mischievous'.[69]

(4) However, 'the unalterable constitution of human nature' is such that the actual aim of rulers, if their powers are unchecked or independent, is to use their power for private and sinister purposes.[70] The check upon, or the counterforce against, the power of rulers therefore must be maximized, as long as the good which, in the shape of security against misrule, is thus produced by the check, is not exceeded by the evil produced by the defalcation made by it from the quantity of power necessary to enable the holder of the power to render, in the highest degree of perfection, the service expected at his hands.[71]

(5) There are two ways of checking power: either by making its exercise dependent upon the will of the governed or by checking its exercise with another co-ordinate power. Bentham adopts the first, since by this means 'the course prescribed by his [the ruler's] particular interest shall on each occasion coincide, as completely as may be, with that prescribed by his duty: which is as much as to say, with that prescribed by his share in the universal interest'.[72] The core idea of Bentham's constitutional design is the dependence of the governors on the governed: different levels of all officials ought to be connected immediately or indirectly to the people by a chain of dependence or

[66] J. Bentham, 'Leading Principles of a Constitutional Code', in Bowring, ii. 269; *Rights, Representation, and Reform*, 411, 415; *First Principles*, 3. *Constitutional Code* (*CW*), 18–9.

[67] Bentham, *Rights, Representation, and Reform* (*CW*), 415; 'Leading Principles', 272.

[68] Bentham, 'Leading Principles', 273. See also G. Postema, *Bentham and the Common Law Tradition* (Oxford: Clarendon Press, 1986), 360.

[69] 'Leading Principles', 273. See also *Rights, Representation, and Reform* (*CW*), 415–6; *Securities against Misrule* (*CW*), 5; Schofield, *Utility and Democracy*, 274, 279.

[70] Bentham, *Constitutional Code* (*CW*), 20; *Constitutional Code*, Bowring, ix. 62.

[71] Bentham, 'Elements of the Art of Packing', in Bowring, v. 69.

[72] Bentham, 'Leading Principles', 273.

subordination.[73] Any circumstance that contributes to the dependence of rulers on the people is to be welcomed:[74]

> In as far as a man who has power is independent, his inclination will be [to] make use of it for his own benefit: in as far as he is dependent upon any one, he will find himself obliged to employ it for the benefit of him on whom he depends. In this there is no jargon, no obscurity. It is founded on the universal, necessary, undisputed and not even to be lamented, property in human nature – the predominance of the self-regarding affections over the social.[75]

Bentham, therefore, argues that every official or power-holder should be dependent immediately or indirectly upon the people: otherwise, he will be in 'a state of incontestable and implacable hostility with the interest and greatest happiness of the greatest number of the members of which the community is composed'.[76] His office is a waste; he will act to promote his sinister interest at the expense of the greatest happiness.[77]

(6) To make rulers dependent upon subjects, the constitution must place the supreme constitutive power in the hands of subjects, whose interest and will it is that the universal happiness be maximized.[78] It is 'the interest of all' that the supreme constitutive power of subjects be maximized.[79] To give supreme constitutive power to subjects is the foundation of popular sovereignty:[80] 'The sovereignty is in the people. It is reserved by and to them. It is exercised, by the exercise of the Constitutive authority', Bentham stipulates in *Constitutional Code*.[81] In relation to the people's supreme constitutive power or sovereignty, all other powers should be subordinate,[82]

[73] Ibid., 270.

[74] Bentham, *Rights, Representation, and Reform* (*CW*), 408, 409, 415; *Securities against Misrule* (*CW*), 226–7.

[75] Bentham, *Rights, Representation, and Reform* (*CW*), 415. See also Schofield, *Utility and Democracy*, 279.

[76] Bentham, *Securities against Misrule* (*CW*), 252–3.

[77] Bentham, *Rights, Representation, and Reform* (*CW*), 407, 415.

[78] Bentham, *First Principles* (*CW*), 407–9; 'Leading Principles', 273; *Constitutional Code* (*CW*), 21; *Constitutional Code*, in Bowring, ix. 107. See also Schofield, *Utility and Democracy*, 235; Halévy, *Philosophic Radicalism*, 411, 416.

[79] Bentham, *First Principles* (*CW*), 30.

[80] Bentham, *Constitutional Code*, in Bowring, ix. 123; *Securities against Misrule* (*CW*), 240.

[81] Bentham, *Constitutional Code* (*CW*), 25.

[82] Bentham, *First Principles* (*CW*), 6.

the end of which is that 'with greater certainty, and if possible even with greater promptitude, the superior will, and at length the supreme will of all, may in each instance receive execution and effect'.[83] The responsibility of these subordinate powers to the body of the people must be maximized.[84] The people should be enabled to 'put a stop to any measures' they do not like.[85] In Bentham's view, popular sovereignty has two crucial mechanisms. One is the public opinion tribunal, and the other is the hierarchical structure of government based upon virtually universal suffrage.[86]

7.5.2 *The Public Opinion Tribunal*

Despite the fact that it may often be prejudiced,[87] the public opinion tribunal is essential to Bentham's constitutional design. In *Constitutional Code*, Bentham states, 'public opinion may be considered as a system of law, emanating from the body of the people . . .. To the pernicious exercise of the power of government it is the only check'; and 'the Public Opinion Tribunal is to the Supreme Constitutive, what the Judiciary is to the Supreme Legislative'.[88] The public opinion tribunal is made effective by the right and facility of the people to manifest their sentiments, which is made possible by the liberties of speech, assembly, political communication, and the publicity of state proceedings:[89] 'it is on the opportunities possessed by the people of manifesting their will that the freedom of a constitution in reality and immediately depends, and not upon any other circumstance such as that of the division of the general mass of power into three independent branches'.[90] The public opinion tribunal can keep the power of the government and judicature (including judges) in check and on the path of the universal happiness

[83] Bentham, *Securities against Misrule* (*CW*), 227.
[84] Bentham, 'Leading Principles', 273.
[85] Bentham, *First Principles* (*CW*), 409.
[86] Bentham, *Rights, Representation, and Reform* (*CW*), 237; Schofield, *Utility and Democracy*, 233.
[87] M. Quinn, 'Popular Prejudices, Real Pains: What Is the Legislator to Do When the People Err in Assigning Mischief?' in *Bentham's Theory of Law and Public Opinion*, ed. X. Zhai and M. Quinn (Cambridge: Cambridge University Press, 2014), 63–89.
[88] Bentham, *Constitutional Code* (CW), 36, 35; also 54.
[89] Bentham, *First Principles* (*CW*), 408–9; also Schofield, *Utility and Democracy*, 236.
[90] Bentham, *First Principles* (*CW*), 413.

by imposing the popular sanction, either punitive or remunerative, upon officials.[91]

Bentham was highly critical of the British government, but he nonetheless considered it 'the best government in the world after the government of the United States', because the House of Commons, in spite of its many serious vices, 'does constitute a sort of permanent delegation of this tribunal [i.e., of public opinion]', which was able to oblige the government to consider 'freely expressed criticisms and complaints'.[92] Bentham disagreed with Burke on many issues. However, he would have endorsed Burke's view that the public opinion tribunal formed the fourth branch of power.[93]

7.5.3 *The Supreme Operative Power*

The public opinion tribunal is necessary but not sufficient. A democratic and hierarchical structure of government is equally indispensable. Bentham, on the one hand, and Locke and De Lolme, on the other, raise the same question: how to guarantee that 'those who enjoy an exclusive authority . . . seek the advantage of all', and 'those who make the laws . . . make only equitable ones'? The solution of Locke and De Lolme is by subjecting the legislators to laws and 'excluding them from all share in the execution of them'.[94] Bentham's answer is to make legislators dependent upon and responsible to the people by giving the people to the power to locate, dislocate, and punish them.

Bentham's constitution allocates the supreme constitutive power to the people, and the supreme operative power to the supreme legislators. The former has the power of locating (or dislocating) and punishing the latter,[95] which makes the latter dependent upon the former: 'the true and efficient cause and measure of constitutional

91 Bentham, *Constitutional Code*, in Bowring, ix. 41; Bentham, *Securities against Misrule* (*CW*), 251–2.

92 Bentham, *Constitutional Code*, in Bowring, ix. 153; also *Constitutional Code* (*CW*), 25.

93 For Burke's reference of newspapers as the fourth estate, see T. Carlyle, *On Heroes, Hero-Worship and the Heroic in History*, 2nd ed. (London: Chapman and Hall, Strand, 1842), 257–8; see also Bentham, *Constitutional Code*, in Bowring, ix. 43.

94 De Lolme, *The Constitution of England* (1771), ed. D Lieberman (Indianapolis: Liberty Fund, 2007), 192.

95 Bentham, *Rights, Representation, and Reform* (*CW*), 407. The specific arrangement is by allowing the supreme legislators to be punished by 'the next supremely operative body', see *First Principles* (*CW*), 31.

liberty or rather security is the dependence of the possessors of efficient [i.e., operative] power upon the originative [i.e., constitutive] power of the body of the people'.[96]

As to the composition of the legislature, Bentham rejects bicameralism: if both chambers represent the people, one of them is useless and needless, and having two of them only complicates and slows down democratic legislation; if one chamber does not represent the people, it is worse than useless: it is maleficent and has to be abolished.[97] Nevertheless, Bentham thinks that division and disagreement between two legislative chambers is not as destructive of the government as that between legislature, judiciary, and administration: 'if the division, the disagreement and the stoppage which obtains in consequence is confined only in the legislative branch, the business of government may yet go on'.[98] Unicameralism, plus annual elections, the people's right to revoke deputies, and the punibility of the deputies by 'the next supremely operative body', Bentham believes, will together ensure the legislators' dependence upon the people.

In addition to standard law-making power, Bentham suggests that the legislature should exercise the powers of declaring war and making peace, of making treaties, and of 'burthening the Nation with debts': it would be unwise to give these powers to the administrative, since war is 'a well-known door to despotism and every mode of political abuse'; furthermore, a declaration of war, or the signing of a treaty, 'suspends a multitude of rights and powers and revives a multitude of others'.[99]

In a large country, it is 'altogether inexpedient and next to impossible' that the supreme legislature should 'engross to itself the whole business of legislation', and it would be better distribute, either explicitly or implicitly, some legislative power to local legislatures in certain cases, on the condition that the latter are subject to its control.[100]

[96] Bentham, *Rights, Representation, and Reform* (*CW*), 409; 407; also *First Principles* (*CW*), 31.

[97] 'Bentham to his Fellow Citizens of France, on the Houses of Peers and Senates', in Bowring, iv. 420–1; Bentham, *Constitutional Code*, in Bowring, ix. 115–6.

[98] Bentham, *Rights, Representation, and Reform* (*CW*), 411.

[99] Ibid., 253–5. See also Bentham, *Preparatory Principles*, 211; Schofield, *Utility and Democracy*, 233.

[100] Bentham, *Rights, Representation, and Reform* (*CW*), 407.

7.5.4 *The Executive*

The essential function of the executive and judicial branches is 'to give execution and effect' to the will declared by the legislative[101] and thereby indirectly to 'the rightly presumed will of the Constitutive'.[102] In order for this to take place, and as a security for moral aptitude, the functionaries exercising the supreme executive power shall be subject, 'in all the modes of subordination', to those exercising the supreme legislative power.[103]

There are two branches of executive power: the administrative and the judicial. Bentham is unwilling to see that both branches have any power of legislation, or any veto on democratic legislation, because this will put them upon a level with the legislature.[104] As a general principle, the legislature should have dislocative and punitive powers over the executive functionaries.[105] Moreover, if the executive disobeys the legislature, the latter can enforce its mandates by itself assuming some executive power.[106] Bentham's view on the legislative-administrative relationship is very different from that of De Lolme and Madison, who are worried about legislative tyranny and therefore argue for the executive's prerogative of veto on the legislature's power.[107]

Interestingly, Bentham also allows the possessors of the supreme operative power to be 'liable to be dislocated by the possessor of the Supreme Executive power', such as by the power of dissolution or the power to prorogue Parliament. In this way, there will be a 'sort of mutual subjection' between them. Bentham does not think this sort of 'mutual subjection' involves any inconsistency: in both cases, an appeal will be 'ultimately made to the people at large in their character of possessors of the supreme constitutive power', because both the wrong dislocation of the supreme administrative functionaries by the supreme operative functionaries, and the wrong dislocation of the supreme operative functionaries by the supreme administrative functionaries, will be punished by the next ensuing supreme operative functionaries located by the people.

[101] Bentham, *First Principles* (*CW*), 6; *Securities against Misrule*, (*CW*) 224; For the details, see *Constitutional Code* (*CW*), 149–56.
[102] Bentham, *Constitutional Code* (*CW*), 149.
[103] Bentham, *First Principles* (*CW*), 33–4.
[104] Bentham, *Preparatory Principles*, 208; *Rights, Representation, and Reform* (*CW*), 237; *Securities against Misrule* (*CW*), 236.
[105] Bentham, *First Principles* (*CW*), 34–5.
[106] Bentham, *Preparatory Principles*, 206–8.
[107] De Lolme, *The Constitution of England*, 192–3.

The mutual subjection is in fact a design that will guarantee the people as the principal and other authorities as their instruments.[108] This explains why Bentham only considers this power of the administrative 'nominal', because 'the utmost effect of which is the preferring an appeal from one set of deputies chosen by the people to a succeeding set of deputies chosen in like manner'.[109]

'Administrative functionaries are *servants* of the Legislature.'[110] To this end, Bentham suggests that the administrative should be kept at a distance from the legislature. The chief executive functionary is not allowed to have a seat in the legislature or take part in its debates, and he is required to communicate with the legislature by message, which Bentham believes will prevent him from being exposed 'to those angry feelings and imputations of sinister conduct, from which, consistently with the nature of man, and the nature of the case, debates, especially when on political subjects, can seldom be altogether free'.[111]

7.5.5 The Judicial Branch

The judiciary is a branch of the executive, whose right and proper end is twofold. First, its 'main and positive' end is 'giving execution and effect to the laws, whatsoever they may be';[112] in this connection, Bentham agrees with Montesquieu that judges are 'la bouche de la loi'. Second, its 'collateral and negative' end is 'avoidance of all needless delay, expence, and vexation in other shapes: all needless delay is injustice while it lasts'.[113]

Commenting on the 1822 Greek Constitution's provision that 'Le pouvoir judiciaire est indépendant des pouvoirs législatif et exécutif', Bentham says, 'such independence is in direct contrariety with my

[108] Bentham, *First Principles* (*CW*), 35; also Schofield, *Utility and Democracy*, 232–3.

[109] Bentham, *Rights, Representation, and Reform* (*CW*), 407. See Schofield, *Utility and Democracy*, 236. The textual support for Bentham's design of 'mutual subjection' is available in 'Division of power' written in 1789 (in *Rights, Representation, and Reform* [*CW*], 407); and in 'Economy as Applied to Office' written in 1822 (*First Principles* [*CW*], 35). In one of his written comments on an early version of this chapter, Schofield says that Bentham rejected this idea of 'mutual subjection' in *Constitutional Code* written between 1822 and 1832 and that this idea is inconsistent with Bentham's overall democratic constitutional thought.

[110] Bentham, *Constitutional Code* (*CW*), 147–8.

[111] Ibid., 148, 152. See also Vile, *The Separation of Powers*, 126.

[112] Bentham, *Securities against Misrule* (*CW*), 252.

[113] Ibid.

principle of absolute and universal dependence on the supreme power of the whole [i.e., the people]'.[114] An independent court 'is dependent on its own passions and caprice. Independence makes virtue as towards this or that man or body of men: but it is dependence that makes virtue as towards the body of the people'.[115] It must be noted that Bentham's denial of independence to the judiciary does not mean at all that the exercise of judicial power is not autonomous or that the legislature, the administrative, or any other party can interfere with judges' adjudication, which must strictly be carried on according to the law.[116]

Bentham welcomes the separation between the judiciary and the administration. Among the fourteen ministers, only the minister of justice is elected directly by the legislative assembly, whereas the other ministers are nominated by the Prime Minister.[117] Halévy notes,

> too much power would be united in the hands of the Prime Minister if he nominated the minister of justice; he could form a coalition with him to pursue some sinister interest. It is in this way that the whig principle of the separation of powers – separation of the legislative and judicial powers, and separation of the judicial and executive powers – finds a place in Bentham's system.[118]

Bentham does not allow the chief executive functionary any share of judicial power, 'whether in the giving direction to the exercise of that power or in the appointment of the persons by whom it shall be exercised'.[119] He argues that 'on the occasion of an ordinary suit between individual and individual, or between government and individual, any such union of the functions of accuser, judge and executioner, would be incompatible with justice'.[120]

Despite his emphasis on the dependence of the judiciary on the people, Bentham in his mature thought opposes popular election of judges and gives their appointment to the minister of justice but allows them to be displaced by the majority of the electors.[121] He gives the following

114 Ibid., 243.

115 UC li (a). 213, as quoted in Postema, *Bentham and the Common Law Tradition*, 363–4.

116 See Bentham, *Rights, Representation, and Reform* (*CW*), 408; also Schofield, *Utility and Democracy*, 237.

117 Bowring, ix. 609.

118 Halevy, *Philosophic Radicalism*, 413.

119 Schofield, *Utility and Democracy*, 236; also Bentham, *Preparatory Principles*, 7.

120 Bentham, *Constitutional Code*, in Bowring, ix. 42.

121 Bentham, *Securities against Misrule* (*CW*), 245. In his works on the judicial organization for France written in 1789, Bentham endorsed the popular election and dismissal of

reasons for this proposal. First, it helps to secure 'consistency and symmetry' to the plan of giving execution and effect to the law. Second, a judge-candidate must be sufficiently apt: on the one hand, the electors do not have sufficient knowledge of his aptitude beforehand; and on the other, 'for the sake of . . . placing in so desirable a situation a confederate of his own, a leader having influence over the people might be apt to raise ungrounded clamour against a sufficiently apt judge'.[122] Third, if the minister of justice makes a poor choice, he can easily be held responsible.[123] Fourth, after a period of experience, the electors are qualified to decide whether a judge is apt or not.

Bentham is clear throughout that judges should not make laws: they are appointed to enforce obedience to laws, and their duty is to obey laws punctually according to their 'decided meaning'; otherwise they will be dismissed.[124] Judges, Bentham insists, should not be allowed to invalidate laws, except an act of subordinate legislation exceeding its proper scope. First, 'place the disagreement between two of those branches, the legislative and the judicial, everything is in confusion. What the one commands, the other forbids. The citizens knows not whom to obey, nor what to do to be at peace'.[125] Second, this kind of judicial review confers on judges 'a controlling power over the acts of the legislature'. Bentham thinks that this is 'a remedy worse than the disease', in that even an undemocratic legislature is still more democratic than judges appointed solely by the administrative branch.[126]

Bentham is, however, happy to give judges some functions or powers that will in fact place some checks upon the legislature. First, the suspensive power. If a judge in a case thinks 'what the letter of the law imports' is not what the legislature 'would have' meant if they had contemplated the case, he is 'authorised, and even required' to suspend the law and to take measures 'necessary to prevent the happening of any irremediable mischief in either event, whether the legislature abide by the law, or alter it'. In this situation, the judge is required to make a report to the legislature, containing statements of the mischief that would ensue if

district judges, which had already been boldly experimented by the French Comité de Constitution. See Schofield, *Utility and Democracy*, 93, 308.

122 Bentham, *Securities against Misrule* (*CW*), 246.

123 Ibid., 245–6.

124 J. Bentham, 'Draught of a Code for the Organization of the Judicial Establishment', in Bowring, iv. 287; also Schofield, *Utility and Democracy*, 307.

125 Bentham, *Rights, Representation, and Reform* (*CW*), 412.

126 Bentham, *Comment/Fragment* (*CW*), 487–8; also *Securities against Misrule* (*CW*), 236.

the letter of the law were observed, the course provisionally taken by him to avoid such mischief, and the alteration of the law most proper for guarding against the mischief.[127] Bentham also calls this power 'the execution-staying function'.[128] Second, the 'contested-interpretation-reporting function' and the 'eventually-emendative function'. By means of these two functions, judges propose to the legislature interpretations or amendments to the law, which will become valid if no action is taken by the legislature within a certain number of days.[129]

According to Bentham's proposal, judges' power of enforcing the law is checked by the quasi-jury and the public opinion tribunal. The quasi-jury, which attends trials and is composed of 'ever changing' lay members convened from 'the body of the people at large'. It has no power to make decisions but serves as a check upon the power of judges.[130] The quasi-jury represents the public opinion tribunal and is internally adopted into and constitutes part of the legal tribunal.[131] In addition, the power of judges is checked by judicial inspectors, that is, spectators at a trial, who form a sort of sub-committee of the public opinion tribunal.[132] In a word, the judiciary must operate under the eye of the public opinion tribunal,[133] and all this presupposes the publicity of the trial: 'doors of the Judicatory constantly open to all visitants. Structure of it, specially adapted to the giving to the greatest number possible the best accommodation possible': 'in judicature, where there is no publicity, there is no justice'.[134]

7.5.6 *The Extraordinary Exercise of the Supreme Legislative Power*

The most distinctive view of Bentham regarding the relationship between the legislature and the executive (comprising the judicial and administrative) is what he terms 'the extraordinary exercise of the

127 Bentham, 'the Organization of the Judicial Establishment', 287–8.
128 J. Bentham, *Constitutional Code*, in Bowring, ix. 508.
129 Ibid., 502–6. See also Schofield, *Utility and Democracy*, 310–1.
130 Bentham, *Constitutional Code*, in Bowring, ix. 465; 'The Elements of the Art of Packing, as applied to Special Juries, particularly in Cases of Libel Law', in Bowring, v. 67–70; for Bentham's quasi-jury, see Schofield, *Utility and Democracy,* 309; Lieberman, 'Bentham, Courts and Democracy'. See also Section 11.3.
131 Bentham, *Constitutional Code*, in Bowring, ix. 41
132 See T. P. Peardon, 'Bentham's Ideal Republic', *The Canadian Journal of Economics and Political Science* 17, no. 2 (1951), 184–203, at 196.
133 Bentham, *Constitutional Code*, in Bowring, ix. 41–4, 155–60.
134 Bentham, *Securities against Misrule* (*CW*), 251–2.

supreme legislative power': the subordinate executive's alleged 'disobedience, tardiness, inaptitude, or casual and momentary want of time [or information]' may necessitate the dislocation, substitution, or punishment of the delinquents or create the necessity for the supreme legislature to assume to itself the whole or part of the judicial or administrative business or functions.[135] In Bentham's view, the legislature 'may without prejudice to liberty possess a portion of judicial power, even in dernier resort, so long as the members of that supreme body are maintained in strict dependence upon the body of the people'.[136] Otherwise, the authority of the legislature would be 'without execution and effect – it would itself be without efficiency or use'; anarchy would be substituted to government.[137]

7.5.7 Will Bentham's Constitutional Structure Lead to Legislative Tyranny?

A worry about Bentham's overall constitutional structure is that it may lead to legislative tyranny. According to Bentham's design, the legislature is superior to the other branches of government and should not be subject to any institutional limitations. So long as the legislature remains dependent upon the people, 'every idea of specific limitation is big with absurdity and inconvenience'.[138] The legislature can locate and dislocate the members of the other branches, and it can intervene with and even take over the latter's powers if it deems it necessary to do so, which, in Madison's view, amounts to giving the legislature an 'overruling influence' over the other branches of power: by 'the encroaching spirit of power', 'the legislative department is . . . drawing all power into its impetuous vortex . . .. the danger from legislative usurpations, which, by assembling all power in the same hands, must lead to the tyranny'.[139]

One of Bentham's core principles of constitutional design is popular sovereignty. Bentham is frank that the people by nature is divided.[140]

135 Bentham, *First Principles* (*CW*), 7; *Constitutional Code*, in Bowring, ix. 203, 124.

136 Bentham, *Rights, Representation, and Reform*, 409. On the legislature's powers to punish judges, see L. J. Hume, *Bentham and Bureaucracy* (Cambridge: Cambridge University Press, 1981), 117.

137 Bentham, *Constitutional Code*, in Bowring, ix. 124.

138 Bentham, *Rights, Representation, and Reform* (*CW*), 237. Schofield, *Utility and Democracy*, 234.

139 *The Federalist*, 262; also 269.

140 Bentham, *Constitutional Code*, in Bowring, ix. 121.

Due to the conflict of interests among the people, the political power cannot 'be possessed by every individual'.[141] Bentham thinks that the perfect constitution should aim at the greatest happiness of all if the happiness of all can be increased without defalcating the happiness of any, which, however, is unlikely in most instances.[142] Therefore, 'to provide for the greatest felicity of the greatest number, is the utmost that can be done towards the maximization of universal national felicity, in so far as depends on government'.[143] However, it may not be fair to accuse Bentham of tyranny of any kind on the grounds that he advocates the greatest happiness of the greatest number and the rule of the majority. As Halévy asks, 'the question is to know whether the real interest of the majority does command it to destroy or to despoil the minority'.[144] Halévy's answer is that 'a "pure representative democracy" does not necessarily tend to the levelling of fortunes; such was the profound conviction of Bentham and of his disciples'.[145] Bentham often uses the United States of America as an example in this respect.[146] He later regretted his formulation of the principle of utility in terms of 'the greatest number' and worried that it might give a misleading message that his principle of utility would allow sacrificing the happiness of a minority as long as the sacrifice increased that of a majority.[147] Schofield argues that Bentham thinks 'the interest of the majority would not necessarily outweigh the interest of the minority' and that Bentham imposes a high threshold on the sacrifice of the interest of the minority.[148] Other defenders of Bentham claim that the illegitimate sacrifice of the interest of the minority would rarely occur under Bentham's constitution because the interests that Bentham's principle of utility and representative democracy protect and promote are

141 Bentham, *Rights, Representation, and Reform*, 409–10.

142 Bentham, *First Principles*, 3.

143 Bentham, 'Leading Principles', 269; *Rights, Representation, and Reform*, 410.

144 Halevy, *Philosophic Radicalism*, 410.

145 Ibid., 428. See also Schofield, *Utility and Democracy*, 101. M. Quinn, 'Bentham, Democracy, Free Government, and the Relationship between Rulers and Ruled'. See Section 2.5.

146 Bentham, 'Leading Principles', 274.

147 Bentham, *Official Aptitude Maximized; Expense Minimized*, ed. P Schofield (Oxford: Clarendon Press, 1993 [*CW*]), 352; Schofield, *Utility and Democracy*, 39.

148 Schofield, *Utility and Democracy*, 39. See also Schofield, 'Intellectual Aptitude and the General Interest in Bentham's Democratic Thought', 000-000 above, and Quinn, 'Bentham, Democracy, Free Government, and the Relationship between Rulers and Ruled'. See Sections 1.1 and 2.5 respectively.

'exclusively common interests in which all have a stake, like interest in public goods'.[149]

Bentham had read *The Federalist*, which contains Madison'sclassic attack on legislative tyranny and his praise of checks and balances.[150] It is indeed strange that Bentham did not explicitly respond to Madison's discussion of legislative tyranny. Bentham might have thought that legislative tyranny of the majority would be obviated by annual popular elections of the deputies, simple fractionization of the legislative power, public and rational legislative deliberation, and public voting.[151] However, as Madison pointed out, 'as little will it avail us that they are chosen by ourselves',[152] and legislative tyranny certainly will take place

> in a representative republic . . . where the legislative power is exercised by an assembly, which is inspired by a supposed influence over the people, with an intrepid confidence in its own strength; which is sufficiently numerous to feel all the passions which actuate a multitude; yet not so numerous as to be incapable of pursuing the objects of its passions, by means which reason prescribes.[153]

Besides, according to Madison, annual elections will cause instability in government:

> every appeal to the people would carry an implication of some defect in the government, frequent appeals would, in a great measure, deprive the government of that veneration which time bestows on everything, and without which perhaps the wisest and freest governments would not possess the requisite stability.[154]

Madison's solution to legislative tyranny is a government in which 'the powers of government should be so divided and balanced among several bodies of magistracy, as that no one could transcend their legal limits, without being effectually checked and restrained by the others'.[155] This

[149] See Postema, 'Introduction', in *Bentham: Moral, Political and Legal Philosophy*, vol. 1, ed. Postema (Aldershot: Ashgate, 2002), xxx.

[150] See Bentham, *Constitutional Code*, Bowring, ix. 123.

[151] For this purpose, Bentham wrote *The Book of Fallacies*, ed. P. Schofield (Oxford: Clarendon Press, 2015 [*CW*]); and *Political Tactics* (*CW*), ed. M. James, C. Blamires, and C. P. Watkin (Oxford: Clarendon Press, 1999).

[152] *The Federalist*, 258–9.

[153] *The Federalist*, 257. For Madison on passions in politics, see *The Federalist*, 262, 264.

[154] Ibid., 262

[155] Ibid., 295.

type of regime, under Bentham's scheme, is a complex fractionization of power, which he fiercely denounces.

7.6 Checks and Balances

The complex fractionization of power is 'where at different times, to acquire its binding force, an act of the constituted authority must have received the consent [or concurrence] of parties [or bodies] more than one'.[156] It presupposes a partial separation of powers,[157] but it is more than that:[158] the same power is conjunctively possessed or shared by different organs, which together Bentham calls 'the compound aggregate'.[159] The same power being concurrently or conjunctively exercised means that each branch has power that blends in or overlaps with the other and that each branch has some control over, or security against the intrusion of, the other,[160] which further implies that they are co-ordinate and that checks and balances are created between them. The typical examples here are bicameral legislatures, unicameral or bicameral legislatures with executive initiative or veto, and the British model of 'King in Parliament' and the American model of separation of powers.[161]

The principle that checks and balances can promote liberty has been famously and frequently reiterated but rarely well argued. Bentham carries out perhaps the most scathing attack on it, condemning it as confused, delusive, nonsensical, and spurious and false and stating that it is at variance with reason, with practice and with itself.[162]

7.6.1 Bentham's Criticisms of Checks and Balances

Bentham's attacks start with the term 'balance', which he thinks is confusing and indeterminate, and which, applied to the three branches

156 Bentham, *First Principles* (*CW*), 8; *Rights, Representation, and Reform* (*CW*), 410–1.

157 For the meaning of a partial separation of powers, see Vile, *The Separation of Powers*, 20; A. Kavanagh, 'The Constitutional Separation of Powers', in *Philosophical Foundation of Constitutional Law*, ed. D. Dyzenhaus and M. Thorburn (Oxford: Oxford University Press, 2016), 223.

158 Bentham, *Constitutional Code*, in Bowring, ix. 123.

159 Bentham, *First Principles* (*CW*), 11.

160 *The Federalist*, 256.

161 Bentham, *Rights, Representation, and Reform* (*CW*), 405.

162 Ibid., 405–7, 414; *Constitutional Code*, in Bowring, ix. 123; *First Principles*, xxiii.

of power, is denounced by him as nonsense. Balance means 'equipoise', i.e. no-action. The business of government is carried on by a series of actions: once there is no action, 'everything falls to pieces, anarchy takes the place of government',[163] and 'the wheels of government are at a stand'.[164] In this situation, government is impossible: if it goes on again, that is because the division is at an end or got over by despotic manipulation.[165]

Bentham believes that the notion of checks and balances is the result of 'a confused idea of an extended application of the old maxim *divide et impera*: the governed are to have the governors under their governance by having them divided amongst themselves'. He argues, 'a still older maxim is that a house divided against itself cannot stand, and supposing both maxims applied to this one subject, I am inclined to think a truer one'.[166] However, the idea of balance, when applied to international relations, is welcomed by Bentham: in this context, it denotes a legitimate object, that is, rest, peace, and prosperity.[167]

Of checks and balances, 'the only way in which it can produce any effect is by producing and keeping up disagreement: the moment the disagreement ceases, the division answers no purpose'.[168] The different branches of power disagree when their interests conflict. With conflicting interests, each will pursue its own interest: 'each interest a little different from each of the two others, and not only different from but opposite to that of the greatest number of the people'. Each will devour as much as it can of the wealth of the people. However, with checks and balances, each is able to prevent the two others from doing anything. When each endeavours to get more than a certain share of the people's wealth, 'it would find itself counteracted by the two others'. 'Whatsoever is in the judgment of any one of them contrary to its own sinister interest, will not be done.' No abuse will be removed if one of them has an interest in preserving and ability to preserve it, and no improvement will be made if

[163] Bentham, The Book of Fallacies, in Bowring, ii. 446–7; Schofield, Utility and Democracy, 237.

[164] Bentham, *Rights, Representation, and Reform* (*CW*), 411.

[165] Ibid.

[166] Ibid., 373; also Schofield, *Utility and Democracy*, 238; R. Harrison, *Democracy* (London: Routledge, 1995), 102.

[167] Bentham, *The Book of Fallacies*, in Bowring, ii. 447.

[168] Bentham, *Rights, Representation, and Reform* (*CW*), 411.

one of them has an interest to prevent it.[169] This will lead to the tyranny of the minority in favour of no-action or stagnation.[170]

This kind of deadlock is beneficial to no one. In order to get out of it, each, therefore, will have to compromise and so 'permit[s] the two others to get their respective shares, and thus it is that harmony is preserved'.[171] Once the harmony or compromise is achieved among the three branches, checks and balances will have no effect: 'whatsoever measure is by them all seen or supposed to be conducive to the aggregate interest of them all, will be carried into effect, how plainly soever it may be contrary to the universal interest of the people'.[172] Bentham summarizes the real logic of checks and balances as this:

> Let a disagreement arise, all three together can do nothing, and anarchy prevails: let them agree among themselves, they can do any thing: they may carry through any measures, be they ever so disagreeable to the people and ever so destructive. [They may]. . . do what was actually done by [the Roman Triumvirate].[173]

The latter scenario is what Bentham really fears: the despotism that 'consists in the interested alliance of all the officials for the exploitation of the people'.[174]

The degrees of power and influence that the three branches of government (i.e., the legislative, administrative, and judicial bodies) possess respectively with relation to their ultimate conjunct action cannot be exactly the same. One body will be superordinate to the other two if their influence on the conjunct action is inferior to the former's. This means that the above-mentioned harmony between different branches of power will be fragile and temporary, and a sort of subordination of the majority to the minority will then exist between these apparently co-ordinate bodies.[175] Referring to an arrangement similar to the American system of judicial review, and judging from its 'general tendency', Bentham claims that it would bring no benefit to the people. In his eyes, it 'transfer[s] a portion of the supreme power from an assembly which

169 Bentham, *The Book of Fallacies*, in Bowring, ii. 445–7.

170 Bentham, *Rights, Representation, and Reform* (*CW*), 410; Bentham, *The Book of Fallacies*, in Bowring, ii. 445–6; see Schofield, *Utility and Democracy*, 235–8.

171 Bentham, *The Book of Fallacies*, in Bowring, ii. 446.

172 Ibid., 445, also 446–7; Schofield, *Utility and Democracy*, 237.

173 Bentham, *Rights, Representation, and Reform* (*CW*), 412.

174 Halevy, *Philosophic Radicalism*, 408–9.

175 Bentham, *First Principles* (*CW*), 11.

the people have had some share, at least, in chusing, to a set of men in the choice of whom they have not the least imaginable share'.[176]

For Bentham, simplicity is a major virtue of constitutional design:

> only in proportion as it [i.e., the political system] is known and understood in time can it be productive of any good effects it aims at: and in so far as it is unknown to, or not understood by, those whose interest is concerned in the knowing and understanding of it, evil is the sure effect of it.[177]

In contrast, 'complication is a Jungle in which sinister interest has its lurking place'.[178] Taking bicameralism as an example, Bentham argues that checks and balances complicate the political system. First, complication means that the political system is opaque, untransparent, and unintelligible. Complication is sinister, because it conceals the operation of the political system from

> the eye of the people at large in their character of members of the Public Opinion Tribunal: and thus the tutelary counterforce opposed by the popular or moral sanction to excess of force on the part of the political including the legal sanction is diminished: the controul exercised by the people in the character of constituents over those official functionaries in question in the character of their Agents is weakened and rendered less efficient.

Second, complication means 'more bodies, more functionaries, and more expence'.[179] Third, complication, including checks and balances, and the plurality of bodies and functionaries involved in undertaking a task, leads to the diminution of responsibility: people have difficulty finding the person or body whom they can hold to account.[180]

7.6.2 Checks and Balances in Democracies

The above discussion is about checks and balances in general. However, depending upon whether the polity is a democracy, Bentham thinks that checks and balances may have very different consequences on the happiness of the community. If the whole of the supreme power is already in

[176] Bentham, *Comment/Fragment* (*CW*), 487–8.
[177] Bentham, *First Principles* (*CW*), 103.
[178] Ibid., 102.
[179] Ibid., 102–3.
[180] Bentham, *Theory of Legislation* (*CW*), 451. See also H. L. A. Hart, *Essays on Bentham* (Oxford: Oxford University Press, 1982), 73–4.

the hands of the people, and the rulers are already dependent on the will of the people and accountable to them, checks and balances between them, or their quarrelling amongst themselves, is 'the worst misfortune that can happen':[181] no additional security is gained, and all the evils of checks and balances will apply.

(1) If all the branches of power are democratic, and if no disagreement exists between them, checks and balances are pointless. In this situation, one branch of power will be sufficient, and any more results in unnecessary complication and waste.[182]
(2) If there is disagreement between them, and if one branch is democratic, the other two will be either unnecessary or mischievous – serving sinister interests at the expense of the universal interest.
(3) Checks and balances might bring three branches into conflict and an 'equipoise' of no-action will result. To get out of this deadlock, one branch will have to overcome the other two. The design of checks and balances may subject the democratic branch to the aristocratic, such as in the United States of America, where the judicial normally overcomes the Congress and the President. Very often, the deadlock may be broken by some strategic manipulation, which will very likely allow a minority to veto proposals supported by a majority.[183]
(4) Checks and balances will make government inefficient by introducing a great deal of wrangling and quarreling into decision-making and the implementation of measures.[184] Within the framework of checks and balances, a democratic measure (statute, policy, or decision) will have to pass through many barriers before it is finally implemented, which leads to 'factitious delay'.[185]

It might be argued that such a delay is justified on the ground that it can help to stop otherwise pernicious measures from being passed by avoiding hasty actions or by preventing decision-making from 'yield[ing] to the impulse of sudden and violent passions'.[186] Bentham disagrees. For

181 Bentham, *Rights, Representation, and Reform* (*CW*), 417; also *Securities against Misrule* (*CW*), 233–4.
182 Bentham, *First Principles* (*CW*), 101.
183 Bentham, *Rights, Representation, and Reform* (*CW*), 237; Schofield, *Utility and Democracy*, 234.
184 Bentham, *Theory of Legislation* (*CW*), 451; *Rights, Representation, and Reform* (*CW*), 411.
185 Bentham, *First Principles* (*CW*), 107.
186 *The Federalist*, 262.

him, this claim is a 'mere matter of presumption'.[187] Experience shows that bicameralism or checks and balances do not reduce the evil of precipitation. According to Bentham, the evil of precipitation or violent passion is prevented by more informed, rational, ordered, and public deliberation and argument. This is the best guarantee that measures promoting particular interests are put aside and those promoting the universal interest are pursued. Factitious retardation is not the means to achieve the right solution and might have the effect of putting aside both the best and the worst. Even if checks and balances can occasionally prevent evil measures by reducing precipitation and constraining passions in decision-making, the evil of universal delay caused by it remains uncompensated. Without checks and balances or the second chamber or judicial review, the people would have opposed a pernicious measures in the first chamber.[188]

7.6.3 'All the Chance the People Have'

What effect will checks and balances have on the universal interest if the power-holders of the community are not accountable to or dependent upon the people? Bentham's answer is that it will tend to produce benefits to the people:[189] checks and balances are useful and should be welcomed under a non-democratically accountable government, which was the norm in Bentham's time.

If the power-holders are not dependent upon the people, one strong possibility, as already mentioned, is that the sinister interest of the ruling few will unite them and prompt them to co-operate in order to depredate and oppress the subject majority, even if these power-holders belong to apparently different branches.[190] However, this strong possibility is not an inevitability. It may happen that the interests of the different branches of power conflict and that the power-holders disagree with each other: in this context, checks and balances will operate in favour of the people. While the possessors of power are independent of the people and they themselves are in conflict, Bentham claims, a system of checks and

[187] Bentham, *Constitutional Code*, in Bowring, ix. 116.
[188] Bentham, *First Principles* (*CW*), 106–7, 112.
[189] Bentham, *Securities against Misrule* (*CW*), 231.
[190] Bentham, *Rights, Representation, and Reform* (*CW*), 410; *Constitutional Code*, in Bowring, ix. 123.

balances is 'all the chance the people have':[191] 'Though incompatible with the only good form of government, it has at times operated as a palliative, how feeble soever, to the mischief produced by a bad one.'[192] What is the greatest misfortune for a genuinely democratic government, Bentham says, then becomes 'the only chance in favour of good government'.[193]

(1) Checks and balances can weaken bad laws. The more undemocratic or despotic the political practice or government, the weaker and more inefficient its laws should be, according to the principle of utility: checks and balance can weaken bad laws by complication, retardation, and expence[194] and thereby create Montesquieu's 'moderate governments' where 'political liberty is found'.[195]
(2) They can create some dependence of governors upon the people. The principle of checks and balances allows different branches of power to disagree: when in disagreement, they will fight for the obedience or good will of the people; in order to prevail, they may find it necessary to appeal to the people, compete for the people's favour, and the people's opinion will, therefore, not be completely ignored. All this will then have the effect of either establishing some arrangement beneficial to the people, transferring some portion of power to the people, or establishing some kind of dependence of the power-holders upon the people; the people will thereby gain some liberty.[196]

Here Bentham in fact offers in a short passage the constitutional history of England in a nutshell. For example, Magna Carta was the product of this type of contest between King and the Barons, and the Bill of Rights between King and Parliament. This explains, first, according to Bentham, why the English system (i.e., a many-headed despotism) is better than those on the Continent (i.e., single-headed despotisms);[197] second, why Bentham says, 'while the possessors of power remain independent of the people, all the chance the people have is in their

[191] Bentham, *Rights, Representation, and Reform* (*CW*), 417.
[192] Bentham, *Securities against Misrule* (*CW*), 231
[193] Bentham, *Rights, Representation, and Reform* (*CW*), 417.
[194] Bentham, *Securities against Misrule* (*CW*), 230, 233.
[195] Montesquieu, *The Spirit of Laws*, 155.
[196] Bentham, *Rights, Representation, and Reform* (*CW*), 410, 414; 417: 'They may appeal to the people: sow jealousy between them, then perhaps they may court the people . . . only to that dependence of the sharers in power on the people of which the division was but the remote and accidental cause.' Also *Securities against Misrule* (*CW*), 23.
[197] Bentham, *Securities against Misrule* (*CW*), 232–3.

quarrelling: and when there is an end of their quarrel, there is an end of their dependence'.[198]

(3) They can contribute to deliberation in the making of law and public policy. In *Fragment on Government*, when dismissing an arrangement anticipating the American system of judicial review, Bentham adds a proviso: this arrangement can bring on 'a public and authorised debate on the propriety of the law . . .. An opportunity is gained of impressing sentiments unfavourable to it, upon a numerous and attentive audience'. Consequently, it has, 'in general, a tendency to answer, in some sort, the purposes of those who espouse, or profess to espouse, the interests of the people'.[199] In this context, Bentham suggested that checks and balances can lessen the danger of ignorance.[200]

Despite the above merits, Bentham emphasizes that these benefits of checks and balances, or their contribution to the moral and intellectual aptitude of the rulers, are only accidental: they 'can take place without it' and can be 'produced with certainty by other means'. The 'other means' that Bentham has in mind is a representative democracy.[201]

7.7 Conclusion

Vile states, 'for all its inadequacy there is a stubborn quality about the doctrine of the separation of powers. It persistently reappears in *differing forms*, often in the very work of those who see themselves as its most bitter critics'.[202] This statement applies especially to Bentham. Bentham opposes the strict separation of powers, in the same way that many oppose it. His opposition to the separation of powers, however, goes far beyond that. He has been widely regarded as the most bitter critic of the doctrine. He constantly dismissed the value of the division of power among rulers[203] and even made such extreme comments as the following: 'suppose all power vested in the hands of one person . . .: in what respect is Constitutional liberty or security the worse, if things are so ordered

198 Bentham, *Rights, Representation, and Reform* (*CW*), 417.
199 Bentham, *Comment/Fragment* (*CW*), 488.
200 See Halévy, *Philosophic Radicalism*, 145
201 Bentham, *Rights, Representation, and Reform* (*CW*), 414–7.
202 Vile, *The Separation of Powers*, 8.
203 Bentham, *Securities against Misrule* (*CW*), 231.

that this person or persons cannot exercise their power but in conformity to the will of the body of the people?' And no harm to universal happiness will take place, even if all powers are accumulated or lodged 'in the hands of one single man', if 'matters are so ordered, and the general powers given as above are subject to such limitations by pre-established laws, that he cannot prevent the people from manifesting their sentiments to each other as well as to himself in all manners of ways and upon all occasions'.[204]

These dismissive comments should be read with caution, and they are better understood as exaggerations for polemical purposes. I have shown that the doctrine of the separation of powers appears in differing forms in Bentham's work.

(1) He embraces the functional division of power and contributes to it by adding to the traditional tripartite division a new division between constitutive and operative powers.
(2) He adopts temporal fractionization of power and the simple fractionization of the supreme constitutive power and the legislative power.
(3) His constitutional design takes the overall shape of the traditional tripartite division of power. This design, however, first, is based on the principle of popular sovereignty and subject to the scrutiny of a fourth power, namely, the public opinion tribunal. Second, there is a relationship of dependence between the sharers of different and divided operative powers, which, instead of being coordinate, belong to different ranks, and among which the legislative branch is superior to the other branches, and subject to no legal limitations, including those of entrenched basic rights. Third, the administrative and judicial branches will normally operate autonomously, and the judicial branch can even exert some influence on the legislative; however, in extraordinary situations, the legislative branch can intervene and even take over the powers of the administrative and judicial branches. According to Bentham, the legislature possesses what Madison called and opposed 'an overruling influence over the others [the administrative and judicial branches] in the administration of their respective powers'.[205] Fourth, for Bentham, the tripartite distribution of power serves such values as the rule of law, impartiality, and checking the abuse of power; and it

[204] Bentham, *Rights, Representation, and Reform* (*CW*), 410, 412–3.
[205] *The Federalist*, 256.

is required by the scientific division of the labour of government and serves the value of efficiency.[206]

(4) What Bentham really opposes is checks and balances. He denounces the idea as nonsense and argues that it leads to anarchy and the exploitation of the majority by the minority. When the polity is democratic, it will lead to complication, waste, and inefficiency. Bentham nevertheless argues that, when the government is independent of the people, checks and balances may be all the chance that the people have to avoid oppression: it can weaken bad laws, contribute to public deliberation of laws, force the power-holders to appeal to the people and thereby make them dependent upon the people.

Bentham's discussion of the separation of powers is abstract, as he makes clear:

> To place in the clearest light the question on which of the two circumstances the security of the people really depends, on the division and balance of power between the different bodies that compose the government or on the obligation on the part of them all to conform [to] the will of the body of the people, the best expedient is to suppose each of these circumstances to take place in the most perfect degree without any mixture of the other, and see what must be the effect.[207]

Checks and balances are of no use when rulers are completely accountable to the subjects. However, in real politics, neither of the two circumstances takes place 'in the most perfect degree', and real democracies are only democratic to a certain degree, and they can never be perfectly democratic. A real political body is always a mixture of democracy and despotism, which seems to suggest that even in Bentham's eyes, both the principle of dependency and that of the separation of powers are necessary and that there is a necessary role for the principle of checks and balances to play in our actual politics. Bentham would agree that, before we enter the constitutional utopia of complete accountability, some kind of checks and balances is necessary and useful to the greatest happiness. The question is how to integrate both principles into a political system in a particular historical context. In direct democracies, or representative democracies complemented with referendums, the separation of powers will have a limited role. However, the more undemocratic the polity is,

[206] Bentham, *Securities against Misrule* (*CW*), 226–7; Halevy, *Philosophic Radicalism*, 422.
[207] Bentham, *Rights, Representation, and Reform* (*CW*), 412.

the more the separation of powers and checks and balances are needed. Bentham would have no difficulty endorsing Madison's following famous argument:

> In framing a government which is to be administered by men over men, the great difficulty lies in this: you must first enable the government to control the governed; and in the next place oblige it to control itself. A dependence on the people is, no doubt, the primary control on the government; but experience has taught mankind the necessity of auxiliary precautions.[208]

[208] *The Federalist*, 269.

PART II

Law and the Courts

8

Between Constructivism and Immanentism

Bentham's Unsettled Conception of Constitutional Law

GUILLAUME TUSSEAU

8.1 Introduction

No domain of the law seems to have escaped Bentham's reformatory activity. Based on a self-proclaimed 'genius for legislation',[1] his ambition was to create a 'complete body of laws' or a *pannomion*.[2] Within this project, constitutional law especially deserves attention. Bentham was concerned with that domain from the very beginning of his career, which started with a criticism of the philosophy of human rights[3] and the resounding *A Fragment on Government*,[4] and which ended with *Constitutional Code*.[5]

Bentham's suggestions on that matter were ignored by his contemporaries. But his failure from the viewpoint of constitutional politics or, as he called it, censorial jurisprudence,[6] has to be distinguished from an appraisal of his expository jurisprudence, and more specifically of the

[1] J. Bentham, *Memoirs and Correspondence*, in *The Works of Jeremy Bentham*, ed. J. Bowring, 11 vols. (Edinburgh: William Tait, 1838–43), x. 27.

[2] J. Bentham, *An Introduction to the Principles of Morals and Legislation*, ed. J. H. Burns and H. L. A. Hart (London: The Athlone Press, 1970 [*CW*]), 305.

[3] J. Bentham, 'Short Review of the Declaration', in *An Answer to the Declaration of the American Congress*, ed. J. Lind (London: T. Cadell, 1776), 119–32.

[4] J. Bentham, *A Comment on the Commentaries and A Fragment on Government*, ed. J. H. Burns and H. L. A. Hart (London: The Athlone Press, 1977 [*CW*]).

[5] J. Bentham, *Constitutional Code: for the Use of all Nations and all Governments Professing Liberal Opinions*, Vol. 1, ed. F. Rosen. and J. H. Burns (Oxford: Clarendon Press, 1991); J. Bentham, *The Works of Jeremy Bentham*, ed. J. Bowring, 11 vols. (Edinburgh: William Tait, 1838–43), ix.; See also J. Bentham, *First Principles Preparatory to Constitutional Code*, ed. P. Schofield (Oxford: Clarendon Press, 1989 [*CW*]); J. Bentham, *Securities against Misrule and Other Constitutional Writings for Tripoli and Greece*, ed. P. Schofield (Oxford: Clarendon Press, 1990 [*CW*]); J. Bentham, *Official Aptitude Maximized, Expense Minimized*, ed. P. Schofield (Oxford: Clarendon Press, 1993 [*CW*]).

[6] J. Bentham, *A Fragment on Government*, ed. R. Harrison (Cambridge: Cambridge University Press, 1988), 397–8.

type of intellectual tools that he decided to use to conceive, think about, and devise a version of constitutional law that was likely to allow for the utilitarian double ambition of understanding social phenomena and carrying out political reform. On that subject, however, Bentham's writings reveal a certain number of uncertainties, hesitations, and tensions.

One may consider it established that, for Bentham, constitutional law was indeed law,[7] unlike his heir, John Austin, who placed constitutional and international law in the category of 'positive morality'.[8] Bentham's conceptual stance is noteworthy, since he seems to have been the very first author to clearly adopt the idea that the constitution does belong to the legal domain. However, beyond that fundamental position, he seems to have hesitated between two ways of understanding the constitution that opposed one another at the time of the American and French Revolutions.

8.2 Between Constitution and Constitutional Law: Bentham's Assertion

8.2.1 The Conceptual Genealogy of the Constitution

The emergence of the modern concept of the constitution has been studied in many works, which have contributed to highlighting the moving mental world and lexical disorder in which Bentham's thought developed.[9] Before 1600 in Europe, the term 'Constitution' referred, in

[7] G. Tusseau, *Jeremy Bentham et le droit constitutionnel. Une approche de l'utilitarisme juridique* (Paris: L'Harmattan, 2001), 81–173.

[8] J. Austin, 'The Province of Jurisprudence Determined and The Uses of the Study of Jurisprudence[1832]', Intro. H. L. A. Hart, (Cambridge: Hackett, 1998), 12, 140–1, 253–68. See also G. Tusseau, 'Positivist Jurisprudents Confronted: Jeremy Bentham and John Austin on the Concept of a Legal Power', *Revue d'études benthamiennes* 2 (2007), 23–37.

[9] See C. McIlwain, *Constitutionalism: Ancient and Modern* (New York: Cornell University Press, 1947); F. Wormuth, *The Origins of Modern Constitutionalism* (New York: Harper & Row, 1949); M. Fioravanti, *Costituzione* (Bologna: Il Mulino, 1999); G. Stourzh, 'Constitution: Changing Meanings of the Term from the Early Seventeenth to the Late Eighteenth Century', in *Conceptual Change and the Constitution*, ed. T. Ball and J. G. A. Pocock (Lawrence: University Press of Kansas, 1988), 35–54; G. Stourzh, 'Vom aristotelischen zum liberalen Verfassungsbegriff', in *Wege zur Grundrechtsdemokratie: Studien zur Begriffs- und Institutionengeschichte des liberalen Verfassungsstaates* (Wien: Böhlau, 1989), 1–34; G. Maddox, 'Constitution', in *Political Innovation and Conceptual Change*, ed. T. Ball, J. Farr, and R. L. Hanson (Cambridge: Cambridge University Press,

civil law as in canon law, to an imperial decree, the status of a corporation, or an unimportant rule that was not linked to politics. In Germany, a '*Konstitution*' referred, for example, to an act, of whatever degree of importance, promulgated by the Emperor, while the rules governing the exercise of power were called '*leges fundamentales*' and were based on a contractual relationship between the governed and the government. The term 'Constitution' was very broadly used in a metaphorical way to talk about the political body as a human being and to refer to its way of being and its configuration. In England, the dominant use of the word was to account for existing institutions in a descriptive way. Some occurrences of a new meaning, associating the idea of the organization of political power and the idea of fundamental law, emerged in the mid-seventeenth century. In 1643, an anonymous work entitled *Touching the Fundamental Laws, or Politique Constitution of this Kingdom* was published. In 1649, the act of accusation of Charles I reproached him with violating the 'fundamental constitutions' of the kingdom. An official text of 1688, relating to James II's abdication, accused him of 'subverting the constitution of the kingdom'. The use of the expression 'British constitution' in the singular was settled only after the Glorious Revolution and referred to the fundamental rules of the organization of the state. In 1733, Bolingbroke could thus explain that, 'by *Constitution* We mean, whenever We speak with Propriety and Exactness, that Assemblage of Laws, Institutions and Customs, derived from certain fix'd Principles of Reason, directed to certain fix'd Objects of publick Good, that compose the general System, according to which the Community hath agreed to be governed'.[10] The constitution became a reference norm for public life and a criterion of assessment of what a good government should be.[11]

The crisis of the British colonial Empire provided the context for a major conceptual development. The word was used on both sides of the Atlantic with obviously opposite purposes. It progressively took on a liberal content, often called by the malleable name of 'English liberties', then by the idea of human rights. Progressively, the idea crept in that

1989), 50–67; H. Mohnhaupt and D. Grimm, *Verfassung. Zur Geschichte des Begriffs von der Antike bis zur Gegenwart: Zwei Studien, 2e Aufl* (Berlin: Duncker & Humblot, 2002); M. Piccinini, *Corpo politico, opinione pubblica, societa politica. Per una storia dell'idea inglese di costituzione* (Torino: G. Giappichelli, 2007).

[10] H. St. J. Bolingbroke, *A Dissertation upon Parties* (London: R. Francklin) Letter X, 108–9.

[11] Mohnhaupt and Grimm, *Verfassung*, 44-48.

'constitution' was not so much a set of descriptive observations on the current organization of political power as a norm stating in a systematic and exhaustive way how the power of the state ought to be organized and exercised and therefore assuming a sort of supremacy over the other elements of the legal order.[12] The first American dictionary testifies to this conceptual shift.[13] In the entry on 'Constitution', it mentions the following meanings:

> CONSTITUTION, noun
>
> 1. The act of constituting, enacting, establishing, or appointing.
> 2. The state of being; that form of being or peculiar structure and connection of parts which makes or characterizes a system or body. Hence the particular frame or temperament of the human body is called its constitution We speak of a robust or feeble constitution; a cold, phlegmatic, sanguine or irritable constitution We speak of the constitution of the air, or other substance; the constitution of the solar system; the constitution of things.
> 3. The frame or temper of mind, affections or passions.
> 4. The established form of government in a state, kingdom or country; a system of fundamental rules, principles and ordinances for the government of a state or nation. In free states, the constitution is paramount to the statutes or laws enacted by the legislature, limiting and controlling its power; and in the United States, the legislature is created, and its powers designated, by the constitution
> 5. A particular law, ordinance, or regulation, made by the authority of any superior, civil or ecclesiastical; as the constitutions of Justinian and his successors.
> 6. A system of fundamental principles for the government of rational and social beings.
>
> The New Testament is the moral constitution of modern society.[14]

[12] D. Grimm, *Die Zukunft der Verfassung*, (Frankfurt am Main: Suhrkamp, 1991) 101, 106–7. On this argumentative dynamics, see esp. D. J. Hulsebosch, *Constituting Empire: New York and the Transformation of Constitutionalism in the Atlantic World, 1664–1830* (Chapel Hill: The University of North Carolina Press, 2005), 6, 28–32, 42–70.

[13] O. Beaud, 'L'histoire du concept de constitution en France. De la constitution politique à la constitution comme statut juridique de l'Etat', *Jus politicum* (2009), vol. 3, accessible at http://juspoliticum.com/article/L-histoire-du-concept-de-constitution-en-France-De-la-constitution-politique-a-la-constitution-comme-statut-juridique-de-l-Etat-140.html; K. M. Baker, 'Constitution', in *Dictionnaire critique de la Révolution française, t. 3 Institutions et créations*, ed. F. Furet and M. Ozouf (Paris: Flammarion), 179–205; Hulsebosch, *Constituting Empire*, 237, 247; G. Sartori, 'Constitutionalism: A Preliminary Discussion', *The American Political Science Review* 56, no 4 (1962), 859; M. Loughlin, 'Burke on Law, Revolution and Constitution', *Giornale di storia costituzionale* 29 (2015), 49–60.

[14] N. Webster, *American Dictionary of the English Language* (1828), accessible at http://webstersdictionary1828.com/Dictionary/Constitution.

Two lexical changes should be highlighted. First, there was a change from the plural to the singular, which gave *the* constitution a unity that the term 'fundamental laws' did not have. Second, the word 'constitution' is self-sufficient, and there is no need to specify that it is the constitution of the state, of the kingdom, of the government, and so on.[15] As Daniel J. Hulsebosch notes, 'although the term "constitution" developed a broad connotation that outlined political society and, for some, prescribed limits on governmental behavior, the term "constitutional law" was all but unknown in the English-speaking world before the American Revolution'.[16]

8.2.2 *The Legal Nature of Constitutional Law*

Bentham fully participated in the legal and political reflection that led to the development of new meanings of numerous words in the political lexicon. Indeed, he was one of the few authors to make an analysis of the notion of the constitution that was fully internal to the legal field.[17] One of the remarkable characteristics of his legal theory is founded on the assertion that constitutional 'law' is indeed law. According to the definition of law that he gave, the constitution – in the sense of norms applicable to the sovereign in a given political society – can perfectly be subsumed under the generic concept of law, which is itself built upon a stipulative re-elaboration and reorganization of the linguistic uses of his time.[18]

Thus, it is possible to find texts throughout his work in which that fully legal nature is taken for granted. In the 1830 *Constitutional Code*, for example, he stated: 'The constitutional branch of law, is that branch, by which designation is made of that person, or those persons, to whose power it is intended, that on each occasion, the conduct of all the other members of the community in question shall be subjected .... Constitutional law has for its object, security against misrule.'[19]

[15] Beaud, 'L'histoire du concept de constitution en France', 4.

[16] Hulsebosch, *Constituting Empire*, 40. See also D. J. Hulsebosch, 'The Constitution in the Glass Case and Constitutions in Action', *Law and History Review* 16, no. 2 (1998), 397–401.

[17] Tusseau, *Jeremy Bentham et le droit constitutionnel*, 81–173.

[18] J. Bentham, *Of the Limits of the Penal Branch of Jurisprudence*, ed. P. Schofield (Oxford: Oxford University Press, 2010), 24–41.

[19] Bowring, ix. 9.

Constitutional law dealt with the distribution of specific powers and corresponding duties. In the edition of *Constitutional Code* that appeared in the *Works of Jeremy Bentham*, which was prepared by Richard Doane and which gathers rather scattered writings that are difficult to date, Bentham thought that such arrangements of constitutional law belonged to civil law. Others, on the contrary, had a penal nature as they were concerned with the establishment of specific crimes and adequate sanctions. Constitutional law – a heterogeneous set of rules that only shared one common point and the only defining feature of which were their subjects and objects – appears to have a hybrid status. Such a statement contradicts what Bentham says in his *Introduction to the Principles of Morals and Legislation*, written in 1780 and published in 1789: 'Besides the civil and the penal, every complete body of law must contain a third branch, the *constitutional*.'[20] In *Of The Limits of the Penal Branch of Jurisprudence*, which continues the reflection begun in *Introduction* at the beginning of the 1780s, the constitutional branch is seen as being of a civil nature.[21] In *Preparatory Principles*, where his reflection on legal concepts was developed in the mid- to late 1770s, he noted that constitutional law essentially belongs to civil law.[22] Conversely, in *Securities against Misrule*, the view expressed is very different. He criticizes the 'depravity [of] the constitutional branch of the penal law, or say the penal branch of the constitutional law',[23] making constitutional law a partial subcategory of penal law, while suggesting that such a classification is the same as making penal law a partial subcategory of constitutional law.

[20] Bentham, *An Introduction to the Principles of Morals and Legislation* (*CW*), 307–8. See similarly J. Bentham, 'Supplement to Papers Relative to Codification and Public Instruction', in *Legislator of the World: Writings on Codification, Law and Education*, ed. P. Schofield and J. Harris (Oxford: Clarendon Press, 1998 [*CW*]), 108, 139 n. b; J. Behtham, 'Letters to the Conde de Toreno', in *On the Liberty of the Press, and Public Discussion and Other Legal and Political Writings for Spain and Portugal*, ed. C. Pease-Watkin and P. Schofield (Oxford: Clarendon Press, 2012 [*CW*]), 223; J. Bentham, *Colonies, Commerce, and Constitutional Law: Rid Yourselves of Ultramaria; and Other Writings on Spain and Spanish America*, ed. P. Schofield (Oxford: Clarendon Press, 1995 [*CW*]), 119.

[21] Bentham, *Of the Limits of the Penal Branch of Jurisprudence* (*CW*), 142–60, 198–200.

[22] Bentham, *Preparatory Principles* (*CW*), 413.

[23] Bentham, *Securities against Misrule and Other Constitutional Writings for Tripoli and Greece* (*CW*), 83 n. a.

Another alternative is presented in *First Principles preparatory to Constitutional Code*, written in 1822: 'The whole body of the law may be considered as divided into two main branches: the immediately operative and the remotely operative branch. The immediately operative is composed of the branches commonly called Penal and Civil taken together: the remotely operative branch is the branch commonly called the Constitutional branch.'[24] Far from being a second-rate component of civil law and penal law or a simple fraction of civil law, constitutional law as such is opposed to the two traditional branches.

These multiple mappings of the legal landscape might make one doubt the consistency of Bentham's thought on the limits of the various branches of jurisprudence.[25] Nevertheless, they should be seen in the light of his theory of language and logic. They testify to his 'perspectivistic' approach, according to which, depending on the speaker's purpose, the raw legal material that the language of the lawmaker offers can be ordered in multiple ways. Consequently, dichotomies and trichotomies are built on demand in a utilitarian way: 'A body [and especially a complete body of law] can be cut in as many parts as one disentangles, and according to the motives one finds to distinguish them.'[26] Besides, this does not alter the fact that, no matter how constitutional law is situated within the *pannomion*, it is constantly and emphatically considered to be law.

Despite the clarity and above all the originality of the definite stance of talking of 'constitutional law' even before the expression appeared in the case law of the United States Supreme Court under Chief Justice John Jay's pen,[27] Bentham's writings and the way he understood the operation

[24] Bentham, *First Principles preparatory to Constitutional Code* (*CW*), 3. See also ibid., 37.

[25] Regarding the distinction between civil law and penal law, see A. Brunon-Ernst, 'Délimiter la branche civile du droit: Bentham et la quête impossible', in *Bentham juriste: l'utilitarisme juridique en question*, ed. M. Bozzo-Rey and G. Tusseau (Paris: Economica, 2011), 177–200; A. Brunon-Ernst, 'Of the Limits of the Civil Branch of Jurisprudence: Background, Definitions and Limits of Bentham's Discussion on Civil Law in Limits', in *The Legal Philosophy and Influence of Jeremy Bentham: Essays on Of the Limits of the Penal Branch of Jurisprudence*, ed. G. Tusseau (London; New York: Routledge, 2014), 134–46; E. de Champs, 'Constitution and the Code: Jeremy Bentham on the Limits of the Constitutional Branch of Jurisprudence', *The Tocqueville Review / La Revue Tocqueville* 32 (2011), 21–42; E. de Champs, 'Towards the Pannomion: Limits and Bentham's French Manuscripts', in *The Legal Philosophy and Influence of Jeremy Bentham: Essays on Of the Limits of the Penal Branch of Jurisprudence*, ed. G. Tusseau (London; New York: Routledge, 2014), 320–37.

[26] UCL xxxiii, 109, quoted in De Champs, 'Constitution and the Code', 29.

[27] *Chisholm* v. *Georgia*, 2 U.S. 419, 479 (1793).

of a constitutional order raise some doubts as to his specific conception of constitutional law.

8.3 Between Constitutional*Taxis* and *Kosmos*: Bentham's Ambiguity

According to Paul Bastid, the word 'constitution' is exposed to a semantic duality.

> Sometimes it applies to an act, which is most of the time voluntary and free, and which transforms an existing situation; sometimes on the contrary it refers to factual data, unrelated to any intervention of man .... Is the constitution a spontaneous product of nature, that is, here, of social reality, in which the share of human genius, of individual initiative would be non-existent? Is it on the contrary a work of art, a voluntary creation which would reflect the ingenuity of the mind? Is it, in short, natural or artificial?[28]

Although those two paradigms were explicitly set the one against the other in Bentham's time, his work seem to oscillate between 'artificialism' and 'immanentism'.

8.3.1 The Obvious Nature of Constitutional Artificialism

Thomas Paine (1737–1809), who, like Bentham, was part of the circle of William Petty, 2nd Earl of Shelburne, 1st Marquis of Lansdowne,[29] offers views that are representative or the first constitutional archetype. According to him,

> a constitution is not a thing in name only, but in fact. It has not an ideal, but a real existence; and wherever it cannot be produced in a visible form, there is none. A constitution is a thing antecedent to a government, and a government is only the creature of a constitution. The constitution of a country is not the act of its government, but of the people constituting its government. It is the body of elements, to which you can refer, and quote article by article; and which contains the principles on which the

[28] P. Bastid, *L'idée de constitution (1962–1963)* (Paris: Economica, 1985), 9–10. See similarly J. S. Mill, *Considerations on Representative Government* (Amherst: Prometheus Books, 1991), 9–25; F. A. Hayek, *Law, Legislation and Liberty: A New Statement of the Liberal Principles of Justice and Political Economy: Vol. 1, Rules and Order* (London: Routledge & K. Paul, 1973), 35–54, opposing 'taxis' and 'kosmos'; P. W. Kahn, *Origins of Order: Project and System in the American Legal Imagination* (New Haven: Yale University Press, 2019).

[29] R. Whatmore, 'Thomas Paine', in *Constitutions and the Classics. Patterns of Constitutional Thought from Fortescue to Bentham*, ed. D. J. Galligan, (Oxford: Oxford University Press, 2014), 414–37.

> government shall be established, the manner in which it shall be organised, the powers it shall have, the mode of elections, the duration of Parliaments . . .; the powers which the executive part of the government shall have; and in fine, everything that relates to the complete organisation of a civil government, and the principles on which it shall act, and by which it shall be bound.[30]

Out of what was at that time a new conceptualization,[31] the idea emerged that a constitution was not the collection of a mass of sources that were more or less indeterminate but a formal instrument, the expression of a political constructivism, which revealed itself to be logically and normatively superior and anterior to the actions of the institutions it defined, empowered and limited.[32] Thus, the political order becomes, in a line that it is possible to trace back to Thomas Hobbes, the object of a human decision.[33] It is not the description of the existing organization of institutions but an artefact.

Many elements rather obviously suggest that it was to that paradigm that Bentham's constitutional thought was linked. A relevant element is the aforementioned fact that he adopted a broad and monistic conception of the law.[34] Each of the elements it included, among which was constitutional law, was understood to be a law. They were uniformly defined as

> an assemblage of signs *declarative* of a *volition* conceived or adopted by the *sovereign* in a state, concerning the conduct to be observed in a certain *case* by a certain person or class of persons, who in the case in question

[30] T. Paine, *Droits de l'homme : en réponse à l'attaque de M. Burke* (Paris: F. Buisson, 1791), accessible at http://classiques.uqac.ca/classiques/paine_thomas/droits_de_lhomme/droits_de_lhomme.html.

[31] On the legislative constructivism that emerges in Europe in the eighteeenth century, see D. Baranger, *Penser la loi. Essai sur le législateur des temps modernes* (Paris: Gallimard, 2018), 200–9.

[32] See similarly Sieyès, *E.-J.Qu'est-ce que le Tiers-Etat?* (Paris: Flammarion, 2009).

[33] See esp. T. Hobbes, *Léviathan. Traité de la matière, de la forme et du pouvoir de la république ecclésiastique et civile*, (Paris: Dalloz, 1999), 173–206 (Ch. XVII–XIX). See generally A. Korshorke, S. Lüdemann, T. Frank, and E. Matala de Mazza, *Der fictive Staat. Konstruktionen des politischen Körpers in der Geschichte Europas* (Frankfurt-am-Main: Fischer, 2007).

[34] See G. Tusseau, 'De Bentham à Kelsen en passant par Merkl, Une trame conceptuelle récurrente de la théorie juridique', in *Questions contemporaines de théorie analytique du droit / Cuestiones contemporáneas de teoría analítica del derecho / Problemi attuali della teoria analitica del diritto, Madrid, Barcelona, Buenos Aires: Marcial Pons*, ed. P. Brunet and F. J. Arena (Madrid: Marcial Pons Ediciones Jurìdicas y Sociales, S. A., 2011), 167–97; G. Tusseau, 'Bentham et le normativisme viennois. Impressions de lecture', in *Bentham juriste. L'utilitarisme juridique en question*, ed. M. Bozzo-Rey and G. Tusseau (Paris, Economica, 2011), 43–105.

> are, or are supposed to be, subject to his power: such volition trusting for its accomplishment to the expectation of certain events which it is intended such declaration should upon occasion be a means of bringing to pass, and the prospect of which it is intended should act as a motive upon those whose conduct is in question.[35]

Although different in two ways, the rules of constitutional law perfectly fit the typology of laws elaborated in *Limits*.[36] First, as regards their addressee, unlike the rules for ordinary individuals – the '*leges in subditos*' or '*leges in populum*' – they are addressed to the sovereign, and are called '*leges in principem*'.[37] Second, the sanction they are coupled with to make sure they are obeyed is also peculiar.[38] Bentham explains:

> Of these sanctions, that which we termed the *physical* is out of the question: for the force in the case in question is supposed to be directed by *design*. There remain the political, the religious and the moral. The force of the political sanction is inapplicable to this purpose by the supposition: within the dominion of the sovereign, there is no one who, while the sovereignty subsists, can judge so as to coerce the sovereign .... But the force of the religious sanction is as applicable to this purpose as to any other .... The same may be said of the force of the moral sanction. Now, the force of the moral sanction as applied to the purpose in question may be distinguished into two great branches: that which may be exerted by the subjects of the state in question acting without, perhaps even against, the sanction of political obligations, acting, in short, as in a state of nature; and that which may be exerted by foreign states. When a foreign state stands engaged by express covenant to take such a part in the enforcement of such a law as that in question, this is one of the cases in which such foreign state is said to stand with reference to such law in the capacity of a *guarantee*.[39]

[35] Bentham, *Of the Limits of the Penal Branch of Jurisprudence* (*CW*), 24–5. See also J. Bentham, *Chrestomatia*, trad. fr., Intro. Cléro J.-P. (Paris, Cahiers de l'Unebévue., 2004), 249.

[36] Bentham, *Of the Limits of the Penal Branch of Jurisprudence* (*CW*), 168.

[37] Ibid. 83–93. For a detailed analysis, see G. Tusseau, 'An Old English Tale? Bentham's Theory of The Force of a Law', in *The Legal Philosophy and Influence of Jeremy Bentham: Essays on Of the Limits of the Penal Branch of Jurisprudence*, ed. G. Tusseau (London; New York: Routledge, 2014), 80–133. In his French writings, Bentham's terminology opposes 'lois *in populum*' and 'lois *in imperium*'. See *Vue générale d'un corps complet de legislation*, in Bentham, *Traités de législation civile et pénale, (1802)*, ed. E. Dumont, préf. M. Bozzo-Rey, A. Brunon-Ernst, and E. de Champs (Paris: Dalloz, 2010), 74.

[38] Bentham, *An Introduction to the Principles of Morals and Legislation* (*CW*), 38–41.

[39] Bentham, *Of the Limits of the Penal Branch of Jurisprudence* (*CW*), 90–92. See also ibid., 87 n. 1.

The voluntarism of Bentham's definition of a law justifies placing him among the proponents of a form of legal positivism and of an imperative theory of law.[40] His insistence upon the idea that the law is first and foremost linked to orders – which are supported by sanctions intended for influencing the springs of individual and collective action in order to direct everybody to behaviour that, when coordinated with that of others, contributes to the realization of the greatest happiness of the greatest number – similarly reveals Bentham's social constructivism.

Moreover, if one goes over the criteria that Paine formulated to define a constitution, it is possible to note a general agreement between his perspective and Bentham's. The fact that he understood the law as being codified, and that he theorized a special method for the expression of the will of the legislator through writing,[41] results in making the law a 'thing', which has a 'real existence' in Paine's sense, a 'visible' element that can be observed and that can rationally influence the behaviour of the holders of public office and citizens. Bentham's constitutional law was completely consistent with the logic of codified law, which is obviously likely to be quoted 'article by article'. The fact that Bentham structured his thought – especially in *First Principles preparatory to Constitutional Code*[42] and later in *Constitutional Code*[43] itself – around the distinction between the powers of the 'supreme constitutive' and those of the 'supreme operative' references the difference between the constituent power and the constituted powers that Paine mentioned when he claimed that the constitution is not created by the government but by the nation. Similarly, the single article of the chapter of the *Code* on 'sovereignty', states: 'The sovereignty is in *the people*. It is reserved by and to them. It is exercised, by the exercise of the Constitutive authority.'[44]

[40] See, e.g., M. El Shakankiri, *La philosophie juridique de Jeremy Bentham* (Paris: LGDJ, 1970). For a discussion, see H. L. A. Hart, *Essays on Bentham: Studies in Jurisprudence and Political Theory* (Oxford: Clarendon Press, 1982); D. Lyons, *In the Interest of the Governed: A Study in Bentham's Philosophy of Utility and Law* (Oxford: Clarendon Press, 1991); G. J. Postema, *Bentham and the Common Law Tradition* (Oxford: Clarendon Press, 1986), 302–36; P. Schofield, 'Jeremy Bentham and H. L.A. Hart's "Utilitarian Tradition in Jurisprudence"', *Jurisprudence* 1, no. 2 (2010), 147–67.

[41] J. Bentham, *Nomography; or the Art of Inditing Laws*, in Bowring, iii. 231–83.

[42] Bentham, *First Principles preparatory to Constitutional Code* (*CW*).

[43] Bentham, *Constitutional Code for the Use of all Nations and all Governments Professing Liberal Opinions*, ed. F Rosen. and J. H. Burns (Oxford: Clarendon Press, 1991 [*CW*]), vol. 1, 27.

[44] Ibid., 25.

The content of *Constitutional Code* itself corresponds closely with the matter of constitutional law as envisaged by Paine. Going well beyond that content, Bentham also dealt, for example, with the army, judicial power, organization of the courts, and local administrative and political organization.[45] In this regard, he joined the demiurgic project of complete reconstruction of the social order that drove the French Revolutionaries after the demise of the *Ancien Régime.*[46] Thus, there is little doubt that the utilitarian philosopher, who is traditionally presented as the upholder of an artificial harmonization of interests,[47] advocated a form of engineering in the constitutional sphere, which made it possible to create a coincidence of duty and interest in public officers to pursue the greatest happiness of the greatest number.[48]

Despite the evidence provided above that Bentham sided with constitutional constructivism, he sometimes seemed to lean towards the immanentist paradigm it opposed.

8.3.2 The Temptation of Constitutional Immanentism

This antagonistic conception was expressed at the time by Edmund Burke (1729–97),[49] whom Bentham himself once opposed regarding government expense,[50] and who was the target of Paine's text. Writing from a completely different conceptual standpoint,[51] Burke had no doubt

45 Bowring, ix. On Bentham's original conception of the book, see P. Schofield, 'Jeremy Bentham', in *Constitutions and the Classics. Patterns of Constitutional Thought from Fortescue to Bentham*, ed. D. J. Galligan (Oxford: Oxford University Press), 235 n. 19.

46 See, e.g., G. Tusseau, 'The Evolution and *Gestalt* of the French Constitution', in *Ius Publicum Europaeum*, vol. 2., ed. A. von Bogdandy, P. M. Huber, P. Cruz Villalón, and S. Ragone (Oxford: Oxford University Press). forthcoming.

47 E. Halévy, *La formation du radicalisme philosophique* (Paris: PUF, 1995), vol. 3, Canto-Sperber M. (rééd).

48 Bentham, *First Principles Preparatory to Constitutional Code* (*CW*), 235.

49 See, e.g., J. G. A. Pocock, 'Burke and the Ancient Constitution: A Problem in the History of Ideas', *The Historical Journal* 3 (1960), 125–43; D. Craig, 'Burke and the Constitution', in *The Cambridge Companion to Edmund Burke*, ed. D. Dwan and C. Insole (New York: Cambridge University Press, 2012), 104–16; M. Loughlin, 'Burke on Law, Revolution and Constitution', *Giornale di storia costituzionale* 29 (2015), 49–60.

50 See *Defence of Economy Against the Right Honourable Edmund Burke*, in Bentham, *Official Aptitude Maximized, Expense Minimized* (*CW*), 39–94.

51 On the way, at the time of the French Revolution, political opinions range from Burke to Paine, see esp. P. Schofield, 'Jeremy Bentham and the British Intellectual Response to the French Revolution', *Journal of Bentham Studies* 13 (2011), accessible at http://discovery.ucl.ac.uk/1333215/1/013%20Schofield.pdf. More generally, see P. Schofield, 'Jeremy

that there was a constitution in England and discoursed at length on its principles, its parts, and whether it had been violated or respected. Far from being the creative fruit of legislative reason and will that constructivism assumes, his logic is more akin to a customary type of constitutionalism, which is made up of tradition and custom and driven not by the deliberate will of men but by the slow and imperceptible evolution of custom and habit, in accordance with the lessons and legacies of the past. According to Burke:

> Our political system is placed in a just correspondence and symmetry with the order of the world and with the mode of existence decreed to a permanent body composed of transitory parts, wherein, by the disposition of a stupendous wisdom, molding together the great mysterious incorporation of the human race, the whole, at one time, is never old or middle-aged or young, but, in a condition of unchangeable constancy, moves on through the varied tenor of perpetual decay, fall, renovation, and progression. Thus, by preserving the method of nature in the conduct of the state, in what we improve we are never wholly new; in what we retain we are never wholly obsolete. By adhering in this manner and on those principles to our forefathers, we are guided not by the superstition of antiquarians, but by the spirit of philosophic analogy. In this choice of inheritance we have given to our frame of polity the image of a relation in blood, binding up the constitution of our country with our dearest domestic ties, adopting our fundamental laws into the bosom of our family affections, keeping inseparable and cherishing with the warmth of all their combined and mutually reflected charities our state, our hearths, our sepulchres, and our altars.[52]

It is only on the basis of 'extravagant and presumptuous speculations'[53] that it is possible, in disregard of prudence, to indulge in constructivism: 'What ought to be the heads, the hearts, the dispositions that are qualified or that dare, not only to make laws under a fixed constitution, but at one beat to strike out a totally new constitution for a great kingdom, and in every part of it, from the monarch on the throne to the vestry of a parish?'[54] The constitution is not strictly speaking created by some will pursuing an objective: it exists, grows, develops, evolves in a constant, slow, imperceptible, incremental, and progressive way, without ignoring

Bentham', in *Constitutions and the Classics. Patterns of Constitutional Thought from Fortescue to Bentham*, ed. D. J. Galligan (Oxford: Oxford University Press, 2014), 231–49.

52 E. Burke, *Reflections on the Revolution in France* (London: British Library, 1970), accessible at www.constitution.org/eb/rev_fran.htm.

53 Ibid.

54 Ibid.

the local circumstances and culture in the name of abstract and universalizing metaphysical ideals.

Even though such a perspective was diametrally opposed to that of Paine, the way Bentham wanted to ensure the efficiency of constitutional law led him to imperceptibly move closer to the immanentist paradigm. In his criticism of the text of Article 16 of the Declaration of the Rights of Man and of the Citizen, which provided the canonical definition of the constitution in its contemporary setting,[55] for example, Bentham contended that:

> According to general import, supported by etymology, by the word constitution something established, something already established, something possessed of stability, something that has given proofs of stability, seems to be implied. What shall we say if, of this most magnificent of all boasts, not merely the simple negative but the direct converse should be true? and if, instead of France's being the only country that has a constitution, France should be the only country that has none! Yet if government depends upon obedience, the stability of government [upon] the permanence of the disposition to obedience, and the permanence of that disposition [upon] the duration of the habit of obedience, this most assuredly must be the case. And if, instead of saying you can't have a constitution unless you make it, it would be much nearer the truth, or rather it would be the plain truth and the only truth, that you can't have a constitution, if you attempt to make one. Your posterity may, if they have good fortune and very good fortune indeed: but you yourselves, the makers of it, can not with propriety be said to have it. So that which has been said of nobility (nobility by descent) in the way of sarcasm may be said of a constitution in good and very good earnest, the way to make it is to sit quietly for so many years in your chair.[56]

That text may bear the marks of circumstances, as Bentham was writing in 1795, after the Terror turned him away from any fondness he might have had for democracy.[57] Thus, becoming more conservative in the face of the extremes of the Revolutionaries, he could rally behind Burke's perspective. However, there seems to exist a dimension of Bentham's thought that, in a structural much more than in a situational way, makes it lean that way. The force of constitutional law depends on the impact of

[55] 'Any society in which the guarantee of rights is not assured, nor the separation of powers determined, has no Constitution.'

[56] J. Bentham, *Rights, Representation, and Reform: Nonsense upon Stilts and other writings on the French Revolution*, ed. P. Schofield, C. Pease-Watkin, and C. Blamires (Oxford: Clarendon Press, 2002 [*CW*]), 373–4.

[57] P. Schofield, *Utility and Democracy: The Political Thought of Jeremy Bentham* (New York: Oxford University Press), 2006.

the popular or moral sanction, which mainly consists in a person losing and gaining the esteem and good will that another could show towards them. Bentham had confidence in its efficiency in political matters.[58] Thus, he pointed to the efficiency of the 1814 French Charter, even though it was only a concession of the king to his subjects and not a superior norm.[59]

The strength of the popular sanction is all the more important when it is understood in the light of Bentham's theory of sovereignty. As early as *A Fragment on Government*, he clearly stated the idea that sovereignty is not a metaphysical entity but the result of facts, which are precisely described as a habit and a disposition to obey one or several persons, driven by a utilitarian calculation.[60] 'The ultimate efficient cause of all power of imperation over persons is a disposition on the part of those persons to obey: the efficient cause, then, of the power of the sovereign is neither more nor less than the disposition to obedience on the part of the people.'[61] That is why the popular sanction, which results from 'each man's spontaneous disposition',[62] is what contributes to the establishment, reinforcement, continuity, limitation, and fall of the sovereign. The moral or popular sanction can act through a feeling of shame or ignominy and in the possible refusal of the people to obey the wishes of the ruler. This last dimension is extremely important in Bentham's theory of the political power. To offer an extreme example illustrating the application of the popular sanction that gives its legal nature to constitutional law, he mentioned the execution of Charles I.[63] That is why, like the individuals who continually compare the utility of conforming to the law and the utility of disregarding it, the sovereign continually compares the utility of imposing such and such a duty, and

[58] *Principles of Penal Law*, in Bowring, i. 453–8. See also Tusseau, 'An Old English Tale?

[59] Bentham, *Securities against Misrule and Other Constitutional Writings for Tripoli and Greece* (*CW*), 140–1.

[60] Bentham, *A Comment on the Commentaries and A Fragment on Government*, (*CW*), 425–48.

[61] Bentham, *Of the Limits of the Penal Branch of Jurisprudence* (*CW*), 42 n. b. See also Bentham, *Preparatory Principles* (*CW*), D180. See also J. Bentham, 'Principes du code penal', in *Traités de législation civile et pénale, (1802)*, ed. E. Dumont, préf. M. Bozzo-Rey, A. Brunon-Ernst, and E. de Champs (Paris: Dalloz, 2010), 393; Bentham, *Securities against Misrule and Other Constitutional Writings for Tripoli and Greece*, (*CW*), 3; Bentham, *Political Deontology*, UC xv, 19 (Thanks are due to Emmanuelle de Champs for allowing me to access her transcription of these manuscripts).

[62] Bentham, *An Introduction to the Principles of Morals and Legislation* (*CW*), 35.

[63] Bentham, *Securities against Misrule and Other Constitutional Writings for Tripoli and Greece* (*CW*), 122–3.

of granting such and such a right, and the probability of being obeyed or resisted. That probability itself is nothing more than the disposition of the people to obey his orders, which is nothing else, in the end, than constitutional law. Covenants, contracts, and so on can represent formalizations of the disposition to obey.[64] Since these instruments can be considered as indications of the conditions under which the popular sanction, which limits the scope of the power of the legislator, will support the exercise of such power, they fully deserve to be understood as 'constitutional law'.

According to Oren Ben-Dor, who presented a reconstruction of the process that is at work, 'constitutional limits are the justificatory conclusions of an interpretive communal process. They are not static entities that one just knows or finds in a code of law. Bearing this interpretative conception of constitutional limits in mind, the reconstruction of Bentham's utilitarian enterprise combines elements of both legal positivism and an interpretative theory of law'.[65] Bentham was led to present a 'a socially dynamic conception of constitutional limits which were to be determined and effectuated by a popular collective judgement'.[66] Laws *in principem* result from the continuous, evolving, dynamic, critical, interactive, and discursive utilitarian assessment of the action of the governors that is conducted by the political community. They express the popular judgement on the limits of political obedience and duty. They determine and apply constitutional limits through the sanction of disobedience and the possible withdrawal of obedience that would result in the end of sovereignty.

This analysis of constitutional law in action is noticeably close to Burke's immanentist perspective. Rather than being created *ab novo*, constitutional law grows and develops incrementally through a multiplicity of social practices over a long period, which is little likely to be rationalized as a whole and departs from the political voluntarism as highlighted by Paine. It seems much more difficult, in the light of constitutional mechanics and of the way they must guide the behaviour of the governing minority, to codify constitutional law. From that point of view, can the code be more than a causal or contributing factor in the realization of an empirical, cultural, and historical

[64] Bentham, *Of the Limits of the Penal Branch of Jurisprudence* (*CW*), 88–9.

[65] O. Ben-Dor, *Constitutional Limits and the Public Sphere: A Critical Study of Bentham's Constitutionalism* (Oxford; Portland: Hart, 2000), 24.

[66] Ibid., 3. See also ibid., 191–233.

situation, made up of a habit and a disposition to obey? More than a norm, constitutional law is then an interactive social practice, which can only evolve gradually, following the pattern that was given its clearest expression by Burke.

According to such a reading, Bentham was not really at the vanguard of the Copernican revolution brought about by constitutionalism at the turn of the nineteenth century. There results a tension that is a priori difficult to understand in his work. The real difficulty is that it was the decisive argument that allowed him to conceive of the fully legal nature of constitutional law in an unprecedented way – that is, resorting to the concept of the popular sanction – that made him turn towards the older antivoluntarist conception of constitutional law. Quite paradoxically and surprisingly, he was the first of the Moderns only thanks to a theory of a sanction that, due to the mechanism of its operation, made him an Ancient.

8.4 Conclusion

An analysis of the way Bentham devised his concept of constitutional law, which, in a way, lay at the crossroads of two legal universes, may give the impression of a confused and undecided conception of the fundamental tools he intended to draw upon in order to establish the utilitarian political order. His work, which extended from the 1770s to the 1830s, was contemporaneous with the two major revolutions that laid the foundations of present day constitutionalism. It was in direct engagement with the crucial stages of that movement that is represented, for example, by the development of the American Republic, the successive French regimes, the Latin-American independence movement starting in 1808, the liberal Spanish Constitution of 1812, and so on. From the point of view of those new legal concepts, or even of the new political culture, which it was then necessary to imagine, Bentham's work illustrates a form of conceptual antagonism between different constitutional cosmologies.

Although he did possess all the conceptual tools of modern constitutionalism (hierarchy of norms making it possible to develop a theory of constitutional validity and rigidity, limitation of the power of the legislator allowing constitutional review by the courts, and so on), he rejected them at the level of legal politics. Thus, even though he 'legalized' the constitution, he nonetheless did not make it the 'supreme law of the land', as some did in the United States, through constitutionality review, or in France, through extremely rigid constitutions.[67] Having renounced those tools in his proposals of reform, he had to fall back on an apparently more 'dated' conception of constitutional law. At the same time, such a choice imposed upon him an important conceptual and practical constraint, which naturally pointed to the role of the deontologist[68] and what he called 'indirect legislation'.[69] Does not that way of governing behaviour – which is so often neglected by Bentham scholars, even though it may represent one of the most innovative and currently relevant dimensions of his work[70] – find its true home in constitutional matters, where what is at stake is to regulate the behaviour of people who, by definition, are in a dominant position within political society and can therefore control direct legislation?[71] One may surmise that, through a sort of stratagem of legal reason, the ultimate refinement of immanentism on which Bentham founded his utilitarian constitutional governance was an immanentism that was organized, configured, and eventually shaped in the most constructivist possible way.

It is in this respect that one of Bentham's fascinating intuitions should be viewed. The control that weighs on the governing minority and guarantees that it pursues the greatest happiness of the greatest number is mainly exercised by the Public Opinion Tribunal.[72] That fictitious

[67] On these two dimensions of contemporary constitutionalism, see G. Tusseau, 'Deux dogmes du constitutionnalisme', in *Penser le droit à partir de l'individu. Mélanges en hommage à Elisabeth Zoller* (Paris: Dalloz, 2018), 835–83. Regarding the rejection of constitutional rigidity, see 'Necessity of an Omnipotent Legislature', in Bentham, *Rights, Representation, and Reform* (*CW*), 263–88. See also *Observations on the Draughts of Declarations of Rights*, in *Rights, Representation, and Reform: Nonsense upon Stilts and Other Writings on the French Revolution* (*CW*), 185–6; Bentham, *Constitutional Code for the Use of all Nations and all Governments Professing Liberal Opinions* (*CW*), vol. 1, 41, 44-45.

[68] See De Champs, 'Constitution and the Code', 32–37, 21–42.

[69] J. Bentham, *Des moyens indirects de prévenir les délits*, in *Traités de législation civile et pénale* 331–405; M. Bozzo-Rey, A. Brunon-Ernst, and A. Van Waeyenberge, eds., 'Nudges: Better Choices?', *The Tocqueville Review/La revue Tocqueville* 37, no. 1 (2016), 7–20. M. Bozzo-Rey, A. Brunon-Ernst, and M. Quinn, eds, 'Indirect Legislation: Jeremy Bentham's Regulatory Revolution', *History of European Ideas* 43 (2017), 1–121.

[70] See esp. the French Nudge Project, http://frenchnudgeproject.fr/.

[71] See, e.g., P. Rudan, 'Influence as a Constitutional Factor: Bentham's Public Ethics', in *La déontologie publique. Trajectoire et présence d'une notion ambiguë*, ed. G. Tusseau (Paris: Institut francophone pour la justice et la démocratie, diffusion LGDJ Lextenso, 2019), 65–77.

[72] G. Tusseau, *Jeremy Bentham. La guerre des mots* (Paris: Dalloz, 2011), 140–57.

body draws its power from the way it administers the moral or popular sanction. Recognized in *Constitutional Code*,[73] it is the object of the following provision:

> Art. 4. Public Opinion may be considered as a system of law, emanating from the body of the people. If there be no individually assignable form of words in and by which it stands expressed, it is but upon a par in this particular with that rule of action which, emanating as it does from lawyers, official and professional, and not sanctioned by the Legislative authority, otherwise than by tacit sufferance, is in England designated by the appellation of Common Law. To the pernicious exercise of the power of government, it is the only check; to the beneficial, an indispensable supplement. Able rulers lead it; prudent rulers lead or follow it; foolish rulers disregard it. Even at the present stage in the career of civilisation, its dictates coincide, on most points, with those of the greatest-happiness principle; on some, however, it still deviates from them: but, as its deviations have all along been less and less numerous, and less wide, sooner or later they will cease to be discernible; aberration will vanish, coincidence will be complete.

The idea that public opinion itself can be understood as a 'legal system' bears the mark of Bentham's panlegalism.[74] It may reveal that far from being spontaneous and immanent, the public opinion that gives constitutional law its legal nature is in reality the object of human design. Bentham's conceptualization of constitutional law as a set of laws depends on his theory of the popular sanction. This theory leads to a form of social interaction that shares most of the characteristics highlighted by the Burkean perspective. But the kind of immanentism that follows in Bentham's writings crucially depends on an active (direct and indirect) legislative and deontological design. As a consequence, constructivism and immanentism seem to reciprocally imply one another, thus highlighting, more than an incoherent legal doctrine, a unique utilitarian jurisprudence.

[73] Bentham, *Constitutional Code for the Use of all Nations and all Governments Professing Liberal Opinions (CW)*, 36.

[74] G. Tusseau, 'An Old English Tale?, 80–133.

9

A Genius for Legislation

Bentham's 'Art and Science' of Legislation and Modern Legisprudence

FRANCESCO FERRARO

The neologism 'legisprudence' refers to 'the name for the branch of legal theory that deals with legislation from a theoretical and a practical perspective'.[1] In what follows, I will present an analysis of Bentham's 'art and science' of legislation and try to show the relevance of his theory for modern legisprudential concerns. A fundamental problem with this field of study concerns its boundaries and its place within the domain of legal science. This is closely related to the question of whether, and possibly how, legal scholars can contribute to legisprudence rather than leaving it (for instance) to sociologists, political scientists, and other experts. I will try to show that, for Bentham, the 'art and science of legislation' was a branch of normative ethics that constituted a completely legitimate and indeed crucial field of research for legal scholars. I will then focus on how Bentham treated the problem of rational law-making and legislative reason-giving, which is central to legisprudence as a 'rational theory of legislation'.[2] Lastly, I confront Bentham's theory with some of the problems that current legisprudence is addressing and examine – including in light of his late constitutional theory – the kinds of answers, if any, he would provide.

[1] L. J. Wintgens, 'Legislation as an Object of Study of Legal Theory', in *Legisprudence: A New Theoretical Approach to Legislation. Proceedings of the Fourth Benelux-Scandinavian Symposium on Legal Theory*, ed. L. J. Wintgens (Oxford; Portland: Hart, 2012), 9–39, at 10.

[2] See L. J. Wintgens, 'Legisprudence as a New Theory of Legislation', *Ratio Juris* 19 (2006), 1–25.

9.1 From the Eighteenth-Century Science of Legislation to Modern Legisprudence

The term 'legisprudence' first appeared in a 1950 article by Julius Cohen.[3] In another article, published thirty-three years later, Cohen lamented that US jurisprudence had 'focused mainly on the judicial side of the legal order'; but 'if, broadly speaking, jurisprudence is a theoretical account of the legal order . . . one would logically expect the legislative side of the legal order also to be within its inquiring ambit'.[4] He suggested that this kind of legal-theoretical enterprise be called 'judicativeprudence', as it limits itself to one part, albeit a very important one, of the field of law. Some plausible causes of this self-limitation on the part of legal theorists were suggested by Cohen. One was the prevalence of a legal-realist approach in North American law schools and their interpretation of Justice Holmes's emphasis on law as the prediction of judicial decisions. Moreover, Cohen emphasized that the legislative part of the legal order was always under suspicion of acting from irrationality and bias, while the judicative part was often seen as a world of rational and careful reflection. From another point of view, this kind of preconception can be seen as marking a borderline between the realm of law and that of politics, thereby excluding the legislative field, seen as part of the latter's dominion, from the scope of jurisprudence.

Cohen also put forward an agenda comprising some of the problems that legisprudence – the branch of jurisprudence focusing on legislation – would have to tackle. Among them, we find the problem of control over legislative meaning, which is due to what we might call the 'semiotic power' of judges as interpreters. This belongs, more generally, to the field of legislative language and the criteria for its adequacy: while a very precise formulation may restrain judicial discretion (although this may not always be the case), thereby favouring predictability and legal certainty, it is also true that, sometimes, such precision is not required or even expedient. Another order of problems arises from the need to evaluate legislation, considered both as a process and as a result. As criteria for evaluation, Cohen suggests the effectiveness of the law (as a means to its purported ends), its systematic or political consistency with

[3] J. Cohen, 'Towards Realism in Legisprudence', *Yale Law Journal* 59 (1950), 886–97.

[4] J. Cohen, 'Legisprudence: Problems and Agenda', *Hofstra Law Review* 11 (1983) 1163–83, at 1163.

other laws, and its moral justifiability. In this last case, of course, we tread the terrain of moral philosophy.

Jeremy Waldron has dug deeper into the motives of the lingering 'embarrassment about legislation'.[5] He holds that the widespread contempt for legislative activity on the part of many illustrious legal thinkers in the common law world, alongside their frequent insistence that legislation is not law, is not merely due to 'a healthy dose of Legal Realism' with its concern for law in court as opposed to law in books.[6] There is more to this dismissive attitude and lack of interest in legislative studies. Aside from socio-political factors – such as the refusal to face the democratic difficulties and counter-majoritarian outputs of judicial review – Waldron identifies two general strands in contemporary thought that contribute nothing at all to the creation of a fertile environment for legislative enquiries. First, we have to take into account the tendency within contemporary legal positivism to revert the traditional pride of place given to legislation and focus on a judicially oriented interpretation of the Hartian rule of recognition. For instance, in Joseph Raz's account, a legal system is such if there is an organized set of law-applying institutions; the centralized production of norms by a legislature is not a necessary condition and, as a matter of fact, is a relatively recent occurrence in the history of legal systems.[7] Second, the anti-constructivist political philosophy of Michael Oakeshott and Friedrich Hayek deemed 'intellectualization in politics' as highly suspect and considered 'the ascendancy of legislative mentality' as a dangerous expression of social rationalism, with its typical preference for deliberate social planning over spontaneous, unselfconscious evolution. Though these two intellectual strands were not immediately connected, Hart's practice conception of social rules is somehow related to Oakeshott's philosophy through the influence of Peter Winch.[8] However, Waldron suggests that the real reason behind the dismissive attitude towards legislation has to do with the appealing myth of the law's neutrality and 'anonymity', much more than with the influence of the philosophical critique of constructivism.

Curiously, in continental legal culture, notwithstanding the central role that legislatures play in civil law systems (and the deep-rooted

[5] J. Waldron, *The Dignity of Legislation* (Cambridge: Cambridge University Press, 1999), 17.
[6] Ibid., 10.
[7] Ibid., 15–6.
[8] Ibid., 17–21.

suspicion of both judge-made law and the rule of binding precedent), legal thought has been characterized by the very same disregard for the study of legislation. Even more curiously, the intellectual roots of this disregard seem to be almost antithetical to those in the common law context. First, continental legal positivism never called into question the centrality of the legislature. During the nineteenth century, the Golden Age of European codification, continental legal positivism prominently included a *theory* of what the *law is*, which assumed that law always features certain characters, one of which is its centralized production at the hands of a legislature. However, continental legal positivism also encompassed a methodology for the study of the law, which prescribed that the jurist should behave as a scientist and a dispassionate observer of what the law is without meddling with the process of its creation. According to this methodological stance – which is due to theoretical concerns that differ somewhat from 'methodological positivism' in contemporary Anglo-Saxon jurisprudence[9] – the law was there to be observed; legal science was supposed to study its object, not to contribute to its creation, an activity that belonged to politics, not to law. The best known example of the heritage of this approach in the twentieth century is Kelsen's 'pure theory of law', which, from the point of view of the separation between the description and moral evaluation of the law, is analogous to Hart's 'morally neutral description'.

Second, continental legal culture has long refused to take into account one of the main legisprudential concerns, that of the justification of law and reason-giving on the part of the legislator, due to two ideological factors. The first was the identification of the legislature as the supreme political authority, which exempted it from explaining its decisions to other powers. The second was the idea that the legislature did not derive its authority and legitimacy from justifiable decisions but from other sources, most prominently democratic elections. Therefore, while in the common-law world suspicion of the role of the legislature as a legal player led to the marginalization of the study of legislation and its justification, in the continental legal world, an opposite cause – that of excessive deference to the legislature – led to the same effect.

Today, due to changes in the legal world, rather than theoretical speculation, the study of legislation in general, and legislative justification and reason-giving in particular, has progressively found its place in

[9] See G. Pino, 'Positivism, Legal Validity, and the Separation of Law and Morals', *Ratio Juris* 27 (2014), 190–217.

jurisprudence and legal theory. National and international courts are increasingly reviewing legislation as a process, to make sure that legislators have done their job properly by making every effort to collect relevant information and extensively discussing measures before they are adopted. Moreover, in many legal systems, judicial review is often carried out with explicit reference to the principle of reasonableness, previously applied only in administrative law. Therefore, we are witnessing the return of legisprudence. I say 'return' because its disappearance has been relatively recent in the history of legal thought. According to J. H. Burns, during the late eighteenth century, 'the notion of a "science of legislation" is widespread, almost commonplace'.[10] We can find it, for instance, in Rousseau; in Adam Smith, with his 'science of a legislator';[11] and on the Italian peninsula, for instance, with *The Science of Legislation* by Gaetano Filangieri, which was translated into French in 1786 and attained immediate success. Bentham, having received from Claude-Adrien Helvétius the inspiration to begin his inquiries into the science of morals and legislation, saw it as the most useful and beneficial enterprise to which his intellect could be devoted.[12]

In comparison with the eighteenth-century science of legislation, modern legisprudence has more problems in setting boundaries to its domain and in finding its proper place among other legal disciplines, at least from the legal scholar's point of view. As noted earlier, Cohen himself assigned a variety of considerably different tasks to legisprudential scholars. Now, it is true that jurisprudence itself comprises doctrinal, philosophical, and sociological approaches and combines them with a number of disciplines, ranging from linguistics to political science, neuroscience, economics, and moral philosophy, to name a few; therefore, it could be seen as unsurprising that the legisprudential subsector also allows for a vast array of approaches and the contribution of many disciplines. Nevertheless, some have observed that legal science, in itself, should not unduly expand into the terrain of what has been called the

[10] J. H. Burns, 'Jeremy Bentham: From Radical Enlightenment to Political Radicalism', *The Bentham Newsletter* 8 (1984), 4–14, at 7.

[11] See K. Haakonssen, *The Science of a Legislator: The Natural Jurisprudence of David Hume & Adam Smith* (Cambridge: Cambridge University Press, 1989).

[12] J. Bentham, *Correspondence*, vol. II, ed. T. L. S. Sprigge (London: Athlone, 1968 [*CW*]), 99 (letter to John Forster, April–May 1778). See also M. Hoesch, 'From Theory to Practice: Bentham's Reception of Helvétius', *Utilitas* 30 (2018), 294–316.

'pragmatic' and 'teleological' rationality[13] of legislation: that is, the actual capacity of statutes to obtain compliance (from both citizens and judges) and to attain the legislator's political and social goals. This kind of rationality is the object of the strand of legal sociology called implementation research. Legal science – so goes the argument – is a non-empirical science of norms, and division of labour should be respected where empirical social and behavioural sciences are assigned the task of ascertaining the efficacy, effectiveness, and efficiency of legislation.[14] Accordingly, if legal scholars are to busy themselves at all with the study of legislation, they should leave empirical enquiries to other disciplines. This stance, of course, presupposes a meta-theoretical framework in which (as in Kelsen's general theory) legal doctrine, unlike legal sociology, is not a 'natural science'.[15] What would be, then, the business of the jurist with regard to the study of legislation? Here, the possible answers diverge according to the kind of general theory of law that we endorse. Methodological legal positivism, as noted above, would rule out the task of the moral evaluation of the law as part of the legal scholar's work. Value considerations could probably be made, albeit only with reference to the interpretation of well-established constitutional principles, fundamental rights, and the like (considered as internal to the legal system and already pertaining to it). Aside from constitutional constraints, which are exclusively or mainly negative (i.e., the legislator cannot do certain things), the legislative power would be seen as practically free in choosing its ends; as indicated above, its democratic legitimacy would exempt it from justifying its decisions, in the sense of giving reasons for them. The legisprudential concerns of the jurists, then, would probably be reduced to analyzing the (usually scarce) use of legal arguments in parliamentary debates, aside from assessments of the formal legitimacy of legislation (deriving from the respect of constitutionalized procedures) and its 'systematic' rationality, that is, its fitting in the legal order without creating inconsistencies (in the sense of normative conflicts). Nevertheless, this is too modest a pursuit for the ambitions of legisprudence, especially if we take into account that both the formal

[13] See M. Atienza, 'Legislation and Argumentation: Towards a Model for the Analysis of Legislative Reasoning', in *Conceptions and Misconceptions of Legislation*, ed. A. D. Oliver-Lalana (Cham: Springer, 2019), 175–206.

[14] See K. Tuori, 'Legislation between Politics and Law', in *Legisprudence*, ed. L. J. Wintgens, 99–107.

[15] See H. Kelsen, *General Theory of Law and State*, trans. A. Wedberg (Union: The Lawbook Exchange, 1999), 162–78.

legitimacy of legislation and its systematic rationality have already been the bread and butter of legal scholars for a very long time. This restricted account of legisprudence would in fact bring us back to the nineteenth-century picture of the legal scientist who studies law as a pre-existing object, without meddling with its creation.

Alternatively, a 'post-positivist' or Dworkinian framework could be adopted by presupposing a general theory of law that is both conceptual and normative. Accordingly, legal scholars are not seen as neutral observers or 'scientists' of law because 'propositions of law' are interpretive and combine elements of description and evaluation without being entirely reducible to either.[16] It has been observed that the Dworkinian and other 'post-positivist' theories have no deep theoretical reason for neglecting the study of legislation and law-making and that such neglect must be merely 'out of habit': if moral reasoning on the part of the legal interpreter is actually required, as such theories claim, and is a proper object for legal studies, there seems to be no reason to disregard instances of such reasoning offered by legislators.[17] However, such disregard on the part of those endorsing this approach probably finds some theoretical ground in Dworkin's well-known distinction between principles and policies.[18] This distinction can easily be interpreted in the sense of a division of labour between legislatures and courts: legislation is seen as preponderantly policy-based, while adjudication is considered more apt for principled reasoning and argumentation. Dworkin himself held that the political process in parliamentary democracies translates majoritarian preferences into legislation, with no filter at all with respect to preferences based on prejudice, which could adversely impact the interests of minorities. 'Therefore constitutional rights are needed.'[19] Dworkin, then, considers that elected legislatures are basically institutional machines for counting and aggregating preferences and that legislators only respond to their constituents' preferences.[20] Thence, judicial review is needed in

[16] See R. Dworkin, 'Law as Interpretation', *Critical Inquiry* 9 (1982), 179–200.

[17] See G. Marcilla, 'Proportionality in Lawmaking: An Attempt of Justification in the Light of a Constitutionalist and Argumentative Conception of Law', in *Conceptions and Misconceptions of Legislation*, ed. A. D. Oliver-Lalana, 153–73, at 160.

[18] See R. Dworkin, *Taking Rights Seriously* (Cambridge, MA: Harvard University Press, 1978), 22–3, 87–8.

[19] R. Dworkin, 'Social Sciences and Constitutional Rights – the Consequences of Uncertainty', *Journal of Law & Education* 6 (1977), 3–12, at 10.

[20] See R. Ekins, *The Nature of Legislative Intent* (Oxford: Oxford University Press, 2012), 77–85.

order to treat issues in political morality as matters of principle, not of policy.[21] Whether this is correct or not, this picture of the role and function of legislatures is incompatible with the view of legislative reasoning as full-fledged legal reasoning, apt for being studied as such by legal scholars. Within this theoretical framework, legisprudence would probably be confined to the analysis of legislation as a product, especially from the point of view of its 'axiological' rationality,[22] namely, its ethical acceptability, assessed with reference to constitutional values and principles. Of course, this is common judicial practice in all contemporary legal systems endowed with the judicial review of legislation. Legal scholars do engage in this kind of evaluation, including with reference to the courts' past decisions and interpretations. However, this is hardly what legisprudence is about: its ambition is to study legislation both as a process and as a result, in all its different dimensions of rationality, and to do so from a juridical standpoint by considering the legislature as a full-fledged player in the legal system – indeed, a central one.

In what follows, I will try to show that Bentham's science of legislation provides a much more suitable theoretical or, rather, meta-theoretical framework for considering legisprudence, with its multifarious aspects, as a perfectly legitimate object of study for legal scholars. Bentham's utilitarian jurisprudence should be seen as different from, and an alternative to, both traditional 'methodological' positivism (with its interpretation of the distinction between the description of the law and its moral evaluation) and 'post-positivist' interpretivism (with its 'pre-Benthamite' refusal of the distinction between law as it is and law as it ought to be).[23]

9.2 The 'Art and Science' of Legislation as a Branch of Ethics

In his memoirs, Bentham recalls that he was drawn by Helvétius to think of 'genius' as the capacity to invent something (as reflected by the etymology of the word 'genius', which is related to the Latin verb *gignere*, 'to generate') and that this led him to recognize his own 'genius for

21 'Judicial review insures that the most fundamental issues of political morality will finally be set out and debated as issues of principle and not political power alone, a transformation that cannot succeed, in any case not fully, within the legislature itself' (R. Dworkin, *A Matter of Principle* [Cambridge, MA: Harvard University Press], 1985, 70).

22 See Atienza, 'Legislation and Argumentation'.

23 See D. N. MacCormick, 'Dworkin as Pre-Benthamite', *The Philosophical Review* 87 (1978), 585–607.

legislation', that is, a talent for the most valuable of all intellectual enterprises.[24] Moreover, Bentham also found the idea of a science of legislation in Francis Bacon, and the place for such science within the all-comprehensive field of human knowledge was arranged by him according to the scheme of the Porphyrian tree, which he had received from both Bacon and d'Alembert.[25] Bentham coupled each science with its corresponding art; the latter was the means of putting into practice the knowledge acquired by the former in order to act to change reality in accordance with the all-comprehensive end of maximizing happiness.

As indicated above, meddling with substantive ethical judgements (such as those required, as Cohen pointed out, by the evaluation of legislation as a product) and political debates (such as those that take place in parliaments) is something that legal scholars would do better to avoid, according to some of the commonplaces inherited from nineteenth-century versions of legal positivism. More generally, however, perplexity regarding the inclusion of such an object into the field of study of jurisprudence or legal theory is understandable; after all, the task of studying existing law seems very different from those of inquiring into how the law was made, of checking whether it respects some basic requirements of instrumental rationality (aside from more substantial ethical judgements), and of verifying or requiring that the legislature offers plausible reasons for it.

Bentham certainly acknowledged the diversity of these tasks and, of course, was perfectly aware of the necessary distinction between the law as it is and the law as it should be – he was actually the first to establish this. However, excluding the study of law-making from the interests of the legal scholar would make absolutely no sense to him. One reason for this, of course, was his 'proto-pragmatist' approach to sciences in general, according to which they had value insofar as they could be turned into techniques capable of acting on reality and changing it – a perspective that had already been embraced by Bacon, Leibniz, and a number of philosophes of the Enlightenment.[26] Therefore, the science of legislation or jurisprudence was inextricably connected with the art of legislation.

[24] J. Bentham, *The Works of Jeremy Bentham*, 11 vols., ed. John Bowring (Edinburgh: Tait, 1838–43), henceforth *Works*, vol. x, 27.

[25] See M.P. Mack, *Jeremy Bentham: An Odyssey of Ideas 1748–1892* (London: Heinemann, 1962), 97, 105–12.

[26] Ibid., 136–7.

If we take a closer look at where the art and science of legislation is located inside Bentham's all-comprehensive 'encyclopedical nomenclature' of arts and sciences, we can see how this field of study fully pertains to the dominion of jurisprudence. First, in *An Introduction to the Principles of Morals and Legislation*, we are told that 'a book of jurisprudence can have but one or the other of two objects: 1. to ascertain what the law is: 2. to ascertain what it ought to be. In the former case it may be styled a book of expository jurisprudence; in the latter, a book of censorial jurisprudence: or, in other words, a book on the art of legislation'.[27] Consequently, the art of legislation corresponds to censorial jurisprudence. In 'Essay on Nomenclature and Classification', we find its proper place in encyclopedical nomenclature:[28] it is an aspect of 'Deontology', that is, of what we would call normative (including applied) ethics. More specifically, it comes at the end of two subdivisions within the field of Deontology and is part of the art and science of 'internal government'. Bentham repeats this point in *Deontology*: 'In so far as the person [whose conduct is] in question is considered as occupying the situation of a member of the ruling few, the art and science of deontology will coincide with the art and science of government: within the field of which art and science is included the art and science of legislation, together with . . . the field of administration.'[29] This suggests that the art of legislation, that is, censorial jurisprudence, is a subdivision of the field of normative (i.e., not merely descriptive) ethics. Expository jurisprudence, for its part, belongs to the science of legislation, which is simply the science corresponding to censorial jurisprudence. Thence, the study of the law as it is – which is usually considered the subject of legal theory and jurisprudence – is part of the field of normative ethics. This might sound strange to modern ears, but it makes perfect sense in terms of Bentham's view of all human knowledge as subservient to the all-comprehensive art of 'Eudaemonics', that is, the art of achieving well-being.

Therefore, we can safely say that Benthamic legisprudence lies legitimately within the domain of jurisprudence since it amounts to its censorial

[27] J. Bentham, *An Introduction to the Principles of Morals and Legislation*, ed. J. H. Burns and H. L. A. Hart (London: Athlone Press, 1970 [*CW*]), 293–4.

[28] See J. Bentham, *Chrestomathia*, ed. M. J. Smith and W. H. Burston (Oxford: Clarendon Press, 1983 [*CW*]), 179–206.

[29] J. Bentham, *Deontology together with A Table of the Springs of Action and Article on Utilitarianism*, ed. A. Goldworth (Oxford: Clarendon Press, 1983 [*CW*]), henceforth *Deontology*, 249.

part, to which expository jurisprudence is subservient. Moreover, all jurisprudence, both expository and censorial, belongs to the field of ethics. The study of law, in its entirety, is an exercise in ethical reasoning; legal scholars can and indeed must engage in value judgements.

I will now focus on the specific place assigned by Bentham to legislation within the larger domain of ethics. Although the art and science of legislation belongs to ethics, this latter realm also includes dominions that are outside the scope of legislative action. Bentham explains as follows: 'By *Deontology* . . . is meant that branch of art and science which has for its object the doing on each occasion what is right and proper to be done . . . in so far as it takes for its subject matter that part of the field to which Government applies itself, Public Deontology is the name that may be employed: in so far as the application of it is considered as confined to those parts of the field of thought and action which Government has left free, Private Deontology is the name that may be employed.'[30]

As noted above, the art and science of government includes (in its internal, not international, subsector) the art and science of both legislation and administration. Private deontology or private ethics 'teaches how each man may dispose himself to pursue the course most conducive to his own happiness, by means of such motives as offer of themselves: the art of legislation . . . teaches how a multitude of men, composing a community, may be disposed to pursue that course which upon the whole is the most conducive to the happiness of the whole community, by means of motives to be applied by the legislator'.[31]

The task of the private deontologist or 'practical moralist',[32] then, is 'to bring out of their obscurity . . . the points of coincidence to the extent of which extra-regarding interest is connected and has by the hands of nature been identified with self-regarding interest'.[33] In other words, the deontologist points to those events and anticipates those consequences of human actions that would, by themselves, motivate men to pursue utilitarian ends and maximize happiness. The legislator, on the contrary, has the task of applying the force of the 'political or legal sanction' in order to provide artificial motives for action, as Bentham's

[30] Ibid., 249.
[31] Bentham, *An Introduction to the Principles of Morals and Legislation* (*CW*), 293.
[32] *Deontology* (*CW*), 250.
[33] *Deontology* (*CW*), 193.

famous definition of 'a law' makes clear.[34] The distinction would seem to be pretty clear-cut.

However, if we look into the Benthamic prescriptions regarding the features of an ideal, all-comprehensive code of laws, there is at least one aspect of the legislator's job that brings it much closer to that of the practical moralist than would seem to be the case at first glance. It has to do with the necessity of giving reasons for every law enacted.

9.3 Legislative Reason-Giving

Bentham argued that it was necessary to attach a rationale to each of the articles in a 'complete code of laws'. The rationale for each norm of the code would accompany 'in the shape of a *perpetual commentary*, the whole mass of imperative or regulative matter'.[35] The 'parts' of the rationale should be 'placed in the most immediate contact with the several arrangements to which they respectively apply'.[36] No preliminary discourse (as in the Napoleonic penal code) would be expedient, in Bentham's view. The rationale would form a substantial part of the very matter of the code: it would not constitute only a formal characteristic of it[37] (as important as the form of the code may be for its success). It would pertain to that 'non-imperative content' that forms a necessary part of the code and includes what Bentham calls 'expository matter'.

The benefits expected from the inclusion of the rationale are numerous. For the legislator, it would serve as a compass (if well disposed), a barrier (if ill-disposed), and support (against criticism). The simple fact that the legislator would be willing to give reasons for the laws constituted, in Bentham's view, a guarantee of 'appropriate aptitude'.[38] For the judge, too, the rationale would serve as a compass, a barrier, and support: it would help determine which interpretation of the legal text best served the legislator's intentions and will.[39] It is worth recalling that the limits of judicial interpretation, both 'strict' and 'liberal', according to Bentham, are marked by a plausible reference to legislative will, be it actual or

[34] See J. Bentham, *Of the Limits of the Penal Branch of Jurisprudence*, ed. P. Schofield (Oxford: Clarendon Press, 2010 [*CW*]), henceforth *Limits*, 24–5.

[35] J. Bentham, *'Legislator of the World': Writings on Codification, Law, and Education*, ed. P. Schofield and J. Harris (Oxford: Clarendon Press, 1998 [*CW*]), henceforth *LW*, 7.

[36] *LW* (*CW*), 257–8.

[37] *LW* (*CW*), 7–8.

[38] *LW* (*CW*), 256–7.

[39] *LW* (*CW*), 142.

presumptive,[40] and to the ends of the law as intended by the legislator (which sometimes diverge from the 'strict import' of the words chosen to express legislative will, thereby making it necessary to interpret liberally).[41]

For citizens at large, the rationale would serve as 'an *anchor* and a *compass*': as a compass for interpretation and as an anchor to fix the details in the memory. More specifically, the rationale would serve as an anchor for the imperative/ordinative part; the latter, in turn, could be used in the same way with regard to the abovementioned 'expository matter'. If the laws were accompanied with a commentary of reasons, 'they would be more pleasantly studied, more easily known, more constantly retained, more cordially approved . . .. The reasons annexed will serve as a kind of technical memory: they will serve as a species of cement, by which to unite all those regulations which would otherwise appear as fragments and dispersed ruins'.[42] However, the rationale would also provide those same citizens with 'a source of security and tranquillity of mind'[43] due to the abovementioned functions of anchor for citizens and compass and barrier for legislators and judges: that is, it would add to legal certainty and predictability by guiding citizens' interpretation of the law, and it would help to secure them against the exercise of arbitrary power on the part of both legislative and judicial power. In their quality of electors, moreover, citizens would find in the rationale a 'Book of Instruction' to evaluate the degree of appropriate aptitude on the part of the candidates. Other advantages of the rationale include the fact that the method of adding rationales to the laws would bring different nations together by making their systems of law more similar and, at the same time, easier to compare.[44] However, the most interesting uses of the rationale would be those related to what we might consider as the relationship between legislation and public morality. One of the uses of the rationale for citizens at large, 'considered in the character of moral and intellectual agents,' is that 'it will serve in the additional character of *a lesson book*: a book of *instruction* in the art and science of *morals*'.[45] This aspect is closely related to what Bentham

[40] *Limits* (*CW*), 175.
[41] See ibid., 175.
[42] J. Bentham, *Essay on the Promulgation of Laws*, in *Works*, vol. i (henceforth *EPL*), 160.
[43] *LW* (*CW*), 142.
[44] *EPL*, 162.
[45] *LW* (*CW*), 142.

considered its 'greatest advantage . . . that which results from conciliating the approbation of all minds, by satisfying the public judgment, and obtaining obedience to the laws; not from a passive principle of blind fear alone, but with the concurrence of the will also'.[46] This is a natural consequence of reason-giving on the part of the legislator. By exhibiting the rationale of each law, every discussion about the law is reduced to the goodness or badness of the rationale. All political discussion revolves around this point. 'All cheats and fanatics' will be disarmed.

The rationale, then, would allow the legislator to address the intellects of its citizens, thereby gaining their approbation for the laws and giving them further motivation to obey them. As stated above, by employing punishments (and, less often, rewards), the legislator provides citizens with artificial motivation, while the practical moralist relies on natural motives by bringing to light how it is in the interest of the agent to act in a way that maximizes happiness for the greatest number of people. When giving reasons for the laws, the legislator resorts to natural motivation: this relies on an explanation that wins citizens' approbation by showing them how a good law is in the interest of everyone. Each citizen is made to understand that obeying the law is also good for them, regardless of the legal consequences of disobeying it. This is why, in a letter to Alexander I of Russia, Bentham wrote that by justifying (i.e., giving reasons for) legislative decisions, the legislator acts not so much as a sovereign but as a father who explains (not by commands but by instructions) the necessity of every obligation imposed.[47] This is what 'the concurrence of the will' mentioned above amounts to: citizens obey the law not because of the fear of sanctions but because their intellect is called into action and made to recognize natural, that is, non-sanction-related, grounds for motivation. In this sense, then, the job of the legislator is much closer to that of the practical moralist than it would seem to be at first glance. 'When a government orders, it but gives its subjects an artificial interest to obey; when it enlightens, it gives them an interior motive, the influence of which they cannot evade.'[48] If accompanied with their rationale, the laws would influence 'the moral nature' of

[46] *EPL*, 161.

[47] *LW* (*CW*), 45.

[48] J. Bentham, *Indirect Legislation*, in *A Bentham Reader*, ed. M. P. Mack (New York: Pegasus, 1969), 182.

the people, and the 'code of public opinion' would be brought into coincidence with the code of laws.[49]

With regard to the modern legisprudential concern for legislative justification, therefore, we could say that Bentham had a clear idea of the necessity and possible functions of such justification. While Bentham was by no means the first political and legal thinker to be concerned with the necessity of the explicit justification of laws – as this concern has been present in Western political thought at least since Plato's *Laws*[50] – the acceptance of such a necessity was anything but commonplace in his predecessors. For instance, Francis Bacon, one of his most admired forerunners in the field of jurisprudence, 'will not allow that reasons should be assigned, because it might lead to disputes concerning the law'.[51] Such an assumption of incompatibility between command and reason-giving was also typical of Thomas Hobbes, who reckoned that explicit legislative justification weakened the effectiveness of laws, even when good reasons are given.[52] The Command Theory of law is thus presented as incompatible with the idea that legislation must be rationally defensible, which is traditionally associated with Natural Law theories. By ascribing a central role to the explicit rationale of laws in his codification projects, Bentham combines an 'imperativist' model of legislation (i.e., the Command Theory of law) with a theory of legislative justification as reason-giving. A huge part of the code will be occupied by non-imperative matter; the rationale is part of this matter that contributes to compliance from citizens. Besides playing a number of other essential functions, the rationale further motivates citizens to comply with the law by addressing their intellect and not merely their will. It is a full-fledged legal material whose purpose is, like all other legal materials, to eventually maximize the happiness of the community by means of the law. Reason-giving does not weaken command but, rather, strengthens the legislator's authority and actually contributes to its legitimacy. We can see this as the other side of the coin with regard to Bentham's claim that the good citizen should '*Obey punctually; censure freely*';[53] the 'commentary of reasons' included in

[49] *EPL*, 161.
[50] See Plato, *Laws*, IV, 690c, 711c, 718b–d, and 722b.
[51] *EPL*, 159.
[52] See T. Hobbes, *De Cive*, English Version, Critical Edition by H. Warrender (Oxford: Clarendon Press, 1983), 30–1.
[53] J. Bentham, *A Comment on the Commentaries and A Fragment on Government*, ed. J. H. Burns, H. L. A. Hart (London: Athlone, 1977 [*CW*]), 399.

the code would be a crucial instrument of accountability by exposing the legislative authority to the critical gaze of public opinion.[54] Therefore, law is also legislative reason-giving, and as an object of study, it includes its explicit justification. The legal scholar would be fully justified in examining such justification and taking it into account, among other things, as a guide for interpretation.

Of course, due to his views on the relationship between legislative power and the judicature, Bentham did not think of a codified rationale as a possible basis for the constitutional judicial review of legislation (although it is not wholly incompatible with his constitutional system, and Bentham himself could presumably approve of it 'for adjudication of charges of formal ultra vires legislative action').[55] However, he was certainly aware of the necessity of legislative justification as a security against both arbitrary power and irrational law-making. Obviously, to draw up the rationalized part of the code requires that the legislator – or, more accurately, the drafter – employs the faculty of intellect, not only power and will, which would suffice for arbitrary legislation.[56] Arbitrariness, here, refers to a decision made on undisclosed, non-public grounds and is the opposite of legal publicity: that is, of the possibility for all the addressees of the law to assess its acceptability. The commentary of reasons included in the code would be a crucial instrument of publicity.[57]

It is worth remarking that, by subjecting the legislative power to the burden of reason-giving, Bentham is placing it in a position much more similar to that of judicial power than is usually thought. The underlying idea is that, although the courts and legislature are differently placed inside the legal system, the decisions of both bodies are ultimately subjected to justification with reference to the greatest happiness principle. For Bentham, while judges have to make reference to both the legislator's will and its application with the least possible 'delay, vexation, and expense', that is, they refer (mainly) indirectly to the

[54] See D. Lieberman, '*Of the Limits* and the Theory of Legislation', in *The Legal Philosophy and Influence of Jeremy Bentham*, ed. G. Tusseau (London: Routledge, 2014), 293–307, at 301.

[55] G. J. Postema, *Utility, Publicity, and Law: Essays on Bentham's Moral and Legal Philosophy* (Oxford: Oxford University Press, 2019), 232.

[56] *LW* (*CW*), 7–8.

[57] G. J. Postema, *Bentham and the Common Law Tradition. Second Edition* (Oxford: Oxford University Press, 2019), 471–4.

greatest happiness principle for justification,[58] the legislator has to give reasons with direct reference to the greatest happiness principle (or, more accurately, to its 'subordinate ends', as we will see in Section 9.4). Legislative activity is by no means free and unbounded as to its ends. Bentham anticipates the modern 'culture of justification' where all state powers are expected to justify their decisions, or at least to be ready to justify them, regardless of their formal legitimacy. Democratic elections do not suffice to exempt elected representatives from giving acceptable reasons for their decisions. Law-making and adjudication are not two fundamentally different models of legal reasoning, although they are placed on different levels, so to say, with regard to their relationship with utilitarian justification (in the sense that law-making has to appeal directly to such justification, while adjudication does so mostly indirectly and by making reference to existing legislation). The idea that legislative and judicial reasoning do not display qualitative differences but at most quantitative ones – such as the degree of discretion in finding solutions to problems – is dear to contemporary legisprudence, especially with reference to balancing and the principle of proportionality (which are considered as characterizing both instances of legal reasoning).[59] What should be clear by now is that none of the methodological or ideological constraints of nineteenth-century legal positivism, which have long stood in the way of legisprudence, belongs to Benthamic jurisprudence as a subsector of the art and science of legislation.

9.4 Contemporary Legisprudential Problems and Benthamic Answers

A few remarks regarding the relationship between Bentham's idea of legislative justification and modern legal 'culture of justification' are necessary, as the latter has paved the way for contemporary legisprudential enquiries. For Bentham, the rationale to be attached to each provision in the code needs to expose the relationship between law and happiness. It is an application of 'arithmetical calculations to the elements of happiness'.[60] Every rationale must show that (1) every new evil imposed by the law is overridden by the preponderant

[58] See F. Ferraro, 'Adjudication and Expectations: Bentham on the Role of the Judges', *Utilitas* 25 (2013), 140–60.

[59] See, for instance, Marcilla, 'Proportionality in Lawmaking', 164–7.

[60] *LW* (*CW*), 251.

amount of good expected, and (2) the same amount of good cannot be obtained by imposing a lesser quantity of evil. In Bentham's words, 'the principle of utility directs all reasons to a single centre: the reasons which apply to the detail of arrangements are only subordinate views of utility'.[61] However, it should be taken into account that, in Bentham's theory of legislative justification, there is room for value pluralism, in that, it is not the principle of utility that should be called into action but, rather, its subordinate principles. Moreover, according to the different (sub-) codes, the rationale will make reference to different subordinate ends of the principle.

> In the civil law, reasons should be drawn from four sources; that is to say, from the four objects, according to which the legislator ought to regulate his conduct in the distribution of private laws: subsistence, abundance, equality, security. In penal laws, the reasons should be drawn from the nature of the evil of offences and from that of the remedies of which they are susceptible. These remedies are of four kinds: preventive remedies, suppressive remedies, satisfactive remedies, penal remedies. In the law of procedure, the reasons should equally derive their source from the different ends that ought to be kept in view: correctness of judgment, quickness, and economy. In financial law, the reasons should be drawn from two principal objects: saving in expense, in order to avoid the evil of constraint; choice of the tax, in order to avoid its accessory inconveniencies.[62]

This kind of approach is fairly close to the modern constitutional balancing of different principles and values. Some have emphasized the need for such balancing and the application of the principle of proportionality, not only in adjudication but also in law-making.[63] Utilitarian balancing is often seen as problematic, but even its critics have allowed room for it when fundamental rights are not at stake, that is, when balancing involves interests rather than rights. When fundamental rights are to be weighed against each other, a different form of balancing is propounded, whereby the number of individuals affected is not taken into account (in order not to tread on minorities).[64]

As is well known, Bentham was hostile to the use of the language of rights in constitutional law. As Gerald Postema has observed, his reasons

[61] *EPL*, 162.

[62] Ibid., 162.

[63] See J.-R. Sieckmann, 'Legislation as Balancing', in *Conceptions and Misconceptions of Legislation*, ed. A. D. Oliver-Lalana, 133–52.

[64] Ibid.

against constitutional rights were not merely conceptual and did not only concern the 'nonsense upon stilts' of natural imprescriptible rights; rather, he thought that the indeterminacy of broad fundamental rights assertions threatened the necessary publicity of the grounds for decision (both judicial and, we may now add, legislative).[65] The language of utility, which Bentham proposes as the means for subjecting the legislator's decisions to public assessment, is very different from the language of rights usually used in modern reviews of legislation. However, the provision of the rationale of laws subjects the legislator to a stricter constraint than those posed by most contemporary constitutions. While these constitutions usually impose negative limits to legislative action, Bentham's reason-giving requirement bounds the legislator to actively pursue happiness maximization. This is in line with the modern legal 'culture of justification', where the courts often expand the scope of justification by not considering themselves limited by the constitutional text. They can review governmental action and demand justification even when, in and by itself, the constitution would prima facie confer legitimacy on such action (as part of the legislator's 'political discretion'). The underlying assumption is that no exercise of power is legitimate unless it is justified,[66] thereby drastically reducing the room for political discretion.

In recent times, legisprudential scholar Luc J. Wintgens has attacked the so-called 'proxy model' of the social contract, which he associates with Hobbes and Jean-Jacques Rousseau, and which confers on the sovereign the power to impose 'external limitations of freedom' on subjects, whatever these limitations may be and independently of the content of the promulgated rules. Against this proxy model, Wintgens puts forward a model of 'legisprudential validity', according to which there are a number of conditions that need to be satisfied in order to produce justified legislative regulations; every rule must actually be justified by the legislator, with explicit reference to these conditions. Moreover, justifiability is not acquired once and for all by the rules; it is subject to scrutiny through time because of changing factual

[65] See Postema, *Utility, Publicity, and Law*, vii.

[66] See M. Cohen-Eliya and I. Porat, *Justification and Authority: Proportionality and Constitutional Culture* (Cambridge: Cambridge University Press, 2013), 120. Conversely, where a legal 'culture of authority' prevails (as opposed to a 'culture of justification'), 'both the government and judiciary are institutions whose legitimacy rests on their authority, not justification. The constitutional text that authorizes the courts to review governmental action is, therefore, of vital importance' (ibid., 119).

circumstances. This means that, if a rule loses its point, it will have to be struck down by the legislature itself or by judicial review.[67] An essential requisite for justifiability and legitimacy, in Wintgens's view, is rationality.[68] We can confidently say that Bentham never adopted the 'proxy model' of sovereignty, not least because, in his late constitutional thought, sovereignty was lodged in the people themselves,[69] that is, in those 'whose interest it is that happiness be maximized'.[70] But the main reason why the 'proxy model' is incompatible with Bentham's perspective is that the legislature was to be kept constantly under the control of the 'subject many' and the Public Opinion Tribunal because this was the only security for 'appropriate aptitude' on the part of its members. The Supreme Legislature, in Bentham's *Constitutional Code*, had no limits to its power but, rather, checks to its exercise in the form of securities.[71] Legislative reason-giving, as we have seen, has among its purposes that of granting effective control over the legislator to the citizens.

As noted above, one reason for the renewed interest in legislative justification is the 'process review' of legislation by the courts. Legislation has to comply with some minimal requirements of rationality in order not to be struck down as purely arbitrary. Usually, the courts are satisfied with merely verifying that there has actually been some debate in the legislature before the approval of the measure in question. Some legisprudential scholars have gone further in analyzing actual parliamentary debates and proposing models for assessing their quality and rationality, thereby looking for justification in the speeches of the members of the legislature rather than some preamble or other part included in the final statute.[72] Bentham considered this kind of approach but dismissed it as much more burdensome, both for the enquirer and the reader.[73]

[67] L. J. Wintgens, *Legisprudence: Practical Reason in Legislation* (Aldershot: Ashgate, 2012), 153–7, 303–4.

[68] L. J. Wintgens, 'The Rational Legislator Revisited: Bounded Rationality and Legisprudence', in *The Rationality and Justification of Legislation: Essays in Legisprudence*, ed. L. J. Wintgens and D. Oliver-Lalana (Cham: Springer, 2013),1–31.

[69] J. Bentham, *Constitutional Code, Vol. I*, ed. F. Rosen and J. H. Burns (Oxford: Clarendon Press, 1983 [*CW*]), henceforth *Constitutional Code I*, 25.

[70] Ibid., 21.

[71] Ibid., 41–2.

[72] See, for instance, D. Oliver-Lalana, 'Rational Lawmaking and Legislative Reasoning in Parliamentary Debates', in *The Rationality and Justification of Legislation*, ed. L. J. Wintgens and A. D. Oliver-Lalana,135–84; also Atienza, 'Legislation and Argumentation'

[73] 'True it is that ... *limits*, to the degree of conciseness, capable of being given to the discourse expressive of the reasons belonging to the ordinances for which the public

However, he also thought that the analysis of parliamentary debates could be useful as a check on legislative power. In *The Book of Fallacies*, he claimed that the disclosure of the employment of fallacies in parliamentary debates would expose the insincerity of those who uttered them and their 'sinister interests'. Bentham thought that his classification and analysis of the political fallacies and their causes could, among other uses, allow them to be pointed out explicitly in notes to printed reports of the debates.[74]

Bentham opposed the constitutional judicial review of legislation; therefore, the 'code of reasons' and the rationale attached to every statute were not meant for judicial control over the legislature's decisions. However, in *Constitutional Code*, the Public Opinion Tribunal, rather than a constitutional court, was the real guardian of the constitution. The Public Opinion Tribunal was the judicial branch of the Supreme Constitutive authority, that is, of the people at large as sovereign.[75] Contrary to other thinkers of the Enlightenment, Bentham conceived of constitutive power not as superior, external, and temporally precedent to the constitution but, rather, as continually existing and watching over all other powers and authorities in the state. For him, 'Public Opinion may be considered as a system of law, emanating from the body of the people'.[76] Now, as we have seen, a proper 'code of reasons' attached to legal provisions would offer a book of instruction in morals and legislation, which would be directed at citizens at large. It would help in moulding public opinion: 'If the laws were founded upon reason, they would infuse themselves, so to speak, into the minds of the people: . . . the code of public opinion would be formed by analogy upon the code of the laws.'[77] By means of the 'code of reasons', the legislature would actually contribute to the shaping of public opinion in accordance with the dictates of utility. From the point of view of the citizens, the legislative rationale would help the people as sovereign in attaining a deeper and

interest presents a demand, cannot but have place: but, small indeed will the quantity be found, in comparison of what might be expected by any workman, who, on taking measure of it in his mind, should look for a pattern, either to the debates of a legislative body, or to the argumentations delivered in a judicatory, on a ground of Common Law' (*LW* [*CW*], 145).

74 See J. Bentham, *The Book of Fallacies*, ed. P. Schofield (Oxford: Oxford University Press, 2015), 72–5.

75 *Constitutional Code I* (*CW*), 35–36.

76 Ibid., 36.

77 *EPL*, 161.

more detailed understanding of their interest and overcoming prejudices and impassioned judgements.

9.5 Conclusion: Bentham's Art and Science of Legislation as a Meta-theoretical Framework for Legisprudence

As I have sought to show, in Bentham's view, the kinds of problems at the core of modern legisprudential enquiries are a perfectly legitimate subject of study for legal theorists. One could say that jurisprudence is part of the study of legislation rather than the other way round. 'Censorial jurisprudence', as we have seen, is just another name for the art of legislation and prescribes how the law should be. This concerns both its substantive content and formal features. Expository jurisprudence, then, amounts to the corresponding science of legislation or, at the very least, a central part of it: namely, that concerned with the analysis of basic legal concepts. It is worth remarking, however, that jurisprudence in both its branches is considered by Bentham as a subsector of Deontology, namely, of normative (that is, not merely descriptive) ethics. Thus, expository (and not only censorial) jurisprudence is also part of normative ethics: it describes law as it is, but it does so as part of the 'censorial' knowledge of what should be done. In other words, both the art and science of legislation are a subsector of normative ethics.

As Xiaobo Zhai has remarked, Bentham's Universal Expository Jurisprudence was ultimately aimed at the maximization of happiness, like all other sciences, as branches of the all-encompassing science of 'Eudaemonics': therefore, it was not a morally neutral description of the kind required by Hartian (and not only Hartian) positivism.[78] Philip Schofield has adopted Stephen Perry's definition of 'methodological legal positivism' as the view according to which legal theory can offer a normatively neutral description of law[79] and, accordingly, has held that Bentham's utilitarian jurisprudence was not an instance of legal

[78] X. Zhai, 'Bentham's Natural Arrangement versus Hart's Morally Neutral Description', *Revue d'études benthamiennes* 10 (2012), doi.org/10.4000/etudes-benthamiennes.603; 'Bentham's Natural Arrangement and the Collapse of the Espositor-Censor Distinction in the General Theory of Law', in *Bentham's Theory of Law and Public Opinion*, ed. X. Zhai and M. Quinn (Cambridge: Cambridge University Press, 2014), 143–83.

[79] See S. R. Perry, 'Hart's Methodological Positivism', in *Hart's Postscript: Essays on the Postscript to the Concept of Law*, ed. J. L. Coleman (Oxford: Oxford University Press, 2001), 311–54, at 311–3.

positivism.[80] Without delving into the question regarding whether the 'legal positivism' tag can be applied to Bentham's jurisprudence, it is clear that many of the usual tenets of legal positivism do not apply to his theory, such as those regarding legal knowledge and the role of jurists as 'legal scientists'. These tenets, as stated above, have long hindered legisprudence as a legitimate enterprise for the legal scholar. At the same time, Benthamic legisprudence avoids the problems of the Dworkinian approach because legislative reasoning is not seen as fundamentally different from judicial reasoning: although the former adopts more direct forms of utilitarian calculation, while the latter is mostly indirectly utilitarian (due to a concern for predictability and respect of law-induced expectations),[81] the distinction is one of degree, not of quality. If adjudication is a conspicuous example of legal reasoning, then so is legislation.

Within the framework of Bentham's utilitarian jurisprudence, a picture of the legal scholar emerges as both a scientist of law and a contributor to its improvement. The task of describing the law as it is, both as an empirical and conceptual enterprise, is as much a legitimate one as the (different but related) task of prescribing how it should be, both with regard to its form and arrangement and its substantive content. Legisprudence finds its place as the primary field of study for legal scholars who wish to provide legislatures with the knowledge necessary for improving the quality of legislation.

[80] See P. Schofield, 'Jeremy Bentham and HLA Hart's 'Utilitarian Tradition in Jurisprudence', *Jurisprudence* 1 (2010), 147–67.

[81] See F. Ferraro, 'Direct and Indirect Utilitarianism in Bentham's Theory of Adjudication', *The Journal of Bentham Studies* 12 (2010), 1–24.

10

Indirect Legislation in Bentham's Late Constitutional Writings

ANNE BRUNON-ERNST

> If of the expedients which we shall proceed to mention under the head of indirect legislation there should be some which may appear referable to the other head, it will be no great matter: nothing of moment will turn upon the accuracy of the division.[1]

10.1 Introduction

This chapter[2] is one of the first attempts to investigate the use of indirect legislation in Bentham's later constitutional writings. However, the epigraph serves as a disclaimer. Bentham acknowledges that his divisions into three categories (civil, penal, and constitutional) might not be as watertight as other parts of his theory.[3] This is a reminder that the explorations of indirect constitutional law presented in the present chapter need to be handled with critical caution as the mechanisms labelled 'indirect' might have shifting boundaries. Moreover, indirect constitutional law holds an unusual position. Indeed, its constitutional branch is

1 Bentham's early writings on indirect legislation are to be found at the University College London collection of Bentham manuscripts (henceforth UC) under the title: 'Projet d'un corps de loix complet, à l'usage d'un pays quelconque: avec les principes et les raisons tant générales que particulières sur lesquelles chaque disposition aura été fondée' (UC xcix. 156; henceforth 'Projet'). The manuscripts containing Bentham's essay 'Indirect Legislation' are accessible at www.ucl.ac.uk/Bentham-Project/transcribe_bentham. The boxes in question are boxes UC lxxxvii (87), lxii. (62), and xcvi (96).

2 The present research originates from an invitation at the University of Macau to speak about Bentham's late constitutional writing as part of an ongoing project directed by Professor Xiaobo Zhai.

3 These divisions are investigated in *Of the Limits of the Penal Branch of Jurisprudence*, ed. P. Schofield (Oxford: Oxford University Press, 2010) (henceforth *Limits* [*CW*]). *Limits* first appeared as *The Limits of Jurisprudence Defined*, ed. C. W. Everett (New York: Columbia University Press, 1945), before being edited for *the Collected Works* by H. L. A. Hart as *Of Laws in General* (London: Clarendon Press, 1970 [*CW*]), and re-edited by Schofield in 2010.

mentioned only, but not described as precisely, as the penal and civil branches of the law. To add injury to insult, the title of the chapter is a misnomer as the phrase 'indirect legislation' itself is hardly mentioned in Bentham's later writings, since the concept had almost disappeared from his writings by 1802.[4]

Notwithstanding these inauspicious beginnings, investigating mechanisms akin to indirect legislation is justified by the use in later writings of instruments labelled 'indirect' in earlier ones. Several instances of this metamorphosis are investigated in this chapter. First, Bentham qualifies some instruments as indirect. It is then possible to trace back the concepts of misrule and public opinion in *First Principles*[5] from the indirect means of promoting good government discussed in *Traités de législation civile et pénale* (hereafter *Traités*).[6] The approach will be to identify mechanisms akin to indirect legislation in Bentham's later writings, even if they are not labelled as such.

The stakes of such an investigation are high, as up to very recently indirect legislation has been a neglected concept in the literature.[7] Identifying indirect mechanisms at work in Bentham's later and more iconic writings may recast indirect legislation as a pivotal concept in his thought, rather than only an early experiment to be discarded.

I here contend that the mechanisms Bentham identified as indirect legislation are still at work in Bentham's later works, especially his constitutional writings. To carry out this study, I will first discuss what

[4] There are some later references to indirect legislation in *The Book of Fallacies*, ed. P. Schofield (Oxford: Oxford University Press, 2015 [*CW*]), 181; and in a manuscript source titled 'Nomography', BL Add MS 33, 548 fo. 257 (24 June 1829). I am indebted to Prof. Schofield for these references.

[5] J. Bentham, 'Economy as Applied to Office', in *First Principles Preparatory to the Constitutional Code*, ed. F. Rosen and P. Schofield (Oxford: Clarendon Press, 1989 [*CW*]), 1–122, at 56–9 (henceforth 'Economy as Applied to Office').

[6] J. Bentham, *Traités de législation civile et pénale*, ed. É. Dumont, 3 vols (Paris, 1802), III, 1–199. For a modern one-volume edition of the *Traités*, see *Traités de legislation civile et pénale*, ed. E. Dumont, with a preface by M. Bozzo-Rey, A. Brunon-Ernst, and E. de Champs (Dalloz: Paris, 2010) (henceforth *Traités*), 381–2.

[7] Very few scholars have investigated Bentham's concept of indirect legislation. Of note are the following works that engage with the concept: M. Mack, *Jeremy Bentham: An Odyssey of Ideas, 1748–1792* (London: Heinemann, 1962), 174n; D. G. Long, *Bentham on Liberty: Jeremy Bentham's Idea of Liberty in Relation to His Utilitarianism* (Toronto: University of Toronto Press, 1977), 135–49; L. J. Hume, *Bentham and Bureaucracy* (Cambridge: Cambridge University Press, 1981), 77; and C. F. Bahmueller, *The National Charity Company: Jeremy Bentham's Silent Revolution* (Berkeley: University of California Press, 1981).

Bentham meant by indirect legislation in his earlier writings.[8] Section 10.3 will be devoted to the study of mechanisms akin to indirect legislation in the later constitutional writings, with a focus on several instances of indirect instruments, such as the Public Opinion Tribunal (hereafter POT), publication and registration schemes, as well as architectural arrangements. The chapter aims to establish that, in more ways than one, indirect legislation is part and parcel of Bentham's system of government.

10.2 Indirect Legislation in Bentham's Earlier Writings

10.2.1 Historiography

Indirect legislation was first publicized in French in Etienne Dumont's widely circulated 1802 edition of the *Traités*. Dumont worked from Bentham's manuscripts, relying on 'Indirect Legislation', which is written in English, and on 'Projet', in French.[9] There are therefore two main published sources: Dumont's *Traités*[10] (which has a whole section on indirect legislation) and Bowring's edition of Bentham's *Works*[11] (which reproduces the former).

There is also a passing reference in *Limits*. Thanks to C. W. Everett's first edition of *The Limits of Jurisprudence Defined* (1945), then to H. L. A. Hart's subsequent edition of *Of Laws in General* (hereafter *Of Laws*) (1970), and to Philip Schofield's final and authoritative edition of *Of the Limits of the Penal Branch of Jurisprudence* (hereafter *Limits*) (2010), the concept has become a noteworthy element in Bentham's corpus.[12] Indeed, although there is only a single reference to the concept in *Limits*,[13] Schofield's editorial choice of associating *Limits* with chapter XVII of *An Introduction to the Principles of Morals and Legislation*

[8] For the full history of Bentham's manuscripts on indirect legislation, see M. Bozzo-Rey, A. Brunon-Ernst and M. Quinn, 'Editors' introduction', *History of European Ideas* 43, no. 1 (2017), 1–10.

[9] See n. 1.

[10] See n. 5.

[11] J. Bentham, 'Principles of Penal Law. Part III. Of Indirect Means of Preventing Crimes', in *The Works of Jeremy Bentham* (Bristol: Thoemmes Press, 1995 [1843]), (henceforth Bowring), i. 533–80.

[12] See S. G. Engelmann, 'Limits and Indirect Legislation', in *The Legal Philosophy and Influence of Jeremy Bentham: Essays on Of the Limits of the Penal Branch of Jurisprudence*, ed. G. Tusseau (London: Routledge, 2014), 308–15.

[13] *Limits* (*CW*), 142

(hereafter *Introduction*),[14] restores it to its place within Bentham's project as a whole and puts indirect legislation on the map of Bentham scholarship. The publication of a special issue of the *History of European Ideas* in 2017 and Quinn's monograph of 2022 worked towards the same goal.[15]

Indirect legislation has also attracted much interest lately on account of two unconnected phenomenon. First, the publication of Foucault's lecture series at the Collège de France and more particularly the volume entitled *Birth of Biopolitics*[16] and second, the growing interest in nudges.[17] Indeed, in later writings, Foucault explores the rise of norms in the era of biopolitics. In doing so, he relies on some of the alternative modes of governance to be found in Bentham's economic writings and practical schemes (Panopticon, police powers, etc.). The growing interest in nudge has also generated corresponding interest in the utilitarian community for the founders of nudging, among whom J. S. Mill is often quoted, and to a lesser extent Bentham.[18] The combination of the edition of Foucault's works on biopolitics and of the promotion of alternative forms of regulation has renewed interest in the theoretical roots of both biopolitics and nudge, thus triggering some of the most interesting scientific research in recent decades in the field of Bentham studies.[19]

[14] J. Bentham, *An Introduction to the Principles of Morals and Legislation*, ed. J. H. Burns and H. L. A. Hart, intro. F. Rosen (Oxford: Clarendon Press, 1996 [*CW*]), henceforth *IPML*.

[15] Bozzo-Rey, Brunon-Ernst and Quinn, 'Editors' introduction', and M. Quinn, *Bentham* (Cambridge: Polity Press, 2022).

[16] M. Foucault, *The Birth of Biopolitics: Lectures at the Collège de France, 1978–1979*, ed. M. Senellart, trans. G. Burchell (London: Palgrave Macmillan, 2008), 65.

[17] The term 'nudge' was coined by Thaler and Sunstein (R. Thaler and C. Sunstein, *Nudge: Improving Decisions about Health, Wealth and Happiness* (London: Penguin, 2008). It is defined as 'any aspect of the choice architecture that alters people's behaviour in a predictable way without forbidding any option or significantly changing economic incentives' (Thaler and Sunstein, *Nudge*, 8. See also C. Sunstein, *Why Nudge? The Politics of Libertarian Paternalism* [New Haven: Yale University Press, 2014], 17).

[18] For a comparative study of Bentham's and Mill's anticipation of nudge theory, see Anne Brunon-Ernst, 'Nudges and the limits of appropriate interference: Reading Backwards from J. S. Mill's Harm Principle to Jeremy Bentham's Indirect Legislation', *History of European Ideas* 43, no. 1 (2017), 53–69.

[19] More recent work by S. G. Engelmann (S. G. Engelmann, '"Indirect Legislation": Bentham's Liberal Government', *Polity* 35 [2003], 369–88); Christian Laval (C. Laval, 'La chaîne invisible: Bentham et le néolibéralisme', *Revue d'études benthamiennes* 1 (2006), https://journals.openedition.org/etudes-benthamiennes/63); a special issue (Bozzo-Rey, Brunon-Ernst, and Quinn, ed., *Indirect Legislation: Bentham's Regulatory Revolution* in *History of European Ideas*, 1–121); and Quinn, *Bentham*; make it possible to reassess the impact of Bentham's concept on his earlier works.

10.2.2 *Direct Legislation Defined*

The concept of 'indirect legislation' has been used several times in the opening paragraphs of this chapter and now needs to be explained. Two additional concepts also need defining: 'indirect constitutional law' as opposed to 'direct constitutional law'. These concepts have precise meaning within Bentham's system and are used at very specific times in his writing.

As 'indirect' legislation presupposes 'direct', direct legislation is a useful tool to understand its converse. To carry out this preliminary task, it is helpful to examine a familiar quote.

> A law may be defined an assemblage of signs declarative of a volition or adopted by a sovereign in a state, concerning the conduct to be observed in a certain case by a certain person or class of persons, who in the case in question are or are supposed to be subject to his power: such volition trusting for its accomplishment to the accomplishment of certain events which it is intended such declaration should upon occasion be means of bringing to pass, and the prospect of which it is intended should act as a motive upon those whose conduct is in question.[20]

The quotation presents three founding elements of Bentham's legal theory. The first is that a law is embedded in language. It is a type of social regulation that does not have any existence other than in words. Laws, which convey the legislator's meaning, are made up of words. These words express either the primary will of the legislator when set out in a statute or his/her delegated will in the case of a decree or any other legal instrument enforceable in court, such as a marriage or employment contract. The second point of note is that a law only applies to those by whom the power to address laws is recognized and accepted, which presupposes habits of obedience. Third, the will of the legislator relies on sanctions. Without sanction, there is no law. However, applying a sanction (fine or imprisonment) will generate pain for the non-compliant party. As utility aims to minimize pain, the rationale for law cannot be punishment but rather the reliance on any legal or non-legal instrument as long as that will make people change their behaviour so that aggregate pleasure be maximized. It becomes clear that nothing in Bentham's definition prevents the inclusion of indirect legislation as law. This point will be discussed further in Section 10.2.3.

[20] *Limits* (*CW*), 24.

'Indirect Legislation', like all of Bentham's writings, has a very complex textual history. When reading the manuscripts and published editions, it is nonetheless possible to identify a certain number of elements that help us to understand what indirect legislation is. First, indirect legislation is always defined in relation to direct legislation; and second, indirect legislation is explained by the use of metaphors, taken, for instance, from drama, hunting, geography, and the weather. These two points give the impression that Bentham is unable to discuss indirect legislation in a direct way, that he has not thought his idea through, and that it cannot operate as a separate system. Indirect legislation is thus best described as legal theory in the making, with three features: indirectness, indeterminacy, and subserviency.[21]

10.2.3 *Indirect Legislation Circumscribed*

The first feature is indirectness. Bentham starts his project of legal reform with direct legislation and explains:

> The same law which is direct in one respect in relation to an end is indirect in relation to another end. This division was perceived by some writers but not determined; and nobody has ever drawn this division to its ultimate conclusion. However, it can be considered as complete.[22]

The quotation provides important information. The first point is that there is direct and indirect legislation in relation to the three branches of law. This is a controversial statement, since, at the same time as Bentham is making this point, he is criticizing the traditional division of the law into three branches.[23] For the sake of clarity, Bentham seems to have sought to make things straightforward for readers by referring to categories of law that would be familiar to them.

The second point is that Bentham gives a rough presentation of the roles of the various branches of the law when he explains that criminal

[21] See A. Brunon-Ernst, 'Indirect legislation and Utility: Study of the Effectiveness of Indirect Legislation', presented at ISUS International Symposium, held in Yokohama University (Japan) on 20–22 August 2014.

[22] UC xxxiii. 111–2.

[23] See A. Brunon-Ernst, 'Délimiter la branche civile du droit: Bentham et la quête impossible', in *Bentham, juriste*, ed. G. Tusseau and M. Bozzo-Rey (Paris: Economica, 2010), 177–200. On Bentham's civil law, see J. Gillardin, 'Les principes du code civil d'après Jeremy Bentham', in *Actualité de la pensée juridique de Jeremy Bentham* (Brussels: Publications des Facultés universitaires Saint-Louis, 1987); Long, *Bentham on Liberty*, 160–70; and Mack, *Jeremy Bentham*, 172.

law is concerned with prohibiting and ordering, that civil law is concerned with attributing title to property, and that constitutional law is concerned with attributing position to individuals. He then states that anything else the law does will be indirect legislation. In doing so, he connects indirect legislation to a wide ranging and open-ended set of elements. Notwithstanding all its inaccuracies, this statement is of interest as it opens up the range of actions for the law. Law is not only about prohibition and command. It includes all the other actions that help achieve a designated target. In Bentham's utilitarian politics, the legislator has now two instruments at his command: the law, with prohibition and command that will seek to implement a given policy; but also other instruments under the heading of indirect legislation and that encompass all the varied courses of action that can be taken to make sure that a given objective is met.

In the quotation above, Bentham states that the division is complete. In light of what has been said so far, this is not a convincing statement. To get a better grasp of what indirect legislation is, the various policies that Bentham listed as indirect legislation must be studied. In the published *Traités* and in the manuscript source headed 'Plan', Bentham gives lists of what is considered as indirect legislation. In the *Traités*, Bentham mentions controlling people through pay,[24] awarding honours to reward certain types of behaviour,[25] regulating data-saving,[26] promoting public education rather than private,[27] freeing the press,[28] indemnifying the victims of crime, and so forth.[29] In the manuscript source named 'Plan', which pre-dates the *Traités*, Bentham notes that the following activities fall within the scope of indirect legislation: procedure, prevention of crimes, benevolence, poor law, prevention of drunkenness,[30] promotion of culture, advocacy of activity on the Sabbath, rules to strengthen the administration of justice, new remedies for crimes of

24 *Traités*, 356.
25 Ibid., 356.
26 Ibid., 369–70.
27 Ibid., 388–90.
28 Ibid., 392f.
29 Ibid., 404–5.
30 Prevention is very much used as synonymous with indirect legislation, see 'Plan': 'Legislation and administration: internal law and international: penal law and civil: private law and public or constitutional: law of procedure, and the as yet undenominated branch of the law which contains the principal matter to the execution of which so much as concerns the law of procedure is subservient. Each of these may be distinguished into direct or ordinary and indirect or preventive.'

honour, provision of information, publicity of public proceeding, marking of individuals, registers, standards of quantity and quality, stamps, account of people (census), and so forth.[31] These lists unfortunately are not very helpful to define indirect legislation as they read like a mass of unrelated elements strung together. However, a closer look at these lists shows that they can, each in their own way, help to achieve a particular utilitarian goal.

Some of the instruments in the list tie into Bentham's later works, such as freeing the press,[32] regulating data saving, controlling people through pay, publicity of official proceedings, provision of information, registers, administration of justice; all these policies are also to be found in Bentham's late constitutional theory. However, at the present stage, it is fair to conclude that these lists of seemingly unconnected policies only exemplify the second feature of indirect legislation: indeterminacy.

The third and final feature is subserviency. Bentham's indirect legislation fits into his hierarchy of norms. Indeed, he writes:

> Indirect legislation may assist direct, but can not supersede [direct legislation]. The one and the other must go hand in hand. The events which call for the infliction of punishment may be more rare: but punishment must always be held up.[33]

Bentham clearly sets out a hierarchy between direct and indirect legislation, with indirect only there to assist direct legislation. In this quote, the term 'assistance' is important because it will reappear in the later constitutional writings. Indeed, some forms of policy are presented as 'assisting' constitutional law. This feature might be the key to identifying forms of indirect legislation in Bentham's late constitutional writing.

Bentham understands legislation, both direct and indirect, as a form of control. His definition of a law is wide and can include both what we understand as law but also many other instruments that would not usually fall under its heading. The reason lies with Bentham's aim: he is first and foremost interested is controlling behaviour. He does so by using both direct and indirect legislation. Stephen Engelmann explains that 'Bentham conceives all legislation as control, and in this sense it is

[31] J. Bentham Project transcript of *Plan*. Courtesy of Michael Quinn (UCL). The manuscripts are to be found in the Bentham fund, at UC, lxxxvii. (87), lxii. (62), and xcvi. (96).

[32] Engelmann, 'Limits and Indirect Legislation', 311.

[33] Appendix B, in *Plan*.

direct and indirect at the same time .... So indirect legislation recommends ways for the legislator to enlist other sanctions'.[34]

This quotation makes it possible to move the study a step further. Indeed, the opening definition of a law associates direct legislation with the infliction of a sanction.[35] It is coeval with the existence of the law. Without a sanction in case of failure to comply, there is no law. Direct legislation enlists the political sanction, that is, legal punishment for crimes or breaches committed. However, when indirect legislation is used, not only the political but also the moral sanctions may be operative.

Thanks to the features established above, indirect legislation can be defined as any attempt by the sovereign to influence the conduct of others, generally without legal punishment in case of non-compliance.[36] Two caveats must be entered in relation to this definition. The first is that the sovereign in *Of Laws* or *Limits* can be replaced by a legislator, either as a single power-wielding individual or as a body of people. The second is that legal punishment can be used with indirect legislation too. Indirect legislation resorts both to the political and the moral sanctions; however, it does not do so in the same circumstances. The circumstances that call for the political or the moral sanction need to be explained as they will help identify certain types of indirect legislation.

10.2.4 Primary and Secondary Forms of Indirect Legislation

To change behaviour, a legislator has two tools: direct legislation and indirect legislation. Direct legislation always imposes the legal sanction, that is, the threat of legal punishment, on the offender.[37] When indirect legislation imposes the legal sanction, it is to target another party, for example, the accessory to a crime: direct legislation would punish the thief, but indirect legislation would also impose a legal sanction on the person who received stolen goods. If the aim of legislation is to stop theft, targeting thieves is not enough. Indeed, in most cases, thieves are not interested in the goods but in the money that they are going to make

[34] Engelmann, 'Indirect Legislation', 372–3. See also Quinn, *Bentham*, 169.

[35] See n. 21.

[36] A. Brunon-Ernst, 'Beyond the Genetic Panopticon: The Limits of Government Intervention on Citizens' Bodies', *Implications philosophiques* 1 (2014), www.implications-philosophiques.org/actualite/une/beyond-the-genetic-panopticon/.

[37] See n. 34.

from their sale. People who buy them are not thieves, as they knowingly (or not) just receive them.[38] In our contemporary legal divisions, they would be accessory to a crime and would be punishable under criminal law. But for Bentham, the offences would fall under two different heads: direct and indirect.

A fine distinction needs to be made between what can be referred to as primary and secondary forms of indirect legislation. The primary form of indirect legislation relies on the legal and political sanction but without targeting the offender. It targets another person who can influence the behaviour of the offender (such as an accessory to a crime).

The secondary form of indirect legislation relies on the moral and popular sanction, as it aims to manipulate personal desires. One of the examples that Bentham gives of this second type of indirect legislation is children in poor houses. He floats the idea of not making them taste cakes.[39] The rationale is that if they have no experience of how sweet cakes taste, they do not risk being frustrated or unhappy because they could not afford to buy them. Bentham is aiming to manipulate people's desires by creating an environment that will force them to behave in certain ways. Most importantly, in this secondary form, it is when he is controlling the levers of behaviour that Bentham's writings connect with nudge theory.[40]

Bentham stops writing on indirect legislation at the turn of the nineteenth century. Assumptions can be made as to the reasons:[41] the concept was vague, as it was not fleshed out properly; Bentham did not need a separate category; or Bentham moved on to different projects. However, although he does not write about indirect legislation anymore, it is evident that what he learnt about indirect legislation is to be found again in his later constitutional writing. Indeed, it could be that indirect

[38] Bentham gives the example of the prostitute. Indirect legislation can complement direct legislation. For instance, enacting legislation to criminalize the purchase of services offered by prostitutes is a clear example of direct legislation as it has the intended effect of prohibiting certain categories of individuals from behaving in certain ways by the threat of a legal sanction. However, it is also to be viewed as indirect legislation as its primary goal is to stop women from turning to prostitution (see *Traités*, 375–7).

[39] J. Bentham, *Outline of a Work entitled Pauper Management Improved*, in Bowring, viii. 369–439, at 439; and J. Bentham, 'Essays on the Subject of the Poor Laws,' in *Writings on the Poor Laws*, ed. M. Quinn (Oxford: Clarendon Press, 2001 [*CW*]), 54.

[40] A. Brunon-Ernst, '"Back to the Sources of Nudges", *Nudges: Better Choices?*', *The Tocqueville Review/ La Revue Tocqueville* 37, no. 1 (2016), 99–122.

[41] A. Brunon-Ernst, 'Le gouvernement des normes: Jeremy Bentham et les instruments de régulation post-modernes', *Archives de philosophie* 78, no. 2 (2015), 309–22.

legislation might be more useful to Bentham when it is not dealt with as a separate category but when it permeates the whole of his system. The rest of the chapter investigates this hypothesis.

10.3 Indirect Constitutional Law in Bentham's Later Writings

10.3.1 Indirect Constitutional Law as Prevention of Misrule

Constitutional law has its direct and indirect legislation. This statement appears early on in the *Traités* in 1802 but is based on manuscripts written around 1780. Bentham explains:

> Constitutional law has its direct and indirect legislation; direct legislation consists in setting up the offices to which public power is allocated .... Indirect legislation consists in general precautions to prevent the misconduct, incapacity or embezzlement among those who administer in chief or as deputies.[42]

This quotation explains what indirect constitutional law does: it sets up precautions to prevent misconduct, incapacity, or embezzlement. Constitutional law is neither interested in people as individual members of society nor in offenders. It deals with the conduct of ruling officials. Its function is to offer 'security against misrule'. Misrule is used sparsely in earlier writings:

> There remains that branch of legislation which is or might be directed against misrule. Even under this head the distinction between direct and indirect legislation may be still preserved; though the limits between those branches are scarcely so distinct, nor is the distinction itself of so much importance, in this case as in the former.[43]

However, it becomes a core concept of Bentham's later constitutional theory. What is security against misrule? It can be defined as follows: 'The security of ordinary subjects of law against the arbitrary exercise of power at the hands of the ruling officials.'[44] These securities can be understood as any protection or precaution to prevent the arbitrary exercise of power or misrule.

[42] *Traités*, 392.
[43] 'Indirect Legislation', UC, lxxxvii, 3.
[44] G. Postema, *Utility, Publicity, and Law: Essays on Bentham's Moral and Legal Philosophy* (Cambridge: Cambridge University Press, 2019), 40.

Bentham explains the causes of misrule.[45] There are three:[46] first, failure of intellectual aptitude; second, failure of active aptitude; and third, failure of moral aptitude. Failure of intellectual aptitude means that people neither have the skills nor the intentions to carry out public functions appropriately.[47] Failure of active aptitude means they do not comply with basic requirements to discharge their duty appropriately, such as to come to work or to carry out the required tasks.[48] Failure of moral aptitude should be understood as corruption or what Bentham terms sinister interest, that is, as public servants, putting their own self-interest first rather than the general interest of the people. Bentham deals with the first very efficiently in creating schools – even schools of legislation where one learns how to write legislation – and by creating a system of competitive examination.[49] This system is meant to ensure that persons are recruited for any official position not only have the required knowledge to do the job but also have the right intellectual and mental capacities, as well as the appropriate skills, to carry out the required duties. Failure of active aptitude is solved mainly by ensuring attendance, thus paying people for their attendance. Money is one handy solution.[50]

Failure of moral aptitude is more complex.[51] First, people's individual interest must not lead them to follow their sinister

[45] Reference to the relationship between indirect legislation and the prevention of misrule is made in chapter 19 of manuscripts (UCL, lxxxvii. 87–107, 109–15, 117, 120, 122–6); and in chapter 21 of *Traités* (sections 9, 11 and 4 are not included in chapter 21 of *Traités*). From this we can conclude that for Bentham during this period, it is delinquency that is the primary concern of indirect legislation. Emphasis comes to be put on misrule in late Bentham. See P. Schofield, 'Bentham on the Identification of Interest', *Utilitas* 8, no. 2 (1996), 223–34.

[46] To have an idea of the importance that the fight against misrule holds for Bentham, through what he calls securities, see the index of volume 1 of the Constitutional Code: 595–8. It is the single most discussed topic in the volume. See also G. Postema, 'The Soul of Justice: Bentham on Publicity, Law and the Rule of Law', in *Bentham's Theory of Law and Public Opinion*, ed. X. Zhai and M. Quinn (Cambridge: Cambridge University Press, 2014), 40–62.

[47] 'Economy as applied to Office', 77.

[48] Ibid., 87–9.

[49] On schools of legislation, see M. Bozzo-Rey, 'Publicity and Nomography: Bentham's School of Legislation', *Journal of Bentham Studies*, 2010, www.scienceopen.com/.

[50] *Traités*, 355.

[51] 'Economy as applied to Office', 13 and 16. In his writings, Bentham opposes the moral aptitude of functionaries to what he calls sinister interest or sacrifice (See, among many recurring references: Bentham, 'Economy as Applied to Office', 13, 17, 28; J. Bentham, 'Identification of Interests', in *First Principles Preparatory to the Constitutional Code*, 128;

interest.[52] In Bentham's constitutional theory, there are two ways in which people can be protected against misrule: first, by imposing legal constitutional limits on governors and second, by promoting publicity. Following Engelmann's interpretation of the place of indirect legislation in Bentham's *Introduction* and *Limits*,[53] the assumption made in this chapter is that publicity is the offspring of indirect legislation. Indeed, on account of the wide-ranging meaning of Bentham's definition of law and the way in which publicity is enlisted to offer protection against misrule, great strength is given to the moral sanction. The moral sanction operates on all areas of public life and, with publicity, contributes to open up the acts of government officials to the scrutiny of the public. It does so thanks to the Public Opinion Tribunal (POT)[54] which is the institutionalized form that the moral sanction takes in the public sphere.

In Bentham's earlier writings,[55] indirect constitutional law sets up precautions to prevent misconduct,[56] incapacity, or embezzlement,[57] Incapacity can be read as what Bentham later recast as intellectual aptitude. It can also cover active aptitude, as 'Bentham's constitutional

J. Bentham, 'Constitutional Code Rationale', in *First Principles Preparatory to the Constitutional Code*, 235 and 276 (henceforth 'Constitutional Code Rationale'); J. Bentham, 'Observations by an Englishman', in *'Securities against Misrule': Writings for Tripoli and Greece*, 250–2 (henceforth *'Securities against Misrule'*); J. Bentham, 'Constitutional Code: Matter Occasioned by Greece', in *'Securities against Misrule'*, 266–7).

52 When an individual seeks his own interest at the expense of the general interest, Bentham says that this individual 'sacrifices' the happiness of the community to advance his own: 'In so far, in the instance of the functionary in question, this identification [of interests] fails to have place, the consequence is – on his part, so far as it depends on his endeavours, the sacrifice of the universal interest to his personal or other particular interest: say, for shortness, *the sinister sacrifice*' ('Economy as Applied to Office', 17). The 'sinister sacrifice' is motivated by 'sinister interest'. If members of the public are expected to follow their best interests, when a servant of the community ('Economy as Applied to Office', 3) does so, it is called 'sinister interest' ('Economy as Applied to Office', 27). The point is to make it the official's best interest to promote the general interest.

53 Engelmann, 'Limits and Indirect Legislation'.

54 For the operations of the POT, see F. Rosen, *Jeremy Bentham and Representative Democracy: A Study of the Constitutional Code* (Oxford: Clarendon Press, 1983); Hume, *Bentham and Bureaucracy*; P. Schofield, *Utility and Democracy: The Political Thought of Jeremy Bentham* (Oxford: Oxford University Press, 2009); and Brunon-Ernst, *Utilitarian Biopolitics*, 67–85.

55 See among others *Traités*, 381–402.

56 See 'Indirect legislation', chapter 7, §4.

57 See ibid., chapter 10, §6.

views underwent significant revision in his lifetime'.[58] Indeed, in between his writings on indirect legislation in the 1780–90s and his writings about misrule in the 1810–20s, Bentham went through the life-changing experience of attempting to buid the Panopticon penitentiary. Thanks to this project, he came in direct contact with the day-to-day working of ministries, of public servants, and people working with or for the government.[59] He got first-hand experience of the way that functionaries, as he calls officials in his later writings, were more concerned to promote their own interest than the general interest. The later concept of failure of moral aptitude can be read back into the earlier opposition to misconduct and embezzlement. The categories are not watertight as misconduct and embezzlement can also be dealt with by direct legislation as crimes. Once there is evidence that misconduct is or will be carried out, preventive action can be taken, such as making sure that people will not even consider embezzling funds or misbehaving because they know that they are under close scrutiny. This policy would also fall within the scope of promoting publicity. Publicity can take different forms, one of them being the POT, which legislates indirectly, at least according to Bentham's earlier categories, and which also acts so that people will internalize any potential future blame or praise that they might receive and thus modify their behavior accordingly.[60]

10.3.2 *Indirect Constitutional Law as Counterforce*

The task set out here is to trace indirect legislation within Bentham's constitutional writings, as well as to find some traces of what has become of indirect legislation in Bentham's later constitutional writing. There are not that many references, as the phrase 'indirect legislation' almost totally disappears.[61] However, Bentham uses other phrases, incorporating the idea of 'indirect' as in 'indirect means' or 'indirect modes'.[62] In these

[58] Engelmann, 'Limits and Indirect Legislation', 310–1.

[59] See, for example, J. Bentham, *Writings on Australia, II. History of Jeremy Bentham's dealings with Lord Pelham*, ed. T. Causer and P. Schofield, 2018 (Digital scholarly resource), www.ucl.ac.uk/bentham-project.

[60] *Traités*, 380–2; 392–402 (for the constitutional use of the popular sanction through the POT).

[61] See n. 4.

[62] There is also a discussion on 'indirect enactments' and 'indirect mandates' in the manuscript source titled 'Nomography', BL Add MS 33, 548 fol. 257 (24 June 1829), at fol. 260 or 263 for instance.

instances, he is very clearly referring to indirect legislation, as the adjective is contrasted to direct. Another comparison that is used is that of a 'counterforce', a telling term as it is also used to describe the POT.[63] Bentham writes:

> By indirect means, understand those by which a counterforce – a force of another class – is employed to the same purpose: brought into action in the view of its opposing itself to the power of the trustees (i.e. functionaries) in question in the event of their engaging on any occasion in the sinister sacrifice, and thereby acting in breach of their trust.[64]

In the quotation, Bentham explains that another means, which is indirect, can be enlisted. The instrument will act as a check and that it is going to be put up in front of the public officer to counteract their desire to follow their personal interest.

In other places in Bentham's later constitutional writings, he resorts once again to references to direct and indirect modes. He writes:

> Be the act what it may, there are two modes in either of which man may be divested of the interest requisite to his performance of [the universal interest]: one is the over-powering force . . . this is the direct mode. The other is – the divesting him of the power of performing that same act . . . this mode may be termed an *indirect* mode.[65]

These ideas of prevention, of divesting, of a counterforce, appear then again in Bentham's later constitutional writing. They are referred to as indirect modes because they do not refer directly to the legal sanction or to any legal punishment but are used in relation to misrule and to ensuring that governors choose to promote the general interest. In this lies the common aim between Bentham's earlier and later constitutional writings.

In Bentham's theory, the sovereign power is held by the people understood as the supreme constitutive, to whom the supreme operative is subordinate.[66] The supreme operative includes all the branches of government: the supreme legislative and the supreme executive, itself including the administrative branch and the judicial branch.[67] Bentham

[63] See, for example, 'Economy as Applied to Office', 29.
[64] Ibid., 17
[65] 'Constitutional Code Rationale', 227–331, at 236.
[66] 'Constitutional Code Rationale', 239; or 'Economy as Applied to Office', 6. See also Oren Ben-Dor, *Constitutional Limits and the Public Sphere* (Oxford: Hart, 2000), 140–1.
[67] For the theoretical foundations of the separation of powers, see J. Locke, *Second Treatise*, para 143, 144, 150, 159; and C. Montesquieu, *The Spirit of Laws* (Chicago: Encyclopaedia Britannica, 1952), 70–84.

posits a hierarchy whereby the supreme legislative takes precedence over the other branches of operative power. To achieve this, it is given a certain number of powers (of location, dislocation, and so forth),[68] as well as the power of legal punishment. As the law emanates from the supreme operative, the main purpose of the supreme constitutive power is to control the supreme operative by locating and dislocating the officials who exercise it. But as this control cannot be carried out on a day-to-day basis, the power it wields against the supreme operative rests in the POT. Indeed, the POT can pass judgement on each one of the acts of the supreme operative.[69] This judgement is then publicized.

In Bentham's theory, people can only be self-interested.[70] The problem therefore is to account for the fact that officials would at some stage desist from promoting their own sinister interest and instead promote the general interest. They would only do so because they have a greater interest in doing it. This is why Bentham advocates a junction of interest and duty,[71] that is, the establishment of a number of mechanisms to make sure that it becomes in the interest of officials to follow their duty. In acting against misrule, that is, sinister interest or abuse of power by government officials, Bentham can use direct constitutional safeguards, but he can also enlist indirect ones. He lists the following safeguards (Table 10.1):

Bentham's lists relating to the direct vs. indirect division are very unsatisfactory, and they are just as unsatisfactory at this later stage than they were in his earlier writings. Although he labels some elements as direct and some of them as indirect, the rationale for doing so is not

[68] By 'locate', Bentham means the allocation of a specific individual to a specific position, by electing or by appointing him/her to the position. To 'dislocate' is thus to remove an individual from a given position, on grounds of misbehaviour, that is, on the grounds that his/her behaviour was not conformable with the active, intellectual, or moral aptitudes required to fulfil his/her duties in the position or in a given circumstance. See 'Economy as Applied to Office', 7, and 32–3; and 'Constitutional Code Rationale', 291.

[69] For references to the POT in *IPML*, 35, n. b; 164; 171, n. o; and 182–4. For references in later works, see, for example, 'Constitutional Code Rationale', 283; or 'Economy as Applied to Office', 29; or '*Securities against Misrule*', 28.

[70] For the purposes of constitutional theory, Bentham assumes that self-interest is the only motive. However, he is well-aware that they may be in fact people who act from other-regarding motives.

[71] The issue of the junction of interests, be it natural or artificial, concerned all writers at the time. See, for example, A. Smith, *An Inquiry into the Nature and Causes of the Wealth of Nations*, ed. C. J. Bullock (New York: F. Collier & Son, 1909), 352; or 'Economy as Applied to Office', 27 and 43.

Table 10.1. *Direct and indirect constitutional safeguards in Bentham's later writings*[a]

Direct constitutional safeguards	Indirect constitutional safeguards
Minimizing the power, money and pay at the disposal of the Operative power.	Maximization of legal responsibility: legal (political) sanction: overpower the force of the conflicting interest.
Exclusion of Factitious Honours.	Maximization of moral responsibility: popular (moral) sanction: prevent the individual from performing an act.
Supreme Constitutive to locate and dislocate members of the Supreme Operative.	
Geographical division of constituencies which each elect a single representative, responsible to his/her electors	
MPs to sit in one chamber, and elected for a year.	

[a] The Table compounds the safeguards listed in 'Economy as applied to Office', 28–9. As Prof. Schofield rightly pointed out, there is a lot missing from this table: secret ballot, no established religion, examination, attendance, economical auction, and so forth.

self-evident. It seems at this later stage that Bentham is using an earlier distinction because it comes in handy.

In the table of the indirect constitutional safeguards (Table 10.1), it is of interest to note that Bentham enlists both the legal political sanction (flowing from primary indirect legislation) and the popular moral sanction (originating from secondary indirect legislation).

10.3.3 Publicity, Information, and Registration in Indirect Constitutional Law

Bentham's POT is an indirect mechanism that is established to prevent sinister interest. It operates as a counterforce to the immense powers that are given to the supreme operative. Reading Bentham's later work from the perspective of his earlier writing, the POT can be seen as an emanation or a continuation of the indirect means of preventing misrule that he identified in the *Traités*. If one is looking at Bentham's theory from the vantage point of his late constitutional works, it is very unlikely that the categories of direct and indirect will be seen as essential in allowing Bentham's overall system of supreme operative, supreme constitutive, and their counterforces, to operate in order to get the best workable political system in place. However, the point the present chapter makes is that the concepts Bentham fleshes out in his earlier writing help him identify the importance of publicity, information gathering, information circulation, blame and praise, for what he later conceives as the POT. Moreover, indirect legislation contributes to his understanding of how praise and blame work at various levels of society and how publicity may be used to deliver the required outcome. Publicity can only operate if there exists a very efficient bureaucracy. In the Western world, an effective bureaucracy comes into existence at the turn of the nineteenth century, precisely at the time when Bentham is writing.[72] In his theory, bureaucracy becomes a means to support the supreme operative and the supreme constitutive, through the POT, in order to bring about a well-functioning political system.

Publicity can only be achieved profitably if other mechanisms are enlisted, such as registration. First, relevant information needs to be registered, and registered in various places and in various ways, so that access to information is secured.[73] Indeed, data is one of the essential tools for decision-making. It needs to be publicized so that everybody can use the information to make decisions in their public and private lives.

Bentham's writings are teeming with references to registration and publication. For example, his 'Table of Admonitory Rules and Notices'[74] and the registration[75] and publication[76] systems developed in *Constitutional Code*. Although they appear in the constitutional writings, these instruments or policies are not constitutional norms. However, they operate as mechanisms that are essential to the proper functioning of

[72] See Hume, *Bentham and Bureaucracy*.

[73] This was a tool used in earlier writings on indirect legislation where registration of dangerous substances is given as an example of appropriate interference on the part of government to prevent crimes. See 'Indirect Legislation', UC lxxxvii. 173: 'Let a particular book be provided, under some such name as the poison-book, in which let the declarations above-mentioned be enter'd, signed with the names and abodes of the buyers and witnesses.'

[74] 'Economy as Applied to Office', 60.

[75] *Constitutional Code*, 159f.

[76] Ibid., 162f.

constitutional law. One can only understand their place in writings on constitutional law, if one bears in mind Bentham's wider understanding of what a law is, that allows the inclusion of mechanisms such as indirect legislation. This comment, combined with the motley list of indirect policies to be found in the manuscript sources and the *Traités* given in Section 10.1, shows to what extent the later use of registration and publication originates in Bentham's earlier explorations of indirect legislation.

10.3.4 *Architecture and Indirect Constitutional Law*

Bentham uses the phrase 'Architectural Arrangements' to head one of his chapters in *Constitutional Code*. He explains:

> Among the *ends in view* . . . in the mode of carrying on the business of the Administrative department . . . are some, which cannot be given to it in so high a degree, without, as with, that assistance, which is not derivable to it from any other source than the art-and-science of *architecture*.[77]

The very presence of a section on architecture in a constitutional code shows the particularity of Bentham's approach to law. This may be one of the few codes ever projected that has provisions for architecture. The reason lies in the fact that constitutional law is both direct and indirect, and, in its indirect means, it can encompass provisions as diverse as modes of publication and architectural considerations. Bentham writes: 'By appropriate architectural arrangements, contribution . . . may be made at the same time to that main end, and to those same collateral aims.'[78]

Architecture makes it possible for Bentham to enlist other forms of sanction, such as the moral sanction. His project includes a crescent-shaped building for ministers, specification of the location of ministerial offices, conversation tubes between the offices, and waiting boxes (private and public) for members of the public.[79] In this project, Bentham is tapping into his previous experiments in population management through panoptic architecture. Bentham describes the Panopticon scheme as nothing more than 'a simple idea in architecture', but it can also become 'a new mode of obtaining power of mind

[77] Ibid., 438.
[78] Ibid.
[79] Ibid., 438–57.

over mind, in a quantity hitherto without example'.[80] In creating an environment where inspectors can see everyone at all times, blame or praise can be automatically allocated. Indeed, architecture becomes a means of enhancing the power and efficacy of the POT. As members can see what is taking place in government offices, they can pass immediate judgement.

If the earlier distinction made between two forms of indirect legislation is applied to the architectural arrangements in *Constitutional Code*, the primary form can use the moral sanction to help the working of the POT, but the secondary form has an effect on the individual psyche. In the ministerial offices, Bentham aims to reproduce a panopticon-like surveillance mechanism, where the inmate can be watched continually by either the inspector or any other person who happens to be in the inspection tower. Bentham conceives of government in the same way. The difference with the ministerial offices is that it is shaped in a semi-circle and ministers can be watched almost at all times by members of the supreme constitutive and by members of the POT, with the result that the behaviour of officials will be modified if they do not conform to the general interest.

This architectural arrangement is part and parcel of constitutional law. In his earlier writings, Bentham would have labelled it indirect constitutional law. In his later works, Bentham does not need to make that distinction, although there are still instances in his work where he distinguishes direct and indirect modes. Bentham's understanding of constitutional law is so foreign to our present understanding that the inclusion of both direct and indirect legislation is unexpected and up to now nearly uncharted.

Architecture does not replace direct legislation but assists it. In this way, indirect legislation is being enlisted to achieve the same ends and views as direct constitutional law. By appropriate architectural arrangements, a contribution may be made to achieve the main aim of constitutional law (which is security against misrule). As noted above, and as the previous Panopticon experiment showed, Bentham does not only rely on architecture alone to safeguard people from misrule but on many other minute indirect instruments that all work towards the success of his utilitarian regimen.

[80] J. Bentham, *Panopticon; or the Inspection-House* in Bowring, iv. 37–172.

10.4 Conclusion

The present chapter offers one of the first attempts to investigate indirect constitutional law. It shows that indirect safeguards rely on an array of techniques that enlist publicity and the moral sanction. Key instruments in Bentham's later writing that tie into earlier indirect policies are as follows: the POT, information gathering and recording, and architecture. Indirect legislation is not often mentioned in Bentham's later writings, but the assumption made here is that a certain number of mechanisms, and maybe also concepts, can be traced back to indirect legislation. This is of importance because it articulates the shift in Bentham's earlier writing, where he was really interested in understanding sovereignty and law, to fleshing out, at the end of his life, a political theory that rests on all the elements he identified earlier.

However, one of the main conclusions to be drawn from the present research is that in his later writings, Bentham does not need indirect legislation any longer because he has constructed, out of his earlier reflections on indirect management, a theory of law that encompasses publicity thanks to the POT amongst other things.

11

Bentham, Courts, and Democracy

DAVID LIEBERMAN

My chapter examines a neglected feature of Bentham's design for representative democracy in his *Constitutional Code.* This is the lengthy plan for the judicial branch of government, set out in the final volume of the three-volume *Code.* Of the many influential advocates for constitutional democracy of his era, Bentham was unique in devoting such systematic attention to courts and judicial procedure. His constitutional programme included a detailed system for a dense network of local courts providing free and rapid adjudication of legal disputes. At the same time, Bentham rejected judicial functions now associated with liberal constitutionalism, such as the protection of entrenched rights and the preservation of constitutional norms. Instead, he emphasized the institutions and public resources required to ensure equal access to justice for the weakest members of the community. This emphasis helps clarify Bentham's larger political strategy for advancing the happiness of the community and the manner in which he understood the specifically democratic character of his judicial plan. The latter theme requires special attention since so much of Bentham's designs for courts and judicial procedure long predated his embrace of democratic radicalism.

11.1 Introduction

The three-volume *Constitutional Code* comprised Bentham's most ambitious contribution to political theory and formed the major intellectual project of the final decade of his long career in law reform (1822–32). A striking, though neglected feature of his constitutional programme was the amount of space and detail devoted to the judiciary. In ordering the component parts of his plan for government, Bentham adhered to a template found in many of the regional, national, and federal constitutions composed over the previous half century. He began with a robust statement of popular sovereignty, insisting that 'sovereignty is in *the people*. It is reserved by and to them'.[1] In elaborating the structure of government powers, he again proceeded conventionally, beginning with the Legislature; then turning to what was often treated as the Executive (here in the form of a Prime Minister, appointed by the elected legislative representatives, who oversaw a network of thirteen administrative ministries); and then presenting his plan for the Judiciary. As was characteristic, Bentham took pains to develop an alternative terminology to delineate more accurately these public authorities. The sovereign people exercised the polity's 'Constitutive authority'. The Legislature, Prime Minister, and the subordinate ministers together formed 'the Government'. The administrative ministries and the judiciary taken together comprised 'the Executive'. The Legislative and the Executive taken together formed 'the Operative' authority, 'as contra-distinguished from the Constitutive' authority of the people.[2]

Bentham was equally unusual in the proportion of attention given to the institutions of justice. He devoted two chapters to the Legislature and the election of legislative representatives, and three chapters to the office of Prime Minister and the thirteen sub-ministries under the Prime Minister's supervision. In contrast, 'the judiciary establishment', which dominated the discussion of the third and final volume of the *Code*, required sixteen chapters.[3] The magnitude of this attention to the judicial branch (to use the more familiar language of modern constitutionalism) can be quickly illustrated through a comparison with the alternative and far more influential example of the first constitution adopted by the National Assembly of France in 1791. Bentham, of course, was a close observer of French politics during the early revolutionary period, commenting extensively and critically on its leading legal and constitutional designs. As in the case of his own constitution, the French Constitution began with the statement of popular sovereignty and designed a system of representative government. The description of public powers started with the elected Legislature, presented in two lengthy chapters that were

1 J. Bentham, *Constitutional Code: Volume 1*, ed. F. Rosen and J. H. Burns (Oxford: Clarendon Press, 1983 [*CW*]), 25.

2 Ibid., 27.

3 Bentham refers to the 'judiciary establishment' at Bowring, ix. 456. He also frequently uses the term 'judicatory' to refer to courts, not liking the monarchical associations of the latter term. Bentham organized *Constitutional Code* into the three volumes; volume 3 additionally covered arrangements for local government. Bentham's three-volume organization of the Code was abandoned by Richard Doane in the version he edited for the Bowring edition. In what follows, I adhere to the three-volume arrangement Bentham planned.

organized into nine separate sections, totaling seventy-two articles. The office of the King, who exercised Executive power as constitutional monarch, occupied two chapters, organized into seven sections and sixty-seven articles. The Judicial Power, however, received a single chapter, undivided into separate sections and containing twenty-seven articles.[4] Taking the constitutional article as the unit of measure, roughly 16 per cent of France's 1791 Constitution addressed Judicial Power. Bentham's *Constitutional Code*, in contrast, devoted nearly one-third of its content – roughly 31 per cent – to the Judiciary. His account of public authority, in effect, reversed the distribution of institutional attention found in the famous French predecessor.[5]

The priority Bentham had come to ascribe to matters of courts and their procedures was nicely captured in a law reform polemic he authored at the time of the *Constitutional Code*. 'On two achievements is based whatsoever can be done in the way of law reform', he maintained, 'appropriate *codification* and appropriate *judiciary establishment*, with its system of procedure'.[6] Unlike his democratic advocacy, Bentham's commitment to codification emerged in the 1770s, at the very start of his writings on law reform. Why, however, should the judiciary establishment have come to acquire such prominence in his reform programme? Why should he have devoted such extensive attention to this area of public authority in his constitutional design? What did he understand as the specifically democratic dimensions of his plan for the courts and procedure?

11.2 Courts and Law Reform

There are obvious and important biographical dimensions to this story. The 1820s in Britain witnessed renewed attention in Parliament and in the press to law reform.[7] A convenient marker of the development was

[4] See 1791 Constitution of France, Title III (Of Public Powers), chapters 1–5.

[5] The same contrast obtains respecting many other contemporary constitutions. The contrast is potentially misleading in that many constitutions left it to subsequent legislation to specify the institutional details for courts that Bentham set out in *Constitutional Code*. However, Bentham's insistence that these matters deserved inclusion in the constitutional document is itself revealing.

[6] Bentham, *Lord Brougham Displayed*, Bowring, v. 609.

[7] These developments are most recently surveyed in the contributions by M. Lobban and P. Polden to volume 11 of the *Oxford History of the Laws of England* (Oxford: Oxford University Press, 2010), which draws on their earlier and valuable research.

provided by Henry Brougham's six-hour speech of 1828 in the House of Commons, which identified, for legislative attention, reform of the superior courts of common law and of common law pleading; the need for inexpensive and accessible local courts; and reform of the laws governing debt, bankruptcy, and tenures. Brougham's marathon oration, however, simply added to an ongoing discussion. Selective reform of the criminal law had been undertaken earlier in the decade under the skilful management of Sir Robert Peel. In 1824, a Royal Commission was appointed to consider long-established complaints concerning the costs and abuses in the Court of Chancery. The publication of Abraham Hayward's 1831 translation of Savigny's famous *Zum Beruf unsrer Zeit für Gesetzgebung und Rechtswissenschaft* was symptomatic of a wider 1820s debate in England concerning the merits of legislative codification.[8] And these debates and parliamentary initiatives received further review and publicity in the prestigious political reviews – the Tory *Quarterly Review*, the Whig *Edinburgh Review*, and the radical *Westminster Review*, and in such recently launched elite law journals as the *Law Magazine*.

Bentham moved promptly to take advantage of the opportunities afforded by these events.[9] He produced two lengthy and unforgiving critiques of the entrenched abuses in English courts and legal process, the 1825 *Indications respecting Lord Eldon* and the 1829 *Justice and Codification Petitions*. His 1832 *Lord Brougham Displayed* set out a scathing condemnation of Brougham's, now Lord Chancellor, proposals for the reform of equity jurisprudence and the establishment of new bankruptcy courts. In 1830 he also published his *Equity Dispatch Court Proposal*, designed to provide litigants with a cheap and speedy alternative to adjudication under England's equity courts. All these works enjoyed a close relationship to *Constitutional Code*. Indeed, it is possible to read Bentham's law reform polemics as a comprehensive presentation

8 A. Hayward, *On the Vocation of Our Age for Legislation and Jurisprudence* (London: Printed by Littlewood & Co. Old Bailey, 1831). I consider the nature of this debate over codification in my 'Legislation in a Common Law Context', *Zeitschrift für Neuere Rechtsgeschichte* 27(2005), 107–23.

9 Schofield provides an insightful survey and assessment of these materials in *Utility and Democracy: The Political Thought of Jeremy Bentham* (Oxford: Oxford University Press, 2006), 304–36. Additional background and important insights are provided by C. Riley in 'Jeremy Bentham and Equity: the Court of Chancery, Lord Eldon, and the Dispatch Court Plan', *Journal of Legal History* 39 (2018), 29–57; and 'The Hermit and the Boa Constrictor: Jeremy Bentham, Henry Brougham, and the Accessibility of Justice', *American Journal of Legal History* (2019), 1–26.

of the abuses and failings that *Constitutional Code*'s alternative plan for the judiciary was designed to eradicate. Bentham himself drew attention to the various connections among these works. His attack on Chancery practice under Lord Eldon was later reissued in the 1830 collection of papers, *Official Aptitude Maximized; Expense Minimized*. The work's contents, Bentham explained at the outset, 'take their common origin' in 'an all-embracing system of proposed Constitutional Law, for the use of all nations professing liberal opinions'.[10] *Indications respecting Lord Eldon*, *Justice and Codification Petitions* and *Equity Dispatch Court Proposal* were each referenced in *Constitutional Code*, along with earlier writings on court reform. The Justice Petitions contained a brief summary of the lengthy judiciary plan elaborated in the *Code*, which supplied the required replacement 'dictated by a real and exclusive regard for the happiness of the community'.[11] By the time of *Lord Brougham Displayed*, much of *Constitutional Code* was already in print. Bentham invoked the *Code* directly for the institutional principles that served as the basis of his denunciation of the 'sham reform' measures proposed by Brougham. The harsh critique then concluded with lengthy extracts from the *Code*'s own treatment of 'judiciaries collectively'.[12]

If the law reform dynamics of the 1820s provided Bentham with extra incentive for devoting himself to courts and legal process, these specific interventions added to a well-developed portfolio of on-topic contributions. As early as the 1789 Preface to *An Introduction to the Principles of Morals and Legislation*, Bentham recognized that his codification programme, initially focused on the composition of a penal code, now included 'principles of legislation in matters of *procedure*'. The 'Procedure Code' reappeared in the preface to the published first volume of *Constitutional Code*, where Bentham promised soon to publish 'a Procedure Code Table' to accompany the constitutional plan.[13] No such Table actually appeared in his own lifetime, though he had already written the materials that would be posthumously published as 'Principles of Judicial Procedure, with the Outlines of the

[10] *Official Aptitude Maximized; Expense Minimized* (1830), ed. Philip Schofield (Oxford: Clarendon Press, 1993 [*CW*]), 5.

[11] *Justice and Codification Petitions*, Bowring, v. 498–504.

[12] *Lord Brougham Displayed*, Bowring, v. 610–2.

[13] *An Introduction to the Principles of Morals and Legislation*, ed. J. H. Burns and H. L. A. Hart (London: Athlone Press, 1970 [*CW*]), 6; *Constitutional Code*, vol. 1 (*CW*), 4.

Procedure Code'.[14] Bentham's single most substantial contribution to legal theory addressed the related topic of legal evidence. This was the five-volume *Rationale of Judicial Evidence*, which a young John Stuart Mill edited for publication in 1827.[15] The plan for judiciary establishment in *Constitutional Code* thus drew upon a unique fund of reflection on courts and their appropriate operations. Indeed, if Bentham is placed within the company of other famous designers of and advocates for republican constitutions of his era, whose political theories drew his critical notice – such canonical figures as Rousseau, Sieyès, Paine, Condorcet, Madison, Godwin – he is exceptional in coming to constitutional creation following such prolonged engagement with this particular branch of public authority.

11.3 Securing Justice

For Bentham, the general goal of the judiciary establishment was to secure justice for the entire community. Justice in this setting was understood in conventional terms, as the 'execution and effect given to the ordinances of the main body of law', which secured 'to every man alike, in so far as may be, the protection of the law, by means of the appropriate services of the functionaries of justice employed for that purpose'.[16] Security was a prerequisite for the pursuit of individual well-being, and legal security was no less vital for the promotion of the community's happiness. In the case of legal disputes between members of the political community, justice was typically frustrated through two distinct kinds of institutional failure, 'misdecision' (an incorrect determination of legal rights) and 'nondecision' (a failure to vindicate legal rights). The avoidance of these failures, in turn, required the minimization of 'expense, vexation, and delay'. While these goals shaped Bentham's treatment of courts and court processes, they implicated large elements of his entire law reform project. Codification and the

[14] Richard Doane, who edited these materials as well as *Constitutional Code* for the Bowring edition, drew attention to these connections in his introduction to the writings on procedure; see Bowring, ii. 1.

[15] Mill was eighteen when he embarked on the editing of the work. The material was first published in 1823 in the version edited by Etienne Dumont as *Traité des Preuves Judiciares*.

[16] *Constitutional Code*, vol. 3, Bowring, ix. 463, 455. Bentham also treated 'justice' in less institutional terms. See, for example, 'The Article on Utilitarianism', in *Deontology*, ed. Amnon Goldworth (Oxford: Clarendon Press, 1983 [*CW*]), 308–9.

elimination of customary law advanced legal certainty and the understanding of legal rights and duties. New principles governing the treatment of evidence and reformed judicial procedures served to secure prompt and accurate adjudication of disputes. Official records registering property titles, contracts, and bequests, as well as concerning births, marriages, deaths, and heirs, settled authoritatively the kinds of factual questions often in dispute in legal contests. In this context, such official information formed a body of what Bentham termed, 'pre-appointed evidence'.[17] Given how many of these elements extended beyond constitutional arrangements, it is unsurprising that these chapters of *Constitutional Code* presupposed and referenced the larger structure of Bentham's Pannomion and the projected codes of procedure, penal, and civil law.

To secure the ends of justice, Bentham designed a network of local courts, 'immediate judicatories', operating under the authority of a Justice Minister appointed by the elected Legislature. As in the case of other contemporary constitutions, Bentham's *Code* specified the process of judicial selection, conditions of service, and procedures for removal from office. Unlike other constitutions, it did not contain lengthy provisions governing matters of jurisdiction and format: whether (as in the case of the North American states) there were to be courts of equity as well as law; whether (as in revolutionary France) different tribunals and process would govern civil and criminal causes; whether (as in Iberia and South America) there would be courts of special jurisdiction (merchant courts, military courts, church courts); how the number and distribution of courts would be shaped by political sub-unit (county, city, municipality, department, arrondissement); how the monetary value of disputes would determine the available legal forum; and so on.

These complexities were eliminated at a stroke. Judges in the immediate courts exercised what Bentham termed 'universal jurisdiction', handling all the disputes that were brought before them, irrespective of their subject matter or monetary value. The immediate courts were publicly financed tribunals, staffed by salaried officials, and available to the members of the community without charge or fees. They provided uninterrupted service – functioning, as circumstances required, at all times of day and night. Hospitals, Bentham reasoned, never closed their doors to those who needed medical assistance; courts should never close

[17] *Constitutional Code*, vol. 3, Bowring, ix. 626; and see *The Rationale of Judicial Evidence*, Book 4.

their doors to those in need of justice. And they were distributed in sufficient numbers so as to be accessible within a single day's journey by foot by each member of the community.[18] (In other contemporary writings, Bentham calculated that this required a local court within twelve miles' distance of the individual.)[19] Allowing six hours for the completion of a typical case, Bentham enthused that 'a grown person, in a state of ordinary health and strength' could access the court and secure judgement 'in the course of any day of 24 hours, without sleeping elsewhere than at home'.

As important as the universality and proximity of these tribunals were the procedures and personnel through which they operated. Presiding over each court was a single appointed judge, an administrative arrangement that embodied the principle of 'single-seatedness', which operated standardly through the *Code*. The immediate judge, moreover, exercised extensive investigatory powers and procedural discretion through a process of adjudication that Bentham referred to as 'natural' or 'summary' procedure. Natural judicial procedure resembled the kind of informal adjudication found in domestic settings and in a variety of jurisdictions in the varied landscape of English law, such as hearings before an individual justice of the peace.[20] The individual judge took responsibility for collecting and receiving evidence and for interrogating litigants and witnesses. Information, arguments, and responses were presented orally by litigants themselves and directly to the judge. Each court was furnished with a small number of salaried officials; among them, advocates representing the government as well as advocates to advise and assist suitors. However, the institution was purposely designed to eliminate the need for and costs of professional representation; and there were no restrictions on the kinds of evidence and testimony the court could receive. The direct participation of the litigants and the procedural discretion given to the judge served, for Bentham, the interests of speedy resolution as well as accurate decision.

The local immediate judicatory functioned as the workhorse of justice in Bentham's constitutional system. He also provided for a system of appellate judicatories that likewise enjoyed universal jurisdiction and

[18] *Constitutional Code*, vol. 3, Bowring, ix. 515–21.

[19] *Justice and Codification Petitions*, Bowring, v. 498.

[20] Bentham's other examples of tribunals adopting natural procedure included statutory Courts of Requests (which adjudicated small debts), Commissions of Bankrupts, and Denmark's Conciliation Courts.

exercised authority to review the decisions by the local courts. Overall, though, appellate review had limited impact on the envisaged structure. In the case of England, Bentham believed that a single appellate court, located in the metropolis, would be sufficient. The appellate court was responsible for reviewing the immediate judge's ruling and the evidence presented at trial. No new evidence was gathered and the litigants themselves were freed from the burden of attendance.[21]

Given the multitude of the immediate courts and the procedural discretion enjoyed by the immediate judge, Bentham turned to the instrument of publicity to ensure the integrity and rectitude of the institution's processes and decisions. Publicity, of course, operated throughout *Constitutional Code* as a general and critical resource against the abuse of power. In the case of the judiciary, however, Bentham believed that publicity functioned with special efficacy. One of the few redeeming features of English law was its system of open courts that enabled the public to monitor the performance of the highest judges. 'Publicity is the very soul of justice', Bentham explained to the legislators of France in 1790. 'It is the keenest spur to exertion, and the surest of all guards against improbity .... It keeps the judge himself, while trying, under trial .... Without publicity, all other checks are fruitless: in comparison of publicity, all other checks are of small amount.'[22]

Bentham reaffirmed these sentiments in the *Code*: 'Only in proportion as publicity has place can any of the checks, applicable to judicial injustice, operate. Where there is no publicity, there is no justice.' Accordingly, his goal for 'every judicial proceeding' was that 'publicity be maximized'.[23] Single-seatedness, while reducing public costs in the form of judicial salaries, at the same time intensified the responsibility and the resulting accountability of each individual judge. With rare exceptions, the immediate courts operated as open tribunals, specifically designed to accommodate outside observers and government monitors. Judges were required to provide full accounts of the reasons behind their rulings; and their decisions were preserved in detailed and standardized official records that would again be available for government and public inspection. The supervising Justice Minister produced an 'Annual Judicial Service Calendar' identifying which judge and court officials staffed each

[21] See *Constitutional Code*, vol. 3, Bowring, ix. 470n, 473–4, 585–8.

[22] *Draught of a Code for the Organization of the Judicial Establishment in France*, Bowring, iv. 306–7.

[23] *Constitutional Code*, vol. 3, Bowring, ix. 493.

immediate court throughout the polity. Official complaint books were maintained, available to all those who participated or casually observed court proceedings, as was the record of cases that received appellate review. The record of complaints was particularly important for determining 'those petty mental and verbal injuries' often caused by those endowed with power and authority. Based on all these records, the performance and productivity of each judge was placed under routine and critical public surveillance.[24] As elsewhere in his plan for government, individualized responsibility and accountability, systematic record keeping, and the inspecting eye of a critical public operated as a check against corruption by officeholders and as a spur to honesty and diligence.

Among the many devices deployed to intensify publicity, Bentham created a novel institution he styled the 'quasi-jury'. The function of the quasi-jury followed from Bentham's analysis of the strengths and weaknesses of the common law petit jury. He had no patience for the conventional rhetoric extolling the jury as the glory of English liberties or the legal voice of community custom. The jury, like much else in English law, was the product of a barbarous past and in no sense equipped to render authoritative legal decisions. Its large size and unanimity requirement actually functioned to reduce individual responsibility and limit dissent among its members. Current practices rendered it vulnerable to manipulation by the bench.[25] Nonetheless, the jury played a critical role under the present conditions of a defective law and corrupt adjudication. The common law jury hindered the application of bad law and resisted government's efforts to censure critics, as in case of seditious libel where the letter of the law actually provided scant protections for press and public freedom. More constructively, the presence of a jury forced the judiciary to provide reasons in its decision-making and thus reveal itself and the law to the community.[26]

The quasi-jury represented a constructive distillation of this analysis. Comprehensive codification and the reformed system of judiciary establishment eliminated at source the kinds of abuses that the traditional jury functioned to obstruct. If 'the principal use' of the common-law jury was

[24] Ibid., 493–4, 498–502.

[25] Bentham's fullest rehearsal of these abuses is found in his polemic against 'jury packing', *The Elements of the Art of Packing, as Applied to Special Juries, particularly in Cases of Libel Law* (published 1821). see Bowring, v. 61–186.

[26] *Constitutional Code*, vol. 3, Bowring, ix. 554–6.

'to undo what legislators and lawyers have done' in creating bad law, then in the opposite situation of laws 'conducive to the greatest happiness of the greatest number', the obstructive function of the jury 'cannot but be prejudicial'.[27] The vital task that instead was left to the jury was to serve as a vehicle for publicity and as a tribunal of first instance for critical public opinion. Like the political press, the quasi-jury comprised an instantiation of democracy's Public Opinion Tribunal. Composed of three members, drawn locally from the large pool of eligible voters, the quasi-jury had no power in determining verdicts. Instead, it functioned as a mandatory court observer, passing judgement on the conduct of cases and especially on the conduct of the judge. Quasi-jurors were paid for their service, which was required by law. The body operated through majority voting. Where the quasi-jury disagreed with the decision of the judge, such disagreement would immediately trigger a review procedure. Where one member of the quasi-jury disagreed with the decision of the judge, a report of the dissent was included in the official record of the court. The 'main uses of the quasi-jury,' Bentham maintained, were twofold: first, 'serving as a check upon the power of the judge' and second, furnishing 'appropriate instruction' to the jurors themselves 'as scholars in the Judicatory, in its character of a *school of justice*'.[28]

Throughout *Constitutional Code*, Bentham's recommendations included frequent reminders of the prevailing abuses that his designs served to eradicate. This was powerfully so in the case with regard to his programme for courts and justice. Just as codification offered a systematic antidote to the pathologies of judge-made customary law, so the publicly funded, single-seated judiciary utilizing natural procedure furnished a systematic remedy to the entrenched abuses of the existing 'technical system of procedure'.[29] In many earlier writings, Bentham delineated at length the opposition between the two court systems. The 1808 *Scotch Reform*, for example, exhibited the stark contrasts between natural and technical processes, presented in two columns in terms of which the failings of the technical system were set against the corrections of the natural system. The dialectical relationship between the two systems was so tight, Bentham explained, that the principal elements of the natural system were themselves 'chiefly of the negative cast;

[27] Ibid., 554.

[28] Ibid., 558. The organization and functions of the quasi-jury are set out in Bowring, ix. 554–68.

[29] *Rationale of Judicial Evidence*, Book 8; Bowring, vii. 196–334.

constituted by the absence of those devices, which constitute so many characteristic features of the technical system'.[30]

For the purposes of *Constitutional Code*, the law reform polemics Bentham composed in the 1820s are particularly relevant and instructive. The 1829 *Justice and Codification Petitions* supplied the British public with draft petitions to Parliament in support of comprehensive law reform. As he insisted in *Constitutional Code*, the key to the vices of the long-entrenched legal order was the practice of imposing court and legal fees, which directly tied the power and material welfare of judges and lawyers to the costs and requirements of the legal process. Rather than aiming at justice, the technical system aimed at the wealth, power, and corrupting sinister interests of 'Judge & Co'. 'One thing is throughout intelligible', Bentham thundered, 'at the bottom of everything are fees . . .. The greater the quantity of gold in the shape of fees . . . the more cruelly will every one of us be . . . delivered over to be tormented' and 'the more insatiably squeezed for fees'.[31] The ordering logic of fees cemented the shared interests of Judge and Co., as it coordinated the conduct of judges, court officials, and legal professionals. 'The more suits the one class gets, the more suits the other gets; and the more money the one gets, the more money the other gets', he explained. Those seeking justice 'are taxed three times over: by payments to the judges, by payments to their subordinates, and by payments to the professional lawyers: the classes of whom are, for the same sinister purpose, multiplied without limit: and not only without use to, but greatly to the detriment of, truth and justice'.[32]

11.4 Courts and Democracy

The cumulative product of the fee-fed 'Judge & Co.' was a towering labyrinth of 'expense, vexation and delay' that masqueraded as justice. The first and most extensive of the *Petitions for Justice*, a massive 207-page text in its original published form, thus set out in enraged detail, the systemic abuses of the technical system. Bentham described fourteen distinct 'Devices' that sustained and magnified the failings of the

[30] *Scotch Reform*, Bowring, v. 8. Bentham drafted the work in response to a statement by Lord Grenville, then Prime Minister, to introduce legislation for the reform of civil justice in Scotland.

[31] *Justice and Codification Petitions*, Bowring, v. 476.

[32] Ibid., 535.

unreformed system. An unwritten and unknowable body of judge-made common law, arcane terminology, feigned legal actions, stylized legal pleadings and exacting court protocols, as well as extensive reliance on legal fictions, created an unintelligible legal order in which the vindication of legal right necessarily required the assistance of lawyers and court officials charging for their services. The search for fees and opportunities to charge litigants inflated the numbers of officials, courts, judges, and jurisdictions, as well as the required stages and forms of legal process. Rules that barred litigants from presenting their own cases in court enabled and multiplied technical rules of evidence, which necessitated the submission of lengthy, costly, and often duplicative documents, and which in turn created new opportunities for extracting fees. Restricted law terms and limited court sittings extended delays and thereby increased costs and vexation. The multiplication of tribunals, distinguished by both territorial and subject-matter jurisdictions, meant the same legal dispute might be bandied from court to court; each court utilizing different procedures and rules of evidence and each requiring new submissions and pleadings; and every step adding further layers of expense and delay. A property dispute appearing before the courts of common law, Bentham reported, 'under the most favorable circumstances' might cost 'upwards of 30 pounds, while, in cases to a large extent, it amounts to hundreds of pounds'. When a property dispute moved 'by appeal from court to court', the cost was raised 'to thousands of pounds'. And when a case came before 'the equity courts', the costs inflated 'to little if anything short of tens of thousands of pounds'. Had the case instead been treated according to a 'mode of procedure really aiming at justice' – that is, the alternative natural procedure – 'the suit would be heard and determined, without any expense in the shape of *money* and at an inconsiderable expense in the shape of *time*'.[33]

For Bentham, the damage caused by the abuses of the unreformed legal order went well beyond the crippling, unnecessary and avoidable expense, vexation, and delay it inflicted on those seeking justice. Two particular consequences received emphasis and regular condemnation. First, the costs of litigation turned the legal order into a weapon the wealthy could use against those lacking comparable resources. What determined an individual to pursue litigation was less the merits of a

[33] Ibid., 535–6. Bentham drafted three separate *Petitions for Justice*. The 207-page length of the first petition refers to the version first published in 1829. The Petitions concluded with a brief summary of the plan for the judiciary detailed in *Constitutional Code*.

legal claim than the resources that could be brought to bear against an opponent. Justice and thus was 'sold', and that at a truly 'ruinous price'.[34] The legal order became 'a graduated system of depredation and oppression' in which each social rank enjoyed 'dominion' over those below it.[35] Second, the expense of litigation simply placed justice beyond the means of the vast majority of the population. The legal establishment conventionally measured the importance of a suit according to the monetary value of the property in question. In addition, entry-costs of litigation were conventionally defended as a useful discouragement to litigiousness. Bentham, however, countered that the importance of the suit was relative to its value for the victim of the alleged injury and that this value necessarily varied according to the material situation of the victim in question. For 'the immense many' who could not afford to pursue a meritorious claim, justice remained simply unavailable. 'Be the pay in each instance but a farthing', he insisted, 'to all that cannot pay the farthing, justice is denied'.[36]

Bentham's polemics against the legal establishment made vivid the institutional revolution encompassed by his constructive constitutional programme. Summary procedure, currently associated with inferior tribunals and disputes of lesser consequence, were elevated as the model forum of justice. What were standardly regarded as the highest forms of adjudication and celebrated as practices maintaining the integrity of judgeship and preserving the liberty of the subject were cast aside as the products of professional avarice and sinister interest.[37] 'No system of judicature hitherto established', Bentham regularly insisted, 'has justice for its object'. His designs, in contrast, for the first time offered 'to every man alike, in so far as may be, the protection of the law, by means of the appropriate services of the functionaries of justice employed for that purpose'.[38]

This priority that the institutions of justice reach all the members of the community extended well beyond the geographic placement of local courts and the free and prompt adjudication these courts delivered. Bentham identified important, additional measures to support those to

[34] Ibid., 444.

[35] *Constitutional Code*, vol. 3, Bowring, ix. 489 and see 474.

[36] *Justice and Codification Petitions*, Bowring, v. 444.

[37] Bentham's *Constitutional Code* did include several 'many seated' judicatories, such as the investigatory and penal tribunals conducted by the legislature. For relevant examples, see Bowring, ix. 457.

[38] *Constitutional Code*, vol. 3, Bowring, ix. 455.

whom justice was previously denied. Litigants had available to them a new official, the 'Eleemosynary Advocate', who provided legal advice and representation to those unable to afford private counsel. Among the measures to ensure 'justice for the helpless' was the creation of a publicly financed 'Equal Justice Fund' to assist with the expenses associated with litigation and court attendance and to help mitigate the imbalance 'between two litigants occupying different stations in the scale of opulence'. Whereas existing abuses enabled the law to function as a weapon of wealth against the poor, Bentham in his constructive programme proved remarkably attentive to the numerous and more subtle ways in which social and economic superiority could hamper the practice of equal justice. In contrast to the elaborate robes and wigs that adorned officials in the highest courts, Bentham specified modest 'habiliments' for judges, designed to reduce rather than magnify the superiority of the individual judge.[39] Judges publicly declared 'not [to] bestow less attention upon the causes of the poor than of the rich' and to recognize 'that the importance' of an individual suit 'depends not upon nominal value, but upon the proportion of the matter in dispute to the circumstances, and its relation to the feelings of the parties'. At the same time, the judge affirmed that 'among my sincere and constant cares' would be 'to avoid wounding, by haughtiness of demeanor, the sensibility of such of my fellow citizens, whose business brings them into communication with me'.[40]

Perhaps most intriguing were the efforts to insulate courts and judges from the corrupting influence of the legal profession. Bentham institutionally severed the professional connections between elite bar and bench by treating professional legal practice as disqualifying for judicial service. Repudiating the well-established English convention that distinction as a barrister provided the proper qualification for elevation to the bench, Bentham emphasized the very different tasks and values appropriate for each role. Talented lawyers inevitably sought employment from wealthy clients whose interests they were hired to advance. Effectiveness in this role required a distinct set of qualities: zeal, partiality, partisanship, and a full commitment to the client's cause. Or, in the characteristically tendentious expression of *Constitutional Code*, successful 'professional lawyers' were those 'who have been for the longest time habituated to

[39] Ibid., 577–9, 490, 540–1.
[40] Ibid., 534.

the practice of profit-seeking and profit-reaping mendacity'.[41] The attributes that made for private wealth and professional eminence, however, were precisely the qualities that proved disastrous in the office of the judge. Here the commitment to justice and the general welfare of the entire community was paramount. Accordingly, Bentham explained of his programme, that 'every expedient that could be found' was embraced 'for bringing the particular interests of the judge as near as possible to coincidence with the universal interest'. In the antithetical case of the private lawyer, whose interest was aligned to the private party whose legal claims he was hired to advance, this kind of alignment between professional interest and universal interest was 'absolutely impossible'.[42]

In the language of modern law, Bentham's constitutional programme gave overwhelming prominence to legal access, legal aid, and equal justice. Or in the rhetorical flourish with which he introduced his *Petitions of Justice*, 'Justice! Justice! Accessible justice! Justice, not for the few alone, but for all! No longer nominal, but at length real justice!'[43] This institutional priority is even more striking given that Bentham at the same time denied to the courts many of the functions now taken as key to constitutional democracy. *Constitutional Code* did not contain a statement of fundamental rights that the judiciary was assigned to protect against violation. The *Code* did not authorize a distribution of public powers that the judiciary was assigned to police and preserve. Judges exercised a weak form of judicial review in that they had authority to identify particular legislative proposals or actions they believed violated the provisions or design of the constitutional system. The impact of such judgements, Bentham believed, would be felt on on political debate and on critical public opinion. Nonetheless, he was explicit that the courts had no authority to invalidate any measures enacted by the legislature. 'If, on any occasion, any ordinance, which to some shall appear repugnant to the principles of this Constitution, shall come to have been enacted by the Legislature, such ordinance is not on that account to be, by any judge, treated or spoken of, as being null and void.'[44]

41 Ibid., 595.
42 Ibid., 592–5.
43 *Justice and Codification Petitions*, Bowring, v. 444.
44 *Constitutional Code Volume 1*, 45. I discuss Bentham's arguments against constitutional entrenchment in 'Declaring Rights: Bentham and the Rights of Man,' in *Philosophy, Rights and Natural Law*, ed. Ian Hunter and Richard Whatmore (Edinburgh: Edinburgh University Press, 2018), 306–37.

While Bentham was thus expansive and resolute concerning the goals and functions of judicial power in his plan of representative government, a critical question emerges concerning what was specifically democratic about this programme? Present-day advocates for enhanced legal access and the better provision of legal services echo Bentham in making clear that the most frequent failures of justice are owing to the systemic impacts of economic disadvantage, power imbalances, the costs of legal process, and the absence of effective legal representation. 'Money often matters more than merit.' an influential American scholar explains, 'and equal protection principles are routinely subverted in practice'. In this discussion, a 'commitment to equal justice' is taken to be 'central to the legitimacy of democratic processes' and affirms 'a respect for human dignity and procedural fairness that are core democratic ideals'. Nonetheless, here as more generally, the emphasis rests on the easily demonstrated and pervasive failures of the legal system to fulfill these ideals and values and to the far-reaching institutional changes required for their realization. The precise democratic nature and ramifications of access to justice are perhaps more frequently invoked than delineated.[45]

The question has particular poignancy in the light of Bentham's own intellectual development. *Constitutional Code* furnished a setting for the constructive elaboration of the institutions of justice, but the plan itself built explicitly on materials that had been assembled earlier, usually in the decades well before he embraced the cause of democratic reform. At the very outset of his career, Bentham recognized that the arcane terminology and procedures of England's unwritten law operated to the benefit of England's lawyers who naturally resisted law reform. The 'grand and fundamental' blemish of William Blackstone's celebrated presentation of English law, he maintained in 1776, was its 'antipathy to Reformation'.[46] As Philip Schofield correctly observes, the 'main features of the judicial establishment which Bentham proposed in the 1820s had been anticipated in "Draught of a New Plan for the organization of the Judicial Establishment in France"', composed some thirty years earlier.[47] Bentham's 1793 *Protest against Law Taxes* denounced the pernicious

[45] D. L. Rhode, *Access to Justice* (Oxford: Oxford University Press, 2004), 3, 9. A valuable recent teatment of these themes is provided by C. Albiston, 'Democracy, Civil Society, and Public Interest Law,' *Wisconsin Law Review* (2018), 187–214.

[46] *A Comment on the Commentaries and A Fragment on Government*, ed. J. H. Burns and H. L. A. Hart (London: Athlone, 1977 [*CW*]), 394.

[47] *Utility and Democracy*, 306.

consequences for the poor of a legal system that charged litigants for the costs of obtaining justice, using arguments and indeed specific language that reappeared in *Constitutional Code*.[48] The 1808 contributions to the debate on judicial reform in Scotland elaborated the dramatic benefits of 'summary procedure' and excoriated the costs, intricacies, and delays of alternative methods of adjudication that so well served the 'sinister interests' (now labelled as such) of the law's 'Judge and Co.' (now identified as such).[49] A full and detailed rehearsal of the case against England's legal institutions and processes was included in the massive *Rationale of Judicial Evidence*, based on manuscripts composed from 1802–12. The work devoted one of ten Books to a strident critique of the 'English system of Technical Procedure'. The discussion, Bentham's talented editor reported, 'may appear not to be so intimately connected with the more limited design of the work which professes to treat of judicial evidence only'. Nonetheless, the 'parenthetical treatise' gave ample opportunity for exposing the abuses of the 'technical system', explaining its 'alliance between the sinister interests of judges and that of professional lawyers' and locating its foundational defect in the goal to promote 'fee gathering' and not substantive justice.[50]

All of these 'pre-radical' discussions of judicial establishment, legal procedure, and judicial evidence were writings Bentham continued to invoke in his democratic constitutional plans. These works explained at length the ways in which his advocated arrangements furthered the greatest happiness of the community. Nevertheless, the earlier contributions left unexplored precisely how these designs advanced democratic interests or the sovereignty of the people. Bentham, in fact, did see important democratic dimensions to the judiciary plan of *Constitutional Code*. These connections, however, need some elaboration, as this was not an instance in which political radicalism led to a comprehensive revamping of a previously developed law reform programme. As occurred in other instances, political radicalism did not transform the content of the programme. Instead, radicalism led Bentham to recognize and emphasize the democratic promise in what was already there. This situation, I previously argued, obtained in the

[48] *A Protest against Law Taxes*, in *Writings on Political Economy Volume 1*, ed. Michael Quinn (Oxford: Oxford University Press, 2016), 269-98.

[49] See *Scotch Reform*, Bowring, v. 6–7, 35.

[50] *Rationale of Judicial Evidence*, Bowring, vii. 199, 201.

case of Bentham's advocacy for codification.[51] In the case of the institutions and practices of justice, the democratic features become plain when we turn to the fundamentals of Bentham's approach to democracy itself.

Like many of the democrats of his era, such as Sieyès and Paine, Bentham arrived at democracy through a critique of monarchy and aristocracy. All political systems, he maintained, divided the community between the 'ruling few' and the 'subject many'.[52] In the unreformed states of Europe and their colonial outposts, the ruling few comprised entrenched elites that controlled the power and resources of the state to advance their own sectional interests at the expense of the general interest. It was the structured and pervasive sacrifice of the general interest of the community that rendered these forms of political rule a system of sinister interests. Democracy, Bentham recognized, likewise created a 'ruling few' exercising government power over a 'subject many'. Crucially, however, democracy offered resources that might systematically combat the tendency for the ruling few to promote their sinister interest against the interests of the community. Frequent popular elections based on a large and equal franchise provided one such resource. But, as in the case of the judiciary, publicity and accountability were especially potent and critical, even in those settings, like the courts, where offices were held by appointment and not by suffrage.

The cumulative effects of sinister interest manifest themselves in the leading features of aristocratic and monarchic politics: large and expensive government structures, bloated military establishments and overseas empires, established churches furnishing official orthodoxies and obstructing public criticism. Governing through a system of 'needless offices, useless offices, overpaid offices, and sinecure offices' provided ample scope for patronage and favouritism, while undermining accountability and responsibility.[53] Political conventions, comprising a mixture of 'authority begotten prejudice' and 'interest begotten prejudice', worked

[51] See my 'Bentham on Codification', in *Selected Writings of Jeremy Bentham*, ed. S. Engelmann (New Haven: Yale University Press, 2011), 470–3.

[52] This following summary draws especially from Bentham's *First Principles Preparatory to Constitutional Code*, ed. P. Schofield (Oxford: Clarendon Press, 1989 [*CW*]). My characterization of Bentham's approach to democracy is heavily indebted to the account provided by Philip Schofield in *Utility and Democracy*.

[53] *Official Aptitude Maximized, Expense Minimized* (1830), ed. P. Schofield (Oxford: Clarendon Press, 1993 [*CW*]), 360.

to mask the corruption and sinister interest of the ruling few.[54] Sinister interest equipped Bentham with a simplifying logic through which he could cut through the variation among existing states and reject established pieties concerning mixed and balanced constitutional forms. As he explained in his 1817 *Plan of Parliamentary Reform*, he would leave familiar descriptions of England's celebrated constitutional achievement to 'Mother Goose and Mother Blackstone'. In reality, England's political order, he reported in *Constitutional Code*, by law comprised 'monarchico-aristocratical despotism with a spice of anarchy'.[55]

Bentham's emphasis that democracy was valuable as an antidote and cure for the destructive rule of entrenched elites additionally meant that this political form was the most promising vehicle for the realization of the larger set of reform projects Bentham had long advocated, ranging from the Panopticon prison to comprehensive codification itself. 'On the texture of the constitutional branch of law', Bentham explained in 1823, 'will depend that of every other. For on this branch of law depends, in all its branches, the relative and appropriate aptitude of those functionaries, on whose will depends, at all times, the texture of every other branch of law'.[56] This instrumentalist reasoning added further weight to the case for democracy itself.[57] At the same time, Bentham's linkage of democracy and public happiness frequently introduced ambiguity and no little sloppiness in his democratic advocacy. Arrangements that promoted the greatest happiness of the community, which naturally included both the ruling few and the subject many, for that reason embodied the 'democratic' or 'universal' interest, as opposed to the 'sinister interest' of a powerful subgroup. Felicific programmes of reforms that were absent and resisted in the current unreformed aristocracies and monarchies of the world became 'democratic' as a result.

This orientation was nonetheless critical to Bentham's understanding of democracy itself. Bentham recognized that popular sovereignty operating through a large and equal democratic franchise did not in itself ensure felicific laws and policies. And he took pains to clarify that the

54 See, as a brief example, Bentham's discussion of the arguments supporting the idea of a 'Second Chamber' in the organization of the legislature; *First Principles Preparatory to Constitutional Code* (*CW*), 106–10. A fuller general discussion appears in *The Book of Fallacies*, ed. P. Schofield (Oxford: Clarendon Press, 2015 [*CW*]), 44–64.

55 *Plan of Parliamentary Reform*, Bowring, iii. 450; *Constitutional Code Volume 1*, 25.

56 'Leading Principles of a Constitutional Code, for Any State', Bowring, ii. 271. 'Leading Principles' first appeared as an article in number 44 of *The Pamphleteer* (London, 1823).

57 I am grateful to Philip Schofield for alerting me to this point.

greatest happiness principle did not license a sacrifice of the interests of a minority to the preferences of the majority.[58] Still, his constitutional programme excluded standard devices for protecting republican and democratic constitutions from the abuse of majority power: bicameral legislatures, declarations of individual rights, super-majoritarian requirements for constitutional change and innovations. For Bentham, the political challenge that representative government faced was emphatically the tyranny of the minority. His favored examples of political abuse tended to dramatize practices of this form of tyranny: Protestant ascendancy in Ireland, the East India Company's rule over millions of 'Hindoos', the government of the master over the slaves in North America, Judge and Co.'s hijacking of justice for the sake of their own wealth and power.

Indeed, courts and legal order supplied Bentham with his leading institutional instantiation of sinister interest and the tyranny of the minority. As we have seen, the leading defects of the law – its perpetuation in unwritten form, its fictions and unfathomable technicality, the expense, vexation and delay that attended its processes – could all be ascribed to the professional interests of judges and practitioners. Rather than implement justice for all members of the community, the legal order advanced the sinister interests of Judge and Co. Significantly, for Bentham, the elite professionals in question were both the beneficiaries and the products of the structures in which they operated. Under the fee-gathering system, judges and lawyers had every incentive to maintain and amplify expense, vexation, and delay, since such conduct was the route to wealth and power. To choose to abandon the technical system and instead advance the goal of substantive justice required a sacrifice of wealth and power for the sake of the general welfare of the entire community. Such a sacrifice of personal interest was entirely possible at the individual level. Nonetheless, the failings of current law made evident the utter folly of relying on such sacrifice at the level of institutional design.[59] 'Men', Bentham explained in his *Petitions for Justice*, 'are the creatures of circumstances'; and although he excoriated against the

[58] This issue led Bentham to abandon his original formulation of the greatest happiness principle – 'the greatest happiness of the greatest number' – and replace it with, 'greatest possible happiness'. See 'Article on Utilitarianism', 309–10.

[59] The need to design institutions and legislation on a presumption of human self-interest was a central tenet of Bentham's reform projects. See *Writings on the Poor Laws Volume 2*, ed. Michael Quinn (Oxford: Oxford University Press, 2010), 353, 373; and *Scotch Reform*, Bowring, v. 15.

cupidity of Judge and Co., he nonetheless acknowledged that, 'placed in the same circumstances', no one else could be confident that his own 'conduct would have been other and better than that'. Or, in the more generous language of his counsel to the reformers of the judicial establishment in France, 'here, as elsewhere, let us blame establishments, which alone, and not individuals, are justly blameable: for individuals are what the laws have made them'.[60]

Bentham's court design and natural procedure, in contrast, created the structures through which the interests of those who dispensed justice were aligned with the interests of the entire community. Judges were separated professionally from the lawyers who served and advocated for the wealthiest clients. The elimination of fees deprived judges and court officials of the opportunity to use adjudication as a means to material profit. They were given the procedural tools to acquire necessary evidence and to resolve disputes quickly. Litigants faced no geographic or financial obstacles to pursue valid claims of legal right. In addition, the relentless mechanisms of intense publicity, direct accountability, and the censorial eye of the quasi-jury gave every encouragement to the rectitude of decision-making. The judge preserved his office and enhanced his professional standing by extending justice and thereby the securities provided by law and the happiness of the entire community.

Bentham's *Constitutional Code* and final set of law reform polemics thus supplied a democratic gloss on reforms that predated the embrace of political radicalism. A further democratic dimension was found in Bentham's increasing emphasis on how the sinister interest of Judge and Co. operated within the larger field of the unreformed British state. The benefits of England's large judicial establishment and technical system of procedure for political rulers received regular rehearsal. Stamp duties on legal documents raised revenue for the state, while the multitude of court offices created abundant opportunities for publicly funded patronage of and rewards for relatives and supporters. The general rule, Bentham maintained, was to '*make the remuneration of all offices as large as the people will endure to see it made*' in order that '*noble and honorable younger sons, and the eldest son during the lives of their respective noble fathers ... may be provided for as nobly as possible*'.[61] Britain's ruling elites clearly benefitted from a legal order that rendered

[60] *Justice and Codification Petitions*, Bowring, v. 506; *Draught of a Code for the Organization of the Judicial Establishment in France*, Bowring, iv. 406n.

[61] *Lord Brougham Displayed*, Bowring, v. 587n.

justice for the rich while neglecting the rights of the poor. However, the benefits came at terrific cost in the expense and professional expertise required to secure many of the basic legal needs of a governing class based on landed wealth: securing dynastic ownership across future generations; mortgaging property to raise funds for building, improvements, and marriage portions; securing dowries; establishing trusts and protecting minor heirs from waste and dilapidation; transferring title; and so on. Why should law reform not have appealed to the powerful who also suffered from avoidable 'expense, vexation and delay'?

Part of Bentham's explanation was ideological. The 'interest begotten' prejudices of Judge and Co. had become dominant orthodoxies among the governing elites. The Blackstonean formula that 'everything is as it should be', which Bentham never tired of invoking, extended from the content of English law to its procedures and practitioners.[62] Coupled with this, comprehensive reform struggled against the fallacy of being thought 'too good to be practicable'. 'So general, not to say universal', Bentham maintained, 'is the preference given to what is old and bad, how bad soever, to what is new and good, how good soever'.[63] But Bentham's case equally rested on specific institutional arrangements that enabled Judge and Co. to exercise an outsize influence on state practices.

In this context, Bentham's fierce attack on Lord Chancellor Eldon, presented in the 1825 *Indications respecting Lord Eldon*, is especially revealing. By the 1820s, the Court of Chancery and English equity jurisprudence were well-established targets for reformers of English law. Eldon's long chancellorship was particularly associated with the endless delays and exorbitant costs of Chancery adjudication. By the mid-1820s, critics of Chancery increasingly focused their attacks on the person of Eldon. Bentham eagerly joined the chorus of detractors. He made ample use of such polemics in his *Indications*, particularly in detailing the notorious length and expense of suits for Chancery litigants. As he explained at the outset, 'finding the practice of the Court of Chancery replete with fraud and extortion, Lord Eldon . . . formed and began to execute a plan for the screwing it up, for his own benefit, to the highest possible pitch'.[64]

62 Bentham first deployed the phrase in 1776. See *Fragment on Government* (*CW*), 407.

63 *Lord Brougham Displayed*, Bowring, v. 581.

64 *Indications respecting Lord Eldon*, in *Official Aptitude Maximized, Expense Minimized*, p. 205. In documenting the abuses in Chancery, Bentham relied heavily on William Vizard, *Letter to William Courtenay* . . . (London, 1824) and *Letter to Samuel Compton*

In his later *Equity Dispatch Court Proposal*, Bentham directly addressed the issue of costs and delays, offering litigants an interim solution to escape the equity courts and have their suits handled by a novel 'Dispatch Court' that included elements of 'natural' procedure.[65] *Indications respecting Lord Eldon*, however, had a different target. This was to make clear the corrupt political processes that enabled Eldon to exploit so ruthlessly the power and material benefits of his office. In this, Eldon provided a perfect foil for Bentham's purposes. As Lord Chancellor, Eldon occupied the highest position in the hierarchy of England's central courts and local tribunals. At the same time, the chancellorship was a major political position, a ministerial official who presided over the House of Lords in both its legislative and judicial capacities. As the member of a succession of ministries and cabinets, Eldon successfully helped to obstruct parliamentary proposals for political and legal reform through the 1810s and 1820s. When a Royal Commission was established in the mid-1820s to investigate Chancery and recommend improvements, Eldon was appointed its nominal head. As Bentham scathingly observed of the arrangements, 'it was by Lord Eldon [that] his Majesty was advised to commission Lord Eldon to report upon the conduct of Lord Eldon'.[66]

As we have seen, Bentham attributed the abuses and defects of justice in England to the foundation source of judicial fees. 'Expense, vexation, and delay' were the cumulative products of the fee-fed judge and the fee-fed lawyer. Eldon's career provided clear and damning evidence of both the judiciary's relentless pursuit of its sinister interests and of the political failings that supported its realization. On several occasions from the bench, Eldon explicitly acknowledged that the fee increases introduced previously at the Court of Exchequer and in the Commission of Bankrupts were 'contrary to the terms of an Order of the Court and sometimes contrary to an Act of Parliament'. Notwithstanding their illicit origins, Eldon declared that he would not attempt to rectify what was now established practice. In the face of mounting complaints against oppressive court fees, the Chancellor simply 'went to Parliament' and secured a statute that 'got the Corruption established'. The legislation in

Cox, Esq. … respecting the practice of that Court [Chancery], (London, 1824). The background to these attacks on Eldon and efforts to reform Chancery are reviewed by Patrick Polden in *Oxford History of the Laws of England*, vol. 11, 646–55.

65 *Equity Dispatch Court Proposal*, Bowring, iii. 297–317.

66 *Indications respecting Lord Eldon*, 237.

question, an act of 1822, gave authority to 'the Judges of the several Courts of Record at Westminster to make regulations respecting the fees of the Officers, Clerks, and Ministers of the said Courts'. Bentham maintained that the legislation gave retroactive parliamentary sanction to what previously occurred without legal authority. Parliamentary sanction of the judicial power to set fees meant that litigants were once more 'delivered up bound, to be plundered in secret, without stint to control, by the hand of these same judges'.[67] Whereas a British government would never dare to raise taxes without the authority of Parliament, judges were authorized to tax suitors in the absence of public scrutiny. Bentham's earlier critique of 'jury packing' showed how the judicial handling of the law of seditious libel protected Britain's governors from much-needed public criticism and dissent. *Indications respecting Lord Eldon*, in turn, displayed how Britain's governors returned the corruption and worked to preserve the sinister interests of Judge and Co. This 'one all-embracing and undeniable truth', Bentham insisted, 'will serve as a key to every thing':

> From the Norman conquest down to the present time, diametrically opposite to the ends of justice, have been the actual ends of judicature .... Suppose that ... Judges would have for the end of action the happiness of suitors? – As well might you suppose that it is for the happiness of negroes that planters have all along been flogging negroes; for the good of Hindoos that the Leadenall Street Proprietors have all along been squeezing and excoriating the sixty or a hundred millions of Hindoos.[68]

11.5 Conclusion

Bentham's elaborate programme for the 'judiciary establishment' proves a singularly fruitful area of attention for understanding basic elements of his constitutional project. It displays particularly well the manner in which his strategy for maximizing the community's happiness worked through a process of extension. The momentous benefits of law and legal security for the first time would be enjoyed by the entire population and especially by those whose lack of wealth previously rendered them victims rather than beneficiaries of the fruits of justice. Here the increase

[67] Ibid., 225, 238–9.

[68] Ibid., 254. The 'Leadenhall Street Proprietors' referred to the stockholders of the East India Company.

in welfare was the product of a radical redistribution of the reach of justice throughout the community.

The judicial plan also provided Bentham with a singularly compelling example of the logic of democracy as an exercise in institutional design. 'Throughout the whole course of my labours', Bentham explained in his polemic against Brougham, his 'one rule' in addressing any 'institution' was 'never to engage in any such attempt is that of pulling it down, but for the purpose, and with the endeavor, to raise up something that to me seemed better, in the room of it'.[69] In the case of the administration of justice, current arrangements magnified the abuses of 'expense, vexation, and delay' and routinely produced injustice in the form of 'misdecision' and 'nondecision'. Well before his embrace of political radicalism, Bentham had identified the foundational source for these abuses in the practice of financing justice through fees and taxes on litigants. Just as customary law enhanced the power and wealth of legal practitioners by forcing the community to require professional expertise in order to navigate a legal system of unwritten and (therefore, for Bentham) unknowable rules, so a hierarchical maze of duplicative tribunals utilizing arcane forms of action and evidentiary rules enhanced the power and wealth of judges, court officials, and elite lawyers by multiplying the opportunities for fees and litigation. The corrupt structure Bentham styled 'the technical system of English law' and the routine failures of justice were the natural results of the fee-fed judge and the fee-fed lawyer.

Bentham's cure for this pathology was a thoroughly reimagined structure of institutional justice comprising a non-hierarchical network of easily accessed local courts, headed by single judges, employing a small number of salaried officials, and utilizing an unencumbered method of 'natural procedure'. These tribunals were organized to eliminate 'expense, vexation, and delay' and to remedy violations of legal right regardless of the social and economic condition of the litigant or the value of the alleged injury. Bentham's local judge enjoyed wide discretion and authority to investigate disputes and decide legal outcomes. However, the combination of individual accountability and intense publicity operated to keep the judge a faithful executor of the law. Given this institutional structure, the judge maintained his office and salary and enhanced his reputation by pursuing justice under law. And thanks to the concurrent operation of a comprehensive code of penal and

[69] *Lord Brougham Displayed*, Bowring, v. 553.

civil law displaying 'the dictates of utility in every title', securing justice advanced the greatest happiness of the entire community.

Bentham's embrace of representative government left in place this critical diagnosis and institutional antidote. Political radicalism supplied a political deepening of the analysis. The rent-seeking conduct of 'Judge and Co.' now figured as one of several privileged elites who commandeered the institutions of the state to enhance their wealth, power and 'sinister interests'. The proposed network of reformed courts and reformed procedures, advancing the welfare of the entire community, were now understood to serve a universal and democratic interest. In addition, political radicalism sustained and enhanced a long lifetime's fury at the failings of current law. 'Astonishment and indignation', Bentham instructed at the opening of his constitutional plan for the judiciary, 'are the sentiments which the perusal of this chapter ... can scarce failed to excite in the breast of every reader ... the effect is certain: the cause is altogether simple'.[70]

The goals of equal justice and legal access that Bentham emphasized in his constitutional programme were, of course, scarcely novel. Bentham himself was fond of quoting Magna Carta to condemn the manner by which justice was routinely sold and denied by England's courts and rulers. The constitutions of his era standardly promised – here in the language of the 1780 Constitution of Massachusetts – that 'every subject ought to obtain right and justice freely, and without being obliged to purchase it; completely, and without any denial; promptly, and without delay; conformably to the laws'.[71] Yet if the goal of free and accessible justice was unexceptional, the attention and care Bentham gave to its institutional realization was quite exceptional. The extraordinary size, specificity, and detail of Bentham's plan for 'judiciary establishment' in *Constitutional Code* can be taken as evidence of the amount of public resource and political commitment that he recognized equal and accessible justice so urgently demanded.

[70] *Constitutional Code*, vol. 3, Bowring, ix. 454.

[71] Constitution of the Commonwealth of Massachusetts (1780), Declaration of the Rights of the Inhabitants, Article XI.

PART III

Codification

12

Ending at the Beginning

Law and Political Theory in 'Pannomial Fragments'

STEPHEN ENGELMANN*

How does one begin an all-comprehensive code of laws? If you're Jeremy Bentham, a pretty good start is the famous beginning of *An Introduction to the Principles of Morals and Legislation* (*IPML*): 'Nature has placed mankind under the governance of two sovereign masters, *pain* and *pleasure*. It is for them alone to point out what we ought to do, as well as to determine what we shall do. On the one hand the standard of right and wrong, on the other the chain of causes and effects, are fastened to their throne.'[1] I suggest that Bentham never managed to improve upon this opening echo of Claude Helvétius's *De l'Esprit*[2] – nor could he. And this even though he was a very busy man indeed between 1780 – when *IPML* was printed – and his death in 1832, never losing sight of his grand ambition, and in his last years still 'codifying like any dragon'.[3]

In his editorial note to 'Pannomial Fragments' (PF), prepared for the third volume of John Bowring's posthumous *Works*, Richard Smith wrote the following:

* Many thanks to Xiaobo Zhai for his invitation to present an early version of this work at the University of Macau Faculty of Law and to him and his students for their hospitality and critical engagement. Thanks also to David Lieberman and Chris Riley for early advice and support, to Guillaume Tusseau for comments, to Mark Canuel for comments and conversations, and to Philip Schofield and Daniel Williams for editorial corrections and suggestions. Finally, many thanks to Tahira Zainulabideen for invaluable research assistance.

[1] J. Bentham, *An Introduction to the Principles of Morals and Legislation* (henceforth *IPML*) (*CW*), ed. J. H. Burns and H. L. A. Hart, with a new introduction by F. Rosen (Oxford: Clarendon Press, 1996 [*CW*]), 11. Bentham intended *IPML* as an introduction to the penal code.

[2] D. Long, 'Claude Adrien Helvétius', in *The Bloomsbury Encyclopedia of Utilitarianism*, reprint ed., ed. J. E. Crimmins (London: Bloomsbury Academic, 2017), 233.

[3] J. Bentham, *Memoirs of Bentham*, in *The Works of Jeremy Bentham*, 11 vols., ed. J. Bowring (Edinburgh: William Tait, 1838–43), xi. 33.

> The MSS. from which the following Chapters are extracted, were written at sundry times, and are in an unfinished state; – the author appears to have designed ultimately to have worked up the sketches he has thus left into an Introduction to a Pannomion, or Complete Code of Laws. Some of the latest sheets are dated June 1831.[4]

In what follows, I examine the manuscript sources of PF and consider allied material and assess Smith's judgement about his editorial product. My tentative conclusions from this study are as follows: (1) the Bowring edition is indeed as unreliable as generations of Bentham scholars have argued, and Smith has here produced another '"Frankenstein" creation';[5] (2) Smith's approach, to honour Bentham's sporadic intention in his final years to produce fresh starts to his proposed code involving statements on its foundations, is nonetheless an admirable, if ultimately impossible, endeavour. Smith's claim that his editorial creation is a collection of Romantic fragments – 'sketches' for a coherent if absent whole – cannot withstand scrutiny. But an investigation of PF provides new insight into a constitutive tension that runs through Bentham's thought. I argue that PF contains elements of two Benthams that cannot finally be reconciled: the critical scientist of the art of government and the utopian legislator. Both have to be present in the code itself because of the code's ambition to be comprehensive and self-explanatory.

In *Leviathan* (1651), Thomas Hobbes tells us that, when writing law, 'perspicuity, consisteth not so much in the words of the Law it selfe, as in a Declaration of the Causes, and Motives, for which it was made. That is it, that shewes us the meaning of the Legislator'.[6] In Bentham's 'Codification Proposal' of 1822, we read that 'the greatest happiness of the greatest number requires, that such [an all-comprehensive] body of law be throughout accompanied by its RATIONALE: an indication of the

[4] J. Bentham, 'Pannomial Fragments', in *Selected Writings: Jeremy Bentham*, ed. S. G. Engelmann, (New Haven: Yale University Press, 2011), 240 (Bowring, iii. 211).

[5] This is Gunhild Hoogensen's memorable label affixed to another Smith effort for the Bowring edition, *A Plan for an Universal and Perpetual Peace*: 'It is difficult to imagine that Bentham wished his various arguments to be dismembered, reconfigured, and arbitrarily sewn together in the sort of "Frankenstein" creation which resulted.' G. Hoogensen, *International Relations, Security and Jeremy Bentham* (Abingdon: Routledge, 2005), 44.

[6] T. Hobbes, *Leviathan*, ed. C. B. Macpherson (London: Penguin Books, 1968), 388 (from chapter XXX, '*Of the* OFFICE *of the Soveraign Representative*').

REASONS on which the several arrangements contained in it are grounded'.[7] The problem of perspicuity, already fraught in Hobbes – we need to know what the sovereign wills so that we can obey – is seriously amplified in Bentham, because Hobbes's legislators can rely on what H. L. A. Hart called the 'content independent and peremptory' authority of their commands.[8] Hobbes has a theory of political obligation. Bentham, by contrast, defines authority in behavioural terms; authority is established and maintained by nothing more or less than obedience, which is driven by habit, interest, or a habitual interest. For Bentham, then, law requires a 'perpetually interwoven rationale'[9] that clarifies the aptness of commands to pleasure and pain as the 'standard of right and wrong' and 'chain of causes and effects', down to nomographic explanations that minutely justify the use of certain phrases and words, and omission of others, in the making of law. Bentham saw this need clearly as early as his first published use of the word 'pannomion', from the concluding note to *IPML*:

> To class *offences* ... is therefore to class *laws*: to exhibit a complete catalogue of all the offences created by law, *including the whole mass of expository matter necessary for fixing and exhibiting the import of the terms contained in the several laws, by which those offences are respectively created*, would be to exhibit a complete collection of the laws in force: in a word a complete body of law; a *pannomion*, if so it might be termed.[10]

[7] J. Bentham, *'Legislator of the World': Writings on Codification, Law and Education*, ed. P. Schofield and J. Harris (Oxford: Clarendon Press, 1998 [*CW*]), 248.

[8] H. L. A. Hart, *Essays on Bentham: Jurisprudence and Political Theory* (Oxford: Clarendon Press, 1982), 243ff. Following Hart on this contrast between Hobbes and Bentham is not an endorsement of his broader reading of Bentham as a legal positivist. On the contrary, Philip Schofield has specified just how mistaken this view is, most recently in P. Schofield, 'Jeremy Bentham and the Origins of Legal Positivism', in *The Cambridge Companion to Legal Positivism*, ed. T. Spaak and P. Mindus (Cambridge: Cambridge University Press, 2021), 203–24. Reading Bentham on his own terms may well point, as Gerald Postema concludes, to a different reconstruction of his thought: 'Bentham never succumbed to the methodological ambition of latter-day positivism to construct a theory of law beholden to no moral or political commitments. His moral, political, and legal theories are interdependent and mutually supporting.' G. J. Postema, *Utility, Publicity, and Law: Essays on Bentham's Moral and Legal Philosophy* (Oxford: Oxford University Press, 2019), 302.

[9] *'Legislator of the World'* (*CW*), 260.

[10] *IPML* (*CW*), 305, emphasis of phrase mine. The note was added when *IPML* was finally published in 1789. 'Pannomion' seems to date in manuscript from the 'Projet' material of the 1780s. See E. de Champs, *Enlightenment and Utility: Bentham in French, Bentham in France* (Cambridge: Cambridge University Press, 2015), 71.

I suspect an introduction to the Pannomion[11] will never see the light of day. Modern editors are not likely to take up Smith's failed project, and not for want of material. Bentham's code can never be begun for the same reason that it cannot ever, on its own terms, be ended.

If Bentham's Pannomion as such is dead, much in his work, however, is living. The critical approach that drags down Bentham's legal project has proliferated throughout, and buoys, the human sciences, which are hard at work enumerating our moral pathologies – that is, our feelings – with governmental intent. Smith's PF is most valuable when it gives clues as to how Bentham thought the principle of utility, or greatest happiness principle, could practically be translated into arrangements for the conduct of conduct.[12] These very translations, however, warn of another problem: they show how uncritical a critical science of government can be. PF's analysis of the subordinate ends of security, subsistence, abundance, and equality, and its enumeration of the axioms of pathology correspondent to them, is beholden to Bentham's middle-period political economy, and this limits the range of vision of his late political radicalism. Perhaps more of the dogmatic spirit that animates the utopian legislator is needed to transcend these limits.

12.1 'Pannomial Fragments' in Bentham Studies

As far as I know this is the first – and it will likely be the last – essay devoted entirely to 'Pannomial Fragments'. The literature not unfrequently cites PF, but in an understandably selective and piecemeal way. Ross Harrison leans on it a bit more than most in his fine philosophical reconstruction, deeming it 'probably reliable enough'.[13] The only treatment of the text as a whole of which I am aware, however, is Mary Mack's brief but enthusiastic note prefacing its inclusion, in lightly abridged form, in her Bentham reader. 'This manuscript [*sic*] has all the

[11] I will from this point capitalize 'Pannomion' throughout, because Bentham almost always does so. Whether some elements of the Pannomion are necessary to all possible pannomions is one of many destabilizing questions that haunt the project.

[12] 'Arrangement' is Bentham's own language, and 'conduct of conduct' descends from Michel Foucault. The latter is government 'in the broad sense, and old sense moreover, of mechanisms and procedures intended to conduct men, to direct their conduct, to conduct their conduct'. M. Foucault, *On the Government of the Living: Lectures at the Collège de France 1979–80*, ed. M. Senellart, trans. G. Burchell (Basingstoke: Palgrave Macmillan, 2014), 12.

[13] R. Harrison, *Bentham* (London: Routledge & Kegan Paul, 1983), 105.

hall-marks of sterling importance in the Bentham canon', she begins, 'above all, in its mathematics-axiomatic structure'. Mack takes on board Smith's own description of his work and even substantially embellishes it: 'Its intended location in the canon was critical. It was meant to be the Introduction to a Pannomion or complete code of laws, the single-minded object of his entire career; and he was still working on these fragmentary pages, perfecting them, trying to make them still more precise and concise, as late as 1831.' Mack concludes: 'But the *Pannomial Fragments* are a coherent whole, intended by Bentham himself to be *the* general introduction to the whole massive work.'[14]

As fundamentally wrong-headed as this description turns out to be, Mack's characterization of PF in intermediate paragraphs is highly suggestive and demonstrates her typically insightful view of Bentham's work as a whole. Warning of its difficulty as a text, she writes: 'In any case, after due patience and care, his meaning is never in doubt.' Bentham 'lays down the fundamental proposition' of the greatest happiness principle as 'a universal normative proposition' and then, 'beginning at the opposite end, he posits the fundamental descriptive data of the human mind to be pleasures and pains. He then must bind these remote elements together – the universal normative with the concrete descriptive-empirical, and this he does in an architecture of axioms'. Thus, 'the structure of Utilitarianism arose on a series of intermediate propositions, the axioms related not directly to or from the universal greatest happiness principle, but indirectly by stages, through axioms related to the four fundamental subordinate principles of security, subsistence, abundance, and equality'. PF is 'really a dictionary,' one that continues Bentham's project, from *A Fragment of Government* onwards, to tie 'what had been mere floating fictions' (e.g., 'happiness, unhappiness, good, evil, end, means, remedy, law . . . obligation, property, possession, power, command') to 'the facts of human feeling, to genuine joy and suffering'. Mack also notes the presence in PF of Bentham's 'favorite medical analogy: his axioms are axioms of mental pathology'. She quotes what she calls a 'key' sentence from the text: 'Experience, observation, and experiment – these are the foundations of all well-grounded medical practice: experience, observation, and experiment – such are the foundations of all well-grounded legislative practice.'[15]

[14] M. P. Mack, ed., *A Bentham Reader* (New York: Pegasus, 1969), 240, 242, emphasis in original.

[15] Ibid., 241, and quoting 'Pannomial Fragments' 266 (Bowring, iii. 224).

I think Mack right to focus the body of this note, as she does, on the four subordinate principles and on the medical metaphor. PF is yet another reminder that, as Michael Quinn has argued, Bentham is not primarily a theorist of 'abstract' utility but is always concerned, as a theorist of the art and science (or, as Mack would insist, art-and-science)[16] of government, with 'concrete manifestations in particular contexts, as modified by prevailing beliefs'.[17] Quinn seems here to be writing primarily about what we call 'cultural' difference and particularity,[18] but the lesson can broadly apply to the primacy of security and the legislator's consequent need to attend to the diversity of existing expectations – no matter how unjust they may be in the abstract. Indeed, Bentham's later writing, alongside often fierce political radicalism, continues to elevate the 'disappointment-preventing principle' as a fundamental tenet of security. And so PF includes material written in February 1828 that describes disappointment-prevention as the 'sole principle' of security as it relates to property.[19] Looking back, the disappointment-preventing principle informs a range of Bentham's proposals, animating, for example, the whole of *Supply Without Burthen* (on revenue reform) in the mid-1790s and his call for the 'euthanasia' of the Church of England in 1818.[20] This

16 Ibid., x.

17 M. Quinn, 'Popular Prejudices, Real Pains: What Is the Legislator to Do When the People Err in Assigning Mischief?', in *Bentham's Theory of Law and Public Opinion*, ed. X. Zhai and M. Quinn (Cambridge: Cambridge University Press, 2014), 72. See also 71–2n, for an illuminating footnote on Bentham on abstract utility and 'Law in the abstract'.

18 His first reference for Bentham on abstract utility is to a passage that follows a brief discussion of sati: 'The clear utility of a law will be as its abstract utility, deduction made of the dissatisfaction and other inconvenience occasioned by it', J. Bentham, 'Place and Time', ed. P. Schofield and S. G. Engelmann, *Selected Writings*, 174.

19 'Pannomial Fragments', 242 (Bowring, iii. 212): 'To civil law, more particularly, apply the axioms relating to security as to property. Sole principle – *the disappointment-preventing principle*.' The sheet from which this is taken (British Library [hereafter BL] Add. MS 33,550, fol. 50) is mostly in Bentham's hand and is headed 'Law Amendment' and 'Propositions' (both in the hand of Bentham's amanuensis John Flowerdew Colls, along with the date), with 'II. Codification' in Bentham's hand in the margin. The emphasis in PF is added by Smith, and Smith mysteriously takes this sentence from its place in the page and surrounds it with material in Bentham's hand from 'Law Amendment or Penal Code' sheets, composed in July 1829, with no reference to a chapter on codification (BL Add. MS 33,550, fols. 142 and 141). Thanks to the British Library for provision of digital images and permission to use, and to the sharp eye and painstaking reconstructive efforts of Tahira Zainulabideen, whose work made the analysis in this chapter possible.

20 J. Bentham, *Supply Without Burthen; or Escheat vice Taxation* ... (London: J. Debrett, 1795); J. Bentham, *Church-of-Englandism and its Catechism examined* ... (London: Effingham Wilson, 1818), no. IV.

general rule for application of the principle of utility as it informs all policy involving property requires plenty of 'experience, observation, and experiment': one must study the past and present in all its empirical richness, and take account of the political complexities of vested interests and their effects on individual expectations, both as strategic matters of implementation (these interests guide the behaviours of rulers and ruled) and justice (these interests are genuine titles that make up the concrete utility of some of the members of the aggregate that is the community in question).

One can almost glimpse from Mack's reading of PF how one might bridge what I call the utopian Bentham and the critical Bentham. But the issue I raise does not map onto the divide between the normative and the empirical, as there are elements of both in each moment. My claim is instead that Bentham the codifier is looking to the future rather than past and present, attempting to map a general and exhaustive anticipation of conduct rather than connecting to any particular account of it. The contrast is similar to that in *Chrestomathia* between the taxonomic tables attempting to map out everything needed for successful instruction, on the one hand, and, on the other, the various and novel arrangements proposed to exploit failures as well as successes in the service of better education.[21] Compare, for example, the encyclopaedic character of Bentham's opening 'Chrestomathic Instruction Tables' with his 'place-capturing principle' and the latter's inventive deployment of features of children's play, with its dynamics of peer esteem and emulation.[22] Bentham's codifying ambitions are analogized, even literalized, in the drive to incorporate place-capturing along with all the other techniques into Table 2's 'Principles of School Management'. Code, as Bentham conceives it, is utopian because it only is what it is when comprehensive, and its comprehensiveness requires, among other things, explicit incorporation – as part of its 'interwoven rationale' – of at least the nuts-and-bolts of the critical project within it.

My contrast between the formal project of the utopian legislator and the substantive work of the critical scientist is definitely not the false opposition sometimes still posed between Bentham the *dirigiste* and Bentham the liberal. Bentham understands all government as an

[21] J. Bentham, *Chrestomathia*, ed. M. J. Smith and W. H. Burston (Oxford: Clarendon Press, 1983 [*CW*]). I owe this illustration of my contrast to a helpful conversation with Mark Canuel. If the analogy holds, this is not to suggest that Bentham's ambitions for the polity as a whole are disciplinary in nature.

[22] Ibid., inserts at 18, 106.

institutionalized process, anchored in law, that relies on agents' own understanding ('rational' or not)[23] and pursuit of their interests, which themselves are always already shaped by law broadly understood.[24] The contrast is instead a variation on Quinn's between the abstract and the concrete. PF and its sources remind us that the late Bentham was still very much both a political realist interested in pragmatic and therapeutic reform and a political idealist whose work demands and founders on its necessary impossibility – the impossibility not of reform and its goals but of the goal of bringing everything into tabular presence. That impossibility is already foreshadowed in some of the formal or nomographic theory and ambition of the early *Limits of the Penal Branch of Jurisprudence*[25] and is apparent in very late manuscript pages possibly intended for the beginning of the Pannomion, composed on the first day of the last year of his life.[26] On New Year's Day of 1832, the eighty-three-year-old formalist dreamer is still hard at work, and he must still incorporate into his impossible text another impulse that both informs and chases after the formal impulse, the substantive impulse to translate his dream into viable reality. Bentham's idealism is driven by his relentless rejection of the common law and its fictions. Therapeutic reform, by contrast, requires a strong dose of acceptance. When we examine the late compositions that go into Smith's PF, we are reminded that the elderly Bentham never wavered from his behavioural conception of authority and from his commitment to the then-young art and science of political economy. But what if the new science and its successors generate categories, explanations, and policies that, like the common law, only

[23] M. Quinn, 'Jeremy Bentham, "The Psychology of Economic Man", and Behavioural Economics', *Œconomia* 6, no. 1 (2016), 3–32.

[24] Thus, the metaphor I have preferred for Benthamic lawmaking is that it is like landscaping. See S. G. Engelmann, 'Imagining Interest', *Utilitas* 13, no. 3 (2001), 289–322.

[25] 'In a map of the law executed upon such a plan, there are no *terræ incognita*, no blank spaces: nothing is at least omitted, nothing unprovided for.' Jeremy Bentham, *Of the Limits of the Penal Branch of Jurisprudence*, ed. P. Schofield (Oxford: Clarendon Press, 2010 [*CW*]), 219n.

[26] See the analysis of Bentham's manuscript work of 1 January 1832 in Section 12.3. Only months earlier (16 July 1831) he wrote, for the first chapter of an essay on nomography, the following definition of Pannomion, which echoes the *Limits* quotation from note 25: 'By a Pannomion understand the entire mass of the matter of law which in the country or say political state in question has the force of law: a mass by which when that extent is given to it which it is capable of having and ought to have, the whole field of law and legislation is comprehended, and the whole surface of it as it were covered.' BL Add. MS 33,548, fol. 12; thanks to Philip Schofield for providing me with transcripts of Bentham's work on nomography.

haphazardly (or worse) link up to subjects' real pains and pleasures and that are sustained by what the old radical might have otherwise identifed as sinister interests?[27] Ironically, it might be Bentham the idealist more than Bentham the realist whom we need in order to face up to the realities of our present predicaments.

12.2 Is it Bentham? 'Pannomial Fragments' and Its Sources

Not much is known about 'Richard Smith, collector of stagecoach duties at the Stamps and Taxes office'. Bentham's initial reference to him, in a letter to Jean Baptiste Say, is as 'a very worthy man' whose government work might be endangered if his superiors were aware of his editorial labors producing *The Rationale of Reward*.[28] Bentham is notorious for having regularly sent off bundles of manuscript with little or no supervision over their editing and publishing; in the same letter to Say, he says of Étienne Dumont's *Théorie des peines et des récompenses* – Dumont's recension that is the basis for Smith's *Rationale* volumes – that 'I never read the Book ... since it was printed, nor perhaps even before'.[29] In a letter to Dumont some sixteen months later, he is much less positive about Smith, who 'though a Republican, is suspected to be a sour religionist, I believe a Calvinist'.[30] Here Bentham shows more assiduity about the work published under his name, having decided that a note from *Théorie* on equality and anarchy was inconsistent with Dumont's earlier recension of Bentham, *Traités de législation civile et pénale*, and finding to his surprise that Smith had already silently omitted it as well as another note on hereditary monarchy. The letter to Dumont generally displays an annoyance with Smith and what Bentham sees as Smith's insufficient credit to Dumont and some struggle over the content of the editorial introduction – which included contemporary remarks from

[27] The 'might have' here is not at all far-fetched when we consider the much more employer-skeptical perspectives of two of Bentham's disciples, both admirers of political economy's potential service to utility: Francis Place, for a political economy that embraced collective bargaining, and William Thompson, for a cooperative political economy to replace competition.

[28] C. Fuller, ed., *The Correspondence of Jeremy Bentham: Volume 11* (Oxford: Clarendon Press, 2000 [*CW*]), 274 & n. (Bentham to Say, 4 August 1823). There might be more about Smith and his relationship to Bentham buried in manuscript; perhaps something will be uncovered with the publication of the remaining correspondence.

[29] Ibid.

[30] L. O'Sullivan and C. Fuller, eds., *The Correspondence of Jeremy Bentham: Volume 12* (Oxford: Clarendon Press, 2006 [*CW*]), 76 (Bentham to Dumont, 14 December 1824).

Bentham – prefacing the 1825 *Rationale*.[31] Regarding the note on hereditary monarchy, Dumont writes back to Bentham that Smith is clearly a fool and a fanatic.[32] In the 'Advertisement' to Smith's 1830 *Rationale of Punishment* there are no remarks from Bentham, but instead we find Dumont's account of his work with the *Théorie*, suggesting a bit more deference to the Genevan editor, not to mention sympathy with one who 'freely used the rights of an Editor' in relation to the prodigious, yet at the same time scattered and incomplete, work of a perpetually newly engaged author.[33]

There is no reason, then, to think that anything that was done with the manuscripts that make up PF was done during Bentham's lifetime and with his blessing. That it was not seems to be confirmed by a note written in Smith's hand sent with 'two sets of fragments' that he recommends be placed either 'immediately after the work on Nomography' or as 'appendices to the General View of a Code of Laws'.[34] Although there is no question from the range of editing he did – including not only *Reward* and *Punishment* but over a dozen works for the Bowring edition – that Smith knew his Bentham well, he followed Dumont in taking a very free hand. And he would often follow Dumont directly as much as he did Bentham: for sundry additional editorial work in the Bowring edition, as for the earlier *Rationale* volumes, he combined manuscript with English translations of Dumont's French, even writing his translations directly into manuscript, for example, in his work with Bentham's 'Place and Time'.[35] The British Library manuscripts catalogued under 'Pannomial

[31] Ibid., 76–8; J. Bentham, *The Rationale of Reward* (London: John and H. L. Hunt, 1825), iii–vi.

[32] 'Je vous dis que votre Calviniste est un sot et un fanatique', in *The Correspondence of Jeremy Bentham: Volume 12* (*CW*), 103 (Dumont to Bentham, late January 1825).

[33] Jeremy Bentham, *The Rationale of Punishment* (London: Robert Heward, 1830), 5.

[34] The note, which is undated and unnumbered, can be found at the beginning of the batch of folios catalogued as 'Pannomial Fragments' in BL Add. MS 33,550. In the end, PF was placed between 'A General View of a Complete Code of Laws' and 'Nomography; or the Art of Inditing Laws' in volume III of Bowring, as its own work. 'General View' is based on a translation of the 'Vue Générale' that makes up the second half of the third volume of Dumont's 1802 *Traités*, and 'Nomography' is based on a then-unpublished essay that Bentham began composing in 1811; both were edited by Richard Smith. On the preparation of the Bowring edition, see M. Otonashi, 'The "Bowring Edition" of The Works of Jeremy Bentham, 1838–1843: Its Formation, Editorial Problem and Editors', Hitotsubashi University Center for Historical Social Science Literature Study Series 29 (1993); http://hermes-ir.lib.hit-u.ac.jp/hermes/ir/re/16637/studys0290000010.pdf.

[35] See, for example, University College London Bentham Papers [hereafter UC], box lxxxviii, fol. 13, where Smith has crossed out a page of Bentham's writing in coloured

Fragments' are a collection of close to one hundred folios from which PF was constructed,[36] and they are quite various. Directly written or authorized mostly by Bentham (some are wholly or partly in the hand of Bentham's amanuensis John Flowerdew Colls), some are written by Smith himself, but usually these copy or paraphrase Bentham from the same collection. It is a haphazard lot. Study of the documents supports what Smith's manuscript note suggests: that finally the most important source of PF as a work is Smith himself, that is, the most important source is the editorial imagination that conceived of this production and assembled and arranged the pieces for it.

The most jarring anomaly in the manuscript collection is the inclusion of several undated eighteenth-century civil law folios, written in French by Bentham, among 1820s and later material, much of which might conceivably be thrown together as axioms/propositions relating to codification. The sheets are faithfully translated by Smith – though not by hand anywhere in this collection – for insertion into the third of four chapters. What was he thinking? It's hard to say, of course. One possibility could be that Smith was intrigued, as I am, by the journey of the four subsidiary ends of legislation – security, subsistence, abundance, and equality – from the civil code to political economy to the Pannomion as a whole. But this is not evidently the case, as the civil code material included is mostly about the grounds of real rights and the attack on imaginary or natural rights. More probable is that Smith, who had edited *Principles of the Civil Code* for Bowring, thought the discussions in question were useful as statements of the distributive correlates and paraphrasis[37] of the penal language – for example, regarding theft – of his previous chapter. And he could reasonably suppose, from the emphasis put by Bentham on the distinctive work that his civil code would do in contrast to others, that something along these lines belonged in an introduction to the

pencil with a note saying 'See the other side'; the other side, in Smith's hand, is almost all translated Dumont. For an analysis of differences between 'Place and Time' and the Dumont and Bowring editions, including several bowdlerizations that show the 'sour religionist' at work, see S. G. Engelmann and J. Pitts, 'Bentham's "Place and Time"', *The Toqueville Review/La revue Tocqueville* 32, no. 1 (2011), 43–66. A much more trivial sign of the work of Smith as religionist in PF is his rendering of Bentham's 'Ce que le God damn your blood est dans la bouche d'un footpad Anglois' as 'what the oath is on the part of the footpad who demands your purse'; BL Add. MS 33,550, fol. 93 and 'Pannomial Fragments' 258 (Bowring, iii. 220).

[36] The collection begins with fol. 48 in BL Add. MS 33,550.

[37] 'Paraphrasis' is Bentham's term for the translation of propositions containing names of fictitious entities into propositions containing names of real entities.

Pannomion.[38] But it is absurd to think that these faithfully translated eighteenth-century manuscripts constitute, as far as Bentham himself was concerned, 'sketches' for such an introduction.

PF's four chapters – General Observations, Consideranda, Expositions, and Axioms – do not correspond to any evident plan of Bentham's. For the first chapter, Smith draws mostly from Bentham's essay on 'Law Amendment', and specifically fragments composed in February 1828, some marked for an intended chapter on codification. For the second, he draws mostly from sheets headed 'Pannomion or Penal Code', the bulk of which are dated in April 1831. The third is mostly a hodge-podge of 'Non-penal or Penal Code' from December 1823, the aforementioned eighteenth-century civil code work, and 'Jurisprudential Entities – Penal Code' from July 1826. The bulk of the fourth and most coherent chapter is material from 'Law Amendment-Propositions', also intended for the chapter on codification in that work, mostly composed in late January 1828. This final chapter of PF – Smith's 'Axioms' – along with the related folios in the first chapter from which it is mysteriously separated, holds great promise as introductory Pannomial material, because it involves more continuous Bentham text than Smith's other sources and is clearly foundational to the project of codification. As far as Bentham's own intentions go, however, it is probably the definitional material from 1831, which Smith labels 'Consideranda', that is most clearly meant for inclusion early in the Pannomion.

12.3 How Would Bentham Begin the Pannomion, and Why?

Much work has been done to reconstruct the main stops and byways on Bentham's long Pannomial journey: from aspirations first articulated in the 1770s through extensive drafting in the 1780s, through a burst of activity in the global proposals of the 1810s and early 1820s, to the more systematic – yet still episodic – labours of his final years.[39] From Fred Rosen through David Lieberman and Philip Schofield to Emmanuelle de Champs, we are getting an increasingly clear picture of Bentham's efforts

[38] See the prolix considerations of the distinctive features of his projected civil code that Bentham thought were important enough to take up the majority of his 1830 preface to the published edition of the first volume of Constitutional Code. Jeremy Bentham, *Constitutional Code: Volume I*, ed. F. Rosen and J. H. Burns (Oxford: Clarendon Press, 1983 [*CW*]), 5–9.

[39] For an excellent one-stop Pannomial overview, see D. Lieberman, 'Bentham on Codification', in *Selected Writings*, 460–77.

over the years to construct an all-comprehensive code of laws, culminating in his last decade in the proposed three volumes of the *Constitutional Code* as the crowning achievement of an ultimately democratic project. Lieberman in particular has insisted on the intimate connections in Bentham's work between the ever-fierce attacks on the common law, the cognoscibility (knowableness) of code, and the ability of the governed to oversee their governors.[40] Schofield has traced how the unmasking of the 'tribe of lawyers', of 'Judge & Co.', became generalized to whole ruling establishments, all wielding their fictions in the service of sinister interests that required comprehensive codification to bring them to heel.[41] De Champs has filled out the early years with intensive work on Bentham's first genuinely pannomial effort, the abandoned 'Projet d'un corps de loix complet' of the 1780s, placing it in its Continental Enlightenment context.[42] And one of many contributions of Rosen's was, with J. H. Burns, to provide an early guide to the Pannomial work of Bentham's final years.[43] I have nothing to add to this except to raise concerns, based on a consideration of some of the latest Pannomial work, regarding Bentham's understanding of and approach to codification.

If a reading of 'Pannomial Fragments', its manuscript sources, and some surrounding material has anything to add, it is simply that Smith is not wrong to see a Bentham who never stopped striving to produce a coherent whole, a Bentham still prone to preoccupation with the Pannomion and its foundations in his last years. And it is foundations – primarily linguistic and what Bentham would call 'pathological' foundations – that I explore here and in Section 12.4. Again, of the material included in PF itself, many of the 'Consideranda' fragments might best reflect Bentham's own late intentions for material to be included early in the Pannomion. The notes, written in April 1831, are marked 'Pannomion or Penal Code', and many also include 'Def.': they make up a kind of glossary of terms (Mack's 'dictionary'). Defined are 'Happiness', 'Unhappiness', 'Good', 'Evil', 'End', 'Means', 'A law'. Some

40 Ibid.; and D. Lieberman, '*Of the Limits* and the Theory of Legislation', in *The Legal Philosophy and Influence of Jeremy Bentham: Essays on* Of the Limits of the Penal Branch of Jurisprudence, ed. G. Tusseau (London: Routledge, 2014), 293–307; D. Lieberman, 'Bentham's Jurisprudence and Democratic Theory: An Alternative to Hart's Approach', in *Law and Public Opinion*, 119–42.

41 See especially P.hilip Schofield, *Utility and Democracy: The Political Thought of Jeremy Bentham* (Oxford: Oxford University Press, 2006), 109ff.

42 De Champs, *Enlightenment and Utility*, 55–91.

43 J. Bentham, *Constitutional Code: I* (*CW*), xxxv–ix.

of the notes then classify the laws of the Pannomion in Bentham's typically hard-to-follow, sometimes cross-cutting fashion: dividing the code into the effective and the constitutive, the directive and the sanctionative, then the sanctionative into the remunerative and the punitive, the expositive as constitutive and part of the directive, thus overlapping the civil and the penal.[44]

Are these 'sketches' intended for an introduction to the Pannomion? No, they are not. They are, however, better candidates for such than the more interesting Law Amendment work of PF chapters 1 and 4 and certainly better candidates than the potpourri of chapter 3. From later manuscript (August 1831) consulted by Smith but not used for PF, it is clear that a glossary of sorts was intended for chapter 1 of the Pannomion, which is not likely the beginning (and which Smith himself doesn't put at the beginning).[45] What might have Bentham meant to put before it? If we go to the beginning of January 1832 – the start of the final calendar year of Bentham's long life – we find text that is clearly intended for an introduction to the Pannomion, and it is similarly linguistic, if far more exhortative in nature. Although most of what I have found in manuscript is in a copyist's hand, we can be quite certain that it is genuine Bentham and was composed on 1 January 1832. How do we know? These pages include a sheet in Bentham's hand, dated by him '1832 Jan. 1', the body of which is faithfully copied. At the top of the Bentham sheet are the following headings: 'Pannomion Nomography Beginning Preliminary Expositions'. When copied, the material is dated 2 January, and is simply headed 'Pannomion'. On another sheet dated 1 January, in the same copyist's hand, also headed 'Pannomion', we have an 'Instructional'. It seems, from the first paragraph, possibly intended for the very beginning of the code:

> Requisite to be had in mind, during the reading or recollection, of every part, of the text of the body of law of which this is the commencement, is the instructional matter which here follows –
>
> Here begin certain considerations and instructions which on all occasions, it will at all times be needful to the person, be he who he may, to have in view.

[44] 'Pannomial Fragments', 245–52 (Bowring, iii. 213–17).

[45] See BL Add. MS 33,549, fol. 322, in Bentham's hand and dated 22 August, headed 'Pannomion', which names the first section of the first chapter 'Consideranda' and has the following note at the top: 'Bring together here all the names of the General Consideranda which throughout the Pannomion there can be need to bring to view.'

> Not excepted on this occasion, are even the legislators of any portion of time future. By no length of time, by no such increase of *knowledge* and maturity of *judgment* – say in one word *wisdom* – as it is in the nature of *experience* to produce, can the needfulness or usefulness, of this same instructional matter be superseded: seeing that at all times, forgetfulness, oversight, unadvisedness, inadvertency are imperfections, to the exemplification of which human nature will at all [times] remain exposed. On this occasion, in two several characters are the members of the community borne in view – namely [in that] of subject-citizens, and in that of legislators. . .
>
> Now then as to the *language* which on this occasion is employed.
>
> *Language* is for ideas of all sorts the instrument of *communication* between man and man: as also of *fixation* in the minds of each.
>
> Pregnant with evil in all its shapes are the *imperfections* of which language is susceptible.
>
> Of the number of these imperfections are *obscurity*, *ambiguity*, and *indistinctness*: – indistinctness or say indistinguishedness, undividedness, unseparatedness, as between one part and another of the subject matter in question – the subject matter the parts of which require, for any purpose, to be distinguished.
>
> Of all these several undesirable qualities the absence is designated by the word *clearness*: in such sort that where this word is employed, the absence of these several imperfections one or more or all of them, will be understood to be meant by it.[46]

He continues, in somewhat repetitive but developing fashion:

> Throughout the whole field of *thought* and *action* and thence throughout the whole field of *law* and *legislation* has place the need of |^^^| and fixation of the intended import of the several locutions which are the sources and seats of the abovementioned imperfections.
>
> Pregnant with evil in all its shapes will be seen to be these same imperfections.
>
> Good, in one shape or other, according to the occasion, is the *end in view* of everything which will have been seen: good, meaning the greatest happiness of the community of which this is the Pannomion.

[46] BL Add. MS 33,549, fol. 316, emphasis in original. The text is in the hand of a copyist, with corrections by Bentham, and headed by him 'Ch. or §1. Preliminary Expositions'. Note that this Pannomial introductory material is explicitly a piece of universal expository jurisprudence (it is for this and really any code 'at all times . . . needful to the person, be he who he may, to have in view') and that it collapses the expositor/censor distinction, i.e., the distinction between describing law as it is and law as it should be ('Pregnant with evil in all its shapes are the *imperfections* of which language is susceptible'). See X. Zhai, 'Bentham's Natural Arrangement and the Collapse of the Expositor-Censor Distinction in the General Theory of Law', in *Law and Public Opinion*, 143–83.

> From every one of these several imperfections flows *evil* in all its shapes; for, in so far as they have place in the body of the law, is liable and wont to be produced *evil* in the corresponding shape unintended.[47]

Bentham goes on to give definitions for the words 'obscurity', 'ambiguity', and 'indistinctness', and he begins to specify sources of these in our language. 'The Purpose for which they are here brought to view is the application of the several remedies of which they are respectively susceptible.'[48] And he brings them to view, first going to sources of ambiguity with regard to number, in the case of the words 'a', 'an', and 'every' (to be repeated with 'any'):

> In such cases *a* or say *an* have the effect of the word *every*, which has again the effect of the word *all*.
>
> In other cases *a* or *an* has not the same effect as the word *every*: in these cases the application made by it of the enactment in which it is enacted is confined to some one and no more than one subject matter: in which case the purpose of the enactment is satisfied, when application has been made of it to the one subject matter of the enactment: in these cases it will not be considered as applying to any more than one. The end in view, as shown by the contrast, will serve for guidance.
>
> Example of the *narrow* or say singular sense of the article *a* or *an*.
>
> Example of the extended or say equivalent to plural sense of the word *a* or *an*.[49]

Keep in mind that this isn't Bentham just working out ideas on paper, or writing draft material for a work on language or on language and law. Something like this belongs in the Pannomion itself, as part of its introduction, perhaps it belongs even at the beginning of its introduction. And engaging in what looks like a potentially very big detour wouldn't be about satisfying the idiosyncratic whims of an infirm elderly man: the work above is in fact admirably consistent with Bentham's lifelong codifying ambitions. Recall that the Pannomion – according to its first mention in a published work, namely *IPML* – must include 'the whole

[47] BL Add. MS 33,549, fol. 317. This sheet is in the copyist's hand but with an insertion by Bentham. It is dated 2 January, but it is cleaner than the previous folio and is almost certainly copying a Bentham composition from 1 January (see n. 48).

[48] Add BL Add. MS 33,549, fol. 318. This sheet, also in the copyist's hand, is dated 2 January but is a faithful copy of the text of BL Add. MS 33,549, fol. 319, which is in Bentham's hand with the 1 January date and the heading (including 'Beginning') described at p. 300 above.

[49] Ibid. At the bottom is written 'Repeat this, *mutatis mutandis*, applying it the word *any*: and give examples'.

mass of expository matter necessary for fixing and exhibiting the import of the terms contained in the several laws, by which those offences are respectively created'.[50] And that is precisely what Bentham thinks he is doing here.

A moment's reflection tells us that the project is an impossible one: we have here an analysis, with no accompanying remedy, of only a few words with respect to one example of one of the 'imperfections' of language. Think about the strangeness of what Bentham is doing: he is codifying the codifying of code – writing down what needs to be known in order to make known (read, or proclaim) what is written down, and it seems necessary to give this a kind of specification well beyond what is actually already written down (for example, there may be a need to explain why some kinds of language are used and not other kinds in what is written down, and in turn write that down). This is not a problem of circularity, and it is not exactly an infinite regress; it is more a kind of bottomless spiral. It shouldn't surprise us that by 3 January 1832 Bentham has again abandoned the Pannomion and its beginnings and is back to feuding over English law reform, writing about bankruptcy for *Lord Brougham Displayed*.[51]

A big part of the problem here is an untenable theory of language. Bentham sees language both as a potentially neutral instrument of communication from mind to mind and as a source of rhetorical effects that are able to do independent work, for better and worse, on listeners and readers.[52] There is a rough consistency in the theory, of course, in that the one kind of language can be effectively unmasked and the other effectively substituted for it. From his early work forward, Bentham tied

50 See n. 10.

51 See UC iv. 459; and J. Bentham, *Lord Brougham Displayed* . . . (London: Robert Heward, 1832). On Bentham and Brougham, see C. Riley, 'The Hermit and the Boa Constrictor: Jeremy Bentham, Henry Brougham, and the Accessibility of Justice', *American Journal of Legal History* 60, no. 1 (2020), 4–29. There is, at BL Add. MS 33,549, fol. 320, a manuscript dated 4 January in Bentham's hand – heading 'Pannomion Beginning Preliminary Expositions' – that continues to be preoccupied with the problem of locutions and their misinterpretation, so he hadn't quite abandoned the effort. But after this, the closest related material I have been able to find – by no means a continuation of the beginning of the Pannomion – is general considerations on language from a few days later (see UC cii. 127).

52 'Table of the Springs of Action' shows both of these possibilities together, presenting 'eulogistic' and 'dyslogistic' terms alongside their neutral alternatives. For an image of the Table itself, from the work printed and published in 1815 and 1817 respectively, see www.ucl.ac.uk/bentham-project/table-springs-action/table-springs-action.

language to power. The fictions of the common law allowed lawyers and judges to abuse litigants and wield arbitrary power.[53] The laws required in place of their current technical arrangement a natural arrangement in conformity with utility.[54]

> It is also necessary that the style of the laws should be as simple as their arrangement; that the language in ordinary use should be employed; that their formulas should have no scientific apparatus; and, in a word, that if the style of the book of the laws were distinguished from the style of other books, it should be by its superior perspicuity – by its greater precision – by its greater familiarity, because it is intended to be understood by all, and particularly by those least enlightened.[55]

The ironies are well-known. The above reads like a brief for the modern plain language movement, a big part of which is involved in reforming the language of government in several countries so that it can be readily understood by the governed.[56] In the eighteenth-century work quoted here, Bentham anticipates that laws founded on utility will only be 'susceptible of a . . . familiar nomenclature'.[57] At least by the time of his mature radicalism, however, he has not only himself generated a host of neologisms – several of which, like 'codification' itself, have managed to catch on – he is quite convinced that 'Neology' is the only way to purify the language, to free it from its capture by sinister interests. This work of 'the friend of the people in the shape of the would be improver of the law' is marked by 'thanklessness', but it is necessary to counter the easier work of 'the enemy of the people in the shape of the fee-fed law practitioner and fee-fed judge'.[58] Yet such work is not only thankless but doomed to

[53] 'The Common Law, as such, is but a series of *ex post facto* Laws.' J. Bentham, *A Comment on the Commentaries and a Fragment on Government*, ed. J. H. Burns and H. L. A. Hart (Oxford: Clarendon Press, 2008 [reissue] [*CW*]), 49n (50) and passim.

[54] 'At the most basic level, Bentham's charge [against the author of the *Commentaries on the Laws of England*] referred to Blackstone's adherence to the technical vocabulary of English law. His retention of such terms as "misprisions, contempts, felonies, praemunires" ensured the technical arrangement could never achieve the practical objective of any system of legal classification.' D. Lieberman, *The Province of Legislation Determined* (Cambridge: Cambridge University Press, 1989), 261.

[55] Bowring, i. 326 ('Principles of the Civil Law').

[56] For the international association, see https://plainlanguagenetwork.org. A Plain Writing Act is now part of the United States Code (see www.govinfo.gov/content/pkg/BILLS-111hr946enr/pdf/BILLS-111hr946enr.pdf). The bill is appropriately short, clear, and direct, but it also explicitly bars enforcement.

[57] Bowring, i. 324 ('Principles of the Civil Law').

[58] BL Add. MS 33,548, fol. 224, 7 June 1827. On the work of 'fee-gathering' in motivating and sustaining or even defining the 'technical system of procedure', see the lengthy

fail at its stated task. Bentham's strictures about language lead to elaborate and impenetrable linguistic inventions, avoidance of active verbs, and other devices. These could, contrary to intent, conceivably produce a viable new specialist science of utilitarian law, but one could never expect the unfamiliar nomenclature and clunky style to produce successful democratic code.

It is crucial to recall the intention behind Bentham's approach to law and language. When writing about codification, he almost never misses a chance to contrast it favourably with the common law and to suggest that in its superiority it will promote the public interest and thwart the mediating work of what he would come to call sinister interest. In his 'Bentham's Fictions', Robert Yelle is right to look back to the Reformation and understand the impulse here as essentially Protestant: Bentham is an iconoclast seeking to smash the idols of the common law and allow the individual access to unmediated, transparent legal scripture, through vernacular code.[59] The analogue to the priesthood here is of course the 'fee-fed' Judge & Co.; judges, like pastors in most Protestant denominations, will see their status diminished and that of laypersons elevated. In the developed Constitutional Code, judges' applications of laws to cases will be overseen by citizen quasi-juries, and their freedom with regard to legal innovation will be restricted to proposals made to legislators.[60] The same code relies heavily on the mobilization of the moral or popular sanction through the Public Opinion Tribunal,[61] which is the enforcer of its numerous equality-enshrining[62] provisions

analysis in J. Bentham, *The Rationale of Judicial Evidence*, Book VIII (Bowring, vii. 196–334).

59 R. A. Yelle, 'Bentham's Fictions: Canon and Idolatry in the Genealogy of Law', *Yale Journal of Law & the Humanities* 17, no. 2 (2005), 151–79. Thanks to David Lieberman for alerting me to this piece. See also Hart: 'Bentham … continually returns to a comparison between the mysteries of the law and lawyer craft and those of religion and priest craft …. Bentham surely recognized in himself the Luther of Jurisprudence', *Essays on Bentham*, 29.

60 For a detailed summary of these and other features of the judicial establishment in the Constitutional Code, see P. Schofield, *Utility and Democracy*, 306–12.

61 Again, regarding this general 'architecture of government', see ibid., 250–71. For specifics on the Tribunal, see *Constitutional Code, Volume I*, 35–41 and passim.

62 Enshrining equality is fundamental to the Constitutional Code. 'The following are the branches of the pannomion, to which the ends immediately subordinate to the greatest-happiness principle respectively correspond: – To constitutional law, the axioms and principles applying to equality.' PF 241 (Bowring, iii. 211), Add MS 33,550. 50 (Law Amendment-Propositions, 14 February 1828 ['The following are' is added in Smith's hand]).

governing the relations between rulers and ruled. The enforcement of the Constitutional Code is one of many ways that laws can be effective without a special class of enforcers. This is how 'indirect legislation' works, according to the Nomography and Constitutional Code work of his final years. In the case of say, licences, it is a decided advantage that activities are regulated without need of 'subsidiary or say effectuative law', without need of a judge and all the 'delay, expence, and vexation' of prosecution. In a sense, then, such law takes care of itself – or at least executes its purpose without aid of Judge & Co., without the mediation of a legal priesthood.[63]

Just as Yelle looks back to the Reformation, Guillaume Tusseau is right to look forward to Marxism and post-Marxism and, in particular, to look from Bentham on legal fictions to the critical legal studies movement's concerns about language and hegemony. Bentham is a forerunner of the unmasking endeavours of the great theorists of suspicion of the nineteenth century and beyond, demystifying fictions to analyze the interests that they serve and sustain.[64] Tusseau suggests that despite the thoroughness of his work, 'atomism and nominalism', as well as 'panlegalism', in the end limit the reach of Bentham's criticism. Bentham's analysis of ideology, in Mannheimian terms, is necessarily local rather than total: he thinks in terms of plots and their perpetrators and so is unable to get to the point of a genuinely structural analysis. Bentham is ultimately, with his code's 'alternative tools', too invested in the law itself, too invested in 'the dogma of law's innocence' – in law's potential, if properly reformed, to be innocent of domination.[65]

Certainly Bentham's alternative tools, in the sense of the Pannomion and the untenable theory of language that animates it, confirm concerns about panlegalism and legal apologetics. But defenders of the reach of the late radicalism would point to its de-personalizing and systemic qualities – both in terms of critique and institutionalization – to suggest that Bentham's approach is, *pace* Tusseau, at least quasi-structural and of expansive critical potential. In the conclusion to his broadside against the 'technical system of procedure' in *Rationale of Judicial Evidence*, he

[63] BL Add. MS 33,548, fols. 258–9, 24–5 June 1829.

[64] G. Tusseau, 'Towards a Linguistic Criticism of Legal Hegemony: Some remarks on Bentham v. Judges and Co.', *Canadian Journal of Law & Jurisprudence* 32, no. 1 (2019), 173-94. Compare again Hart, *Essays on Bentham*, 21–6.

[65] Tusseau, 'Towards a Linguistic Critique of Legal Hegemony', 190–3, quoting V. Kerruish, *Jurisprudence as Ideology*.

writes regarding 'judicial character' that 'it is not the *individual*, it is the *species* that has been struck at: nor yet the species, but in respect of that *situation* in which the conduct of any other part of the human species would have been the same'.[66] And in his constitutional work, Bentham institutionalizes, according to several of its admirers, the structural framework for a democratic attack on various hegemonies and their subjection to the operations of an evolving critical public opinion.[67] In Section 12.4, however, I return to PF and its way of introducing the Pannomion to air concerns that share affinity with those expressed by Tusseau.

12.4 'Pannomial Fragments' and Benthamic Legacies

'Pannomial Fragments' begins as follows:

> By a Pannomion, understand on this occasion an all-comprehensive collection of law, – that is to say, of *rules* expressive of the will or wills of some person or persons belonging to the community, or say society in question, with whose will in so far as known, or guessed at, all other members of that same community in question, whether from habit or otherwise, are regarded as disposed to act in compliance.[68]

Bentham wrote the note reproduced here in June 1831.[69] As a candidate for the beginning of Pannomion, the choice is reasonable; it shows that Bentham's command conception of law and behavioural conception of obligation to law stayed with him until the end. The statement is open as to whether to proceed to Pannomial matter, Pannomial form, or a

66 Bowring, vii. 329. For a contrast with how John Stuart Mill – the editor of Bentham's *Evidence* – views character, see S. G. Engelmann, 'Mill, Bentham, and the Art and Science of Government', *Revue d'études benthamiennes* 4 (2008), doi.org/10.4000/etudes-benthamiennes.178.

67 The boldest and most far-reaching of these sympathetic readings – democratically deconstructing sovereignty, and reading utility not as a potentially rigid foundational principle but instead as a kind of participatory discursive field of changing moral possibilities – is offered by O. Ben-Dor in *Constitutional Limits and the Public Sphere: A Critical Study of Bentham's Constitutionalism* (Oxford: Hart, 2000).

68 'Pannomial Fragments', 240 (Bowring, iii. 211).

69 BL Add. MS. 33,550, fol. 49. This is in Bentham's hand, dated '1831 June 5', under the heading 'Pannomion', with the marginal 'A Pannomion, what'. MS reads '*laws*' rather than 'law', followed by a dash, in the first sentence. The rest of the sheet is written by Smith (and follows in PF), most but not all of which can be found in Bentham's hand in the same collection.

statement on matter and form.[70] We saw above that Bentham turns to form for his beginnings the following New Year's Day, and that he dives into definitions for a first chapter, but he could just as well move on to matter. That is what Smith chooses to do. But in doing so, Smith jumps to material composed in early 1828 for an essay on Law Amendment.[71] The initial Law Amendment selection introduces the four ends – security, subsistence, abundance, and equality – as means to the 'all embracing end' of happiness; Smith follows with a confusing and incomplete mix of Pannomial branches (constitutional law, etc.) and 'axioms of moral and political pathology' as they relate to the four ends and to one another. This thread and its source material, which continues and completes the chapter, is taken up again in the 'Axioms' chapter that concludes PF.

Bentham appears to have stopped writing 'Law Amendment' in February 1828. This makes sense if it is what it appears to be, a text written with the expectation that it could be useful for a law reform initiative that Bentham hoped his then-ally Henry Brougham would advance in Parliament.[72] On 7 February 1828, Brougham gave a speech on law reform that was a huge disappointment to Bentham; in fashioning his response, Bentham appears to have soon moved on from the essay. On the one hand, the Law Amendment material makes no sense for inclusion as introductory Pannomion material; it is not intended as such. On the other hand, it makes perfect sense. Bentham is elucidating fundamental principles of morals and legislation, much of it for a chapter on codification. Smith is right, I think, that Bentham should begin the Pannomion in this way and not with the linguistic considerations that clutter his late intentions for it.

Why? Bentham's subordinate ends and correspondent moral pathologies combined with an introduction to the branches of the Pannomion serve to elaborate on pain and pleasure as 'sovereign' of both standard of right and wrong and chain of causes and effects and to illustrate how legal divisions and rules can acknowledge and realize these within a generalized utilitarian art of government. The intimate connections between what at one point Bentham presciently labels 'political

[70] See, for example, the material quoted in n. 26.

[71] He does this following a statement of the greatest happiness principle, one that reads very much like Bentham but that I have been unable to trace.

[72] Much of the text is preoccupied with duelling and its abolition. Thanks to Chris Riley for providing me with transcripts.

psychology'[73] and the dictates of the principle of utility are manifest in the need to know what makes people happy in order to legislate in service of happiness. But, as Mack hints in her paean to PF, without the mediation of the four subordinate ends, it is inconceivable that fact and principle could be consistently conjoined within a stable framework of rule. And the particular axioms of moral pathology relating to each of the four ends – for example, that pain from loss is greater than any pleasure from the equivalent gain, that there is a diminishing marginal utility to wealth, etc. – are crucial both for figuring out what to do and figuring out how to do it when it comes to codifying the laws. Bentham's framework suggests the need for trade-offs of various sorts, for example, between equality and security, where security (the most important of the four ends) might allow for minimizing inequality (the least important) but only up to a certain point. Such trade-offs – basic to a flexible and pragmatic utilitarian art of government – are a challenge to the spirit animating Bentham's codifying impulse. Although Bentham is careful throughout his career to warn against any possibility of perfection in politics, his own version of the republican drive to shove aside the rule of men and make way for the rule of law[74] has at once too much and too little faith in the latter project. Too much faith is evident in the desire to anchor everything in law *qua* law; too little faith is evident in the suspicion that to leave doubt as to what law says courts disaster.[75]

73 See Add MS 33549. 251. In the margin, Bentham has added 'or say Axioms of political psychology or say pathology' underneath 'Ch. Axioms pathological' on a sheet that was originally headed 'Law Amendment' from January 1828 but seems to have been repurposed for 'Penal Code For Pannomion'.

74 Frank Lovett and Philip Pettit deploy Bentham as a foil in theorizing non-domination. This is surprising considering the very Benthamic character of their liberal neorepublicanism, which neatly matches up with the strengths and limitations of Bentham's attack on sinister interest. F. Lovett and P. Pettit, 'Neorepublicanism: A Normative and Institutional Research Program', *Annual Review of Political Science* 12 (2009), 11–29; see also P. Pettit, 'Freedom in the Market', *Politics, Philosophy & Economics* 5, no. 2 (2006), 131–49.

75 Gerald Postema offers a powerful account of the meaning of the rule of law, arguing persuasively that it is incompatible with the idea of sovereignty and incompatible more generally with a limited conception of who instantiates and reproduces law's rule. But the central idea animating his account – that in order to rule, law has always to be normatively and existentially more-than-law – cannot, I think, be successfully translated into Bentham's own account of the sanctions (first specified in *IPML*, 34–7) and the relationships between them. Postema wants Bentham's emphasis on publicity to carry the weight of Postema's conception of the rule of law. But despite remarkable and expansive anticipations for the Public Opinion Tribunal – including the fecund idea that 'Public Opinion may be considered as a system of law, emanating from the body of the people'

Thus, even though it is not Bentham's intuition as to where he should begin, Smith's beginning is the right move: a statement of the principle of utility should be followed by a statement of the four ends and their relationship to the divisions of the Pannomion (Constitutional Code, Civil Code, Penal Code, and Procedure Code), followed by axioms of mental pathology relating to these and other cross-cutting categories and divisions. Linguistic analysis should wait, and it shouldn't be allowed to overrun the rest. This is, I think, what Smith's PF tries to do. But it does what it does in shabby, incomplete, and disordered form. There is, for example, no mention of the Procedure Code – a full branch of the Pannomion – until towards the end of the third of four chapters. The Constitutional Code is given almost no treatment. We can read PF and hardly be aware that this is late Bentham: that this is the Bentham who did so much to systematize securities against misrule, that this is the Bentham who was concerned to join duty and interest not only for the subject many, but for the ruling few, to the point where the latter would no longer have any exclusive 'constitutive authority' whatsoever.[76]

Even if Smith had done a better job of it, though, this beginning would only make us more aware of a significant problem. Although the four ends and their related axioms of pathology allow Bentham to join utility to code, they blunt his radicalism in a way that makes PF's curious omission of anything but the faintest allusion to democracy seem appropriate. An anomaly early in the General Observations of chapter 1 betrays one major limitation. In this introductory section, having assigned equality and its axioms to constitutional law, and security and its axioms to penal and civil law, PF reads as follows:

> To political economy apply the axioms and principles relating to subsistence and abundance. To political economy – that is to say, to those portions of the penal and civil codes in the rationale of which considerations suggested by the art and science of political economy are applicable and have place.[77]

(*Constitutional Code: I* [*CW*], 36) – Bentham does not and ultimately cannot understand law's work in Postema's terms. See G. Postema, 'Law's Rule: Reflexivity, Mutual Accountability, and the Rule of Law' followed by 'The Soul of Justice: Bentham on Publicity, Law, and the Rule of Law', in *Law and Public Opinion*, 7–62.

[76] 'The sovereignty is in the *people*. It is reserved by and to them. It is exercised, by the exercise of the Constitutive authority.' *Constitutional Code: I* (*CW*), 25.

[77] 'Pannomial Fragments', 242 (Bowring, iii. 212). Add MS 33550. 50 (headed 'Law Amendment', with 'Propositions' and 'Ch. II Codification' in the margin, dated 14 February). Bentham is here writing about axioms of pathology in relation to branches of the Pannomion, just as faithfully reproduced by Smith in PF.

Instead of a branch of the Pannomion, Bentham introduces here a branch of the art and science of government, that branch concerned with wealth. He clarifies that he does this is in order to supply portions of the penal and civil codes. But what this acknowledges is that the way utility is to be translated into these codes is not necessarily through subsidiary ends as commonly understood but through subsidiary ends that have place as categories in a scientific discourse that studies and authoritatively specifies their relations. The problem here goes beyond a general problem of the social sciences: that disciplines rising alongside emerging democracy to aid in self-government – disciplines in which each is to count for one and no more than one[78] – could produce expert-generated techniques of domination in the service of new ruling classes. Specific to Bentham is the problem that tendentious assumptions locked into his political economy – about, for example, the necessity of poverty and broader tensions between equality, on the one side, and subsistence and abundance, on the other – become codified into law. And this might make us wonder whether a new set of fictions of service to a limited class are substituting for the old in the very matter of the laws.

Paola Rudan's 'Society as a Code' argues that Bentham's political economy, and his legislative project as a whole, is fundamentally about protecting a newly visible society from itself.[79] In light of Rudan, we can see how the mysterious journey of the four ends from civil law to political economy to the entire Pannomion makes perfect sense. Property in wealth – the source of all subsistence – and the sexual and other hierarchies that sustain it must be secured and enhanced.[80] This begins with the civil code but branches out into a broader art of government informed by political economy; consider, for example, how, *contra* Adam Smith, usury is to be taken out of the penal code on the basis of Smith's

[78] *Rationale of Judicial Evidence*, Bowring, vii. 334.

[79] P. Rudan, 'Society as a Code: Bentham and the Fabric of Order', *History of European Ideas* 42, no. 1 (2016), 39–54.

[80] On the domination of women and its relationship to the politics and political economy of the time, see William Thompson, *An Appeal of One Half of the Human Race, Women, Against the Pretensions of the Other Half, Men, to Retain them in Political, and thence in Civil and Domestic, Slavery; in reply to a paragraph of Mr. Mill's celebrated 'Article on Government'* (London: Longman et al., 1825). The book argues that finally only a cooperative system of production is compatible with women's emancipation. Thompson collaborated with Anna Wheeler; both were familiars of Bentham and his circle. Despite a mixed record on suffrage for women and private misgivings about James Mill's position, Bentham excludes women from the franchise without comment in *Constitutional Code: I* (*CW*), 29, though not from the Public Opinion Tribunal (35).

own science. The very developments that enhance wealth, however, produce consequences – foremost among them indigence – that must be carefully managed, for example, through colonization, so as not to threaten security. Rudan describes poor panopticons – domestic colonies[81] – in these terms; in addition to training the indigent to the hard truths of political economy, they preclude a potentially subversive association between the indigent and the employed poor.[82] In the final 'Axioms' chapter of PF this concern about a threat from within is demonstrated by Bentham's worry about the Malthusian dynamics of enrichment and population and the eventual limits to foreign colonization.

> The consequence is, that sooner or later, on every habitable part of the earth's surface, the community will be composed of three classes of inhabitants: – 1. Those by whom ... [matter of subsistence] ... is possessed in a quantity sufficient for the preservation of life and health; – 2. Those ... [without matter of subsistence] ... on their way to speedy death; – 3. Those who to save themselves from impending death are occupied in waging war upon the rest, providing the means of subsistence for themselves at the expense of the security of all.[83]

Bentham, in order to reconcile provision for the indigent with the dynamic that marches toward this dystopia, recommends 'a quiet solution of these difficulties': no doubt referencing infanticide, which of course demands revision of the penal code.[84] The remainder of the 'Axioms' chapter takes up the relative merits of adding to wealth rather than people (re abundance), and includes a vigorous discussion of the diminishing returns of wealth that promotes redistribution in combination with a warning about the disastrous effects of the 'levelling system' (re equality). In the discussion of equality, concerns about disruption of Rudan's 'fabric of order' are front and centre, and Bentham speaks of the

[81] See B. Arneil, 'Jeremy Bentham: Pauperism, Colonialism, and Imperialism', *American Political Science Review* 115 (2021), 1147–58, and more broadly B. Arneil, *Domestic Colonies: The Turn Inward to Colony* (Oxford: Oxford University Press, 2018).

[82] Rudan, 'Society as a Code', 50n.

[83] 'Pannomial Fragments', 273 (Bowring, iii. 227–8); headed 'Law Amendment', dated 28 January 1828, with 'Propositions' and 'Ch. II Codification' in margin.

[84] Ibid. The statement including these words is written in very tiny letters in the margin. On 'excess of population', and the decriminalization of infanticide and abortion in relation to women's reputation and health, see J. Bentham, *Of Sexual Irregularities, and Other Writings on Sexual Morality*, ed. P. Schofield, C. Pease-Watkin, and M. Quinn (Oxford: Clarendon Press, 2014 [*CW*]), 25–8 and 98–9.

virtues of gradual gradations of wealth and the imperatives to maximize wages and minimize profits.[85]

In all this, the conclusions of political economy are decisive, and so it might be said that a branch of the art and science of government – specifically a dominant contemporary strain of that branch – is conducting the whole. This is not to take away from Bentham's abiding preoccupation with sinister interest, which is often also construed by him in political-economic terms, that is, as wasteful.[86] But whereas for Bentham sinister interest stood in the way of needed reforms and could even, in the case of Judge & Co.'s common law, breed serious insecurity, something like the levelling system would in his view produce more complete destruction. The legacy today of Bentham's concern for society might, ironically, be found in the preservation of a political-economic system that promises destruction, given growing ecological catastrophe. But the tensions in his approach are evident already in contemporary terms. Partha Chatterjee in *I Am the People* writes about passive revolutions of capital and the evolving condition of the rupture between the subject of interest and the citizen; although Bentham repeatedly declares these latter to be one and the same, there is clearly a difference between his ordinary subject of law and his vigilant member of the Public Opinion Tribunal. As members of democratic publics, we are formally equals, but today, according to Chatterjee, the tactical contractions of the neoliberal state and tactical extensions of the populist state are seriously exacerbating, in contexts of widening wealth gaps, the problem of sorting legitimate from illegitimate inequality.[87] Economics, psychology, political science, and allied fields seem to have addressed the problem by more actively trying to manage it, as 'from the 1970s onward, if not earlier, all social science disciplines have been mobilized for the task of contributing to the technical administration of populations as things'.[88] Bentham paved the way for this administration with his marrying of obligation and rule to motivation and measurable

[85] 'Pannomial Fragments', 275–9 (Bowring, iii. 229–30). Smith adds a final fragment venturing beyond wealth to equality with respect to power, rank, and reputation.

[86] J. Bentham, *Official Aptitude Maximized, Expense Minimized*, ed. P. Schofield (Oxford: Clarendon Press, 1993 [*CW*]).

[87] P. Chatterjee, *I Am the People: Reflections on Popular Sovereignty Today* (New York: Columbia University Press, 2020).

[88] Ibid., 66.

well-being, contributing to the conversion of law into policy. Perhaps now we need less of this flexible, successfully inventive, and pragmatic Bentham and more of the rigid spirit that drove the failed codifier. This is the spirit that aims to seek out and slay the fictions generated by sinister interests – fictions that operate today, as before, well beyond the confines of the law.

13

Bentham's Constitutional Code and His Pannomion

MICHIHIRO KAINO

13.1 Introduction

Bentham aspired to be the 'legislator of the world'. At first, his aim was for the Pannomion to serve as a complete code of laws, consisting of the constitutional code, civil code, penal code, and procedural code. He tried to convince many countries to adopt his system. There have been many criticisms of Bentham's theory of codification, some of which can be answered by examining his constitutional code. In this chapter, I will discuss two categories of criticism.

It is well known that Bentham was fiercely critical of the common law as 'judge-made law' and tried to limit the role of judges to the enforcement of the Pannomion. However, Bentham was fully aware that it was not possible to foresee every case that might arise. In response to criticism that the Pannomion would be unable to keep up with social change, Bentham, in his constitutional code, empowered judges to suggest amendments to the Pannomion to the legislature. I will also discuss Bentham's distinction between an individual offence and a species of offence. For instance, in 'A General View of a Complete Code of Laws', Bentham pointed out that, although punishable offences could not be foreseen individually, they might be foreseen in their species. In 'Pannomial Fragments', Bentham suggested that when individual offences could be foreseen in their species, adding them to an existing species of law could be left to judges. Thus, in Section 13.2, I argue that Bentham had the resources to ensure that his Pannomion could keep up with social change.

According to Philip Schofield, Bentham realized in 1817 or 1818 that constitutional reform was a precondition for introducing his Pannomion. During the same period, Bentham began to advance the idea of the 'contagious influence of reason', namely, that if one government adopted the Pannomion, the Pannomion would spread around the world.

However, Bentham's strategy of legal transplantation in his early years was an incremental one, which seems to stand in sharp contrast to his later optimistic radicalism. In 'Place and Time', written around 1780, Bentham discussed the problem of legal transplantation and emphasized the importance of freedom of the press and public discussion. In Section 13.3, I will discuss whether Bentham's theory of legal transplantation changed and explore how his early incrementalism can be reconciled with his later optimistic radicalism.

13.2 Bentham's Pannomion and His Theory of Interpretation

13.2.1 Bentham's Pannomion

It is well known that Bentham's discontent with the common law led him to propose the Pannomion concept. For instance, in 'Justice and Codification Petitions', Bentham complained that, in common law cases,

> on each occasion, the rule to which a judge gives the force of law, is one which, on this very occasion, he makes out of his own head: and this – not till the act for which the man is thus dealt with has been done: while, by these same judges, if the same thing were done by the acknowledged legislature, it would be spoken of as an act of flagrant injustice, designated and reprobated, in their language, by the name of an *ex post facto* law.[1]

Bentham's criticisms of the common law were wide-ranging, but as seen in the excerpt above, one of the problems with the common law was its 'confusion of the functions of law-making and law-applying'.[2]

For Bentham, the common law provided only particular commands and punishments. In addition, Bentham was of the view that, in the common law, it was by unauthoritative and arbitrary inference from the grounds of past cases that rules were established.[3] Common lawyers might have opposed this argument with their 'declaratory theory', meaning that the judges did not make law but only found it. However, as Gerald Postema states, Bentham could easily refute these arguments by pointing out that common law judges actually produced rules with the help of 'legal fictions, abstract and largely empty notions like

[1] J. Bentham, 'Justice and Codification Petitions', Bowring, v. 437–548, at 546.

[2] G. Postema, *Utility, Publicity, and Law: Essays on Bentham's Moral and Legal Philosophy* (Oxford: Oxford University Press, 2019), 165.

[3] See M. Lobban, *The Common Law and English Jurisprudence 1760–1850* (Oxford: Oxford University Press, 1991), 121.

"reasonableness", "policy", "natural law", and Latinized principles',[4] which gave them no concrete guidelines and allowed them to decide as they thought fit. Thus, for Bentham, common law judges were not applying the law. They were, in fact, making *ex post facto* laws. Against this backdrop, where law and individual rights were defined only after a judgement was rendered, Bentham thought that it was necessary to introduce 'a body of law, from the respective parts of which we may, each of us, by reading them or hearing them read, learn, and on each occasion know, what are his rights, and what his duties'.[5]

Already in his early thirties, Bentham began the project of developing a body of law, the Pannomion, which became his life's work. In 'Of Nomography', written in his mature years, Bentham defined a Pannomion as follows:

> By a pannomion, understand the entire mass of the matter of law which in the country, or say, political state in question, has the force of law: – a mass by which, when that extent is given to it which it is capable of having, and ought to have, the whole field of law and legislation is comprehended, and the whole surface of it, as it were, covered.[6]

Bentham's Pannomion was supposed to comprise a penal code, civil code, constitutional code, and procedural code. Bentham published only the first volume of the constitutional code. The most original points in Bentham's theory of codification are his scheme for penal and civil codes and his view on the relationship between them.

In *Of the Limits of the Penal Branch of Jurisprudence*, Bentham defined law as follows:

> A law may be defined an assemblage of signs *declarative* of a *volition* conceived or adopted by the *sovereign* in a state, concerning the conduct to be observed in a certain *case* by a certain person or class of persons, who in the case in question are, or are supposed to be, subject to his power.[7]

Thus, Bentham's analysis of law was based on an imperative theory of law, which reflected his discussion about the relationship between penal and civil laws. According to Bentham:

4 Postema, *Utility, Publicity, and Law*, 167.
5 Bentham, 'Justice and Codification Petitions', Bowring, v. 547.
6 J. Bentham, 'Of Nomography', Bowring, iii. 231–95, at 234.
7 J. Bentham, *Of the Limits of the Penal Branch of Jurisprudence* (henceforth *Limits* [*CW*]), ed. P. Schofield (Oxford: Clarendon Press, 2010 [*CW*]), 24.

> [T]he civil branch of each law... is but the *complement* of the penal: it is on the penal that every proposition which can be found in a book of law depends for its obligatory force.[8]

Bentham's division between the penal law (code) and the civil law (code) was unconventional. For Bentham, 'a law', as defined above, served 'as a pattern to which the contents of a statute or any number of statutes may be reduced'.[9] According to Bentham, 'it will probably be found convenient that every law should have, a civil branch as well as a penal'.[10] More specifically, in 'A General View of a Complete Code of Laws', Bentham pointed out that:

> It is proper that the legislator should form two catalogues: the one containing the events which confer a right to the possession of each thing – the other containing the events which destroy this right . . ..
>
> All laws that have no penal clauses, or that only prescribe the obligation of restitution when any one has become possessed of the property of another without evil intention, may be placed in the civil code. All laws that direct a punishment over and above simple restitution – for example, imprisonment, forced labour or fines – may be reserved for the penal code.[11]

It is important to note that Bentham's concept of penal law was broader than the modern concept. For Bentham, those laws addressing breach of contract and tort were also penal laws. Thus, 'of the offences enumerated and defined in the Penal code, non-performance of services due by contract, or more shortly non-performance of contract, must necessarily be one'.[12]

Bentham, then, emphasized the point that it was only 'when the imperative clause or clauses to which a clause that is not imperative is traced out and understood, the true nature and efficacy of such clause is clearly understood: till then, it remains in darkness'.[13] Bentham proposed a system of cross-referencing whereby each part of the civil code would be linked to the correspondent part of the penal code:

[8] Ibid., 221.
[9] Ibid., 35.
[10] Ibid., 221.
[11] Bentham, 'A General View of a Complete Code of Laws', Bowring, iii. 154-210, at 161.
[12] J. Bentham, 'First Lines of a Proposed Code of Law', in *'Legislator of the World': Writings on Codification, Law, and Education* (henceforth *LW* [*CW*]), ed. P. Schofield and J. Harris (Oxford: Clarendon Press, 1998[*CW*]), 189–239, at 238.
[13] *Limits* (*CW*), 221.

> Each civil law forms a particular head, which ought to rest upon a penal law. Each penal law is the consequence, the continuation, the termination of a civil law.[14]

Bentham's views concerning the relationship between the penal and civil laws had important implications for his Pannomion. In *An Introduction to the Principles of Morals and Legislation*, Bentham stated:

> So many different sorts of *offences* created, so many different laws of the *coercive* kind: . . .
>
> To class *offences* . . . is therefore to class *laws:* to exhibit a complete catalogue of all the offences created by law . . . would be to exhibit a complete collection of the laws in force: in a word, a complete body of law, a *pannomion,* if so it might be termed.[15]

To understand the nature of Bentham's Pannomion, it is necessary to understand what Bentham meant when he stated, 'to class *offences* . . . is therefore to class *laws*'.

As in *IPML*, in 'A General View of a Complete Code of Laws', Bentham divided offences into (1) private offences, (2) self-regarding offences, (3) semi-public offences, and (4) public offences.[16] He continued to subdivide each of these classes of offence. For instance, he subdivided private offences into offences against the person, offences against reputation, offences against property, and offences against condition in life.[17] He went further, for instance, by subdividing offences against property into offences affecting the right of property and offences affecting the use of property,[18] in the latter of which such species of offence as endamagement, wrongful occupation, theft, fraudulent acquisition, and non-payment of debts, were included.[19] As to theft, Bentham wrote:

> [W]hat is meant by *a man's having a* title *to take a thing?* To be complete, the law must have exhibited, amongst a multitude of other things, two catalogues; the one of events to which it has given the quality of *conferring title* in such a case; the other of the events to which it has given the quality of *taking it away.* [20]

14 Bentham, 'A General View of a Complete Code of Laws', Bowring, iii. 161.

15 J. Bentham, *An Introduction to the Principles of Morals and Legislation* (henceforth *IPML* [*CW*]), ed. J. H. Burns and H. L. A. Hart with a new Introduction by F. Rosen (Oxford: Clarendon Press, 1996 [*CW*]), 305.

16 See Bentham, 'A General View of a Complete Code of Laws', Bowring, iii. 164.

17 See ibid.

18 See ibid., 166.

19 See ibid.

20 *IPML* (*CW*), 304.

As we have seen, in Bentham's Pannomion, the civil code, for instance, would confer proprietary rights, whereas the penal code would include offences and punishments for the violations of those proprietary rights.

On the other hand, Bentham argued that civil laws were exceptive clauses to penal laws:

> Now every law in which there is an exceptive clause may be resolved into two provisions. These provisions where the law is ... of the negative or prohibitive kind are 1. a primordial mandate of the prohibitive kind, the more extensive of the two: 2. a superventitious mandate of the permissive kind which is the least extensive of the two, being revocative but revocative *pro tanto* only and not *pro toto* of the former. No man shall meddle with the field (describing it): Praetextatus and such other persons as he allows may meddle with the field.[21]

For Bentham, every civil law, which confers rights, is an exceptive clause of the corresponding penal law, which deals with offences. Therefore, it was, for instance, possible for Bentham to list all of the laws conferring property rights by listing all of the offences related to property. This was what he meant when he said that '[t]o class *offences* ... is therefore to class *laws*'.[22]

13.2.2 *Judges' Functions in Bentham's Pannomion*

As I stated at the beginning of this chapter, there have been many critics who have argued that Bentham's Pannomion, his 'complete code of laws', was impractical. For example, the American legal philosopher Richard Posner implies that the Pannomion is out of touch with reality:

> Bentham wanted to shift the center of legal rule making from the courts to a suitably reformed Parliament, which he hoped would draft detailed codes covering every area of law and would thereby minimize judicial discretion. The judges would be minor bureaucrats rather than politicians parading in phony oracular colors – minor because the codes would be drafted in ordinary language and so require no professional training to decipher and because they would be so comprehensive that judges would have no scope for legislating in the guise of filling gaps left by legislators.[23]

[21] J. Bentham, *Of Laws in General*, ed. H. L. A. Hart (London: The Athlone Press, 1970 [*CW*]), 177. This part is not included in the new edition of *Limits* (*CW*).

[22] See n. 15.

[23] R. Posner, *The Problems of Jurisprudence* (Cambridge, MA: Harvard University Press, 1993), 13.

> This view led him to suppose that a legal code could be drafted that would establish an undistorted path of communication between the legislators on the one hand and the judges and citizens on the other, and would make the interpretation and application of law mechanical – a task for low-level civil servants.[24]

This type of interpretation of Bentham's Pannomion has been widely accepted, at least outside of Bentham scholars. However, this interpretation unfairly oversimplifies the Pannomion as a collection of static codes by suggesting that the role of judges would be minor.

As we will see below, Posner's remark that, with the Pannomion in place, 'judges would have no scope for legislating in the guise of filling gaps left by legislators' is correct. However, his remark that Bentham tried to 'make the interpretation and application of law mechanical – a task for low-level civil servants' is quite wrong.

The role of Judges was extensively explained in Bentham's mature work, *Constitutional Code*, where he gave judges three functions whereby they might suggest amendments to the Pannomion.[25]

First, under the contested-interpretation-reporting function, the Judge Immediate (trial judge), along with the appellants, could propose amendments to the wording of the Pannomion to the Judge Appellate (appellate judge). The Judge Appellate could then propose those amendments, as well as his or her own, to the Justice Minister, who could in turn submit them, as well as his or her own, to the Legislation Minister. Finally, the Legislation Minister could pass the proposals on to the Contested Interpretation Committee, which could decide to amend the relevant wording of the Pannomion according to one of the proposals.[26]

Second, under the eventually emendative function, the Judge Immediate would, 'when, in any part of the law, the need of amendment presents itself, on the occasion of a suit brought before him',[27] bring the amendment forward to the Judge Appellate and the Justice Minister. If the Judge Appellate and the Justice Minister agreed with the amendment and the Legislature did not take any action, the relevant part of the Pannomion would be amended accordingly. Thus, in this function,

[24] Ibid., 13–4.

[25] See P. Schofield, *Utility and Democracy: The Political Thought of Jeremy Bentham* (Oxford University Press, 2006), 310–1. For Bentham's view on the interpretations of law developed in his early works, see X. Zhai, 'Bentham on the Interpretation of Laws', *The Journal of Legal History* 38, no. 3 (2017), 282–307.

[26] See Bentham, 'Constitutional Code', Bowring, ix. 502–4.

[27] Ibid., 504.

> by the tacit consent of the Legislature, an amendment, proposed by a Judge Immediate, will, as if proposed by a Member of the Legislature, and adopted, receive the force of law, and be aggregated to the body of the laws.[28]

This seems to give judges as much power as that of legislators. However, Bentham added that it would be

> only for some alleged oversight in the wording, in consequence of which the words employed fail, it is supposed, of being expressive either of the desire actually entertained by the legislature, or of the desire which it is believed would have been thereby entertained, if the circumstances mentioned as forming the ground of a justificative cause of the demand for the amendment had been respectively present to its mind . . .. For if it be in respect of the design and policy of the law that a change presents itself as beneficial, an appropriate authority more competent to the reception of the supposed amendment, is the Legislature.[29]

Although Posner is right that, in the Pannomion, 'judges would have no scope for legislating in the guise of filling gaps left by legislators',[30] it should by now be clear that Posner's understanding of the role of judges under the Pannomion – the mechanical application of law – is wrong. It is also possible to argue that Bentham's Pannomion was a dynamic code of laws rather than a static one, as implied by Posner's remarks, if we examine the third function, namely, the pre-interpretative function.

Under the pre-interpretative function, potential litigants or ordinary people as well as judges had an important role:

> To this function exercise is given, in so far as an application is by any person made, bringing to view a particular portion of the Pannomion, and requesting to know of the Judge, what, in case of a suit thereupon grounded, will be the import by him ascribed to it, and the opinative decree pronounced in consequence: all such other points in the Pannomion as are deemed to bear upon the point in question, being at the same time contemplated.
>
> . . . If to the Judge, it shall, on this occasion, appear, that, by a correspondent amendment, ambiguity or obscurity may be cleared up, and that, by the benefit of such clearance, the evil, produced by the addition, if any, made thereby to the bulk of the rule of action, will be outweighed, – he will accordingly make transmission of such proposed amendment to the superordinate authorities.[31]

28 Ibid.
29 Ibid., 506.
30 See n. 23.
31 Bentham, 'Constitutional Code', Bowring, ix. 511.

We will see later that Bentham was aware that the contested-interpretation-reporting function and the eventually emendative function might lead to *ex post facto* law. Thus, for Bentham, 'the advantage of the preinterpretative over the interpretative function [contested-interpretation-reporting function and eventually-emendative function] was that certainty might be achieved without the need for litigation'.[32] Moreover, it is worth stressing that a wide range of amendments were covered by this function:

> Note here, that need of interpretation may have place, without deficiency on the part of the Legislator in any point of appropriate aptitude: without either sinister policy, on his part, or relative ignorance, or erroneous judgment, or so much as oversight: for, it may be, that at the time of enactment, the reason of the case requiring a certain species of objects to be included in the law, the existence of no individual belonging to that species was at the time realized, or could so much as have been anticipated.[33]

Posner's interpretation of Bentham's code as a static code might have been derived from his misunderstanding of Bentham's concept of the 'completeness' of his codes. We have seen that Bentham defined the Pannnomion as 'a complete body of law'. Accordingly, it is quite logical for Posner to argue that Bentham's Pannomion consisted of 'detailed codes covering every area of law and would thereby minimize judicial discretion'.[34] However, to understand the nature of Bentham's Pannomion, we need to look at his views on the division of offences and the species of offence more closely.

The division of offences was the cornerstone of the Pannomion. In Bentham's theory, if the division of offences were 'comprehensive', the division of legal rights would be so as well. Bentham's method was that of bipartition. It was 'based on contradictory formula: what was classed in one division would thus be contradictory to what was classed in the other'.[35] The division of offences would be continued until different offences, such as wrongful destruction, wrongful occupation, theft, fraudulent acquisition, among others, were specified.

It is tricky but, as Francesco Ferraro argues, in the Pannomion, 'only the method of classification is established *ex ante* and could actually be

[32] Schofield, *Utility and Democracy*, 311.
[33] Bentham, 'Constitutional Code', Bowring, ix. 511.
[34] See n. 23.
[35] Lobban, *The Common Law and English Jurisprudence 1760–1850*, 164.

described *a priori* . . . but the final result of this method, that is, the classification itself, is not predetermined nor established *ex ante*, but is rather left to the will of classifier to determine'.[36] Ferraro's interpretation is supported by the pre-interpretative function, where, at the instigation of potential litigants, judges would propose amendments to the Pannomion, which would cure the deficiency, for instance, due to an oversight of a species of offence by legislators.

Ferraro's interpretation is also supported by Bentham's theory of legal transplants, which will be discussed in Section 13.3.2. Bentham admitted that different communities could add species of offence that were indigenous to their countries to the Pannomion.

If we understand, as Ferraro shows, that in Bentham, '"completeness" is the same as "all-comprehensiveness"',[37] we can see why Bentham thought that additions of new species of offence to his 'complete' Pannomion were possible. A genus of injury introduced into the division of offences, such as corporal injury, would be capable of including – or comprehending – new species of offence. That Bentham's division of offences was 'all-comprehensive' or 'complete' meant that his bipartite division based on contradictory formula could include every species of offence, including new ones.

13.2.3 The Legal Reasoning of the Common Law and Bentham

Importantly, Bentham was aware of the criticisms of common lawyers against legislation. As summarized by David Lieberman, Lord Kames, for instance, argued that legislators relied too much on a small number of cases to make laws of general application and produced short-sighted measures, whereas judges could make general rules incrementally from the induction of many cases.[38] Bentham relied on the 'comprehensive' nature of his division and the idea of species of offence to counter this criticism. In 'A General View of a Complete Code of Laws', he stated:

> It is objected to the forming a code of laws, that it is not possible to foresee every case which can happen. I acknowledge that it is not possible to foresee them individually, but they may be foreseen in their species; for

[36] F. Ferraro, 'Adjudication and Expectations: Bentham on the Role of Judges', *Utilitas* 25, no. 2 (2013), 140–60, at 144.

[37] Ibid., 148.

[38] See D. Lieberman, *The Province of Legislation Determined: Legal Theory in Eighteenth Century Britain* (Cambridge: Cambridge University Press, 1989), 163.

> example, a person may be assured that every species of offence are comprised in the tables which this work includes, although he may not be assured that every possible individual offence has been foreseen.[39]

In 'Pannomial Fragments', which was, according to the editor Richard Smith, 'written at sundry times'[40] through to June 1831, Bentham explained the nature of the species of offence more fully. He at first articulated more generally the nature of the species of offence than he did in his explanation of the pre-interpretative function:

> By *power of classification* a species of legislative power is exercised. Thus when an enactment to any effect has been framed, if by any proposition bearing the form of a command or a rule, enlargement or retrenchment is applied to the genus, or say class of objects which contribute to constitute the subject-matter of the command; – by this means, in a sort of indirect way, by and with the help of the other words which enter into the composition of the enactment, is produced the effect of a different enactment: one of the classes of which that same subject-matter is composed receives thereby *contraction* or enlargement, and a fresh classification is made thereby.[41]

Although Bentham did not go into detail in the explanation of the pre-interpretative function in *Constitutional Code*, in 'Pannomial Fragments', he made it clear that 'by no other authority than the legislative can the power [of adding a species of offence to Pannomion] be exercised'.[42] In 'Pannomial Fragments', on the other hand, he also discussed 'locative power':

> Of this same function – of this same power, exercise is made by any functionary, or set of functionaries, belonging to a department other than, and thence inferior to, the *legislative;* for in no other way can classes be filled up by individuals, and reality given to general ideas. Call this power, power of location, or say *locative* power. But what difference there is between this case and the preceding consists in this: in the former case, by no other authority than the legislative can the power be exercised – the effect produced: in the latter case it is produced in virtue of a general authorization given by the legislative authority, and by that authority is never produced, unless it be in consequence of some extraordinary occurrence.[43]

39 Bentham, 'A General View of a Complete Code of Laws', Bowring, iii. 205.

40 J. Bentham, 'Pannomial Fragments', in *Selected Writings: Jeremy Bentham*, ed. S. Engelmann (New Haven; London: Yale University Press, 2011), 240–79, at 240.

41 Ibid., 249.

42 Ibid., 250.

43 Ibid.

Thus, according to Bentham, locative power, which assigned individual cases to the relevant species of offence, could be exercised by judges and would be acquiesced in by the legislature with very few exceptions. This locative power reminds us of analogical reasoning in common law practice.

For instance, rights generated by contracts were protected by penal laws, prohibiting a species of offence, such as wrongful occupation.[44] In his civil code, Bentham included property rights generated by bilateral agreements, such as '1. Exchange. 2. Sale and purchase. 3. Exchange of money. 4. Purchase of bills of exchange. 5. Purchase of rent without mortgage. 6. Purchase of rent with mortgage'.[45] Analogy was commonly used by judges in developing the common law. For instance, Austin argued that, in common law cases, 'it often (perhaps, most commonly) happens, that he [a judge] derives the new rule, by a consequence built on analogy, from a rule or rules actually part of the system'.[46] Austin also noted that a rule on a bill of exchange was deduced from a rule on a promissory note by analogy.[47] Thus, although not included originally in the Pannomion, Bentham might have allowed that rights generated by purchase of a promissory note as well as those generated by bills of exchange would be protected, through analogy, by a penal law prohibiting a species of offence such as wrongful occupation.

In Section 13.2.1, we saw that Bentham criticized the common law as *ex post facto* law through its confusion of the functions of law-making and law-applying. The basis of this criticism was Bentham's emphasis on 'expectation utility'. Expectation utilities were, according to Postema, 'those linked to the fulfillment or disappointment of expectations regarding only certain future events' and 'those which have their origins in beliefs regarding the likely behavior of persons, private or official'.[48] Bentham thought that expectation utility or security of expectation was important because the well-being of people consisted in the security of expectations as well as the pleasures of the moment.[49] Bentham even defined 'justice' as 'legitimate expectation'.[50] Thus, in his *Constitutional*

[44] See Lieberman, *The Province of Legislation Determined*, 275–6.
[45] Bentham, 'A General View of a Complete Code of Laws', Bowring, iii. 192.
[46] J. Austin, *Lectures on Jurisprudence or the Philosophy of Positive Law*, 2 vols., 4th ed., ed. R. Campbell (London: John Murray, 1879), vol. 2, 660.
[47] See ibid.
[48] Postema, *Utility, Publicity, and Law*, 150.
[49] See ibid., 151.
[50] Ibid., 149.

Code, when discussing the pre-interpretative function, Bentham stated, from the viewpoint of justice or expectation utility:

> On this occasion, an evil against which the Judge and the several superordinate authorities will be on their guard, is – the danger of doing injustice to other interests, which, by, or in consequence of, the statement made by the applicant, may not have been sufficiently brought to view. Accordingly, no such preinterpretation will the Judge ever afford, without having taken effectual measures for preserving all such interests from being injured, for want of adequate faculty of contestation and counter-evidence.[51]

However, according to Bentham, when judges were exercising locative power and putting individual cases into the existing and relevant species of offence, they were not disturbing societal expectations, as individual offences 'may be foreseen in their species'.[52] This was the case even when judges were dealing with novel cases and were putting them in some species of offence in the Pannomion where similar cases had been included. It is possible to regard Bentham's locative power as identical to the common lawyers' analogical reasoning, the value of which Bentham fully recognised. According to Postema:

> Bentham noted that even in novel cases – cases to which no established rules or past decisions directly apply – common-law judges are bound to decide only by appeal to analogy to established rules and past decisions, and not by appeal, to utility or convenience .... Analogy is, he maintained, 'more easily agreed upon' than utility.[53]

Bentham thought that judges' locative power, as well as analogical reasoning, could guarantee people's expectations. Like the common lawyers, whose main device for developing the law was through analogy, Bentham's judges could have located novel cases in the existing and relevant species of offence without disturbing people's expectations. Thus, Bentham appears to have sufficient resources to argue that his Pannomion would keep up with social change.

However, another typical criticism of Bentham and of codification in general was developed by James Carter in New York in the late nineteenth century. In *The Province of the Written and the Unwritten Law* of 1889, he strongly opposed the codification scheme of Edward Livingston,

[51] Bentham, 'Constitutional Code', Bowring, ix. 511.
[52] See n. 39.
[53] Postema, *Utility, Publicity, and Law*, 158.

who corresponded and exchanged works with Bentham. Carter compared the legal reasoning of written (or codified) and unwritten law. In unwritten law, according to Carter, the judge starts with a body of rules ascertained and declared by his predecessors. If he finds that the case at hand is not different from some similar class, he assigns it to that class and his work is done. However, if the case does not have any definitively similar class, he has to decide whether the difference is a material one, and whether the case ought to go 'into a new class to be made for it with different legal consequences for its characteristic'. Carter then indicated, the judge 'was to apply to the case the social standard of justice . . . to make an original application of it [justice]'.[54] On the other hand, in the system of written law, when a judge deals with a new case, Carter argued that the only point would be whether the relevant rule would apply to the case or not.

Carter's criticism can certainly be applied to Bentham, who argued that, according to the eventually emendative function, judges should not make amendments to the law, 'if it be in respect of the design and policy of the law'.[55] We have also seen that Bentham, in 'Pannomial Fragments', argued that adding a new species of punishable offence or a new species of law to the Pannomion should be left to legislators. Certainly, in terms of law's responsiveness to social change, the common lawyers' technique discussed by Carter – the technique of 'distinction' – seems preferable. However, Bentham had a counterargument to this criticism. In *Constitutional Code*, after discussing the pre-interpretative function, Bentham noted that:

> In English practice, a known distinction has place between deciding *according to the strict rules of law,* and deciding *according to the merits* . . .. But how much better the effect would be if the innovation were authorized by real law, and accompanied by the obligation of making communications to the Legislature, as in the here proposed mode, – is sufficiently evident.[56]

Although Bentham, in *Constitutional Code*, did not elaborate his criticism of the technique of distinction, his point might have been that the device of distinction would disturb people's expectations, unlike innovations made by legislature.

[54] J. Carter, *The Province of the Written and the Unwritten Law* (New York: Banks & Brothers, 1889), 26.

[55] See n. 29.

[56] Bentham, 'Constitutional Code', Bowring, ix. 514.

It is now clear that Bentham's Pannomion can withstand the criticism that it was a static and unrealistic enterprise. However, Bentham's theory of legal transplants, it might be suggested, was unrealistic. Now, I will turn to this criticism.

13.3 Bentham's Theory of Legal Transplants

13.3.1 Bentham's Later Optimism about Legal Transplants

It might be argued that Bentham's theory of legal transplants, particularly after 1817 or 1818, was unrealistic. In this section, I will first compare Bentham's later theory with his earlier theory of legal transplants.

Bentham offered his penal, civil, and constitutional codes to the newly elected Portuguese government. When, in 1822 Bentham received news that the Portuguese Cortes had accepted his offer, he began drawing up his Pannomion. As noted by Schofield, Bentham began first to draft the constitutional code, because 'seeing how unavoidably dependent in principle & even in tenor, the non penal [i.e., civil] and penal Codes, are on the Constitutional, it is with that I have begun'.[57] Related to this is his idea of 'contagious influence of reason', which, according to Schofield, 'would ensure that once an all-comprehensive, rationalized code had been adopted by one government, it would be difficult for other governments to resist demands to reform their law upon similar principles'.[58]

Already by 1814, Bentham seems to have had this idea of 'the contagious influence of reason'. In that year, he wrote to Simon Snyder, the Governor of Pennsylvania, that:

> [S]eeing that neither to establish, any more than to pen, a Code, supported throughout by reason, is a thing impossible, government will, in this or that other state, become ashamed of giving out codes, altogether destitute of this support. But it is by the nature of things, that reasons, in so far as they are good ones, are made: made they can not be, as laws may be and are, by any man that has power – by any such man at pleasure. Giving reasons every where, rulers will not, every where, without giving such as they would be ashamed to give, be able to give reasons, nor therefore to give laws, altogether different from ours: and thus, you see, our empire spreads itself.[59]

[57] J. Bentham, *The Correspondence of Jeremy Bentham*, Volume XI, ed. C. Fuller (Oxford: Clarendon Press, 2000 [*CW*]), 334, quoted in Schofield, *Utility and Democracy*, 249.

[58] Schofield, *Utility and Democracy*, 246.

[59] J. Bentham, 'Papers Relative to Codification and Public Instruction', in *LW* (*CW*), 3–185, at 79.

According to Schofield, Bentham came to the view that constitutional reform was a precondition for introducing his Pannomion at some point between the summer of 1817 and the spring of 1818.[60] In non-Western countries, he seems to have gone further. In 1823, in his 'Letters to John Quincy Adams', Bentham developed a strategy for introducing his reforms into Tripoli:

> Tripoli would be the country for the Revolution to take its commencement. In that country, there exists not any regular trained or paid armed force whatever. Not so much as a body-guard in the condition of a standing army has the Sovereign of the state .... [T]he despotism continues because no man, with a hundred others to stick by him, has ever been found to stand up and propose any thing better. Could they but rely on their chief and on each other, the hundred men with whom our Henry 7th. commenced his standing army, or even the fifty men with whom Pisistratus set up his tyranny, would suffice for establishing a popular constitution.[61]

Bentham added that, in Tripoli, Tunis, Algiers, and Morocco, the value of security against misrule was unknown to the body of people. He also stated, 'with respect to this matter, how scanty so ever in detail, so efficient is the state of knowledge as to generals, that a popular representative government, if established in any one, would spread over every other as a matter of course'.[62] These optimistic views seem to have been ungrounded, especially when we see that Bentham, in his earlier years, had held a more cautious view of legal transplants.

13.3.2 Bentham's Theory of Legal Transplants in His Early Years

Bentham developed his theory of legal transplants in 'Place and Time', which was written around 1780. It is interesting to see that the idea of the species of law, or of offence, discussed above, was also important in his theory of legal transplants as well. In 'Place and Time', Bentham stated:

> The plain truth of the matter is this: there are certain acts which admit of laws, which, if worded in a certain manner, may stand good, and be equally applicable to all places and times ... such as murder, theft,

[60] See Schofield, *Utility and Democracy*, 247.

[61] J. Bentham, 'Jeremy Bentham to John Quincy Adams', in *Securities against Misrule and Other Constitutional Writings for Tripoli and Greece*, ed. P. Schofield (Oxford: Clarendon Press, 1990 [*CW*]), 145–52, at 145–6.

[62] Ibid., 149.

> adultery, perjury, and the like. Let no one commit murder; let no one commit theft; let no one commit adultery; let no one commit perjury; and so on. Upon this plan, we might make a variety of laws, of which the expediency might without impropriety be termed universal and immutable.[63]

Bentham continued:

> [L]aws, while the expression of them is confined to terms so loose and so extensive, will never be found precise and clear enough for use. The act thus vaguely described must, before it can be thoroughly understood and perfectly distinguished, be broken down into *species*: . . . Now, of these qualifying provisions, some, it will be found, ought, in point of expediency, to be different in one country from what they are in another; different in the same country at one time from what they are at another: and this is the secret history of the universality and immutability of these universal and immutable laws.[64]

In Section 13.2.2, I mentioned that Bentham expected different communities to add different species of offence to his Pannomion. And he maintained this idea throughout his career. In a letter to the Russian Emperor in 1815, Bentham stated:

> Among the circumstances by which a demand for legislation is produced, some are of *universal* growth, others only of *local* growth: to such only as are of universal growth, could a foreign hand undertake to afford *in terminis* an adequate supply of legislative provision, with any sufficient ground for confidence. In this outline will accordingly be contained so much of the proposed code as can be proposed to stand *in terminis*. For the filling up of this outline, notwithstanding the utmost degree of ability with which it can possibly be penned, whatsoever matter of detail, adapted to circumstances of *local* growth, may be necessary, must be prepared by some *native* hand: at any rate by some person, to whom those circumstances have been made sufficiently known by *residence*.[65]

Here, what Bentham had in mind when he wrote about 'the circumstances of *local* growth' must have been identical with what he meant when he wrote about species of offence, and Bentham's 'the circumstances of *universal* growth' was confined to the genera of offences.[66]

[63] J. Bentham, 'Place and Time', ed. P. Schofield and S. Engelmann, in *Selected Writings: Jeremy Bentham*, 152–219, at 205.

[64] Ibid.

[65] Bentham 'Papers Relative to Codification and Public Instruction', in *LW* (*CW*), 93.

[66] See R. Loring, 'The Role of Universal Jurisprudence in Bentham's Legal Cosmopolitanism', *Revue d'études benthamiennes* 13 (2014), 8.

In Section 13.2.1, we saw that Bentham's method of the division of offences was that of bipartition based on contradictory formula. Offences were firstly divided into (1) private offences, (2) self-regarding offences, (3) semi-public offences, and (4) public offences. However, Bentham's theory of punishment was, of course, based on the theory of utility. Bentham set forth as his premise that offences could be committed only against individuals and that there were no such offences as those against religion or order in that no definable harm to individuals was implied.[67] In 'Place and Time', Bentham divided the influence of the circumstances of the country to where laws were to be transplanted into two classes:

> [T]he first, consisting of those in which the influence of circumstance operating as a ground of variation is unsurmountable: the other, consisting of those in which that influence is not necessarily and absolutely unsurmountable .... In the former predicament stand all those cases in which the ground of variation is brought about by causes purely physical .... Of this nature are the circumstances of climate and texture of earth .... Of the opposite nature come the circumstances of government, religion, and manners.[68]

With regard to the first class of circumstances, one of Bentham's examples was related to an offence related to avalanches. Bentham divided semi-public offences into the genera of those 'operating through calamity' and those 'operating merely by delinquency'. Writing about the former, Bentham stated:

> In mountainous countries, great mischief is sometimes done by falls of snow, which, in the neighbourhood of the Alps, are called *avalanches*, and by which whole villages are sometimes overwhelmed. A sudden concussion given to the air, by means so inconsiderable as the discharge of a pistol, will sometimes, it is said, be sufficient to give rise to a catastrophe of this sort. I forget what traveller it is who says, that on this account the discharge of fire-arms is made penal in some parts of that mountainous region.[69]

These cases were dependent on what Bentham called 'circumstances of *local* growth'. In such cases, Bentham recognized that different species of offence might be added to the Pannomion by different communities. From his discussion of the circumstances of universal and local growth, it

[67] See P. Schofield, 'Jeremy Bentham and HLA Hart's "Utilitarian Tradition in Jurisprudence"', *Jurisprudence* 1, no. 2 (2010), 147–67, at 154–5.

[68] Bentham, 'Place and Time', 167.

[69] Ibid., 160.

seems that Bentham admitted that locals could add offences to his Pannomion under the genera of any offences. However, as we have seen above, Bentham argued that the influence of government, religion and manners was 'not necessarily and absolutely insurmountable'. In 'Place and Time', Bentham argued that 'a bad form of government, a bad set of opinions on matters of religion, or a bad system of manners, may be changed into a better'.[70] Thus, there seems to be a contradiction between his discussion of the circumstances of universal and local growth, on the one hand, and that of the influence caused by the circumstances of government, religion and manners, on the other hand.

This apparent contradiction can be overcome when we examine Bentham's approach to cultural diversity. In 'Place and Time', Bentham set out rules for legal transplants, one of which was that 'the clear utility of the law will be as its abstract utility, deduction made of the dissatisfaction and other inconvenience occasioned by it'.[71] Bentham suggested that the sensibilities of particular community when they were at odds with the principle of utility should be changed incrementally:

> [A]s a means of obviating dissatisfaction, indirect legislation should be preferred to direct: gentle means, to violent: example, instruction, and exhortation should precede or follow, or, if possible, stand in the place of law.[72]

Thus, Bentham allowed that particular communities might recognize species of offence that were at odds with the principle of utility, but he thought that they might be persuaded to abolish such laws. Freedom of the press and public discussion had a critical role in Bentham's view. He thought that, through freedom of the press and public discussion, people would discover their true interests and would stop, for instance, punishing species of offence that did not cause harm to other individuals.

13.3.3 *Finding Continuity in Bentham's Theory of Legal Transplants*

As I wrote at the beginning of this chapter, there seems to be an obvious discontinuity between Bentham's early theory of legal transplants and his later one based on 'the contagious influence of reason'. It seems that

[70] Ibid., 167.
[71] Ibid., 174.
[72] Ibid.

Bentham came to hold the optimistic view that his Pannomion would spread irresistibly around the world. Why, then, did he come to believe in the idea of 'the contagious influence of reason'? I think the answer is quite simple and is related to a change in his constitutional theory in the global context.

In 1815, when Bentham offered to draft a Pannomion for Polish statesman Adam Czartoryski, Bentham explained the nature of each code:

> [M]y expectations are much more *extensive,* as well as sanguine [than in relation to the constitutional branch], in relation to the *penal* and the *civil* branches: including, in both cases, (though, so far as concerns the organization of the *judicial establishment,* it belongs to the *constitutional* branch,) the *system of procedure.* Why? Because, in the *civil* branch, there will be a good deal of matter, – and in the penal a good deal *more,* – applicable alike to the circumstances of *all countries;* and therein applicable, with little or no difference, under *any form of government* .... whereas, in regard to *constitutional* law, in which is included the *form of government,* it would be folly for me to pretend to originate anything considerable. What is the monarch willing to *leave,* or to *concede,* to your nobles, and the great body of the people, taken together? ... All this, if known to anybody, is known to you: not a particle of it to me.[73]

Although Bentham in the excerpt above was arguing that the civil and penal branches of his Pannomion were 'applicable alike to the circumstances of *all countries*', we will see that Bentham did not change his approach to cultural diversity and continued to recognize that particular communities would add particular species of offence to the Pannomion. However, it was not the case with the constitutional branch of his Pannomion. As Schofield argues, as to the question of 'what form of government was best', which also appears in the extract above, 'Bentham's theory of sovereignty did not in itself prescribe a particular constitutional structure .... It was only when he eventually came to consider what form of government would be most desirable that he needed to relate his theory of sovereignty to the constitutional structure in question'.[74]

In 1815, Bentham asked Czartoryski, 'what is the monarch willing to *leave,* or to *concede,* to your nobles, and the great body of the people, taken together?' However, around 1817 to 1818, Bentham began to offer

[73] Bentham, 'Papers Relative to Codification and Public Instruction', in *LW* (*CW*), 108.
[74] Schofield, *Utility and Democracy*, 227–8.

his Pannomion to 'nations professing liberal opinions', in other words, democratic countries. Around this time, Bentham discarded his tolerance of a diversity of constitutional laws in the world and committed himself to the idea of the 'contagious influence of reason'. However, Bentham did not change his views on the penal and civil codes. In 'Codification Proposal', printed in 1822 (after accepting the idea of the 'contagious influence of reason'), Bentham restated the distinction between universally applying laws and exclusively applying laws, equivalent to the distinction between universal and mutable laws in 'Place and Time'. In 'Codification Proposal', Bentham wrote:

> Of whatsoever country the draughtsman be a native, these circumstances, which are of universal occurrence and applicability, may be equally and perfectly present to his notice. For those shades of difference, which are peculiar to his own country, the native, as compared with the foreigner, will be – if not exclusively, at least preferably, qualified.[75]

Bentham did not change his stance from that developed in 'Place and Time' and continued to rely on members of the various communities in question to add species of offence to the Pannomion. For instance, in 'Codification Proposal', as to the genera of simple mental injuries, Bentham wrote that 'in some countries, and in the case of some persuasions on matters of religion, the description of the thus injurious discourse, or exhibition, will be of one sort; in others, of another'.[76]

And again:

> [S]o far as depends on particular arrangements conceived *in terminis*, he [i.e., Bentham himself] is not competent to the filling up of the outline; – yet, by virtue of his comparatively greater command over the whole field, it might be in his power, by means of *instructions* furnished by him in general terms, to afford, to any natives, on whom the task devolved, superior assistance: assistance, of such sort, as should enable them to give a more apt execution to it, than without him it would have been in their power to give to it.[77]

We have seen that Bentham, in 'Place and Time', hoped that through instruction and exhortation, or more specifically through the freedom of the press and public discussion, people would stop punishing species of offence that did not cause harm to other individuals. Bentham conceived

[75] Bentham, 'Codification Proposal', in *LW* (*CW*), 243–388, at 293.
[76] Ibid., 292.
[77] Ibid., 293.

of his own role as that of providing instruction, exhortation and assistance. It is certainly true that Bentham was too optimistic in believing that his Pannomion would spread irresistibly around the world. What changed with him in 1817–8 was that he began to address himself directly to the people of the world, and that the diversity of constitutional laws around the world, which had forced him to offer the Pannomion separately to each country, no longer raised a barrier for his theory of legal transplants.

14

Bentham's Cosmopolitan Constitutionalism

PETER NIESEN

14.1 Introduction

Throughout his long career, Jeremy Bentham wrote on law and politics both domestic and international. His first co-publication was a pamphlet on the American Revolution, and throughout his later writings, the emancipation of nations from the Ottoman, Spanish, and Portuguese Empires was a main concern.[1] In all periods of his work, Bentham commented on questions of foreign policy, on border-crossing political economy, on the atrocities committed in war and colonial settlement, and on international law as part of an all-comprehensive legal code. But although his writings are routinely celebrated, following John Stuart Mill, for 'their cosmopolitan character',[2] there exists no consensus on what exactly his contribution to the cosmopolitan canon is. This may be the reason why, in marked contrast to the popularity of Immanuel Kant's writings on the same topic, which continue to inform and shape today's approaches in political theory,[3] there exist few systematic attempts to link Bentham's imputed cosmopolitan attitude to contemporary debates. This is a serious lacuna in the literature, given that Bentham's legal and political thought, and especially his global political thought, have attracted genuine and detailed interest in recent decades. His reflections on global order, empire, and colonialism have been thoroughly re-evaluated, and there is no shortage of works on his international political

[1] [J. Bentham and J. Lind], 'Short Review of the Declaration' [1776], *The Declaration of Independence*, ed. D. Armitage (Cambridge, MA: Harvard University Press, 2007), 173–86; J. Bentham, *Legislator of the World.* (Oxford: Clarendon Press, 1998 [*CW*]).

[2] J. S. Mill, *Collected Works*, vol. XVII (Toronto: University of Toronto Press, 1984), 1812. See G. Varouxakis, 'Cosmopolitan Patriotism in J. S. Mill's Thought and Activism', *Revue d'Études Benthamiennes* 4 (2008), doi.org/10.4000/etudes-benthamiennes.188.

[3] The late David Held has done more than anyone to connect Kant's ideas to contemporary cosmopolitanism. See his *Cosmopolitanism: Ideals and Realities* (Cambridge: Polity, 2010).

thought.[4] Still, the label 'cosmopolitan' has been tacked onto Bentham's writings largely as a complimentary gesture, commending a benign impartial global outlook rather than characterizing specific features of his normative political theory. Despite its enormous progress with regard to Bentham's global thought, current research has not established exactly where its 'cosmopolitan potential'[5] lies. In this, today's literature has not advanced much over J. S. Mill's blanket recommendation.

This chapter attempts to lay the groundwork for an interpretation of Bentham's legal and political writings as a specific type of cosmopolitanism. It suggests that the way of probing its exact contours is through Bentham's constitutional, not his international law writings, thereby building on the scholarly work on Bentham's democratic constitutionalism.[6] It may seem counter-intuitive at first to look at Bentham's constitutionalism for his cosmopolitan stance, since nowhere does his conception of the scope of constitutional law go beyond the perimeters of the nation-state. In contrast to Kant's understanding of a 'cosmopolitan constitution' and current ideas of 'global constitutionalism',[7] Bentham's cosmopolitan orders are state constitutions. Accordingly, Bentham's key cosmopolitan innovation does not lie in a specific conception of global order but in a re-invention of statehood, specifically of claims to political participation. He argues for transnationalizing existing constitutional processes and thus strives for a cosmopolitan constitutionalism 'within one country', in every country. The central mechanism of his cosmopolitan constitutionalism is the opening up of nation-state borders to outsiders' political influence.

[4] D. Armitage, 'Globalizing Jeremy Bentham', in *History of Political Thought*, 32 (2011), 63–82; J. Pitts, *A Turn to Empire* (Princeton: Princeton University Press, 2005), 103–22; B. Bourcier, 'Bentham's International Political Theory', *Utilitas* (2021), 1–17; G. Postema, 'Utilitarian International Order', in *Utility, Publicity, and Law* (Oxford: Oxford University Press, 2019), 247–66.

[5] D. Lieberman, *The Province of Legislation Determined* (Cambridge: Cambridge University Press, 1989), 241.

[6] F. Rosen, *Jeremy Bentham and Representative Democracy* (Oxford: Oxford University Press, 1983); O. Ben-Dor, *Constitutional Limits and the Public Sphere* (Oxford: Hart, 2000); P. Schofield, *Utility and Democracy* (Oxford: Oxford University Press, 2007), chap. 9; D. Lieberman, 'Bentham's Constitutional Code and the Politics of Information', MS 2007; X. Zhai and M. Quinn, eds., *Bentham on Law and Public Opinion* (Oxford: Oxford University Press, 2015).

[7] For Kant, see his *Theory and Practice*, 304n. and *Toward Perpetual Peace*, 329, both in I. Kant, *Practical Philosophy* (Cambridge: Cambridge University Press, 1996). For global constitutionalism, see A. Lang and A. Wiener, eds., *Handbook Global Constitutionalism* (Cheltenham: Edward Elgar, 2017).

In what follows, I treat Bentham's recommendations for transnationalizing state constitutions across various contexts not as ad hoc ideas but as so many elements of a conception of a cosmopolitanism in one country, to be embraced by all states.[8] Although his writings undergo development and change, it seems possible to distill some conceptual and institutional features concerning constituent subjects and constitutional form and to reveal the elements and the normative principles on which his transnationalizing constitutionalism is built. I argue that Bentham's cosmopolitan constitutionalism is characterized by border-crossing, not border-obliterating features. It does not invoke post-statist ideas of regional or global authority and legitimacy, but it does correct the statist model of constitutionalism by perforating states' boundaries for foreign involvement, by incorporating foreign citizens into the polity in varying modes and functions. The cosmopolitanism Bentham advocates is one of degrees of open membership in overlapping political communities, where each such community extends some state membership rights to every inhabitant of the globe, making it virtually universal in intake but not authority. In picturing cosmopolitan orders independently from a presumptively single global commonwealth, as a way of relating foreigners and existing states, Bentham's conception is certainly not a blueprint for addressing all the issues that globalization has created. But, as I will point out in the conclusion, it is not at all toothless when intervening in contemporary debates.

14.2 Bentham's Cosmopolitanism: Two False Starts

In this section, I discuss and reject two types of arguments that seem to invite conclusions about Bentham's conception of cosmopolitanism. The two main routes explored in the past are through Bentham's utilitarianism and through his internationalism. Before commenting on their respective deficits, a brief discussion of terminology is in order. A first conceptual distinction is that between cosmopolitanism and internationalism. Contemporary philosophical cosmopolitanism has driven home the point that cosmopolitanism deals with relations among persons, or

[8] As we will see, Bentham addresses his constitutional designs to populations 'professing liberal opinions' as far as popular sovereignty is concerned but recommends much the same securities in draft constitutions for reform-minded autocracies. See J. Bentham, *Securities against Misrule and other Constitutional Writings for Tripoli and Greece* (Oxford: Oxford University Press, 1990 [*CW*]).

between persons and states, while internationalism deals with the relations among states, peoples, or nations.[9] As is clear from their etymological roots in Greek and Latin, cosmopolitanism refers to individuals, internationalism to collectives. Bentham underlined the need for conceptual clarity when, in 1780, he reserved the term 'international law' for the legal relations between 'sovereigns', that is, heads of state,[10] precluding its application to any matters involving individual foreigners. International law is an intergovernmentalist notion, in that governments represent their citizenries when they declare war and enter into peace treaties on their behalf. In contrast, Bentham is clear that border-crossing relations between 'mere' individuals are of no concern to international law: in 'any transactions which may take place between individuals who are subjects of different states, these are regulated by the *internal* laws ... of one or the other of these states'.[11] Bentham goes on to explain that even foreign heads of state, in border-crossing relations of a private nature, should be treated no differently from foreign individuals. He does not, however, mention the case of individual citizens' relations to foreign states or governments. In Section 14.3, we will see that this is where cosmopolitan constitutional law comes in.

The second contemporary distinction concerns different types of cosmopolitanism. Although the field is complex, I will restrict myself to a binary distinction between moral and institutional cosmopolitanism. In current discussions, moral cosmopolitanism is characterized as the view that all human beings are equal units of moral concern or have equal moral worth.[12] While moral cosmopolitans claim that all individuals are the ultimate units of moral concern, it is controversial whether this should be taken to entail that all individuals are bearers of a universal

[9] It is thus no longer possible to identify forms of 'liberal internationalism' as versions of 'consequentialist cosmopolitanism'. D. Weinstein, 'Consequentialist Cosmopolitanism', in *Victorian Visions of Global Order*, ed. D. Bell (Cambridge: Cambridge University Press, 2007), 267–90.

[10] J. Bentham, *Introduction to the Principles of Morals and Legislation* (*IPML*) (Oxford: Oxford University Press, 2005), chap. XVII, § 25n. (296f.). The term was introduced there in the printed material of 1780, although the work was published only in 1789. For Bentham's parallel use of 'international relations', see his *Book of Fallacies*, Bowring, ii. (Edinburgh: Tait, 1843), 447.

[11] *IPML* XVII, § 25, 296, emphasis is mine.

[12] T. W. Pogge, 'Cosmopolitanism and Sovereignty', *Ethics* 103 (1992), 48–75, at 49; G. Brock and H. Brighouse, 'Introduction', in *The Political Philosophy of Cosmopolitanism*, ed. G. Brock and H. Brighouse (Cambridge: Cambridge University Press, 2005), 1–9, at 4.

and equal legal and political status vis-a-vis each other and all governmental actors. For our purposes, therefore, a distinction is necessary between a moral understanding of cosmopolitanism as an interactional category governing all interpersonal relationships and an institutional understanding of cosmopolitanism as a legal and political status conferring rights and duties on individuals. While moral cosmopolitans believe that obligations are global in scope, not all of them want to see those obligations institutionally entrenched in the form of universal legal and political rights. Contemporary institutional cosmopolitans, in contrast, believe that cosmopolitan rights and duties are to be enacted in the form of law, usually through permanent authoritative organizations with global scope. In Miriam Ronzoni's words,

> for institutional cosmopolitans ... all human beings should be part of the same political-juridical community, and therefore be fellow citizens of the world (*kosmopolites*) in a literal sense. In their view, the most important moral and political problems can only be tackled through the establishment of global institutions with universal reach and (at least some) sovereign powers.[13]

Bentham's position is hard to map onto these two conceptual distinctions. First, it is generally presumed that utilitarianism is a form of moral cosmopolitanism, since nothing stands in the way of applying the principle of utility to an all-comprehensive group of persons.[14] I will discuss this reading in Section 14.2.1. But Bentham is nothing if not an institutionalist, in the sense that he generally takes normative terms such as 'rights' and 'duties' to refer to coercive mechanisms of one kind or another. For the most part, he is prepared to reject normative language as meaningless if not backed up by institutions. He is not averse to seeing global institutions installed 'with universal reach', although, as we shall see in Section 14.2.2, in an internationalist, not a cosmopolitan sense. His internationalist vision of global order does reveal one aspect of his

[13] M. Ronzoni, 'For (Some) Political and Institutional Cosmopolitanism, (Even If) against Moral Cosmopolitanism', in *Cosmopolitanism versus Non-cosmopolitanism*, ed. G. Brock (Oxford: Oxford University Press, 2013), 156–72, at 158.

[14] This understanding of Bentham's utilitarianism is dominant in normative International Relations Theory. 'Bentham is not an advocate of world government ... but he is a cosmopolitan. The state has no value as such.' See C. Brown, *International Relations Theories: New Normative Approaches* (New York: Columbia University Press, 1992), 43. While it is true that the state, for Bentham, has no value as such, nothing, apart from happiness, has value as such for Bentham. It is impossible to derive cosmopolitanism or refute internationalism based on utilitarian axiology alone.

cosmopolitanism but in a way that bypasses the issue of unified global sovereign powers in Ronzoni's sense. Both a utilitarian and an internationalist approach thus miss what is distinctive about Bentham's institutional cosmopolitanism, which is to empower local institutions with border-crossing reach.

14.2.1 Cosmopolitanism versus Utilitarianism

One intuitive interpretation builds on his utilitarianism as a moral theory, on the principle of utility as a principle that in the default case extends to all human beings.[15] The principle of utility 'approves or disapproves of every action whatsoever, according to the tendency which it appears to have to augment or diminish the happiness of the party whose interest is in question' and applies to individuals as well as state governments.[16] In the calculation of the greatest aggregate happiness, the principle treats all members of the 'party whose interest is in question' as moral equals. This raises two questions, one about the universalist, morally cosmopolitan character of the 'party', the other about the derivation of institutional from moral cosmopolitanism.

In an influential interpretation, David Lyons has argued that the principle of utility is always to be understood in a context-relative, 'parochial' sense, identifying 'the party whose interest is in question' with the local political community or even the individual herself and never in a universalist sense. Lyons claims that under the principle of utility, an agent is not committed to considering 'everyone who might be affected by an act or its alternatives' but rather 'those under one's 'direction', that is, 'those subject to one's direction, influence or control'.[17] He concludes that 'the interests to be promoted are the interests of those being "directed" rather than those who may be "affected".[18] In a systematic way, this foreshadows today's distinction between two main understandings of the criterion establishing political community, as governed by an 'all affected' principle, on the one hand, or by an 'all subjected' principle,

[15] B. Bourcier, 'Le Plus Grand Bonheur pour le Plus Grand Nombre de Jeremy Bentham: un Utilitarisme Cosmopolitique', *Philosophical Enquiries: Revue des Philosophies Anglophones* 9 (2017), 59–77.

[16] *IPML* I, § 2.

[17] D. Lyons, *In the Interest of the Governed* (Oxford: Oxford University Press, 1973), 24, 31

[18] Ibid., 32.

on the other.[19] It is worth stating that the difficulty raised by Lyons does in no way sabotage our way of thinking of Bentham as a moral cosmopolitan.[20] There is no systematic reason to think that Bentham does not have 'the wider interests of humanity' at heart.[21] An 'all affected' reading may be available for his moral cosmopolitanism, but the 'all subjected' reading may still be correct for all institutional relations. The question is rather whether utilitarian morality stands in any systematic connection to institutional cosmopolitanism.

We do not have to commit to Lyons's controversial reading of utilitarianism as a form of moral anti-cosmopolitanism to see that his reading poses a problem for deriving institutional cosmopolitanism from utilitarianism. There is no doubt that the 'parochial' institutional reading describes a genuine case of Benthamite utilitarianism. Institutions, under a natural reading, put people under the direction, influence, and control of others. Those 'directed' will then have a claim that 'government should serve the interests of those governed'.[22] Whoever is doing the directing, according to Lyons, will have to worry that 'the interests of a powerful nation might tragically conflict with the interest of mankind at large, and one . . . could therefore find himself endorsing conduct detrimental to the welfare of mankind as a whole'.[23] Bentham says as much in manuscripts posthumously collected as 'Principles of International Law', where he takes seriously the question whether the government of a particular state, being under an obligation to provide for the greatest happiness of its population, is permitted to commit itself to global utility. What would the duty of a utilitarian legislator for a particular country be? 'That moderation, which would be a virtue in an individual acting for his own interests, would it become a vice, or treason, in a public man commissioned by a whole nation? . . . [W]ould the course he would

[19] For 'all affected' vs. 'all subjected', see N. Fraser, *Scales of Justice* (London: Polity, 2008), 24–5, 65–7. For 'all affected interests' and 'all subjected persons', see D. Owen, 'Constituting the Polity, Constituting the Demos', *Ethics and Global Politics* 5, no. 3 (2012), 129–52.

[20] Bentham's one sustained attempt at systematic ethics, *Deontology* (Oxford: Oxford University Press, 1983), is inconclusive as to the disagreement referenced here. But see J. Dinwiddy, 'Bentham on Private Ethics and the Principle of Utility', in *Bentham: Selected Writings*, ed. J. Dinwiddy (Stanford: Stanford University Press, 2004), 134–54.

[21] H. L. A. Hart, 'Bentham's Principle of Utility and Theory of Penal Law', in J. Bentham, *IPML*, xcvi.

[22] Lyons, *In the Interest*, 85.

[23] Ibid., 26.

pursue be unjust or equitable?'[24] In Section 14.2.2, I will look at Bentham's attempted reconciliation between parochial ('all subjected') and universalist ('all affected') demands on state government's duties. Here, it suffices to conclude that in the absence of global institutions, not only do we lack a position from where the interests of mankind could be effectively considered, but those who do have political influence or control have strong reasons not to let considerations detracting from the happiness of the governed enter the calculation. In a nutshell: utilitarianism as a moral theory may be cosmopolitan, while institutional utilitarianism, in the absence of global government, is not.

14.2.2 Cosmopolitanism versus Internationalism

One way of bypassing the inconclusive relationship of moral utilitarianism and institutional cosmopolitanism is to argue that, for Bentham, there exists a moral requirement to instal a global institutional order. However, I will argue in this section that Bentham's actual plan for global order is internationalist, not cosmopolitan. In Section 14.2.1, I mentioned the collection of fragments entitled 'Principles of International Law' where Bentham reflects on the lack of co-ordinated activity in the international realm. In these manuscripts, he advocates establishing a 'Congress or Diet' among (European) nations, to which a non-coercive 'common court of judicature for the decision of differences between the several nations' is to be attached.[25] Besides a brief reference to the circumstances of extradition, there is no indication that he conceives of these institutions as negotiating the claims of individuals, let alone as establishing a border-crossing juridical-political community with individuals as its members. Neither the envisaged court nor the 'Congress or Diet' have a corresponding unified 'people'.[26] For the stability of an international legal order, Bentham mainly trusts in the power relations among states. A head of state who aims to maximize domestic utility at the expense of international utility, Bentham says, 'cannot fail always to experience a certain resistance', and repeated confrontation with other

[24] J. Bentham, 'Objects of International Law', in 'Principles of International Law', Bowring, ii. 537–40, at 537.

[25] J. Bentham, 'Plan for an Universal and Perpetual Peace', in *Principles of International Law*, Bowring, ii. 546–60, at 547. For a recent interpretation, see Bourcier, 'International Political Theory', 8–10.

[26] Bourcier, 'International Political Theory', 9.

states will lead him to seek out a 'line of least resistance'. 'The point of repose will be that in which all the forces find their equilibrium.'[27]

Although textual caution is in order,[28] most scholars approach the topic of cosmopolitanism in Bentham from the 'Principles of International Law' fragments and the (partly French) manuscripts on which they are based, since they seem to contain one of its unproblematic sources. Their first essay, 'Objects of International Law', starts out with the following passage:

> If a citizen of the world had to prepare an universal international code, what would he propose to himself as his object? It would be the common and equal utility of all nations: this would be his inclination and his duty.[29]

There are two relevant phrases in this short quotation. I will address the term 'citizen of world' first and the formula of the 'common and equal utility of all nations' in the next paragraph. Since the term 'cosmopolitan' and its derivatives do not occur in Bentham's writings, the phrase 'citizen of the world' is one of the few explicit terminological sources. The phrase first made its appearance in the preface to Bentham's first book, *A Fragment on Government* (1776), likewise in a context *de lege ferenda.* In *Fragment,* Bentham distinguishes two perspectives on law, that of an 'expositor', who presents law as it is, and that of a 'censor', who criticizes existing legal practice from the perspective of law as it should be: 'The Expositor, therefore, is always the citizen of this or that particular country: the Censor is, or ought to be the citizen of the world.'[30] While the expositor can only reconstruct existing law, the censor can serve in the function of a teacher to the future legislator. A citizen of the world is then somebody who brings a competent, 'disinterested',[31] independent,

[27] J. Bentham, 'Objects of International Law', 538.

[28] G. Hoogensen, *International Relations, Security, and Jeremy Bentham* (London: Routledge, 2005), 40–54.

[29] Bentham, 'Objects of International Law', 537.

[30] J. Bentham, *Fragment on Government* (Cambridge: Cambridge University Press, 1988), 8. Note the global context of 'censorial jurisprudence' in that *Fragment* implicitly refers to the American Revolution. For the relation, see the doctoral dissertation by P. Rudan, 'Dalla Costituzione al Governo. Jeremy Bentham e le Americhe' (University of Bologna, 2007). Rudan reads Bentham's later anti-colonial writings as cosmopolitan in intent, uniting 'the censorial jurisprudence of Jeremy Bentham, citizen of the world, and the utility of emancipation' ('Dalla Costituzione al Governo. Jeremy Bentham e le Americhe', 269).

[31] Bentham, 'Objects of International Law', 539.

and benevolent mindset, undistorted by loyalty to a given political system, to the task of formulating a critique or a normative legal program. This authorial understanding is firmly in place from Bentham's earliest writings, and his contacts around the globe would commend his legislative initiatives as those of a 'citizen of the world', a 'friend of mankind'.[32] I will come back to the authorial meaning of cosmopolitanism later, in Section 14.3.3. What is important in our context is that authorial uses of the term 'citizen of the world', be they hypothetical (as in the designing of an international code) or actual (in drafts of foreign legislation), do not vouch for a legislative output that is institutionally cosmopolitan rather than internationalist.

What should give us pause here is the puzzling phrase of 'common and equal utility of all nations'. Critics and friends alike see an inferential relation between this much-quoted formula and Bentham's cosmopolitanism. They argue that 'early utilitarian cosmopolitans like Jeremy Bentham … defended their cosmopolitanism by pointing to the "common and equal utility of all nations",[33] or hold that the "common and equal utility of all nations" has a "cosmopolitan purpose'.[34] But what exactly are the cosmopolitan credentials of this singular occurrence of a powerful phrase, which Bentham used exclusively in the present context and is absent from all of his other writings? How to explain the fact that it occurs side by side with the much more straightforward notion of 'common utility', that is, the 'greatest happiness of all nations taken together'?[35] The first thing to notice is that the hypothetical world citizen-legislator is in both cases concerned with the utility of nations, not the utility of persons. This has two implications. First, the fact that international law relates nations through their 'sovereigns' to each other has the consequence of excluding any entitlements of stateless individuals and non-state peoples from an international code. Despite Bentham's general anti-colonial stance, this means that members of non-state peoples cannot appeal to his *Principles of International Law* for protection but will have to turn to states' 'internal' laws instead. A second, more systematic observation concerns the questionable coherence of the

[32] Bentham, *Legislator of the World* (*CW*), 319, 335.

[33] P. Kleingeld and E. Brown, 'Cosmopolitanism', *Stanford Encyclopedia of Philosophy*, 2019, https://plato.stanford.edu/archives/win2019/entries/cosmopolitanism/.

[34] J. Pitts, '"Great and Distant Crimes": Empire in Bentham's Thought', in *Jeremy Bentham: Selected Writings*, ed. S. Engelmann (New Haven: Yale University Press, 2011), 478–99, at 481.

[35] Bentham, 'Objects of International Law', 538.

phrase 'common and equal utility' of nations with Bentham's utilitarianism. Under Bentham's own formula, the utility of a community is the aggregate happiness of its individuals.[36] Committing to 'equal utility' among nations means that the total happiness of a small country would be of equal weight to that of one with a numerous population. The principle of 'common and equal utility of nations' is thus not 'a principle of utility for international law',[37] since it is not a principle of aggregation. Consequently, the 'common and equal utility' of nations is as anti-cosmopolitan as it is anti-utilitarian in that its concern for the equality of collectives entails a differential concern for individuals. While exchanging aggregation for equality may produce similar prescriptions in cases where international law ordains not to harm other nations, it will also entail large differences in welfare where 'doing the greatest good possible to other nations'[38] is mandated.

Now it could be objected that there is a way to reconcile the formula of 'common and equal utility' with utilitarianism as a form of moral cosmopolitanism. Recall that 'the common and equal utility of all nations' sets the task (the 'object') for the legislator of an international code. There is no contradiction in holding that, in her decision-making, a Benthamite citizen-of-the-world legislator may be expected to use a criterion different from the one Bentham the political theorist will use for the overall utilitarian evaluation of legislative outcomes. Making a distinction between the standard mandated for decision procedures and the standard of right action is not alien to utilitarian theorists; in fact, it has been used to characterize indirect forms of utilitarianism in Mill and in Sidgwick.[39] Applying this distinction to Bentham on international law, then, would mean distinguishing between a legislation procedure committed to the '*object*' of legislation, that is, the 'common and equal utility of all nations', and the criterial '*end* that a disinterested legislator upon

[36] 'The community is a fictitious body, composed of the individual persons who are considered as constituting [it]. The interest of the community then is, what? – the sum of the interests of the several members who compose it.' *IPML* I, § 4.

[37] Postema, 'Utilitarian International Order', 255. See also Bourcier, 'International Political Theory', 8.

[38] Bentham, 'Objects of International Law', 538.

[39] For an introductory account, see D. Brink, 'Mill's Moral and Political Philosophy', *Stanford Encyclopedia of Philosophy*, 2018, https://plato.stanford.edu/archives/spr2022/entries/mill-moral-political/. With regard to Bentham, the indirect utilitarianism hypothesis has mainly been explored with regard to concrete policy questions, not codification procedure. See P. J. Kelly, *Utilitarianism and Distributive Justice: Jeremy Bentham and the Civil Law* (Oxford: Oxford University Press, 1990).

international law would propose to himself', that is, the 'greatest happiness of all nations taken together'.[40] In contrast to equal utility, as the 'object' to be pursued by the hypothetical international legislator, aggregate global utility would not serve as the guiding principle of the legislative process itself.

Does this attempted reconciliation of Bentham's utilitarianism with his internationalism help in deriving institutional cosmopolitanism from internationalism? Note that what links the aggregative end of international politics with an equality-oriented decision procedure is an empirical assumption. Given the circumstances of politics, if a legislator is to have a chance of realizing 'common utility' through her international code, she should aim at codifying for 'common and equal utility'. But, according to Bentham, realizing the common and equal utility of nations accords with the domestic duties of the heads-of-states only under the assumption of a balance of power, where respecting other nations' utility is the way of 'least resistance'. Indirectly, utilitarian international legislation would be wise to take the roughly equal threat-potential of states or alliances into account. There is no parallel empirical argument yielding a concern for individuals and non-state peoples along a 'line of least resistance'. Take the security challenge posed by indigenous Australians, which can be largely disregarded from the perspective of European settlers and cannot be addressed from within Bentham's conception of international law.[41] Insofar as his argument from an envisaged harmony between the morality and prudence of reciprocity will not be forthcoming for the relationship between states and non-state peoples, or states and individuals, an indirect utilitarian global lawgiver could not afford to build the latter's interests into his global code. As neither individuals nor non-state peoples can credibly threaten retaliation, a global code might leave governments free to take advantage of them or be under obligation to their subjects to do so. I conclude that the indirect utilitarian reading of 'common and equal utility' strengthens the interpretation that international obligations do not unequivocally entail any

[40] Bentham, 'Objects of International Law', 538, my emphasis.

[41] Bentham's works on an Australian 'Colonization Society' discount the security challenge of 'uncivilized' Australian aborigines. MS Colonization Society, UC box 8, 155. For a critique, see P. Niesen, 'The West Divided? Bentham and Kant on Law and Ethics in Foreign Policy', in *Rethinking Ethical Foreign Policy*, ed. D. Chandler and V. Heins (London; New York: Routledge, 2007), 93–115.

normative commitments to individuals, hence does not reveal anything of substance about Bentham's cosmopolitanism.[42]

In this section, I have tried to show that two intuitive routes to the cosmopolitan character of Bentham's political thought are unavailable. There is no direct route to an institutional variant of cosmopolitanism from Bentham's utilitarianism in moral theory, nor is there one from his internationalist theory of global law. While the one true cosmopolitan feature discovered in Bentham's writings on international law, the authorial role of a draughtsperson of an international code, does show 'cosmopolitan potential', for a systematic expression of Bentham's cosmopolitanism we must look elsewhere.

14.3 Bentham's Cosmopolitan Constitutionalism

Bentham's central work on constitutional law is the three-volume *Constitutional Code*, volume one of which was published in 1830.[43] It is the high point of his life-long concern with democratic theory, setting out a draft model constitution alongside the reasons for its allocation of competences and duties. Bentham had begun to develop many of the radical ideas proposed in the *Code*, including its strategy of including elements of institutional cosmopolitanism, in earlier periods, and in what follows I will sketch a broadly chronological picture in four steps.

14.3.1 Foreigners' Rights to Be Elected

A first element of Bentham's cosmopolitanism is granting to foreigners rights to be elected and to fill political office. He developed this idea in manuscripts sent to France during the convocation of the Estates General, advising continental thinkers and politicians on constitutional matters. The manuscripts from late 1788 to 1792, collected in the volume *Rights, Representation, and Reform*, demonstrate that Bentham radicalized his egalitarianism concerning electoral law and that in successive writings he gradually came to advocate universal suffrage for men and women,

[42] This interpretation also vindicates Nancy Rosenblum's view that Bentham's internationalism, because of its 'realism', is hard to square with cosmopolitanism. N. Rosenblum, *Bentham's Theory of the Modern State* (Cambridge, MA: Harvard University Press, 1978), 106. For the opposite view, see Bourcier, 'International Political Theory', 2.

[43] J. Bentham, *Constitutional Code*, vol. 1 (Oxford: Oxford University Press, 1983 [*CW*]).

suggesting the abolition of all property qualification.[44] What is less well known is that he suggested the same radical extension in the right to stand for election and fill public office not only for women but also for foreigners. Even before the French revolutionary constitutions of 1791 and 1793 provided for easy naturalization of foreigners, Bentham argued that the holding of political office in France ought not to be limited to French citizens. While conceding that only French citizens should be entitled to vote (again, under conditions of swift naturalization), he demanded that 'from the capacity of being elected no human creature whatsoever shall be excluded'.[45] In his characteristic style of mixing insight with insult, Bentham asks: 'Why throw open to all the world the right of being elected? . . . Would you admit for example an idiot, a child in arms, a woman, a negro, or a convicted murderer?' After having made clear that neither 'idiot' nor child nor murderer would escape their confinement were they to be elected, he changes tack and insists that the election of a black or female candidate would constitute a triumph of talent over prejudice. It would attest to the candidates' having a 'degree of merit superior to any that was to be found among whites and among men'.[46] If elections are to serve a meritocratic function, this will trigger a requirement of admitting foreigners as candidates, since only by including all-comers will it be possible to pick the best candidate for the job.

Bentham's prime example for the admission of foreigners to elections is the prominent figure of Jacques Necker, Genevan banker, expert administrator and sometime financier of the *Ancien Régime*: 'In France, it seems to be no uncommon opinion that M. Necker, a Citizen of Geneva, is not of all men the least deserving of the confidence of French men.'[47] Thus, the cosmopolitan entitlement, at first glance, seems to hold the nascent French Republic to standards established by its autocratic predecessor regime.[48] However, Bentham insists that

[44] J. Bentham, *Rights, Representation, and Reform* (Oxford: Clarendon Press, 2002 [*CW*]), 67–96. See P. Schofield, *Democracy and Utility*, 78–108.

[45] Bentham, *Rights, Representation, and Reform* (*CW*), 231. In French, he reiterates his point: 'To whose advantage is it to exclude from the choice of an electoral district any living featherless biped? Be they Turk, Chinese, Negro from Guinea, or even English?' *Rights, Representation, and Reform*, 91, translated by Peter Niesen.

[46] Bentham, *Rights, Representation, and Reform* (*CW*), 250.

[47] Ibid.

[48] In a later work, Bentham also refers approvingly to the medieval and Renaissance practice of appointing a foreigner as caretaker dictator, in periods of constitutional emergency. Bentham, *Legislator of the World* (*CW*), 29.

foreigners' appointments cannot bypass the support of a republican electorate.[49] In stressing not technocratic superiority but recognition of their qualification and virtue, Bentham treats foreigners' inclusion as a way of securing the interests of the domestic population. The normativity of his proposal's 'cosmopolitan potential' does not rest on any assumption to the effect that restrictions would violate any claims or entitlements of non-citizens desiring to stand for elections. It is the citizens themselves whose interests may be hurt by foreigners' exclusion. Any restriction on the choice of delegates to the National Assembly would be 'an infringement of the right of the elector'.[50] Electors would be harmed if they were kept from choosing from the largest possible pool of those willing and capable of filling an office, and their support would be sufficient to quell suspicions of sinister motivations on the part of the office-holder. Eclipsing considerations of 'all subjected persons' as well as of 'all affected interests', cosmopolitan institutional inclusion appears to rely on an 'all available talents' principle.

14.3.2 Foreigners' Rights to Political Representation

The second feature of Bentham's cosmopolitan constitutionalism concerns the rights and opportunities of political representation of and by foreigners. This idea is not identical to awarding them a right to be elected, which would commit potential foreign holders of mandates to representing the domestic interest exclusively. The idea is rather partly to represent foreign interests, partly to take advantage of foreign expertise. Again, Bentham developed a version of this idea in writings on parliamentary proceedings during the early stages of the French Revolution. Another variant he discussed with his South American interlocutors after their emancipation from the Spanish empire.

The first version, a model of 'reciprocal representation', is still systematically wedded to an internationalist idea of reciprocity. Bentham developed it in the context of the Franco-English confrontation induced by the French Revolution. In such a situation, reciprocal representation could be conducive to peace: 'Were the French and English legislature to interchange a few Members, there could not be a more powerful means of wearing away those national antipathies and jealousies which as far as

[49] Bentham, *Rights, Representation, and Reform* (*CW*), 91.
[50] Ibid., 250.

they prevail are so disgraceful and so detrimental to both countries.'[51] The term 'reciprocal representation' was coined by Philippe Schmitter, who suggested that neighbouring states as a rule should accord each other two or three seats in their respective assemblies.[52] According to Schmitter, such representatives should have debating rights and rights of documentation but not voting rights. While Bentham is non-committal about voting rights at this stage, we will see that he makes up his mind later on. Reciprocal representatives could supplement the normal channels of diplomatic relations by publicly highlighting problems that might arise and thus embody an 'early warning system' (Schmitter) for policies that could negatively affect the citizens of their respective home countries. Bentham's suggestion is more universal in scope as it does not require that representatives belong to neighbouring states. But note that although the proposed exchange of delegates is to counter nationalistic sentiment, Bentham's suggestion is not yet evidence of a cosmopolitan mindset. Bentham's suggestion is designed to accommodate foreign states, and it does not seem far-fetched to argue that reciprocal representation echoes his affirmation of the old system of appointing 'war residents' in enemy countries.[53] His idea is still internationalist since foreign representatives would sit in parliament in an official role, not as citizens of the world but as delegates of their own constituted authorities.

Despite the fact that it was a non-starter at the time of the French Revolution, Bentham returned to the same point in the nineteenth century, when working on his mature constitutional theory. In an 1822 proposal, Bentham suggests opening up parliaments to foreign delegates in a unilateral mode:

> In the case of a legislative body the members of which are freely chosen by the people, why should not they aggregate to themselves a few members, selected by them from other political states, associates, whose constitution bears more or less analogy to theirs. In the case of these foreign associates, to the right of speech and motion need not, nor should, be added the right

51 Ibid.

52 P. Schmitter, 'Exploring the Problematic Triumph of Liberal Democracy', in *Democracy's Victory and Crisis*, ed. A. Hadenius (Cambridge: Cambridge University Press, 1997), 297–307, at 303–5.

53 Bentham, 'A Plan for an Universal and Perpetual Peace', 545: 'When war has broken out, a palliative for its evils might perhaps be found in the appointment of war-residents, to provide for prisoners and to prevent violations of the laws of war .... A resident of this character could always be employed as a channel of communication, if an accommodation were desired.'

> of suffrage: for, to any use, derivable from information, afforded by a man in the character of a witness or an advocate, would be applied – not addition but subtraction, by any share, given to him in the power of a Judge. Power, it would not be competent to them to give: information, so it but afforded any the least promise of being of use, no man can be incompetent to receive . . .. An aggregation of this sort would be - not only a source of information, but a bond of fellowship.[54]

This suggestion leaves reciprocal internationalism behind and moves towards a unilateral, individualist orientation, even though it restricts the intake of foreign parliamentarians. Given that constitutions should bear 'more or less analogy' to each other, the arrangement is not yet fully cosmopolitan. However, the restriction seems to be motivated mainly by the need to identify experienced and trustworthy candidates and not by an expectation of their ideological conformity. Their selection is not engineered through foreign secondment but through a process of co-option by the elected members of the legislature themselves. Bentham believes that foreign parliamentarians might be especially welcome in cases of recent liberal constitutional transformation, such as in early nineteenth century Portugal and Spain, and of decolonization, where constitutional and legislative consolidation is the order of the day. In 'the case of Spain', he asks, 'what should hinder the Legislative body, in that country, from calling in the assistance of a few distinguished individuals, one or more from each one of several foreign countries? Portugal, Italy, Germany, France, and England, for example'.[55]

It is significant that Bentham offers only initiative and deliberative rights to the transnational members of parliament. Such rights are important in influencing parliamentary agenda-setting and opinion-formation, but they characteristically lack decisional impact. This is in line with Bentham's deliberative understanding of parliamentarism.[56] The foreign members' competence concerns first of all the deliberative

[54] Bentham, *Legislator of the World* (*CW*), 295f. n. The text ('Codification Proposal Addressed by Jeremy Bentham to All Nations Professing Liberal Opinions') was first printed in 1822.

[55] Bentham, *Legislator of the World* (*CW*), 295n. For a recent adaptation, see H. Landemore, *Open Democracy* (Princeton: Princeton University Press, 2020), 215.

[56] His early manuscripts were first published in 1816 as *Tactique des Assemblées Déliberantes*, although the term 'deliberating' is not Bentham's. See J. Bentham, *Political Tactics* (Oxford: Clarendon Press, 1999 [*CW*]); and P. Niesen, 'Une Petite Mappemonde du Chaos: La Délibération Parlementaire chez Bentham et Dumont', in *Bentham et la France: Fortune et Infortunes de l'Utilitarisme*, ed. E. de Champs and J.-P. Cléro (Oxford: Voltaire Foundation SVEC, 2009), 129–41.

'influence of understanding over understanding', in contrast to an 'influence of will over will', as manifested in voting rights.[57] Whereas the reciprocal scheme could leave open the question of voting rights, the unilateral opening up of a state parliament gives the ideal of a cosmopolitan constitutionalism more characteristic contours, in that it privileges foreigners' epistemic contribution, not dissimilar to the competence requirement discussed earlier (Section 14.3.1) over claims to a representation of foreigners' interests. If we look for an underlying normative principle for cosmopolitan entitlement, it will again neither be of the 'all subjected' nor the 'all affected' variety but secure eligibility for 'all available talents' under a process that selects for competence.

14.3.3 Foreigners' Authorship in Lawmaking

The third feature of Bentham's cosmopolitanism 'in one country' will be familiar to readers of his works and can here be treated briefly for reasons of space. It consists in the freedom to draft and publicly propose codes of law, especially constitutional codes.[58] We have already come across a variant of this feature, in Bentham's assigning the responsibility for drafting an international code to a 'citizen of the world' (see Section 14.2.2). As is well known, Bentham advocates holding open competitions for the drafting of codes, in order to maximize both moral aptitude and intellectual talent on the part of the drafters. He styles this 'the open mode' of codification.[59] With great patience, he rejects objections levelled against that method: that invoking a foreigner's expertise would subject the nation to a foreign yoke or expose it to that stranger's ignorance of its particularities, or that it would shame the nation's pride.[60] On the contrary, while a foreigner's intellectual aptitude can be judged publicly against his domestic competitors, he is at a clear advantage in terms of his moral trustworthiness: by not having a stake in the finished product, his work can be more single-mindedly directed toward the greatest happiness of the domestic order.[61] Although Bentham admits that local knowledge is not to the greatest degree at the disposal of the foreign expert,

[57] Bentham, *Rights, Representation and Reform* (*CW*), 422.

[58] Bentham, *Legislator of the World* (*CW*), 243–97, esp. 281.

[59] Ibid., 262; cf. 85, where Bentham adds that one virtue of the open mode is the possibility of public deliberation about drafts.

[60] Ibid., 22–9.

[61] Cf. ibid., 91. Foreigners, in contrast to nationals, tend to be free from 'sinister interests and affections, from the irresistibly-tempting and seductive influence'. Ibid., 290.

and therefore his intellectual aptitude diminished, he stresses the foreigner's greater aptitude in terms of judgement: he may succumb to his own, but not to 'local prejudices'.[62] Again, as in Sections 14.3.1 and 14.3.2, participation in foreign constitution-making does not flow from any supra-positive entitlement on the part of the draughtspersons but is derived from their presumptive competence and usefulness from the point of view of the domestic legal order:

> The greatest happiness of the greatest number requires, that, for the drawing of the original draught, all foreigners be admitted into the competition: and that, in so far as applicable, unless it be in all particulars taken together decidedly inferior, the draught of a foreigner be employed in preference.[63]

Although the draftsperson's most striking qualities will be disinterestedness and impartiality, Bentham does not for a moment suggest that capacities to try one's hand at codification will be equally distributed and does not use the language of universal empowerment. The most plausible reconstruction of the underlying normative principle will therefore yield a version of the 'all available talents' principle, standing exclusively in the service of the electorate.

14.3.4 Foreigners' Stakes in Popular Sovereignty

It is only in *Constitutional Code* (1830) that Bentham formulates his cosmopolitan constitutionalism in a universal deontological form. Here, he brings together various perspectives on the political inclusion of foreigners, both as contributors to and beneficiaries from domestic politics. As might have been expected from the author of 'Nonsense upon Stilts',[64] the *Code* is not strong on outlining catalogues of individual rights. All the more significant is the fact that the book does invoke one single supra-positive right, which is cosmopolitan in scope. Before analyzing the normative basis of Bentham's cosmopolitan constitutionalism (Section 14.3.4.2), it will be useful to examine the various features that document the *Code's* cosmopolitan orientation (Section 14.3.4.1).

[62] Ibid., 290–2.
[63] Ibid., 289.
[64] Bentham, *Rights, Representation and Reform* (*CW*), 317–402.

14.3.4.1 Cosmopolitan Rights under Constitutional Code

In *Constitutional Code*, all political authority is derived from the sovereignty of the people.[65] The meaning of the term 'the people', however, is indeterminate and depends on its concomitant Electoral Code.[66] It needs fixing through a bootstrapping process. In *Constitutional Code*, Vol. 1, this is done by means of a residency requirement, not through a membership condition. Constitutive authority is said to lie 'in the whole body of the inhabitants, who … are resident on the territory of the state'.[67] In formulations that appear in the Bowring edition of *Constitutional Code*, Bentham had still resorted to membership. There, constitutive authority is still said to lie 'in the whole body of active *citizens*', not residents or inhabitants.[68] But already an earlier pamphlet entitled *Radical Reform Bill* (1819) had made eligibility as an elector conditional on six months of residency, not on naturalization.[69] Bentham's mature constitutional theory identifies the sovereign 'people' through their subjection to government, not through their prior belonging to the citizenry. A second feature of the *Code* concerns eligibility for election and public office. Although the texts of *Constitutional Code* and *Radical Reform Bill* do not explicitly corroborate Bentham's earlier position on foreigners' candidatures for parliament, an indication is given by the fact that even the office of Prime Minister does not require naturalization. Excluded from eligibility are only those who have not 'either in a resident or migratory state, passed at least … years, in some part or other of the territory of this State'.[70] In filling the ministerial posts in his cabinet, the Prime Minister is free to choose 'any person at pleasure'.[71] As far as political input is concerned, Bentham exclusively follows principles of 'talent and trust'.[72]

[65] Bentham, *Constitutional Code*, vol. 1 (*CW*), 25.

[66] 'For prevention of uncertainty, reference must be made to the election code, where the requisite determinateness is given to it.' Bentham, *Constitutional Code*, Bowring, ix. 97. In *Constitutional Code*, vol. 1 (*CW*), Bentham had outsorced considerations on the Electoral Code to an earlier work. Bentham, *Radical Reform Bill*, Bowring, iii. 558–97. See the introduction by F. Rosen, *Constitutional Code*, vol. 1 (*CW*), xxv.

[67] Bentham, *Constitutional Code*, vol. 1 (*CW*), 29. This rules out 'passengers', ibid., 27.

[68] Bentham, *Constitutional Code*, Bowring, ix. 98, my emphasis.

[69] Bentham, *Radical Reform Bill*, Bowring iii. 564.

[70] Bentham, *Constitutional Code*, vol. 1 (*CW*) 157. Bentham leaves open the period required.

[71] Ibid., 311.

[72] Ibid., 313.

As far as political output is concerned, the best indicator for the cosmopolitan imprint of Bentham's constitutionalism is the 'Legislator's Inaugural Declaration'. *Constitutional Code* requires that all members of the Legislative Assembly, upon election, take this solemn oath, which consists of fourteen sections.[73] In the section entitled 'In International Dealings, Justice and Beneficence Promised', the 'Declaration' includes the following two paragraphs:

> On every favourable occasion – my endeavours shall be employed to the rendering, to the subjects, and for their sake to the constituted authorities, of every foreign State, all such positive good offices, as can be rendered thereto, without its being at the expense of some other State or States, or against the rightly presumable inclination, as well as at the expense, of the majority of my fellow-countrymen, in this our State.
>
> Never, by force or intimidation, never by prohibition or obstruction, will I use any endeavour to prevent my fellow-countrymen, or any of them, from seeking to better their condition in any other part, inhabited or uninhabited, of this globe. In the territory of this State, I behold an asylum to all: a prison to none.[74]

The first paragraph signals an important development from Bentham's internationalism in his 'Principles of International Law'. It specifies that when involved in 'international dealings', elected representatives need to attend to the interests of the citizens of foreign states. Positive duties are owed to the 'subjects . . . of every foreign State' and only in a mediated way (as far as their subjects profit) to their governments. Although still oriented to international stability through the absence of war and the renouncement of conquest, the 'Legislator's Declaration' obligates state officials to take into account foreign individuals' interests. In an earlier passage of the 'Declaration', the rejection of distant colonization and imperial domination is said to be owed directly to 'the inhabitants of such [colonized] territory', given that they normally will not see their interest tracked by the legislature of the mother country. Bentham here exhibits a concern not for the collectives but for 'the subject many, in both States'.[75]

The interpretation of the second paragraph is more challenging. What does it mean to say that a constitutional order is a prison to none, yet an 'asylum to all'? What is clear is that nation-state borders are to remain

[73] On the various functions of the declaration, see Rosen, *Jeremy Bentham and Representative Democracy*, 67–75.

[74] Bentham, *Constitutional Code*, vol. 1 (*CW*), 144.

[75] Ibid., 143.

constantly open for emigration. But to whom is 'asylum' offered under the *Constitutional Code*? Under a narrow construal, the 'asylum to all' protects the legislator's 'fellow-countrymen' collectively and individually, in enjoying complete security under their domestic constitution.[76] But Bentham is well aware of various bona fide reasons for seeking refuge – in the *Code*, he discusses ships admitting 'persons taking refuge from shipwreck, from famine, from enemies, from pirates, from mutineers'.[77] In his writings on pauper management, he provides for large groups of 'new-comers', for example, 'emigrant foreigners, driven from home in multitudes at a time' as well as 'shipwrecked persons . . . cast destitute on any part of the English coast'.[78] Under a broad construal that takes into account Bentham's expressed concern for 'subjects . . . of every foreign state', I conclude that 'asylum for all' can be understood to extend to non-citizens, giving foreign individuals a constitutional claim to apply for refuge.

14.3.4.2 An 'All-Cognizant' Principle for Cosmopolitan Constitutionalism

Given the *Constitutional Code*'s cosmopolitan orientation in both political input and output, in documenting foreigners' claims to institutional eligibility, concern, and refuge, it is now time to review the normative source of Bentham's cosmopolitan constitutionalism. *Constitutional Code* locates sovereignty 'in the people' and entrusts its exercise to a constitutive authority (co-extensive with the electorate). The constitutive authority is supreme among the hierarchically ordered set of authorities. Its competences lie in delegating and revoking the members of the legislature and, if necessary, holding them legally accountable. Besides its operations as an electoral or constitutive body, a complementary feature of the constitutive authority is the Public Opinion Tribunal, envisaged as a judicial body. This body, although it belongs to the constitutive authority, is not made up exclusively of electors or residents but also of foreigners: It comprises 'of all other political communities, all such members, to whom it happens to take cognizance of the question,

[76] For an in-depth reading of Bentham on security, see A. Marciniak, *Politische Sicherheit* (Frankfurt: Campus, 2015), 162–259.

[77] Bentham, *Constitutional Code*, Bowring, ix. 421.

[78] J. Bentham, 'Tracts on Poor Laws and Pauper Management, Table of Cases Calling for Relief', Bowring, viii. 364–5.

whatever it may be'.[79] Every such Tribunal consists of all domestic individuals and all members of all other political communities who have taken notice of the goings-on in their country. The right to participate in the exercise of the Public Opinion Tribunal is conferred equally on them. Thus, when Bentham states that 'Public Opinion may be considered as a system of law, emanating from the body of the people',[80] his notion of the people is even wider than that of the constitutive body. Singularly among theorists of popular sovereignty, Bentham's 'people' encompasses both the members of the constitutive body and those making up the Public Opinion Tribunal.

Cosmopolitan participation in the Public Opinion Tribunal brings full circle Bentham's earlier understanding of citizenship 'of the world' as an authorial and, predominantly, critical practice. The functions of the Tribunal are 'statistic' (informational), 'censorial' (expressing blame or praise), 'melioration-suggestive' and 'executive' (in bringing about punishment or reward for those blamed or praised). In a dramatic passage, Bentham invokes the cosmopolitan constituency of *Constitutional Code*:

> To every person, elector, inhabitant, or foreigner, – to every individual of the human species, *belongs the right of exercising*, in relation to the condition of every department of this government, and the conduct of every functionary thereto belonging, the statistic, executive, and melioration-suggestive functions .... So likewise the Censorial: how strong soever the terms, in which the approbation or disapprobation stands expressed.[81]

In contrast to the recruitment of talented foreigners for political posts, which were ultimately derived from the 'rights of the elector', the participation rights in the Public Opinion Tribunal are subjective entitlements, universal constitutional rights to participation, directly owed to the foreign individuals themselves. In contrast to the 'all available talents' principle invoked in Sections 14.3.1–14.3.3, its basic principle is of an 'all cognizant' type. In order to see that this global scope for the composition of the Public Opinion Tribunal is a new development, compare the position developed in *Constitutional Code* to the position in *Securities against Misrule*. In this latter work of 1822, Bentham is supporting a liberal, but not necessarily democratic, constitutional revolution for

79 Bentham, *Constitutional Code*, vol. 1 (*CW*), 35.
80 Ibid., 36.
81 Ibid., 39. My emphasis.

Tripoli in North Africa.[82] Already here, Bentham toys with an 'all cognizant' principle when he says that 'all those by whom any cognizance is taken of public affairs may be considered as constituting the Tribunal of Public Opinion, a sort of Committee' where every member 'who chooses to attend, attends accordingly, and has a voice'.[83] But the cosmopolitan impulse of this passage is stifled when, later in the same work, Bentham restricts membership in the Tribunal to members of the political community under an 'all subjected' reading. 'Take any political community – the British empire for example. Of the aggregate of all the persons belonging to it, rulers and subjects taken together, will the Public Opinion Tribunal be composed.'[84] This position is then corrected and expanded in *Constitutional Code*. Disregarding their subjection or belonging, as well as their competence or expertise, under the 'all cognizant' reading everybody who takes notice of a domestic phenomenon is entitled to communicate their thoughts across borders.

No global institutional development will be necessary to generate such a tribunal, nor does it require the existence of a single integrated global public sphere. Bentham's constitutionalism is designed for a plurality of overlapping public spheres, all with global intake and local focus, accompanying and controlling the workings of the domestic institutional orders. This leads us to the question: what kind of binding character can Bentham's institutional cosmopolitanism aspire to? Contemporary global institutional cosmopolitans insist that only through institutions universal in reach, with some sovereign competences, can such binding power be achieved.[85] This is not what Bentham has in mind or what can be secured through constitutional law. Although foreigners' entitlements are to be entrenched in the constitutional codes of every country and have the status of fundamental law, it is not immediately clear how breaches and violations of individuals' claims by a given state are to be confronted. Two cases need to be distinguished here. The first is clear-cut: against democratic constitutional change, even if it were to do away with foreigners' rights, there is no bulwark except bottom-up public pressure. Bentham explicitly forbids the judiciary to invalidate presumptively unconstitutional legislation and leaves the defence of the

82 Bentham, *Securities against Misrule*, 23–112.

83 Ibid., 28.

84 Ibid., 57.

85 See the discussion of Ronzoni's understanding of institutional cosmopolitanism (Section 14.2).

constitution to the electorate.[86] The other case is less clear-cut and concerns governmental violations of an existing constitution, once a draft like *Constitutional Code* is adopted. Here, it is not implausible to think that cosmopolitan entitlements both of political input (foreigners' communication, association, standing for election etc.) as well as of output (asylum, foreign policy concerns) could find coercive protection through domestic courts controlling governmental behaviour. As long as legislators are at least paying lip service (in form of the 'Inaugural Declaration') to foreigners' claims, the judiciary could block administrative agents attempting to detract from them.

14.4 Conclusion

In conclusion, I want to recapitulate the normative principles that have been found to play a role in Bentham's cosmopolitan constitutionalism and say briefly how his conception connects with contemporary issues. Cosmopolitan constitutional law fixes the rights of foreigners in relation to states of which they are not members. It goes beyond Bentham's qualification, in *Introduction to the Principles of Morals and Legislation*, of 'internal' law as dealing with the private relations of citizens, in relating individuals to existing state governments. In Section 14.2, we have seen that not much can be inferred in terms of institutional consequences from reading Bentham as a moral cosmopolitan. Section 14.3 showed that in contrast to today's global institutional cosmopolitanism, Bentham's does not depend on overarching institutional mechanisms placed above the several states. Its characteristic feature is that it entrenches cosmopolitan entitlements in the constitutional arrangements of every single state. The democratic character of those constitutions gives normative plausibility to the 'all available talents' principle, under which mandates and offices are open to all foreign individuals, given that the people have a claim to select from the best candidates on the basis of 'talent and trust'. Normatively speaking, this institutional cosmopolitanism is nothing but a reflex, dependent on an epistemic understanding of democratic government. Next, we learned from the *Constitutional Code* that the 'people' incorporate resident foreigners and that officials can be

[86] 'If, on any occasion, any ordinance, which to some shall appear repugnant to the principles of this Constitution, shall come to have been enacted by the Legislature, such ordinance is not on that account to be, by any judge, treated or spoken of, as being null and void.' Bentham, *Constitutional Code*, vol. 1 (*CW*), 45.

recruited from them without naturalization. In accounting for the composition of the electorate, this builds on an 'all subjected' (as opposed to a membership-based) conception of the political community. The most extraordinary feature of the *Code* is perhaps the fact that the notion of the constitutive authority of the people, operating in the form of the Public Opinion Tribunal, encompasses 'every individual of the human species' as an equal participant. Such empowerment of foreigners corresponds to a strict political division of labour: while the 'all subjected' principle determines who is to be involved in decision-making, the 'all cognizant' principle governs who is to be included in debate. Again, foreigners' empowerment largely concerns the epistemic contribution they will be able to make but is based on their individual right to do so. Foreign members of the Tribunal can provide information and help to influence domestic governments, but most characteristically they will, in their 'censorial' function, communicate criticism and inform legislative authorship, as evidenced by Bentham's own plans for an 'open mode' of codification, underlining the central role envisaged for the authorial aspects of cosmopolitan inclusion. This will not guarantee that all material cosmopolitan concerns will remain entrenched beyond the 'Legislator's Declaration' under unwilling governments but will make sure that public pressure is increased on governments failing to honour them. The 'all cognizant' principle, lying at the basis of overlapping Public Opinion Tribunals for every country, shows democratic government to be defective if it does not involve the entire global population in its constitutional and legislative debates. Cosmopolitanism 'in one country' is a requirement of democratic constitutionalism.

Bentham's conception of cosmopolitan constitutionalism helps identify a key contemporary challenge for cosmopolitan legal development. This challenge does not lie in the slowing momentum toward international organizations and global institutions that we are currently witnessing[87] but in the closing down of state borders for foreign communicative influence by all those 'cognizant' of domestic violations of rights and justice. Wherever they limit, control, or punish border-crossing political communication and civil society activities or criminalize foreign funded media or civil society organizations,[88] states signal that they are

[87] A. Schäfer and M. Zürn, *Die demokratische Regression* (Berlin: Suhrkamp, 2021).

[88] J. Wolff and A. E. Poppe, *From Closing Space to Contested Spaces: Re-assessing Current Conflicts over International Civil Society Support* (Frankfurt: Peace Research Institute, 2015).

sliding toward autocracy. The past quarter century has witnessed a significant 'defunding' trend, where the monitoring and education activities of foreign philanthropic or political foundations have been limited and their staff endangered.[89] Where border-crossing news agencies or oppositional groups are criminalized as 'foreign agents', states immunize themselves against any consequences that could follow from outsiders taking cognizance of domestic injustice.[90] Bentham's brand of cosmopolitanism 'within one country' could encourage the contemporary debate to distinguish more clearly between foreign governmental (i.e., internationalist) and cosmopolitan communicative interventions, with the latter claiming complete freedom as an external corollary of domestic democracy. An isolated Public Opinion Tribunal consisting exclusively of those subjected to a given government may be less attentive, will be less pluralistic and comprehensive, and easier to control. Hence, where foreigners' access to public debates on domestic issues is being restricted, this will violate the claims of the members of foreign communities but also the rights of the electorate. The 'cosmopolitan potential' of Bentham's constitutionalism lies not least in the intimate connection it displays between the political inclusion of foreigners' perspectives and the unimpeded functioning of constitutional democracies.[91]

[89] D. Christensen and J. Weinstein, 'Defunding Dissent: Restrictions on Aid to NGOs', *Journal of Democracy* 24, no. 2 (2013), 77–91. Unfortunately, the authors do not distinguish between governmental and non-governmental funding for border-crossing NGOs.

[90] A. Roth, 'Putin approves law targeting journalists as "foreign agents"', *Guardian* 3 December 2019.

[91] I owe thanks to Julian Culp, Marcus Willaschek, Angela Marciniak, Miriam Ronzoni, and Jens Steffek and audiences at Darmstadt, Frankfurt, Fudan, Macao and New York Universities for comments on earlier versions.

BIBLIOGRAPHY

Manuscript Collections

Grote Papers, British Library Additional Manuscripts (BL Add. MS) 33.
University College London collection of Bentham manuscripts (UC), boxes i–clxxvi.

Works by Jeremy Bentham

1774 *White Bull* (London: J. Bew).

1776 'Short Review of the Declaration', in *The Declaration of Independence: A Global History*, ed. D. Armitage (Cambridge, MA: Harvard University Press), 173–86.

1776 'Short Review of the Declaration', in *An Answer to the Declaration of the American Congress*, ed. J. Lind (London: T. Cadell), 119–32.

1778 *View of the Hard-Labour Bill; being an abstract of a pamphlet intituled 'Draught of a bill, to punish by imprisonment and hard labour, certain offenders; and to establish proper places for their reception'. Interspersed with observations relative to the subject of the above draught in particular, and to jurisprudence in general* (London: T. Payne).

1795 *Supply Without Burthen; or Escheat vice Taxation* (London: J. Debrett).

1802 *Traités de législation civile et pénale*, ed. É. Dumont, 3 vols. (Paris).

1808 *Scotch Reform; considered, with reference to the Plan, proposed in the Late Parliament, for the regulation of the Courts, and the Administration of Justice, in Scotland: with Illustrations from English Non-reform: in the course of which divers imperfections, abuses, and corruptions, in the Administration of Justice, with their causes, are now, for the first time, brought to light. In a series of Letters, addressed to the Right Hon. Lord Grenville* (London: Richard Taylor and Co.).

1811 *Scotch Reform* (London: J. Ridgway).

1817 *Plan of Parliamentary Reform* (London: R. Hunter).

1818 *Church-of-Englandism and its Catechism Examined* (London: Effingham Wilson).

1821 *The Elements of the Art of Packing, as applied to Special Juries, particularly in cases of libel law* (London: Effingham Wilson).

1823 *Traité des Preuves Judiciares*, ed. E. Dumont (Paris: Bossange Frères).
1823 'Leading Principles of a Condtitutional Code, for any state', *The Pamphleteer* 22, no. 44, 476–86.
1825 *The Rationale of Reward*, ed. R. Smith (London: John and H. L. Hunt).
1827 *Rationale of Judicial Evidence, specially applied to English practice*, 5 vols. ed. J. S. Mill (London: Hunt and Clarke).
1830 *The Rationale of Punishment* (London: Robert Heward).
1832 *Lord Brougham Displayed* (London: Robert Heward).
1843 *The Works of Jeremy Bentham*, published under the Superintendence of his Executor, J. Bowring, 11 vols. (Edinburgh: William Tait).
1896 *Theory of Legislation*, trans. R. Hildreth (London: Kegan Paul, Trench, Trubner & Co.).
1954 *Jeremy Bentham's Economic Writings, Volume 3*, ed. W. Stark (London: Allen & Unwin).
1968 *Correspondence, Vol. 2, 1777–1780*, ed. T. L. S. Sprigge (London: Athlone (*CW*)).
1968–2022 *The Collected Works of Jeremy Bentham*, ed. J. H. Burns, J. R. Dinwiddy, F. Rosen, and P. Schofield (Oxford: Clarendon Press; London: Oxford University Press), henceforth (*CW*).
1969 'Indirect Legislation', in *A Bentham Reader*, ed. M. P. Mack (New York: Pegasus).
1970 *Of Laws in General*, ed. H. L. A. Hart (London: The Athlone Press [*CW*]).
1970/1996 *An Introduction to the Principles of Morals and Legislation*, ed. J. H. Burns and H. L. A. Hart (London: Athlone Press [*CW*]). Republished with a new introduction by F. Rosen (Oxford: Clarendon Press [*CW*]).
1977 *A Comment on the Commentaries and a Fragment on Government*, ed. J. H. Burns and H. L. A. Hart (London: Athlone [*CW*]).
1983 *Constitutional Code, Volume I*, ed. F. Rosen and J. H. Burns (Oxford: Clarendon Press [*CW*]).
1983 *Chrestomathia*, ed. M. J. Smith and W. H. Burston (Oxford: Clarendon Press [*CW*]).
1983 *Deontology together with A Table of the Springs of Action and Article on Utilitarianism*, ed. A. Goldworth (Oxford: Clarendon Press [*CW*]).
1988 *A Fragment on Government*, ed. J. H. Burns and H. L. A. Hart (Cambridge: Cambridge University Press).
1989 *First Principles Preparatory to Constitutional Code*, ed. P. Schofield (Oxford: Clarendon Press [*CW*]).
1990 *Securities against Misrule, and Other Constitutional Writings for Tripoli and Greece*, ed. P. Schofield (Oxford: Clarendon Press [*CW*]).
1993 *Official Aptitude Maximized; Expense Minimized*, ed. P. Schofield (Oxford: Clarendon Press [*CW*]).

1995 *Colonies, Commerce, and Constitutional Law: Rid Yourselves of Ultramaria; and Other Writings on Spain and Spanish America*, ed. P. Schofield (Oxford: Clarendon Press [*CW*]).

1998 *'Legislator of the World': Writings on Codification, Law, and Education*, ed. P. Schofield and J. Harris (Oxford: Clarendon Press [*CW*]).

1999 *Political Tactics*, ed. M. James, C. Blamires, and C. P. Watkin (Oxford: Clarendon Press [*CW*]).

2000 *The Correspondence of Jeremy Bentham: Volume 11*, ed. C. Fuller (Oxford: Clarendon Press [*CW*]).

2001 *Writings on the Poor Laws: I*, ed. M. Quinn (Oxford: Clarendon Press [*CW*]).

2002 *Rights, Representation and Reform: Nonsense upon Stilts and other writings on the French Revolution*, ed. P. Schofield, C. Pease-Watkin, and C. Blamires (Oxford: Clarendon Press [*CW*]).

2004 *Chrestomatia*, ed. J.-P. Cléro (Paris: L'Unebévue).

2006 *The Correspondence of Jeremy Bentham: Volume 12*, ed. L. O'Sullivan and C. Fuller (Oxford: Clarendon Press [*CW*]).

2008 *A Comment on the Commentaries and a Fragment on Government*, ed. J. H. Burns and H. L. A. Hart (Oxford: Clarendon Press [*CW*]).

2010 *Of the Limits of the Penal Branch of Jurisprudence*, ed. P. Schofield (Oxford: Clarendon Press [*CW*]).

2010 *Traités de législation civile et pénale*, ed. E. Dumont, pref. M. Bozzo-Rey, A. Brunon-Ernst, E. de Champs (Paris: Dalloz).

2010 *Writings on the Poor Laws: II*, ed. M. Quinn (Oxford: Clarendon Press [*CW*]).

2011 *Church-of Englandism and its Catechism Examined*, ed. J. E. Crimmins and C. Fuller (Oxford: Clarendon Press [*CW*]).

2011 *Selected Writings: Jeremy Bentham*, ed. S. G. Engelmann (New Haven: Yale University Press).

2012 *On the Liberty of the Press, and Public Discussion and other Legal and Political Writings for Spain and Portugal*, ed. C. Pease-Watkin and P. Schofield (Oxford: Clarendon Press [*CW*]).

2013 *Not Paul, but Jesus. Vol. III. Doctrine*, ed. P. Schofield, M. Quinn, and C. Pease-Watkin (London: University College London Press).

2014 *Of Sexual Irregularities, and Other Writings on Sexual Morality*, ed. P. Schofield, C. Pease-Watkin, and M. Quinn (Oxford: Clarendon Press [*CW*]).

2015 *The Book of Fallacies*, ed. P. Schofield (Oxford: Clarendon Press [*CW*]).

2016 *Preparatory Principles*, ed. D. G. Long and P. Schofield (Oxford: Clarendon Press [*CW*]).

2016 *Writings on Political Economy: I*, ed. M. Quinn (Oxford: Clarendon Press [*CW*]).

2018 *Writings on Political Economy, Volume III: Preventive Police*, ed. M. Quinn (London: Bentham Project).

2018 *Writings on Australia, II. History of Jeremy Bentham's dealings with Lord Pelham*, ed. T. Causer and P. Schofield, www.ucl.ac.uk/bentham-project.

2019 *Writings on Political Economy: II*, ed. M. Quinn (Oxford: Clarendon Press [*CW*]).

2022 *Panopticon versus New South Wales and other writings on Australia*, ed. T. Causer and P. Schofield (London: University College London Press [*CW*]).

Works by Other Authors

Albiston, C. 2018 'Democracy, Civil Society, and Public Interest Law', *Wisconsin Law Review* 2, 187–214.

Armitage, D. 2011 'Globalizing Jeremy Bentham', *History of Political Thought* 32, 63–82.

Arneil, B. 2018 *Domestic Colonies: The Turn Inward to Colony* (Oxford: Oxford University Press).

2021 'Jeremy Bentham: Pauperism, Colonialism, and Imperialism', *American Political Science Review*, 115, 1147–58.

Atienza, M. 2019 'Legislation and Argumentation: Towards a Model for the Analysis of Legislative Reasoning', in *Conceptions and Misconceptions of Legislation*, ed. A. D. Oliver-Lalana (Cham: Springer), 175–206.

Austin, J. 1879 *Lectures on Jurisprudence or the Philosophy of Positive Law*, 4th ed., 2 vols., ed. R. Campbell (London: John Murray).

1998 *The Province of Jurisprudence Determined and The Uses of the Study of Jurisprudence* (first published 1832), ed. H. L. A. Hart (Indianapolis; Cambridge: Hackett).

Bahmueller, C. 1981 *The National Charity Company: Jeremy Bentham's Silent Revolution* (Berkeley: University of California Press).

Baker, K. M. 2017 'Constitution', in *Dictionnaire critique de la Révolution française, t. 3 Institutions et creations*, ed. F. Furet and M. Ozouf (Paris: Flammarion), 179–205.

Ball, T. 1980 'Utilitarianism, Feminism and the Franchise: James Mill and His Critics', *History of Political Thought* 1, 91–115.

1980 'Was Bentham a Feminist?', *The Bentham Newsletter* 4, 25–31.

Baranger, D. 2018. *Penser la loi. Essai sur le législateur des temps modernes* (Paris: Gallimard).

Bastid, P. 1985. *L'idée de constitution, [1962–1963]* (Paris: Economica).

Beauchamp [G. Grote], P. 1822 *Analysis of the Influence of Natural Religion* (London: R. Carlile).

Beaud, O. 2009. 'L'histoire du concept de constitution en France. De la constitution politique à la constitution comme statut juridique de l'Etat.' *Jus politicum*, 3, http://juspoliticum.com/article/L-histoire-du-concept-de-constitution-en-France-De-la-constitution-politique-a-la-constitution-comme-statut-juridique-de-l-Etat-140.html.

Bedau, H. A. 2000 '"Anarchical Fallacies": Bentham's Attack on Human Rights', *Human Rights Quarterly* 22, 261–79.

Ben-Dor, O. 2000 *Constitutional Limits and the Public Sphere: A Critical Study of Bentham's Constitutionalism* (Oxford: Hart).

Blackstone, W. 1765–9 *Commentaries on the Laws of England* (Oxford: Clarendon Press).

1975 *Commentaries on the Laws of England* (Chicago: University of Chicago Press).

Bolingbroke, H. St. J. 1735 *A Dissertation Upon Parties* (London: R. Francklin).

Bourcier, B. 2017 'Le Plus Grand Bonheur pour le Plus Grand Nombre de Jeremy Bentham: un Utilitarisme Cosmopolitique', *Philosophical Enquiries: Revue des Philosophies Anglophones* 9, 59-77.

2021 'Bentham's International Political Theory: Taking States' Responsibilities Seriously', *Utilitas*, 33, 287–303, doi:10.1017/S0953820820000448.

Bozzo-Rey, M. 2010 'Publicity and Nomography: Bentham's School of Legislation', *Journal of Bentham Studies*, doi:10.14324/111.2045-757X.037.

2011 'Bentham et le management des fonctionnaires: utilité, transparence et management de soi', raison-publique.fr.

2011 'La transparence chez Jeremy Bentham: de l'invisibilité d'un concept à sa publicité', *The Tocqueville Review/La revue Tocqueville* 32, 89–111.

Bozzo-Rey, M., Brunon-Ernst, A., and Quinn, M. (eds.) 2017 'Indirect Legislation: Jeremy Bentham's Regulatory Revolution', *History of European Ideas* 43, no. 1, 1–121.

Bozzo-Rey, M., Brunon-Ernst, A., and Van Waeyenberge, A. (eds.) 2016 'Nudges: Better Choices?', *The Tocqueville Review / La revue Tocqueville* 37.

Brink, D. 2018 'Mill's Moral and Political Philosophy', *Stanford Encyclopedia of Philosophy*. https://plato.stanford.edu/entries/mill-moral-political/.

Brock, G., and Brighouse, H. 2005 'Introduction', in *The Political Philosophy of Cosmopolitanism*, ed. G. Brock and H. Brighouse (Cambridge: Cambridge University Press), 1–9.

Brown, C. 1992 *International Relations Theories: New Normative Approaches* (New York: Columbia University Press).

Brunon-Ernst, A. 2007 'Les métamorphoses panoptiques: de Foucault à Bentham', *Cahiers critiques de philosophie* 4, 60–71.

2010 'Délimiter la branche civile du droit: Bentham et la quête impossible', in *Bentham, juriste*, ed. G. Tusseau and M. Bozzo-Rey (Paris: Economica), 177–200.

2014 'Beyond the Genetic Panopticon: The limits of Government Intervention on Citizens' Bodies', *Implications philosophiques* 1, www.implications-philosophiques.org/actualite/une/beyond-the-genetic-panopticon/.

2014 'Of the Limits of the Civil Branch of Jurisprudence: Background, Definitions and Limits of Bentham's Discussion on Civil Law in Limits', in *The Legal Philosophy and Influence of Jeremy Bentham. Essays on Of the Limits of the Penal Branch of Jurisprudence*, ed. G. Tusseau (London; New York: Routledge), 134–46.

2014 'Indirect legislation and Utility: Study of the Effectiveness of Indirect Legislation', ISUS International Symposium, Yokohama University, Japan, 20–22 August 2014.

2015 'Le gouvernement des normes: Jeremy Bentham et les instruments de régulation post-modernes', *Archives de philosophie* 78, 309–22.

2016 'Back to the Sources of Nudges, Nudges: Better Choices?', *The Tocqueville Review/ La Revue Tocqueville* 27, 99–122.

2017 'Nudges and the limits of appropriate interference: Reading Backwards from J. S. Mill's Harm Principle to Jeremy Bentham's Indirect Legislation', *History of European Ideas* 43, 53–69.

Burke, E. 1790 *Reflections on the Revolution in France, 1790*, www.constitution.org/eb/rev_fran.htm.

Burns, J. H. 1966 'Bentham and the French Revolution', *Transactions of the Royal Historical Society* 16, 95–114.

1973 'Bentham on Sovereignty', *Northern Ireland Political Quarterly* 24, 133–51.

1984 'Jeremy Bentham: From Radical Enlightenment to Political Radicalism', *The Bentham Newsletter* 8, 4–14.

2005 'Happiness and Utility: Jeremy Bentham's Equation', *Utilitas* 17, 46–61.

Campos Boralevi, L. 1980 'In Defense of a Myth', *Bentham Newsletter* 4, 33–44.

1984 *Bentham and the Oppressed* (Berlin: W. de Gruyter).

Carlyle, T. 1842 *On Heroes, Hero-Worship and the Heroic in History*, 2nd ed. (London: Chapman and Hall, Strand).

Carter, J. 1889 *The Province of the Written and the Unwritten Law* (New York: Banks & Brothers).

Cattaneo, L., and Chapman, A. 2010 'The Process of Empowerment: A Model for Use in Research and Practice', *American Psychologist* 65, 646–59.

Chatterjee, P. 2020 *I Am the People: Reflections on Popular Sovereignty Today* (New York: Columbia University Press).

Chernock, A. 2005 'Extending the "Right of Election": Men's Arguments for Women's Political Representation in Late Enlightenment Britain', in *Women, Gender and Enlightenment*, ed. S. Knott and B. Taylor (Basingstoke: Palgrave Macmillan), 587–609.

Christensen, D., and Weinstein, J. 2013 'Defunding Dissent: Restrictions on Aid to NGOs', *Journal of Democracy* 24, 77–91.

Christie, I. R. 1984 *Stress and Stability in Late Eighteenth-Century Britain: Reflections on the British Avoidance of Revolution* (Oxford: Clarendon Press).

Church-of-Englandism, and its Catechism Examined. *British Critic* 10 (November 1818), 519–28.

Church-of-Englandism and its Catechism Examined. *Quarterly Review* 21 (1 January 1819), 167–77.

Church Establishment. *Examiner* 894 (20 March 1825), 177.

Clark, A. 2003 *Scandal: The Sexual Politics of the British Constitution* (Princeton: Princeton University Press).

Cohen-Eliya, M., and Porat, I. 2013 *Justification and Authority: Proportionality and Constitutional Culture* (Cambridge: Cambridge University Press).

Cohen, J. 1950 'Towards Realism in Legisprudence', *Yale Law Journal* 59, 886–97.

1983 'Legisprudence: Problems and Agenda', *Hofstra Law Review* 11, 1163–83.

Cornett, J. M. 1997 'Hoodwink'd by Custom: The Exclusion of Women from Juries in Eighteenth-Century English Law and Literature', *William and Mary Journal of Race, Gender and Social Justice* 4, 2–89.

Cornish, W., Anderson, J. S., Cocks, R., Lobban, M., Polden, P., and Smith, K. 2010 *The Oxford History of the Laws of England: Volume XI* (Oxford: Oxford University Press).

Cot, A. 2003 '"Let there be no distinction between the sexes": Jeremy Bentham on the Status of Women', in *The Status of Women in Classical Economic Thought*, ed. R. W. Dimand and C. Nyland (Cheltenham: Edward Elgar), 165–89.

Craig, D. 2012. 'Burke and the Constitution', in *The Cambridge Companion to Edmund Burke*, ed. D. Dwan and C. Insole (Cambridge; New York: Cambridge University Press), 104–16.

Crimmins, J. E. 1990 *Secular Utilitarianism: Social Science and the Critique of Religion in the Thought of Jeremy Bentham* (Oxford: Clarendon Press).

1994 'Bentham's Political Radicalism Reexamined', *Journal of the History of Ideas* 55, 259–81.

2001 'Bentham's Religious Radicalism Revisited: A Response to Philip Schofield'. *History of Political Thought* 22, 494–500.

Crompton, L. 1978 'Jeremy Bentham's Essay on "Paederasty": Part 2', *Journal of Homosexuality* 4, 91–107.

Davidoff, L., and Hall, C. 1987 *Family Fortunes: Men and Women of the English Middle-Class, 1780–1850* (London: Routledge).

De Champs, E. 2006 'Les fonctionnaires dans le Code Constitutionnel', *Revue d'études benthamiennes* 1. doi.org/10.4000/etudes-benthamiennes.59.

2008 *'La déontologie politique' ou La pensée constitutionnelle de Jeremy Bentham* (Geneva: Droz).

2008 'Propriété et statut personnel chez Jeremy Bentham', in *Le libéralisme au miroir du droit. L'Etat, la personne et la propriété*, ed. B. Bachofen (Paris: ENS éditions), 117–43.

2011 'Constitution and the Code: Jeremy Bentham on the Limits of the Constitutional Branch of Jurisprudence', *The Tocqueville Review/La revue Tocqueville* 32, 21–42.

2014 'Towards the *Pannomion*: *Limits* and Bentham's French Manuscripts', in *The Legal Philosophy and Influence of Jeremy Bentham. Essays on Of the Limits of the Penal Branch of Jurisprudence*, ed. G. Tusseau (London; New York: Routledge), 320–37.

2015 *Enlightenment and Utility: Bentham in French, Bentham in France* (Cambridge: Cambridge University Press).

Dinwiddy, J. R. 1975 'Bentham's Transition to Political Radicalism, 1809–10', *Journal of the History of Ideas* 36, 683–700.

2004 'Bentham on Private Ethics and the Principle of Utility', in *Bentham: Selected Writings*, ed. W. Twining (Stanford: Stanford University Press), 134–54.

Dworkin, R. 1977 'Social Sciences and Constitutional Rights – the Consequences of Uncertainty', *Journal of Law & Education* 6, 3–12.

1978 *Taking Rights Seriously* (Cambridge, MA: Harvard University Press).

1982 'Law as Interpretation', *Critical Inquiry* 9, 179–200.

1985 *A Matter of Principle*, (Cambridge, MA: Harvard University Press).

Ekins, R. 2012 *The Nature of Legislative Intent* (Oxford: Oxford University Press).

El Shakankiri, M. 1970 *La philosophie juridique de Jeremy Bentham* (Paris: LGDJ).

Elster, J. 2013 *Securities against Misrule: Juries, Assemblies, Elections* (Cambridge: Cambridge University Press).

Engelmann, S. G. 2001 'Imagining Interest', *Utilitas* 13, 289–322.

2003 '"Indirect Legislation": Bentham's Liberal Government', *Polity* 35, 369–88.

2008 'Mill, Bentham, and the Art and Science of Government', *Revue d'études benthamiennes* 4.

(ed.) 2011 *Selected Writings: Jeremy Bentham* (New Haven; London: Yale University Press).

2014 'Limits and Indirect Legislation', in *The Legal Philosophy and Influence of Jeremy Bentham: Essays on Of the Limits of the Penal Branch of Jurisprudence*, ed. G. Tusseau (London; New York: Routledge), 308–15.

Engelmann, S. G., and Pitts, J. 2011 'Bentham's "Place and Time"', *The Toqueville Review/La revue Tocqueville* 32, 43–66.

Ferraro, F. 2010 'Direct and Indirect Utilitarianism in Bentham's Theory of Adjudication', *The Journal of Bentham Studies* 12, 1–24.

2011 'Moral Aptitude and The Moral Sanction in Bentham's Institutional Architecture: Is There Any Room for Non-Egoistic Motivation?', in *Philosophy and Public Issues–Filosofia E Questioni Pubbliche* 1, 11–19.

2013 'Adjudication and Expectations: Bentham on the Role of the Judges', *Utilitas* 25, 140–60.

Fioravanti, M. 1999 *Costituzione* (Bologna: Il Mulino).

Foucault, M. 1975 *Surveiller et punir – Naissance de la prison* (Paris: Gallimard).

2008 *The Birth of Biopolitics: Lectures at the Collège de France, 1978–1979*, ed. M. Senellart, trans. G. Burchell (London: Palgrave Macmillan).

2014 *On the Government of the Living: Lectures at the Collège de France 1979–80*, ed. M. Senellart, trans. G. Burchell (Basingstoke: Palgrave Macmillan).

Fraser, N. 2008 *Scales of Justice: Reimagining Political Space in a Globalizing World* (London: Polity).

Fuller, C. 2008 'Bentham, Mill, Grote, and *An Analysis of the Influence of Natural Religion on the Temporal Happiness of Mankind*', *Journal of Bentham Studies* 10, 1–15.

2010 '*Utility of Religion a Subject yet Little Examined*: A Survey of Bentham's Writings on the Utility of Religion', *Revue d'études benthamiennes* 6, 1–16.

Gillardin, J. 1987 'Les principes du code civil d'après Jeremy Bentham', in *Actualité de la pensée juridique de Jeremy Bentham* (Brussels: Publications des Facultés universitaires Saint-Louis), 549–76.

Grimm, D. 1991 *Die Zukunft der Verfassung* (Frankfurt am Main: Suhrkamp).

Guidi, M. E. L. 2008 '"Everybody to count for one, nobody for more than one": The Principle of Equal Consideration of Interests from Bentham to Pigou', *Revue d'études benthamiennes* 4, doi.org/10.4000/etudes-benthamiennes.182.

Haakonssen, K. 1989 *The Science of a Legislator: The Natural Jurisprudence of David Hume & Adam Smith* (Cambridge: Cambridge University Press).

Halévy, E. 1934 *The Growth of Philosophic Radicalism*, trans. M. Morris (London: Faber & Faber).

Halévy, E. 1995 [1901–4] *La formation du radicalisme philosophique*, 3 vols., ed. M. Canto-Sperber (Paris: PUF).

Hamilton, A., Jay, J., and Madison, J. 2001 *The Federalist*, ed. G. W. Carey and J. McClellan (Indianapolis: Liberty Fund).

Harrison, R. 1983/2008 *Bentham* (London: Routledge & Kegan Paul).

Hart, H. L. A. 1982 *Essays on Bentham: Jurisprudence and Political Theory* (Oxford: Clarendon Press).

2005 'Bentham's Principle of Utility and Theory of Penal Law', in *An Introduction to the Principles of Morals and Legislation*, ed. J. H. Burns and H. L. A. Hart (Oxford: Oxford University Press), lxxix–cxii.

Hayek, F. A. 1973 *Law, Legislation and Liberty: A New Statement of the Liberal Principles of Justice and Political Economy. 1, Rules and Order* (London: Routledge & Kegan Paul).

Held, D. 2010 *Cosmopolitanism: Ideals and Realities* (Cambridge: Polity).

Helvétius, C. A. 1988 *De l'esprit* (Paris: Fayard).

Hobbes, T. 1968 *Leviathan*, ed. C. B. Macpherson (London: Penguin Books).

1986 *De Cive: English Version*, ed. H. Warrender (Oxford: Clarendon Press).

1999 *Léviathan. Traité de la matière, de la forme et du pouvoir de la république ecclésiastique et civile* (Paris: Dalloz).

Hoogensen, G. 2005 *International Relations, Security and Jeremy Bentham* (Abingdon: Routledge).

Howley, W. 1814 *A Charge Delivered to the Clergy of the Diocese of London* (London: T. Bensley).

Hulsebosch, D. J. 1998 'The Constitution in the Glass Case and Constitutions in Action', *Law and History Review* 16, 397–401.

2005 *Constituting Empire: New York and the Transformation of Constitutionalism in the Atlantic World, 1664–1830* (Chapel Hill: The University of North Carolina Press).

Hume, D. 1739–40 *A Treatise of Human Nature: Being an Attempt to Introduce the Experimental Method of Reasoning into Moral Subjects*, 3 vols. (London).

Hume, L. J. 1981 *Bentham and Bureaucracy* (Cambridge: Cambridge University Press).

Jacques, S., and Schofield, P. (eds.) 2021 *Jeremy Bentham on Police: The Unknown Story and What It Means for Criminology* (London: University College London Press).

James, M. 1981 'Public Interest and Majority Rule in Bentham's Democratic Theory', *Political Theory* 9, 49–64.

1986 'Bentham's Democratic Theory at the Time of the French Revolution', *Bentham Newsletter* 10, 5–16.

Kahn, P. W. 2019 *Origins of Order: Project and System in the American Legal Imagination* (New Haven: Yale University Press).

Kant, I., 1996 'On the Common Saying: This May Be Correct in Theory, but It Is of No Use in Practice', in *Practical Philosophy*, ed. M. Gregor (Cambridge: Cambridge University Press), 273–309.

1996 'Toward Perpetual Peace', in *Practical Philosophy*, ed. M. Gregor (Cambridge: Cambridge University Press), 311–51.

Kavanagh, A. 2016 'The Constitutional Separation of Powers', in *Philosophical Foundation of Constitutional Law*, ed. D. Dyzenhaus and M. Thorburn (Oxford: Oxford University Press), 223.

Kelly, P. J. 1990 *Utilitarianism and Distributive Justice: Jeremy Bentham and the Civil Law* (Oxford: Oxford University Press).

Kelsen, H. 1999 *General Theory of Law and State*, trans. A. Wedberg (Union: The Lawbook Exchange).

Kerruish, V. 1992 *Jurisprudence as Ideology* (London: Routledge).

Kleingeld, P., and Brown, E. 2019 'Cosmopolitanism', *Stanford Encyclopedia of Philosophy*, https://plato.stanford.edu/entries/cosmopolitanism/.

Koh, T. Y. 2019 'Bentham on Asceticism and Tyranny', *History of European Ideas* 45, 1–14.

2019 'Bentham and the Pleasures of Cruelty', *History of Political Thought* 40, 699–716.

Korshorke, A., Lüdemann, S., Frank, T., and Matala de Mazza, E. 2007 *Der fictive Staat. Konstruktionen des politischen Körpers in der Geschichte Europas* (Frankfurt-am-Main: Fischer).

Lacey, N. 1998 'Bentham as proto-feminist? Or an Ahistorical Fantasy on "Anarchical Fallacies"', *Current Legal Problems* 51, 441–66.

Landemore, H. 2020 *Open Democracy: Reinventing Popular Rule for the Twenty-First Century* (Princeton: Princeton University Press).

Lang, A., and Wiener, A. (eds.) 2017 *Handbook on Global Constitutionalism* (Cheltenham: Edward Elgar).

Laval, C. 2006 'La chaîne invisible: Bentham et le néolibéralisme', *Revue d'études benthamiennes* 1, https://journals.openedition.org/etudes-benthamiennes/63.

Legrand, S. 2007 *Les normes chez Foucault* (Paris: Presses Universitaires de France).

Lieberman, D. 1989 *The Province of Legislation Determined* (Cambridge: Cambridge University Press).

2005 'Legislation in a Common Law Context', *Zeitschrift für Neuere Rechtsgeschichte* 27, 107–23.

2007 'Bentham's Constitutional Code and the Politics of Information'. Unpublished paper.

2011 'Bentham on Codification', in *Selected Writings of Jeremy Bentham*, ed. S. Engelmann (New Haven: Yale University Press), 460–77.

2014 'Of the Limits and the Theory of Legislation', in *The Legal Philosophy and Influence of Jeremy Bentham: Essays on Of the Limits of the Penal Branch of Jurisprudence*, ed. G. Tusseau (London: Routledge), 293–307.

2014 'Bentham's Jurisprudence and Democratic Theory: An Alternative to Hart's Approach' in *Bentham's Theory of Law and Public Opinion*, ed. X. Zhai and M. Quinn (Cambridge: Cambridge University Press), 119–42.

2019 'Declaring Rights: Bentham and the Rights of Man', in *Philosophy, Rights and Natural Law. Essays in Honour of Knud Haakonssen*, ed. I. Hunter and R. Whatmore (Edinburgh: Edinburgh University Press), 306–37.

Lind, J. 1775 *Remarks on the principal acts of the Thirteenth Parliament of Great Britain. By the author of Letters concerning the present state of Poland. Vol. I. Containing remarks on the acts relating to the colonies. With a plan of reconciliation* (London: T. Payne).

Lobban, M. 1991 *The Common Law and English Jurisprudence 1760–1850* (Oxford: Clarendon Press).

Locke, J. 1988 'Second Treatise of Government', in *Two Treatises of Government*, ed. P. Laslett (Cambridge: Cambridge University Press), 267–428.

Lolme, J. L. de. 2007 *The Constitution of England (1771)*, ed. D. Lieberman (Indianapolis: Liberty Fund).

Long, D. 1977 *Bentham on Liberty: Jeremy Bentham's Idea of Liberty in Relation to His Utilitarianism* (Toronto: Toronto University Press).

2017 'Claude Adrien Helvétius', in *The Bloomsbury Encyclopedia of Utilitarianism*, reprint ed., ed. J. E. Crimmins (London: Bloomsbury Academic), 233.

Loring, R. 2014 'The Role of Universal Jurisprudence in Bentham's Legal Cosmopolitanism', *Revue d'études benthamiennes* 13. doi.org/10.4000/etudes-benthamiennes.749.

Loughlin, M. 2015 'Burke on Law, Revolution and Constitution', *Giornale di storia costituzionale* 29, 49–60.

2015 'The Constitutional Imagination'. *The Modern Law Review* 78, 1–25.

Lovett, F., and Pettit, P. 2009 'Neorepublicanism: A Normative and Institutional Research Program', *Annual Review of Political Science* 12, 11–29.

Lyons, D. 1973 *In the Interest of the Governed* (Oxford: Oxford University Press).

1991 *In the Interest of the Governed: A Study in Bentham's Philosophy of Utility and Law* (Oxford: Clarendon Press).

MacCormick, D. N. 1978 'Dworkin as Pre-Benthamite', *The Philosophical Review* 87, 585–607.

Mack, M. P. 1962 *Jeremy Bentham: An Odyssey of Ideas, 1748–1792* (London: Heinemann).

Maddox, G. 1989. 'Constitution', in *Political Innovation and Conceptual Change*, ed. T. Ball, J. Farr, and R. L. Hanson (Cambridge: Cambridge University Press), 50–67.

Marcilla, G. 2019 'Proportionality in Lawmaking: An Attempt of Justification in the Light of a Constitutionalist and Argumentative Conception of Law', in *Conceptions and Misconceptions of Legislation*, ed. A. D. Oliver-Lalana (Cham: Springer), 153–73.

Marciniak, A. 2015 *Politische Sicherheit. Zur Geschichte eines umstrittenen Konzepts* (Frankfurt: Campus).

McIlwain, C. H. 1947 *Constitutionalism: Ancient and Modern* (Ithaca: Cornell University Press).

Mill, J. S. 1981 *Autobiography and Literary Essays* (Toronto: University of Toronto Press).

1984 *Collected Works XVII*, ed. J. Robson (Toronto: University of Toronto Press), 1812.

1991 *Considerations on Representative Government* (Amherst: Prometheus Books).

Mohnhaupt, H., and Grimm, D. 2002 *Verfassung. Zur Geschichte des Begriffs von der Antike bis zur Gegenwart: zwei Studien*, 2nd ed. (Berlin: Duncker & Humblot).

Montesquieu, C. 1952 *The Spirit of Laws* (Chicago: Encyclopaedia Brittanica).

1989 *The Spirit of the Laws*, ed. A. M. Cohler, B. C. Miller, and H. S. Stone (Cambridge: Cambridge University Press).

Newman, J. H. 1893 *The Idea of a University Defined and Illustrated* (London: Longmans, Green and Co.).

Niesen, P. 2007 'The West Divided? Bentham and Kant on Law and Ethics in Foreign Policy', in *Rethinking Ethical Foreign Policy*, ed. D. Chandler and V. Heins (London; New York: Routledge), 93–115.

2009 'Une Petite Mappemonde du Chaos: La Délibération Parlementaire chez Bentham et Dumont', in *Bentham et la France: Fortune et Infortunes de l'Utilitarisme*, ed. E. de Champs and J.-P. Cléro (Oxford: Voltaire Foundation SVEC), 129–41.

Oliver-Lalana, D. 2013 'Rational Lawmaking and Legislative Reasoning in Parliamentary Debates', in *The Rationality and Justification of Legislation*, ed. L. J. Wintgens and A. D. Oliver-Lalana (Cham: Springer), 135–84.

Otonashi, M. 1993 'The "Bowring Edition" of The Works of Jeremy Bentham, 1838-1843: Its Formation, Editorial Problem and Editors', Hitotsubashi University Center for Historical Social Science Literature Study Series 29, http://hermes-ir.lib.hit-u.ac.jp/hermes/ir/re/16637/studys0290000010.pdf.

Owen, D. 2012 'Constituting the Polity, Constituting the Demos: On the Place of the All Affected Interests Principle in Democratic Theory and in Resolving the Democratic Boundary Problem', *Ethics and Global Politics* 5, 129–52.

Paine, T. 1791 *Droits de l'homme; en réponse à l'attaque de M. Burke* (Paris: F. Buisson), http://classiques.uqac.ca/classiques/paine_thomas/droits_de_lhomme/droits_de_lhomme.html.

Peardon, T. P. 1951 'Bentham's Ideal Republic', *The Canadian Journal of Economics and Political Science* 17, no. 2, 184–203.

Perry, S. R. 2001 'Hart's Methodological Positivism', in *Hart's Postscript: Essays on the Postscript to the Concept of Law*, ed. J. L. Coleman (Oxford: Oxford University Press), 311–54.

Pettit, P. 2006 'Freedom in the Market', *Politics, Philosophy & Economics* 5, 131–49.

Pezet, E. 2007 *Management et conduite de soi. Enquête sur les ascèses de la performance* (Paris: Vuibert).

Philip, P. 2014 *Reforming Ideas in Britain: Politics and Language in the Shadow of the French Revolution, 1789-1815* (Cambridge: Cambridge University Press).

Piccinini, M. 2007 *Corpo politico, opinione pubblica, societa politica. Per una storia dell'idea inglese di costituzione* (Torino: G. Giappichelli).

Pino, G. 2014 'Positivism, Legal Validity, and the Separation of Law and Morals', *Ratio Juris* 27, 190–217.

Pitts, J. 2005 *A Turn to Empire: The Rise of Imperial Liberalism in Britain and France* (Princeton: Princeton University Press), 103–22.

2011 '"Great and Distant Crimes". Empire in Bentham's Thought', in *Jeremy Bentham: Selected Writings*, ed. S. Engelmann (New Haven: Yale University Press), 478–99.

Pocock, J. G. A. 1960 'Burke and the Ancient Constitution: A Problem in the History of Ideas', *The Historical Journal* 3, 125–43.

Pogge, Thomas W. 1992 'Cosmopolitanism and Sovereignty', *Ethics* 103, 48–75.

Posner, R. 1993 *The Problems of Jurisprudence* (Cambridge, MA: Harvard University Press).

Postema, G. J. 1986 *Bentham and the Common Law Tradition* (Oxford: Clarendon Press).

2002 'Introduction', in *Bentham: Moral, Political and Legal Philosophy*, vol. 1, ed. G. Postema (Aldershot: Ashgate).

2014 'Law's Rule: Reflexivity, Mutual Accountability, and the Rule of Law', in *Bentham's Theory of Law and Public Opinion*, ed. X. Zhai and M. Quinn (Cambridge: Cambridge University Press), 7–39.

2014 'The Soul of Justice: Bentham on Publicity, Law, and the Rule of Law', in *Bentham's Theory of Law and Public Opinion*, ed. X. Zhai and M. Quinn (Cambridge: Cambridge University Press), 40–62.

2019 *Utility, Publicity, and Law: Essays on Bentham's Moral and Legal Philosophy* (Oxford: Oxford University Press).

2019 *Bentham and the Common Law Tradition*. 2nd ed. (Oxford: Oxford University Press).

Quinn, M. 2014 'Popular Prejudices, Real Pains: What Is the Legislator to do When the People Err in Assigning Mischief?', in *Bentham's Theory of Law and Public Opinion*, ed. X. Zhai and M. Quinn (Cambridge: Cambridge University Press), 63–89.

2016 'Jeremy Bentham, "The Psychology of Economic Man", and Behavioural Economics', *Œconomia* 6, 3–32.

2019 'Bentham on Preventive Police: The Calendar of Delinquency in Evaluation of Policy, and the Police Gazette in Manipulation of Opinion', *International Criminal Justice Review*, https://journals.sagepub.com/doi/10.1177/1057567719827343.

2022 *Bentham* (Cambridge: Polity Press).

Rawls, J. 1999 *A Theory of Justice* (Cambridge, MA: Harvard University Press).

Rhode, D. L. 2004 *Access to Justice* (Oxford: Oxford University Press).

Riley, C. 2018 'Jeremy Bentham and Equity: The Court of Chancery, Lord Eldon, and the Dispatch Court Plan', *Journal of Legal History* 39, 29–57.

2019 'The Hermit and the Boa Constrictor: Jeremy Bentham, Henry Brougham, and the Accessibility of Justice', *American Journal of Legal History*, 1–26.

Ronzoni, M. 2013 'For (Some) Political and Institutional Cosmopolitanism, (Even If) against Moral Cosmopolitanism', in *Cosmopolitanism versus Non-cosmopolitanism: Critiques, Defenses, Reconceptualizations*, ed. G. Brock (Oxford: Oxford University Press), 156–72.

Rosen, F. 1983 *Jeremy Bentham and Representative Democracy: A Study of the Constitutional Code* (Oxford: Clarendon Press).

1983 'Introduction'. In Bentham, J., *Constitutional Code Vol. 1*, ed. F. Rosen and J. H. Burns (Oxford: Oxford University Press)

1992 *Bentham, Byron, and Greece: Constitutionalism, Nationalism, and Early Liberal Political Thought* (Oxford: Clarendon Press).

2003 *Classical Utilitarianism from Hume to Mill* (London: Routledge).

Rosenblum, N. 1978 *Bentham's Theory of the Modern State* (Cambridge, MA: Harvard University Press).

Roth, Andrew 'Putin approves law targeting journalists as "foreign agents"'. *Guardian* 3 December 2019, www.theguardian.com/world/2019/dec/03/putin-approves-law-targeting-journalists-foreign-agents.

Rudan, P. 2007 *Dalla Costituzione al Governo. Jeremy Bentham e le Americhe*. University of Bologna, http://amsdottorato.cib.unibo.it/193/1/Rudan._Jeremy_Bentham_e_le_Americhe.pdf.

2016 'Society as a Code: Bentham and the Fabric of Order', *History of European Ideas* 42, 39–54.

2019 'Influence as a Constitutional Factor: Bentham's Public Ethics', in *La déontologie publique. Trajectoire et présence d'une notion ambiguë*, ed. G. Tusseau (Paris: Institut francophone pour la justice et la démocratie, diffusion LGDJ Lextenso), 65–77.

Sartori, G. 1962. 'Constitutionalism: A Preliminary Discussion', *The American Political Science Review* 56, 853–64.

Schäfer, A., and Zürn, M. 2021 *Die demokratische Regression* (Berlin: Suhrkamp).

Schmitter, P. 1997 'Exploring the Problematic Triumph of Liberal Democracy and Concluding with a Modest Proposal for Improving Its International Impact', in *Democracy's Victory and Crisis*, ed. A. Hadenius (Cambridge: Cambridge University Press), 297–307.

Schofield, P. 1996 'Bentham on the Identification of Interests', *Utilitas* 8, 223–34.

1999 'Political and Religious Radicalism in the Thought of Jeremy Bentham', *History of Political Thought* 20, 272–91.

2003 'Jeremy Bentham's "Nonsense upon Stilts"', *Utilitas* 15, 1–26.

2006 *Utility and Democracy: The Political Thought of Jeremy Bentham* (Oxford: Oxford University Press).

2010 'Jeremy Bentham and HLA Hart's 'Utilitarian Tradition in Jurisprudence', *Jurisprudence* 1, 147–67.

2011 'Jeremy Bentham and the British Intellectual Response to the French Revolution', *Journal of Bentham Studies* 13, http://discovery.ucl.ac.uk/1333215/1/013%20Schofield.pdf.

2014 'A Defence of Jeremy Bentham's Critique of Natural Rights', in *Bentham's Theory of Law and Public Opinion*, ed. X. Zhai and M. Quinn (New York: Cambridge University Press), 208–30.

2014 'Jeremy Bentham', in *Constitutions and the Classics*, ed. D. J. Galligan (Oxford: Oxford University Press), 231–49.

2021 'Jeremy Bentham and the Origins of Legal Positivism' in *The Cambridge Companion to Legal Positivism*, ed. T. Spaak and P. Mindus (Cambridge: Cambridge University Press), 203–24.

Schwartzberg, M. 2007 'Jeremy Bentham on Fallibility and Infallibility', *Journal of the History of Ideas* 68, 563–85.

Scott, J. W. 1997 *Only Paradoxes to Offer* (Cambridge, MA: Harvard University Press).

Shocking and Pernicious Absurdities of Bigotry. *Examiner*, 559 (13 September 1818), 578–9.

Sieckmann, J. R. 2019 'Legislation as Balancing', in *Conceptions and Misconceptions of Legislation*, ed. A. D. Oliver-Lalana (Cham: Springer), 133–52.

Sieyès, E.-J. 2009. *Qu'est-ce que le Tiers-Etat?* (Paris: Flammarion).

Smith, A. 1909 *An Inquiry into the Nature and Causes of the Wealth of Nations*, ed. C. J. Bullock (New York: P. F. Collier & Son).

Smith, H. L. 2002 *All Men and Both Sexes: Gender, Politics, and the False Universal in England, 1640–1832* (University Park: Penn State University Press).

Sokol, M. 2011 *Bentham, Law and Marriage: A Utilitarian Code of Law in Historical Contexts* (London: Continuum).

Splichal, S. 2003 'Bentham, Kant, and the Right to Communicate', *Critical Review* 15, 285–305.

Steintrager, J. 1971 'Morality and Belief: The Origin and Purpose of Bentham's Writings on Religion', *Mill Newsletter* 6, 3–15.

1980 'Language and Politics: Bentham on Religion', *Bentham Newsletter* 4, 4–20.

1988 '*Constitution*: Changing Meanings of the Term from the Early Seventeenth to the Late Eighteenth Century', in *Conceptual Change and the Constitution*, ed. T. Ball and J. G. A. Pocock (Lawrence: University Press of Kansas), 35–54.

1989 'Vom aristotelischen zum liberalen Verfassungsbegriff', in *Wege zur Grundrechtsdemokratie: Studien zur Begriffs- und Institutionengeschichte des liberalen Verfassungsstaates*, ed. G. Stourzh (Wien: Böhlau), 1–34.

Sunstein, C. 2014 *Why Nudge? The Politics of Libertarian Paternalism* (New Haven: Yale University Press).

Thaler, R., and Sunstein, C. 2008 *Nudge: Improving Decisions about Health, Wealth and Happiness* (London: Penguin).

Thompson, W. 1825 *An Appeal of One Half of the Human Race, Women, Against the Pretensions of the Other Half, Men, to Retain them in Political, and thence in Civil and Domestic, Slavery; in reply to a paragraph of Mr. Mill's celebrated 'Article on Government'* (London: Longman et al.).

Tuori, K. 2002 'Legislation between Politics and Law', in *Legisprudence: A New Theoretical Approach to Legislation. Proceedings of the Fourth Benelux-Scandinavian Symposium on Legal Theory*, ed. L. J. Wintgens (Oxford; Portland: Hart), 99–107.

Tusseau, G. 2001 *Jeremy Bentham et le droit constitutionnel. Une approche de l'utilitarisme juridique* (Paris: L'Harmattan).

2007 'Jeremy Bentham on Power-Conferring Laws', *Revue d'études benthamiennes* 3, 48–77.

2007 'Positivist Jurisprudents Confronted: Jeremy Bentham and John Austin on the Concept of a Legal Power', *Revue d'études benthamiennes* 2, 23–37.

2011 'De Bentham à Kelsen en passant par Merkl, Une trame conceptuelle récurrente de la théorie juridique.' in *Questions contemporaines de théorie analytique du droit / Cuestiones contemporáneas de teoría analítica del derecho / Problemi attuali della teoria analitica del diritto*, ed. P. Brunet and F. J. Arena (Madrid; Barcelona; Buenos Aires: Marcial Pons), 167–97.

2011 'Bentham et le normativisme viennois. Impressions de lecture', in *Bentham juriste. L'utilitarisme juridique en question*, ed. M. Bozzo-Rey and G. Tusseau (Paris: Economica), 43–105.

2011 *Jeremy Bentham. La guerre des mots* (Paris: Dalloz).

2014 'An Old English Tale? Bentham's Theory of The Force of a Law', in *The Legal Philosophy and Influence of Jeremy Bentham. Essays on Of the Limits of the Penal Branch of Jurisprudence*, ed. G. Tusseau (London; New York: Routledge), 80–133.

2018 'Deux dogmes du constitutionnalisme', in *Penser le droit à partir de l'individu. Mélanges en hommage à Elisabeth Zoller* (Paris: Dalloz), 835–83.

2019 'Towards a Linguistic Criticism of Legal Hegemony: Some Remarks on Bentham v. Judges and Co.', *Canadian Journal of Law & Jurisprudence* 32, 173–94.

(forthcoming) 'The Evolution and *Gestalt* of the French Constitution', in *Ius Publicum Europaeum*, vol. 2., ed. A. von Bogdandy, P. M. Huber, P. Cruz Villalón, and S. Ragone (Oxford: Oxford University Press).

Twining, W. L. 1975 'The Contemporary Significance of Bentham's Anarchical Fallacies', *Archiv fur Rechts–und Sozialphilosophie* 61, 325–56.

Varouxakis, G. 2008 'Cosmopolitan Patriotism in J.S. Mill's Thought and Activism', *Revue d'études benthamiennes* 4. doi.org/10.4000/etudes-benthamiennes.188.

Vermeule, A. 2015 'Open-Secret Voting', in *Secrecy and Publicity in Votes and Debates*, ed. J. Elster (Cambridge: Cambridge University Press), 215–29.

Vile, M. J. C. 1998 *Constitutionalism and the Separation of Powers* (Indianapolis: Liberty Fund).

Voltaire 2008 *Prix de la justice et de l'humanité* (Oxford: Voltaire Foundation).

Von Savigny, F. C. 1831 *Of the Vocation of our Age for Legislation and Jurisprudence*, trans. A. Hayward (London: Littlewood & Co.).

Waldron, J. 1999 *The Dignity of Legislation* (Cambridge: Cambridge University Press).

2016 *Political Political Theory* (Cambridge, MA: Harvard University Press).

Webster, N. 1828 *American Dictionary of the English Language*, http://webstersdictionary1828.com/Dictionary/Constitution.

Weinstein, D. 2007 'Consequentialist Cosmopolitanism', in *Victorian Visions of Global Order*, ed. D. Bell (Cambridge: Cambridge University Press), 267–90.

Whatmore, R. 2014 'Thomas Paine', in *Constitutions and the Classics: Patterns of Constitutional Thought from Fortescue to Bentham*, ed. D. J. Galligan (Oxford: Oxford University Press), 414–37.

Williford, M. 1975 'Bentham on the Rights of Women', *Journal of the History of Ideas* 36, 167–76.

Wintgens, L. J. 2006 'Legisprudence as a New Theory of Legislation', *Ratio Juris* 19, 1–25.

2012 'Legislation as an Object of Study of Legal Theory', in *Legisprudence: A New Theoretical Approach to Legislation. Proceedings of the Fourth Benelux–Scandinavian Symposium on Legal Theory*, ed. L. J. Wintgens (Oxford; Portland: Hart), 9–39.

2013 'The Rational Legislator Revisited. Bounded Rationality and Legisprudence', in *The Rationality and Justification of Legislation: Essays in Legisprudence*, ed. L. J. Wintgens and A. D. Oliver-Lalana (Cham: Springer), 1–31.

Wolff, J., and Poppe, A. E. 2015 *From Closing Space to Contested Spaces: Re-assessing Current Conflicts over International Civil Society Support* (Frankfurt: Peace Research Institute).

Wormuth, F. D. 1949 *The Origins of Modern Constitutionalism* (New York: Harper & Row).

Yelle, R. A. 2005 'Bentham's Fictions: Canon and Idolatry in the Genealogy of Law', *Yale Journal of Law & the Humanities* 17, 151–79.

Zhai, Xiaobo 2012 'Bentham's Natural Arrangement Versus Hart's Morally Neutral Description', *Revue d'études benthamiennes*. doi.org/10.4000/etudes-benthamiennes.603.

2014 'Bentham's Natural Arrangement and the Collapse of the Expositor-Censor Distinction in the General Theory of Law', in *Bentham's Theory of Law and Public Opinion*, ed. X. Zhai and M. Quinn (Cambridge: Cambridge University Press), 143–83.

2017 'Bentham on the Interpretation of Laws'. *Journal of Legal History* 38, 282–307.

2017 'Bentham's Exposition of Common Law'. *Law and Philosophy* 36, 525–60.

Zhai, X., and Quinn, M. (eds.) 2014 *Bentham's Theory of Law and Public Opinion* (New York: Cambridge University Press).

INDEX

For EU product safety concerns, contact us at Calle de José Abascal, 56–1°,
28003 Madrid, Spain or eugpsr@cambridge.org.

www.ingramcontent.com/pod-product-compliance
Lightning Source LLC
LaVergne TN
LVHW052026200926
848481LV00005B/1595